MW01002643

The Political Economy
of China's Belt and Road Initiative

Series on China's Belt and Road Initiative

Print ISSN: 2591-7730
Online ISSN: 2591-7749

Series Editors: ZHENG Yongnian *(National University of Singapore, Sinapore)*
Kerry BROWN *(King's College London, UK)*
WANG Yiwei *(Renmin University of China, China)*
LIU Weidong *(Chinese Academy of Sciences, China)*

This book series showcases the most up-to-date and significant research on China's Belt and Road Initiative (BRI) by leading scholars from inside and outside China. It presents a panoramic view on the BRI, from the perspectives of China's domestic policy, China's foreign investment, international relations, cultural cooperation and historical inheritance. As the first English book series on the BRI, this series offers a valuable English-language resource for researchers, policymakers, professionals and students to better understand the challenges and opportunities brought by the BRI.

Published:

Vol. 1   *The Political Economy of China's Belt and Road Initiative*
by ZOU Lei
translated by ZHANG Zhiping

Series on China's Belt and Road Initiative – Vol. 1

The Political Economy
of China's Belt and Road Initiative

ZOU Lei

Shanghai Administration Institute, China

Translated by ZHANG Zhiping

The Navy Medical University in Shanghai, China

World Scientific

EW JERSEY · LONDON · SINGAPORE · BEIJING · SHANGHAI · HONG KONG · TAIPEI · CHENNAI · TOKYO

Published by

World Scientific Publishing Co. Pte. Ltd.
5 Toh Tuck Link, Singapore 596224
USA office: 27 Warren Street, Suite 401-402, Hackensack, NJ 07601
UK office: 57 Shelton Street, Covent Garden, London WC2H 9HE

Library of Congress Cataloging-in-Publication Data
Names: Zou, Lei, 1986 November–   author.
Title: The political economy of China's Belt and Road Initiative /
    Lei Zou (Shanghai Administration Institute, China).
Description: New Jersey : World Scientific, [2018] | Includes bibliographical references.
Identifiers: LCCN 2017053866 | ISBN 9789813222656
Subjects: LCSH: China--Foreign economic relations. | China--Commercial policy. |
Economic development--China. | Regionalism--China.
Classification: LCC HF1604 .Z38849 2018

British Library Cataloguing-in-Publication Data
A catalogue record for this book is available from the British Library.

Published by arrangement with Shanghai People's Publishing House.

Sponsored by Chinese Fund for the Humanities and Social Sciences

Copyright © 2018 by World Scientific Publishing Co. Pte. Ltd.

All rights reserved. This book, or parts thereof, may not be reproduced in any form or by any means, electronic or mechanical, including photocopying, recording or any information storage and retrieval system now known or to be invented, without written permission from the publisher.

For photocopying of material in this volume, please pay a copying fee through the Copyright Clearance Center, Inc., 222 Rosewood Drive, Danvers, MA 01923, USA. In this case permission to photocopy is not required from the publisher.

For any available supplementary material, please visit
http://www.worldscientific.com/worldscibooks/10.1142/10508#t=suppl

Desk Editor: Dong Lixi

Typeset by Stallion Press
Email: enquiries@stallionpress.com

Printed in Singapore

Contents

About the Author

ZOU Lei is an assistant professor of International Relations at the Shanghai Party Institute of CCP & Shanghai Administration Institute. He received his BA, MA and PhD in International Relations from Fudan University (Shanghai, China) in 2008, 2010 and 2013 respectively. Dr. Zou focuses his research on China's Belt and Road Initiative, China's Economic Diplomacy, China's National Security, and Religion and International Security. He is the author of *The Political Economy of China's Belt and Road Initiative* (Chinese version, Shanghai People's Publishing House,2015) and *The Belt and Road: China's Global Initiative for Win-Win Cooperation* (Chinese version, Shanghai People's Publishing House, 2016), and the co-editor (with Professor Xu Yihua) of *Religion and China's Foreign Relations* (Chinese version, Shanghai People's Publishing House, 2014). From 2015 to 2016, he was invited to be the chief writer of the CCTV (China Central Television) documentary series, *The Belt and Road*, which were guided by the Office of the Leading Group for Belt and Road and broadcasted in China and many countries in Chinese, English, Russian, French, Spanish and Arabic. Dr. Zou will welcome suggestions and criticism on this book via leizou10@163.com

About the Translator

ZHANG Zhiping is an associate professor of the Navy Medical University in Shanghai, China. Dr Zhang received PhD in international politics from Fudan University (Shanghai, China) in 2014. She was a visiting scholar to University of Virginia from December 2011 to May 2013, and her research focuses on American politics, social conservatism, and New Christian Right Movement.

Introduction

In the period between the 2nd century BC, when Zhang Qian was sent as the Emperor's envoy to the then Han Dynasty's western neighbors, and the 15th century AD, when Zheng He was sent on expeditionary voyages, there was a long trade route connecting China and the rest of Asia, Africa and Europe. Known as the "Silk Road", it traversed vast grasslands, deserts and oceans, and was named after its most famous commodity, silk. The name "Silk Road" was first used by German geographer Ferdinand von Richthofen, and was made famous, thanks to the eponymous book published in 1983, by the Swedish explorer Sven Hedin.[1] At first, "Silk Road" was mainly used to describe the overland trade route that existed before the rise of the modern Western world. It started from China and extended as far as Europe, with China, Central Asia and West Asia at its core. Gradually, it became the name for the complex cobweb formed by the ports,

---

[1] Daniel C. Waugh, "Richthofen's 'Silk Roads': Toward the Archaeology of a Concept," *The Silk Road*, vol. 5, no. 1, Summer 2007, p. 4; Sven Hedin, *The Silk Road: Ten Thousand Miles through Central Asia*, translated by F. H. Lyon, New York: E. Pl Dutton & Company, Inc, 1938.

trading posts, commodities, ideas, cultures, regions and ethnicities along the way. Instead of referring to only one route, it became a generic term that people used to describe the several trading routes between Europe and Asia, including the original "Oasis Route" that crossed the desert in the Middle East, plus the "Maritime Route", "Steppe Route" and "Southwest Route".

Countless Chinese specialties, such as silk, porcelain and tea leaves, together with millet, rice, sorghum, cinnamon, ginger, musk and the Four Ancient Chinese inventions, namely, compass, gunpowder, papermaking skills and printing techniques were introduced westward by the Sogdians, Persians and the Arabians, making great contributions to the development of civilizations. In the meantime, precious and exotic animals, spices, jewelry, currencies, music, dance, food and clothes made their way to China through the overland or maritime Silk Roads. A number of plants found in ancient Chinese literature and archives with the word "foreign" in their name, including foreign peach (walnut), foreign melon (cucumber), foreign pepper (black pepper) and foreign turnip (carrot) were also introduced to China this way. It is fair to say it was because of the "Silk Road" that the Chinese culture was able to absorb foreign cultural elements, thus obtaining its diversity. Over the course of more than 1000 years, the Chinese, Indians, Arabians, Persians, Javanese as well as people from Europe, East Africa and other Asian countries and their religions including Buddhism, Zoroastrianism, Nestorianism, Manichaeism and Islam all left their imprints on this road.

Due to the temporal succession of the decline of the ancient "Silk Road" and the rise of the modern Western world, the political, economic and cultural bonds between ancient China and other non-Western countries created and maintained by the "Silk Road" were seen as a direct reference to the modern political and economic order forcefully imposed by the West. Standing in between the East and the West, ancient and modern, plus being a direct mirror of the power shift between the East and the West, the ancient "Silk Road" has always been a center of attention. It is seen as the most symbolic of the political, economic, religious, cultural and ethnic engagements and interactions between Asia and Europe before the West came to the center stage. As a result, rebuilding the long-lost geo-economic bond in the Eurasia continent in the name of rejuvenating the "Silk Road" became a consensus. Since the end of the Cold War, the United Nations, the United States, Russia, Turkey, Kazakhstan, Iran, South Korea and Japan all proposed their versions of a "New Silk Road".

As the most important country at the east end of the ancient "Silk Road", the rise and decline of China's national power was intimately associated with the road's ups and downs. On September 7, 2013, Chinese President Xi Jinping proposed, during his speech at the Nazarbayev University in Kazakhstan,

> In order to make economic ties closer, mutual cooperation deeper and the space of development broader between Eurasian countries, we can innovate the mode of cooperation and jointly build the "Silk Road Economic Belt" step by step to gradually form overall regional cooperation.[2]

On October 3, 2013, when addressing the Indonesian Parliament, he suggested that,

> Southeast Asia has since ancient times been an important hub along the ancient maritime Silk Road. China will strengthen maritime cooperation with ASEAN countries to make good use of the China-ASEAN Maritime Cooperation Fund set up by the Chinese government and vigorously develop maritime partnership in a joint effort to build the 21st-Century Maritime Silk Road.[3]

His proposal marked the new Chinese government's official invitation, hundreds of years after the decline of the ancient Silk Road, to

---

[2] Xi Jinping, "Promote Friendship between Our People and Work Together to Build a Bright Future — Speech at Nazarbayev University", *People's Daily*, September 8, 2013, p. 3. (习近平:《弘扬人民友谊共创美好未来——在纳扎尔巴耶夫大学的演讲》 (2013 年 9 月 7 日, 阿斯塔纳), 载《人民日报》2013 年 9 月 8 日, 第 3 版。)
[3] Xi Jinping, "Jointly Building China-ASEAN Community of Shared Interest—Speech at Indonesian Parliament", *People's Daily*, October 4, 2013, p. 2. (习近平:《携手建设中国—东盟命运共同体——在印度尼西亚国会的演讲》 (2013 年 10 月 3 日, 雅加达), 载《人民日报》2013 年 10 月 4 日, 第 2 版。)

relevant countries to jointly build the "Belt and Road". Gradually, the Initiative was expanded to include other relevant countries in Asia, Europe, Africa and Oceania and is open to all countries. Its reach is far wider than the ancient Silk Road.

Since September 2013, the Belt and Road Initiative (BRI) has become a central topic in conversations inside China and between China and other countries. It is also a core topic in discussions in the central and local governments, among market participants, in policy discussions and in academic symposiums. Ideas as grand as global governance structure, central government departments' work arrangements and investment and operations decisions by companies are increasingly influenced by it.

Even ordinary people in China and other countries along the Belt and Road are increasingly feeling its influence, be they fruit farmers in west China's Xinjiang Autonomous Region, computer assembly workers in central China's Chongqing municipality, bank clerks in charge of cross-border RMB business in east China's Fujian province, young scholars studying international relations in Shanghai, restaurant owners along the "West Europe–West China Highway" in Kazakhstan, primary school students who suffer from constant blackouts in Pakistan's mountain areas, crane operators working in the Port of Colombo in Sri Lanka, workers from Qingdao Port who are currently in Myanmar's Maday Island building—an oil terminal, a joint venture by China and Myanmar, workers from China and Indonesia who are working on the high-speed railway connecting Jakarta and Bandung, textile workers in the Suez Economic and Trade Cooperation Zone in Egypt, Russian university students who shop on AliExpress, traders who sell Chinese commodities in Madrid, Chinese and French engineers who are building the Hinkley Point nuclear station in the United Kingdom. Voluntarily or not, they are feeling the influence of the BRI on their work, study and every aspect of life.

It is safe to say that the BRI is reshaping the world we are in today and more and more government departments, companies and individuals are used to thinking under the framework of the Belt and Road. The Belt and Road Forum for International Cooperation held in May 2017 showed that the BRI is one of the hottest topics in the field of international political and economic relations. At the 19th National Congress of the Communist Party of China (CPC) held in October 2017, the Belt and Road Initiative was stressed in Xi Jinping's political report and was also incorporated into the new CPC Constitution. Cementing international cooperation in building the Belt and Road has become an important part of major-country diplomacy with Chinese characteristics in the New Era. Supportive or not, everybody has to take it seriously.

But that said, what exactly is the Belt and Road Initiative? It refers to the most important initiative for international cooperation and national development strategy proposed by China. Although borrowing its name from the ancient Silk Road, it reflects China's new thinking and vision on regional development and international cooperation in this new era. Importantly, China wants to build partnerships with countries in Asia, Europe and Africa with economic, cultural and people-to-people exchanges as the main theme. Currently, work on the East and the West, the ocean routes and the land routes, the domestic and international fronts is being pushed forward simultaneously.

For countries along the Belt and Road, it represents China's proposal for international cooperation. For China, it is a major national development strategy in the new era. After confirmations by the Neighborhood Diplomacy Work Conference, Central Conference on Work related to Foreign Affairs, Central Economic Work Conference, Central Conference by the Central Financial and Economic Leadership, National People's Congress, the Chinese People's Political Consultative Conference, the Third Plenary Session of the 18th Central Committee of the Communist Party of China and the 13th 5-Year Plan for Economic and Social Development, the Belt and Road Initiative was sealed as a national development strategy, one of the three major strategies during the 13th 5-Year Period, together with the strategy of "Promoting Coordinated Development of Beijing, Tianjin and Hebei" and the strategy of "Building a Yangtze River Economic Belt".

But how is the importance of and the attention at the highest level to the BRI manifested? According to President Xi Jinping, the BRI is a major strategic measure for expanding the opening-up and top-level design for economic diplomacy. It is a key area for development in the next phase.[4] Vice Premier Zhang Gaoli, head of the Leading Group for the Belt and Road Initiative pointed out that the BRI is a key strategy in China's opening-up.[5] The National Development and Reform Commission (NDRC) and the Ministry of Commerce (MOFCOM), among other central government departments tasked with executing the BRI, commented that, "jointly building the Belt and Road is a major initiative proposed by President Xi Jinping to relevant countries, and the guiding principle in China's opening-up and foreign cooperation in the period to come."[6] To better implement the Initiative, the Central Leading Group for Financial and Economic Affairs, China's supreme economic affairs decision-making body, convened in November 2014 to discuss ways to push forward the BRI. Local governments, central departments and commissions as well as state-owned companies directly managed by the central government all submitted their execution plans. During Chinese leaders' overseas visits and when they receive foreign leaders, the BRI is always one of the most frequently discussed topics. Such a high level of attention and the amount of resources devoted fully demonstrate the strategic importance of the BRI.

The sixth Ministerial Meeting of China–Arab States Cooperation Forum held in June 2014 was the first major diplomatic move themed

---

[4] Xi Jinping, "Speech at the Second Plenum of the Fifth Plenary Session of the 18th Central Committee of the Communist Party of China" (October 29, 2015), *Qiu Shi*, no. 1, 2016. [习近平:《在党的十八届五中全会第二次全体会议上的讲话（节选)》(2015 年 10 月 29 日), 载《求是》2016 年第 1 期。]

[5] Zhang Gaoli, "To Form a Better Development *Philosophy*", in The Writing Group eds., *Understanding Recommendations for the 13th Five-Year Plan for Economic and Social Development,* Beijing: People's Publishing House, 2015, p. 19. (张高丽:《完善发展理念》, 收入本书编写组:《<中共中央关于制定国民经济和社会发展第十三个五年规划的建议>辅导读本》, 北京:人民出版社 2015 年版, 第 19 页。)

[6] The National Development and Reform Commission of PRC, "Promoting Development and Opening-up of Key Border Areas as Important Props for the Belt and Road", January 11, 2016, http://www.sdpc.gov.cn/xwzx/xwfb/201601/t20160111_771029.html, log-in time: March 15, 2016. (国家发改委:《推进沿边重点地区开发开放步伐 构筑推进"一带一路"建设重要支撑》, 2016 年 1 月 11 日。)

"jointly building the Belt and Road" since the proposal of the Initiative. It brought back memory of China and Middle Eastern countries working together to build the ancient Silk Road (also known as the Road of Spice and the Road of Porcelain). In fact, archaeological findings show that compared with the intermittent and sporadic cultural and trade exchanges between China's Han Dynasty and the Roman Empire, exchanges of commodities, people, religions and cultures between China's Tang and Song Dynasties and the Islamic world in the Middle East were more direct, sustaining and extensive. They reflected something far deeper.[7]

In fact, long before the proposal of the BRI, the spontaneously formed "Modern Silk Road" from China to the Middle East since the beginning of this century has already attracted a lot of attention. As a lot of observers noticed, driven by energy trade, the exchanges of commodities, energy, people and money between Asian countries such as China, India, Japan and Singapore on one hand and Middle Eastern oil states on the other significantly quickened up since the beginning of this century. The long-severed economic and trade ties between the two regions were reconnected and the name "Modern Silk Road" captured this new geo-economic phenomenon.[8] As a

---

[7] Ma Wenkuan, "An Examination of the Cultural Exchanges between China's Tang and Song Dynasties and the Islamic World Unveiled by Archaeological Findings", *Archaeological Research on Han and Tang Dynasties and Border Areas*, Beijing: China Science Publishing & Media Ltd, no. 1, 1994, p. 245. (马文宽:《从考古资料看中国唐宋时期与伊斯兰世界的文化交流》, 载中国社会科学院考古研究所《汉唐与边疆考古研究》编委会:《汉唐与边疆考古研究》(第一辑), 科学出版社 1994 年版, 第 245 页。)

[8] Dominic Barton, Kito de Boer, and Gregory P. Wilson, "The New Silk Road: Opportunities for Asia and the Gulf", *The McKinsey Quarterly*, July 2006, pp. 1–2; Economist Intelligence Unit, *Near East Meets Far East: The Rise of Gulf Investment in Asia*, New York: The Economist Group, 2007; Afshin Molavi, "The New Silk Road", *The Washington Post*, April 9, 2007; Stephen Glain, "The Modern Silk Road," *Newsweek*, May 26/June 2, 2008, pp. 32–33; Miria Pigato, *Strengthening China's and India's Trade and Investment Ties to the Middle East and North Africa*, Washington, D.C.: World Bank, 2009; Mikkal E. Herberg et al., *The New Energy Silk Road: The Growing Asia-Middle East Energy Nexus*, Washington, D.C.: The National Bureau of Asian Research, 2009; Christopher Davidson, *The Persian Gulf and Pacific*

result, the economic influence of Asian countries, such as China and India, in the Middle East grew quickly.[9] On the other hand, countries in the Middle East were increasingly looking eastward.[10] Both phenomena pointed to the power shift between China/Asia, the Middle East and the United States/the West. According to the Australian observer Ben Simpfendorfer, the popularity of the "Modern Silk Road" shows that the Middle East is rebuilding its once close ties with China, something that stands in sharp contrast to its gradual dissociation from the United States/the West after 9/11.[11]

Hence, as a major national development strategy articulated by the Chinese government, the BRI should be examined by reference to at least two parameters, the ancient Silk Road and the "Modern Silk Road". The core purpose of the book is thus to illustrate how people should understand its strategic importance and how it fits this very new era. More specifically, the book will focus on the following three interwoven questions.

Asia: From Indifference to Interdependence, London: Hurst & Co., 2010; Alshin Molavi, "The New Silk Road, 'Chindia,' and the Geo-Economic Ties that Bind the Middle East and Asia", in Bryce Wakefield and Susan L. Levenstein, eds., *China and the Persian Gulf: Implications for the United States,* Washington, D.C.: Woodrow Wilson International Center for Scholars, 2011, pp. 45–53.

[9] Manochehr Dorraj and Carrie Currier, "Reconstructing the Silk Road in a New Era: China's Expanding Regional Influence in the Middle East," in Emilian Kavalski, ed., *China and the Global Politics of Regionalization,* New York: Ashgate Publishers, 2009, pp. 165–176; Geoffrey Kemp and Abdulaziz Sager, eds., *China's Growing Role in the Middle East: Implications for the Region and Beyond,* Washington, D.C.: The Nixon Center, 2010; Geoffrey Kemp, *The East Moves West: India, China, and Asia's Growing Presence in the Middle East,* Washington, D.C.: Brookings Institute Press, 2010; Christina Lin, *The New Silk Road: China's Energy Strategy in the Greater Middle East,* Washington, D.C.: Washington Institute for Near East Policy, 2011.

[10] Emile Hokayem, "Looking East: A Gulf Vision or A Reality?", in Bryce Wakefield and Susan L. Levenstein, eds., *China and the Persian Gulf: Implications for the United States,* Washington, D.C.: Woodrow Wilson International Center for Scholars, 2011, pp. 38–44; Jaqueline M. Armijo and Lina M. Kassem, "Turning East: The Social and Cultural Implications of the Gulf's Increasingly Strong Economic and Strategic Relations with China", *Singapore Middle East Papers,* Vol. 1, 2012, pp. 22–45.

[11] Ben Simpfendorfer, *The New Silk Road: How a Rising Arab World is Turning Away from the West and Rediscovering China,* New York: Palgrave Macmillan, 2009, pp. 7–27.

First, compared with the ancient Silk Road, how has the BRI inherited from its ancient counterpart, and what is new about it? What are the similarities and differences between the two in geography, trade and religion?

Second, compared with the so-called "Modern Silk Road", what makes the BRI more strategic? In particular, how should we understand its strategic planning for a new international political and economic order?

Third, how to understand the measures that China is taking or about to take to build the Belt and Road? How to evaluate and respond to the potential risks or possibilities of setbacks as China implements this initiative?

1. Literature Review

With the growing international influence of the Belt and Road Initiative, more and more people show interest in it and devote time in deciphering it. But most of the existing research focuses on its strategic considerations, implementation and risk evaluation. To help foreign readers better understand the BRI, research findings mainly by the Chinese scholars and officials are listed as follows:

1.1 *The Strategic Considerations of the BRI*

1. *Background*: According to Yang Shu, director of the Institute for Central Asian Studies at Lanzhou University, the Silk Road Economic Belt Initiative was by no means a compromise proposed following China's setback in implementing its ocean strategy nor a countermeasure in response to America's "Rebalancing towards the Asia Pacific". Rather, it is in line with China's all-round opening-up and development strategy.[12] Wang Xiaoquan, researcher at the Public

---

[12] Yang Shu, "What Kind of New Silk Road Does West China Need—From Beijing's Strategic Planning to Lanzhou's Practical Needs", *People's Forum: Frontiers*, no. 1, December 2013, p. 14–15. (杨恕:《中国西部地区需要什么样的新丝绸之路——从北京的战略构想到兰州的现实诉求》, 载《人民论坛•学术前沿》2013 年 12 月上, 第 14–15 页。)

Diplomacy Institute of Shanghai Cooperation Organization (SCO) at Shanghai University, believes that the "Silk Road Economic Belt" came as China started to change its traditional focus in international economic and trade cooperation, from solely on the ocean routes in the East to paying equal attention to the East ocean routes and West land routes.[13] Mei Xinyu, researcher at the Academy of International Trade and Economic Cooperation of MOFCOM pointed out, when the BRI was first proposed, what China had in mind was merely to build the middle of the land routes, so as to establish a new economic order in West Asia that includes the Middle East, Afghanistan and Iran, against the backdrop of America and North Atlantic Treaty Organization's (NATO) withdrawal from Afghanistan and the change in international economic landscape. This route would take the place of the American version of the "New Silk Road" and help China prevent political power change and the resultant chaos in the region, thus helping it better counter the threats of terrorism, extremism and separatism. It was only later that China expanded this proposal to include a North Route, South Route and Maritime Silk Road. He also believed that at a time when Europe has become China's largest trading partner, the "Silk Road Economic Belt" will help ease the potential pressure on the China–Europe trade route possibly arising as a result of the chaos in the Arab world.[14] Some Western scholars pointed out that the proposal of building a "21st-Century Maritime Silk Road" was China's answer to America's so-called "String of Pearls Strategy". It aims at reducing other countries and people's concern about China's ocean strategy by emphasizing economic cooperation.[15]

---

[13] Wang Xiaoquan, "Strategic Thinking on Building the Silk Road Economic Belt", *Economic Herald*, Issue March 2014. (王晓泉:《建设"丝绸之路经济带"的战略思考》, 载《经济导刊》2014 年 3 月号。)

[14] Mei Xinyu, "Understanding the Underlying Intention of the New Silk Road", *People's Forum: Frontiers,* no. 1, December 2013, p. 38. (梅新育:《新丝绸之路的深意》, 载《人民论坛·学术前沿》2013 年 12 月上, 第 38 页。)

[15] Shannon Tiezzi, "The Maritime Silk Road vs. The String of Pearls", http://thediplomat.com/2014/02/the-maritime-silk-road-vs-the-string-of-pearls/, log-in time: July 11, 2014.

2. *Strategic positioning*: Scholars like Hu Angang, professor at Tsinghua University, believe that the Silk Road Economic Belt Initiative is an integration of China's ideas on international political and economic relations, domestic development and foreign engagement. It inherits from the past yet transcends its historical counterpart. It reflects the country's policy of combining opening-up to its western neighbors with developing its western region. It was developed on the basis of the national security and economic strategies proposed by the previous generations of central leadership. It is manifested by the several transformations of China's national security strategy, including from passive strategic defense to active strategic movements, from singular focus on its own border security to focus on holistic multinational cooperation, from separating internal development from international engagement to integration.[16] He Maochun, director of the Centre for Economic Diplomacy at Tsinghua University and Zhang Jibing, a researcher at the same institute, pointed out that the Silk Road Economic Belt is China's vision on a new model of cross-regional economic cooperation that was born in an era of regional economic integration and economic globalization. It is aimed at reviving the ancient Silk Road. Compared with Japan's "Silk Road Diplomacy", America's "New Silk Road" and the "North–South Corridor" proposed by Russia, India and Iran, China's initiative is most practicable and strategically valuable. Wen Yang, scholar at the China Institute of Fudan University, observed that thanks to its partial inheritance from the ancient Silk Road, China's new "Silk Road" carries an inherent message, engaging not just the region that was the center of the world before the West's domination, but the wider region that was influenced by ancient China and Chinese idea of seeking peace, friendship and win-win cooperation. It was a world where there was no geostrategic ambition or any attempt to control the world. These characteristics set China's Belt and Road Initiative

---

[16] Hu Angang, Mawei and Yan Yilong, "Silk Road Economic Belt: Strategic Considerations, Positioning and Implementation Routes", *Journal of Xinjiang Normal University (Social Science Edition)*, no. 2, 2014, pp. 1–10. (胡鞍钢、马伟、鄢一龙:《"丝绸之路经济带":战略内涵、定位和实现路径》, 载《新疆师范大学学报》(哲学社会科学版) 2014 年第 2 期, 第 1–10 页。)

apart from either the American version or the UN's version of "New Silk Road".[17]

3. *Strategic importance*: According to China's Minister of Commerce, the Belt and Road Initiative will contribute to China's all-round opening-up strategy that features opening by land and sea routes, to the East and the West. It allows B&R countries to share each other's advantages for win-win results. It also helps the region to become a community of shared interest and common future.[18] Cao Yun, director of a consulting center in Zhejiang province, pointed out that the Silk Road Economic Belt at least serves four strategic objectives: national security (geopolitical balancing, counter-terrorism and national energy security), opening-up, development of west China and finding new engines for economic growth.[19] Zhan Hao, a famous commentator, observed that the two new Silk Roads have the following strategic functions: solidifying strategic and economic security, expanding space for international cooperation, promoting development of central and west China, countering international terrorism and accelerating industrial upgrading. Moreover, the Silk Road Economic Belt is a countermeasure to America's "New Silk Road" strategy. It facilitates Eurasian integration. The 21st-Century Silk Road, while helping China break away from America's maritime encirclement and counter its Air-Sea Battle strategy, helps China enhance economic ties with countries in Southeast Asia and along the Indian Ocean, so that China is not economically insulated by the United States' Trans-Pacific Partnership (TPP) initiative.[20] Speaking

---

[17] Wen Yang, "Historical Heritage of China's New Silk Road", March 2, 2014, guancha.cn, http://www.guancha.cn/wen-yang/2014_03_02_209999.shtml, log-in time: March 11, 2014. (文扬：《中国版"新丝路"的历史含义》，观察者网，2014 年 3 月 2 日。)

[18] Gao Hucheng, "Deepening Economic and Trade Cooperation to Jointly Build a More Glorious Future", *People's Daily*, July 2, 2014, p. 11. (高虎城：《深化经贸合作 共创新的辉煌》，载《人民日报》2014 年 7 月 2 日，第 11 版。)

[19] Cao Yun, "The Four Strategic Objective of the Silk Road Economic Belt", *China Social Sciences Today*, January 11, 2014, p. A07. (曹云：《丝绸之路经济带具四重战略目标》，《中国社会科学报》2014 年 1 月 11 日，A07 版。)

[20] Zhan Hao, "The Strategic Considerations of the Two Silk Roads", *Social Eyes*, no. 1, 2014, p. 39–41. (占豪：《两条丝绸之路的战略考量》，载《社会观察》2014 年第

from the perspective of economic, trade and financial strategies, Guo Tianyong, professor of finance and economics at the Chinese University of Finance and Economics, pointed out that the BRI is conducive to China's industrial upgrading, logistics and cross-border commerce development, financial market development and RMB globalization.[21]

1.2 Policy Implementation of the BRI

1. *Government level*: Wang Yi, China's Foreign Minister proposed that the main thread of the BRI is economic cooperation and people-to-people exchanges. Priorities are interconnectivity and trade and investment facilitation, by way of equal consultation and securing gradual progress to achieve win-win cooperation and build a community of shared interest.[22] Gao Hucheng, China's former Minister of Commerce said that the BRI is an open and inclusive economic cooperation initiative. It does not favor one country over another. Nor is it a closed entity. Any country and economy that is willing to join can be part of, support, and benefit from it.[23] Zhong Shan, the current Minister of Commerce said that the Silk Road Economic Belt will fully rely on existing bilateral and multilateral mechanisms, take advantage of existing regional cooperation platforms and enrich

---

1 期, 第 39–41 页。)

[21] Guo Tianyong and Li Qiong, "Strategic Role of the New Silk Road on Economics, Trade and Finance," *People's Forum: Frontiers,* December 2013, p. 64–70. (郭田勇、李琼:《"新丝绸之路"的经贸金融战略意义》, 载《人民论坛•学术前沿》2013 年 12 月上, 第 64–70 页。)

[22] "Meeting the Press at the Second Plenary Session of the 12th National People's Congress by His Excellency, China's Foreign Minister, Wang Yi on China's Foreign Policy and Diplomatic Relations", *People's Daily,* March 9, 2013, p. 3. (《王毅在十二届全国人大二次会议举行的记者会上就中国外交政策和对外关系答中外记者问》, 载《人民日报》2014 年 3 月 9 日, 第 3 版。)

[23] Gao Hucheng, "Deepening Economic and Trade Cooperation to Jointly Build a More Glorious Future". (高虎城:《深化经贸合作 共创新的辉煌》, 载《人民日报》2014 年 7 月 2 日, 第 11 版。)

them.[24] Li Pumin, Secretary General of the National Development and Reform Commission, proposed that in building the Silk Road Economic Belt, economic cooperation is the core pursuit. Countries should follow the rules of "friendship, sincerity, mutual benefit and inclusiveness" and the principles of collective consultation, joint building and sharing. Countries should promote policy coordination, facilities and infrastructure connectivity, unimpeded trade, financial integration and people-to-people bonds. They should use major cooperation projects as a lever to improve cooperation mechanisms.[25] Liu Cigui, the former chief of the State Oceanic Administration believed that building maritime partnership is the most important objective in developing the 21st-Century Maritime Silk Road. Countries should improve maritime connections, enhance marine economy and industry cooperation, advance cooperation in the area of nonconventional maritime security, and expand cooperation in people-to-people exchanges to build such partnership.[26]

2.   *Nongovernmental/semigovernmental/think-tank level*: A report issued by the Chongyang Institute for Financial Studies at Renmin University of China suggested that the implementation of the Silk

---

[24] Zhong Shan, "Deepening Mutually Beneficial Economic and Trade Cooperation to Push for Solid Progress in Building the Silk Road Economic Belt—Speech at the International Symposium on the Silk Road Economic Belt", June 26, 2014, http://www.scio.gov.cn/ztk/dtzt/2014/31055/31059/Document/1373660/1373660.htm, log-in time: September 15, 2014.(钟山:《深化互利共赢的经贸合作 扎实推进丝绸之路经济带建设——在丝绸之路经济带国际研讨会上的演讲》, 2014 年 6 月 26 日, 乌鲁木齐。)

[25] Li Pumin, "Jointly Building the Silk Road Economic Belt to Share New Opportunities from Development and Prosperity—Keynote Speech at the International Symposium on the Silk Road Economic Belt", June 26, 2014, Urumqi, http://www.scio.gov.cn/ztk/dtzt/2014/31055/31059/Document/1373923/1373923.htm, log-in time: September 15, 2014. (李朴民:《共建丝绸之路经济带 共享繁荣发展新机遇——在丝绸之路经济带国际研讨会上的主旨演讲》, 2014 年 6 月 26 日, 乌鲁木齐。)

[26] Liu Cigui, "An Look at Developing Maritime Partnership to Promote the 21st-Century Maritime Silk Road", *International Studies*, Issue 4, 2014, pp. 1–8. (刘赐贵:《发展海洋合作伙伴关系推进 21 世纪海上丝绸之路建设的若干思考》, 载《国际问题研究》2014 年第 4 期, 第 1–8 页。)

Road Economic Belt Initiative be divided into three phases spanning 35 years. The first phase is from when the report came out to 2016. The focus during this phase was on domestic and international mobilization. The second phase, from 2016 to 2021, would focus on strategic planning. And the third phase, from 2021 to 2049 would be about strategic implementation.[27] Liu Huaqin and Li Gang, two researchers at the MOFCOM held that in building the Silk Road Economic Belt, there should be some basic principles, such as combining immediate and long-term interests, trade and investment as well as bilateral and multilateral engagement, maximizing common interests and finding new market-based cooperation models. Gradually, a strategic map comprising three levers, three routes and three regions within the sphere of influence of the three levers will take shape. The first lever is the SCO, supporting Commonwealth of Independent States (CIS) countries. The second is the Gulf Cooperation Council (GCC) for West Asian countries. The third are the China–Pakistan Economic Corridor and the Bangladesh–China–India–Myanmar Economic Corridor which will lead the development of South Asian countries. But the most important lever should be the SCO.[28]

Professor Zheng Yongnian from National University of Singapore suggested that the Belt and Road Initiative could learn from the "Marshall Plan", America's proposal after the World War II to help rebuild Europe, but should transcend its geopolitical ambitions. In terms of execution, the Chinese central government can set up an international development institution to facilitate Chinese companies' international endeavors and coordinate their overseas activities. It can leverage its strong financial capabilities and infrastructure building

---

[27] Chongyang Institute for Financial Studies of Renmin University eds., *The Eurasian Age—Silk Road Economic Belt Blue Book 2014–2015*, Beijing: China Economic Publishing House, 2014, p. 243. (中国人民大学重阳金融研究院主编：《欧亚时代——丝绸之路经济带蓝皮2014–2015》, 北京: 中国经济出版社, 2014 年, 第 243 页。)
[28] Liu Huaqin and Li Gang, "Overall Strategy and Architecture of the Silk Road Economic Belt", *International Trade*, no. 3, 2013, pp. 6–7. (刘华芹、李钢:《建设"丝绸之路经济带"的总体战略与基本架构》, 载《国际贸易》2014 年第 3 期, 第 6–7 页。)

prowess, and by building an open Silk Road, ease other countries' geopolitical concerns.[29] Zhu Surong, governor of the Urumqi Central Subbranch of the People's Bank of China, pointed out that the Silk Road is in essence a trade route, supported by finance. So we should fully leverage the central role of finance in supporting "road connectivity" and "unimpeded trade". We should promote regional cooperation by facilitating financial integration and thus facilitate trade and investment.[30] Wei Jianguo, Deputy Director of China Central for International Economic Exchanges, suggested that the 21st-Century Maritime Silk Road should be supplemented with a platform, a fund and a mechanism. The platform should be comprised of forums with attendees from countries along the road. The fund, that is, the Silk Road Fund is a natural result of the interconnectivity on the road. And there should be a mechanism of mayor's meeting attended by mayors of cities along the road to be held regularly.[31]

1.3 *Risk Evaluation of the BRI*

1. *Economic/institutional risks:* A group of researchers at Sha'anxi Province's Academy of Social Sciences held that the difficulty in coordination among counties and different regional cooperation mechanisms, sluggish infrastructure building in Central Asia and the weak cooperation among customs departments will pose severe challenges to the Silk Road Economic Belt.[32] Yang Shu, director of the Institute

---

[29] Zheng Yongnian, "New Silk Road—What to do and How to do?", June 24, 2014, Zao bao.com, http://www.zaobao.com/forum/views/opinion/story 20140624-358341/page/0/1, log-in time: 11 July 2014. (郑永年:《新丝绸之路——做什么、怎么做?》, 2014 年 6 月 24 日。)

[30] Zhu Surong, "Financial Support to the Silk Road Economic Belt", *China Finance*, no. 24, 2013, pp. 77–78. (朱苏荣:《丝绸之路经济带的金融支持》, 载《中国金融》2013 年第 24 期, 第 77–78 页。)

[31] Xiao Yingying, "Wei Jianguo's Three Suggestions on Developing the Maritime Silk Road", 23 February 2014, chinanews.com, http://www.hi.chinanews.com/zt/2014/0408/39372.html, log-in time: July 11, 2014. (肖莹莹:《魏建国为"海上丝绸之路"下一步发展提三点建议》, 2014 年 2 月 23 日。)

[32] Focus Group at Shaan Xi Academy of Social Sciences, "Analysis and Prospect of the Silk Road Economic Belt", in Ren Zongzhe et al., eds., *Annual Report on Development of the Silk Road (2014)*, Beijing: Social Sciences Academic Press, 2014.

for Central Asian Studies at Lanzhou University, pointed out that the severe imbalance of economic development among countries and regions along the road, the different track gauges, and the competition for the two Arctic Passages are all potential setbacks for the Silk Road Economic Belt.[33] Zeng Xianghong, also professor at Lanzhou University, said that, the different interests of Middle Eastern countries and different levels of economic development will make coordination more difficult.[34] Cheng Yunjie, professor at Xinjiang University of Finance and Economics, attributed the challenges in the economic and trade cooperation among countries along the Belt and Road to the competition for markets by America, Europe, Russia, Japan and South Korea; the trade diversion effect of the Customs Union of Belarus, Kazakhstan and Russia; cross-border transportation restrictions and the trade barriers in some countries.[35]

2. *Political/security risks*: Yongnian believes that the biggest challenge to the new Silk Road is the geopolitical issue. Therefore, China should properly handle its relationship with Russia, Association of Southeast Asian Nations (ASEAN) and India.[36] Citing Kazakhstan as an example, Zhou Ming, a scholar of Lanzhou University, pointed out that Kazakhstan only has a vague idea of China's geopolitical

---

(陕西省社会科学院课题组:《丝绸之路经济带建设形势分析与展望》, 载任宗哲、石英、白宽犁主编:《丝绸之路经济带发展报告(2014)》, 北京: 社会科学文献出版社, 2014 年。)

[33] Yang Shu and Wang Shusen, "Silk Road Economic Belt, Strategic Vision and Challenges", *Journal of Lanzhou Universit (Social Science Edition)*, no. 1, 2014, pp. 28–29. (杨恕、王术森:《丝绸之路经济带:战略构想及其挑战》, 载《兰州大学学报》(社会科学版) 2014 年第 1 期, 第 28–29 页。)

[34] Zeng Xianghong, "How the Middle East Sees the Silk Road Economic Belt and What They Expect", *Contemporary World*, no. 4, 2014, p. 40. (曾向红:《中亚国家对"丝绸之路经济带"构想的认知和预期》, 载《当代世界》2014 年第 4 期, 第 40页。)

[35] Cheng Yunjie, "New Opportunities and Challenges to China's Foreign Trade from Silk Road Economic Belt", *Economic Review*, no. 6, 2014, p. 95. (程云洁:《"丝绸之路经济带"建设给我国对外贸易带来的新机遇与挑战》, 载《经济纵横》2014 年第 6 期, 第 95 页。)

[36] Zheng Yongnian, "Several Major Issues for China's Revival of the Silk Road", June 17,2014,Zaobao.com,http://www.zaobao.com/forum/views/opinion/story20140617-355672, log-in time: July 11, 2014. (郑永年:《中国重返丝绸之路的几个重大问题》, 联合早报网, 2014 年 6 月 17 日。)

position, and some people are concerned that the cooperation will disproportionately benefit China. This has cast a shadow over the prospect of Kazakhstan's long-term participation in and identification with the Silk Road Economic Belt. So all participants have to seriously think about how to increase their people's knowledge and understanding of China and ensure all participants shall benefit equally.[37] Xinyu reminded that, given the possibility that Islamic extremism will continue to expand at least in the next 20 years, China should be mindful of being trapped by some Western forces into the "Islamic chaos" and risking depletion of its national power and therefore losing out in the triangular power struggle among China and Russia, the West and Islamic extremism.[38] Zhang Wenmu, expert on international relations, pointed out that with Russia's tactical withdrawal from the Middle East after the fall of the Soviet Union and America's withdrawal of its troops from Afghanistan, a threat similar to that of Abbasid Dynasty in the 8th century is emerging along China's western frontiers. China is under increasing pressure as regional terrorist forces fight for control of the strategic vacuum. The gradual concentration of "extremist, terrorist and separatist forces" in the southern part of China's Xinjiang Autonomous Region is a vivid reminder of the historical pattern by separatist forces in Xinjiang. At a time when the disputes in the East China Sea are becoming its main security concern, China should be cautious in the west.[39] Another report published by the Centre for China in the World Economy at Tsinghua University, holds that, in addition to infrastructure backwardness,

---

[37] Zhou Ming, "Geopolitical Imagination and Pursuit of Benefits: Review of Kazakhstan's Participation into the Silk Road Economic Belt", *Foreign Affairs Review*, no. 3, 2014, p. 136–156. 周明:《地缘政治想象与获益动机——哈萨克斯坦参与丝绸之路经济带构建评估》, 载《外交评论》2014 年第 3 期, 第 136–156 页。

[38] Mei Xinyu, "Guarding against Falling into the Islamic Trap in Building the Silk Road", June 4, 2014, Ifeng, http://city.ifeng.com/special/chinacity46/, log-in time: July 25, 2014.(梅新育:《丝绸之路谨防深陷"伊斯兰陷阱"》, 2014 年 6 月 4 日。)

[39] Zhang Wenmu, "Silk Road and Security of China's West Border: On the Historical Conditions and Laws of the Rise of Forces in the Middle East and Suggested Responses", *World Economics and Politics*, no. 3, 2014, pp. 4–27. (张文木:《丝绸之路与中国西域安全——兼论中亚地区力量崛起的历史条件、规律及其因应战略》, 载《世界经济与政治》2014 年第 3 期, 第 4–27 页。)

issues such as religious and ethnic relationship complexity, different national governance structures and historical legacies also pose threats to the Silk Road Economic Belt. If they want to realize the prospect for cooperation and development, countries along the Belt have to push for cooperation in economy, finance, education, tourism and counter-terrorism immediately.[40]

In a nutshell, since the proposal of the BRI, there have been more and more research efforts devoted to it. As we have explained in the literature review section, existing research to certain extent helps people understand its strategic considerations, implementation plans and risk evaluation.

However, current research work still has a lot of room for improvement, and its focus is too confined to just one or two aspects of a far more comprehensive concept. Since interest in decoding this grand initiative mainly sprang from it being a national strategy, most researchers focus their efforts on understanding its implications and making policy suggestions. If you compare the statements made by researchers and scholars and relevant government departments such as the National Development and Reform Commission, the Ministry of Foreign Affairs and the Ministry of Commerce, you will find a high degree of similarity and overlap. This was, undoubtedly understandable and even helpful, during the period immediately after its proposal. Over time, however, the limitations of this kind of policy-decoding-oriented research become increasingly salient. One example is that in talking about the natural link between the BRI and the ancient Silk Road, most researchers only see the latter as a historical symbol that helps justify the new policy, without digging deeper into the lessons that the ancient Silk Road could provide. Nor do they spend much time trying to understand the similarities and differences between the two from a comparative historical research perspective. Thus their findings are sporadic and unsystematic. In making

---

[40] Centre for China in the World Economy of Tsinghua University, *The Silk Road Economic Belt: Prospects and Policy Suggestions*, May 20, 2014. (清华大学中国与世界经济研究中心:《丝绸之路经济带——发展前景及政策建议》, 2014 年 5 月 20 日。)

suggestions on implementation, most researchers show the tendency of valuing conclusion over reasoning process and overall picture over details. In particular, few conducted detailed analysis by tracking all the specific measures taken by the government, or tried to unveil a general model. Given the previous reasons, we hold the opinion that while existing research provides us with some valuable lessons, it is still a work in process.

2. Book Structure

First, we look at the three core issues (geography, trade and religion) in the evolution of ancient Silk Road to get a historic view on the Belt and Road Initiative. Specifically, analysis of the alternating rise and decline of maritime and land transportation routes helps understand the reason behind simultaneously proposing the "Belt" and the "Road". Examination of international trade (in particular, trade of commodities and finance) helps with understanding the different international economic and political orders reflected by the ancient Silk Road, the Modern Silk Road and the BRI. Analysis of the spread of religions (mainly the Islamic influence on the Silk Road) helps understand the complicated role played by religious elements on the "Modern Silk Road" and the BRI. The spread of Islam to the eastern Chinese city of Yiwu through its trade with the Islamic world, the natural opening-up of China to its West neighbors due to the religious ties between China's Ningxia Autonomous Region with the Arab world, the state–religion relationship and state-building predicament in countries along the "Belt" and the constant threats posed by "extremism, terrorism and separatism" are all related to the historical expansion of Islam. Hence, understanding the transmission of religions along the ancient Silk Road is helpful for understanding the interactions between religion and trade and religion and politics at different periods.

Second, by comparing the "Modern Silk Road" between China and the Middle East, we aim to provide a reference for the contemporary Belt and Road. Instead of making instinctive descriptions of the commodities, energy, people and capital flow along the Modern

Silk Road as some other observers do, this book focuses on the structural conditions that lay the foundation for its development and the modern political and economic order and structure reflected by this bilateral relationship. Analysis shows that compared with the ancient Silk Road, the "Modern Silk Road" has some distinctive modern characteristics. Yet compared with the BRI, it is a mere demonstration of the interactions between China's domestic development strategy and the "triangular trade structure" under the framework of the modern international political and economic relationship. In this light, this book rejects Western observers' exaggerated recognition of the strategic importance of the "Modern Silk Road", proposing that while the revival of this trade route is a blow to the geo-economic landscape centered around Europe and the United States, it in essence only reflects the flow of Chinese manufactured goods to the Middle East and the latter's oil to China at a time when the US dollar is the dominant currency. Instead of promising to change the existing international political and economic landscape, it reflects some profound strategic dilemma. The "Modern Silk Road" is only unique because it came at a time when a new order was ready to challenge the old. This provides a modern reference to the BRI.

Third, by comparing the BRI with the ancient Silk Road and the "Modern Silk Road", the book tries to explain the former's strategic planning. The comparison with the ancient Silk Road helps with the understanding of the historical conditions giving rise to the BRI, and especially, the intertwining domestic and foreign political, economic and technological conditions. Based on this analysis, the book distinguishes between the practical considerations and ultimate pursuits of the BRI. In terms of practical considerations, the BRI overcomes the limitations of the "Modern Silk Road" between China and the Middle East. For example, by opening up to its West neighbors and developing its West, the BRI helps reverse the tendency of China's economy being overly concentrated in the coastal area and by diversification, it helps reduce China's excessive reliance on the Middle East for oil. It is also China's response to some practical domestic and foreign issues. For example, by expanding Chinese companies' avenues in going global, the BRI helps alleviate the problem of over-capacity and too much money chasing too few assets in China. It also further improves the trade link between Asia and Europe. In terms of ultimate pursuits, it includes overall planning for domestic, especially regional development and opening-up as well as proposing a new international political and economic order. This is where the BRI has greater strategic meaning than both the ancient Silk Road and the "Modern Silk Road".

Fourth, the book evaluates the specific measures that China is taking or about to take as well as some risk responses. Then, it tries to make generalizations of some common models behind these specific measures. In analyzing risk management, the book focuses on the long-term and structural political and security risks that are either real or possible. These risks include political turbulences in key B&R countries, threat posed by "extremism, terrorism and separatism" and arm-wrestling among major powers. These risks intertwine and interact. They have deep historical and modern roots. Therefore, the book will pay most attention to their interactions (such as the interaction between the Afghan situation and "the three forces", the interaction among opium trade, weaponry and terrorism) and strive to illustrate their historical roots (such as the Islamic influence on the ancient Silk Road). Starting from that, the book will make constructive suggestions on China's responses, in terms of both principles and strategies.

The book is divided into three parts: introduction, main body and conclusion. The main body includes eight chapters. The first two chapters provide some historical and modern background for understanding the BRI. Chapters 3–8 discuss about its practical consideration, future vision, cooperation framework, multiple opportunities, government actions, new achievements and risk management, respectively.

Specifically, Chapter 1 reexamines the rise and fall of the ancient Silk Road in order to get some historical background on the BRI in the new era. In particular, discussions focus on the geo-economic and political, trade and religious dimensions.

Chapter 2 looks at the conditions that gave rise to the "Modern Silk Road" and its form and essence so as to provide a modern reference for the BRI.

Chapter 3, building on the previous two chapters, examines the historical background, practical considerations and future vision of the BRI to help readers better understand its importance in the new era.

Chapter 4 discusses how China intends to jointly build the Belt and Road. Chapter 5 analyzes the opportunities that the BRI will bring about for global development, China, markets around the world and ordinary people. Chapter 6 introduces specific measures the central and local governments have taken or will take. Chapter 7 tracks the progress in policy coordination, infrastructure connectivity, unimpeded trade, financial integration, and closer people-to-people bond.

Chapter 8 focuses on the political and security risks that are either real or possible, including political turbulences in key B&R countries, threat of "extremism, terrorism and separatism" and great power competitions and based on that, proposes some tentative responses.

The conclusion of the book tries to sum up the core idea based on discussions in the previous chapters and understand the changed and unchanged in the Belt and Road Initiative compared with the ancient Silk Road and the "Modern Silk Road".

Chapter

1

Reflections on the Ancient Silk Road

As the most important political, economic, cultural and religious link connecting Europe and Asia before the rise of the modern Western world, the Silk Road has become a key concept for describing the continuous communication between the East and West in the ancient times. Since the 20th century, various economic cooperation projects either within Asia or between the two continents have been carried out in the name of a "New Silk Road". The Belt and Road Initiative is another large-scale cooperative initiative that adopts the historical symbol of the Silk Road.

From the perspectives of geography, trade and religion, this chapter aims at portraying a historical horizon for understanding the Belt and Road Initiative in the new period, in view of the reflection over the rise and fall of the ancient Silk Road. Firstly, the evolution of the Silk Road — how did it connect ancient China with Eurasian countries via land and sea-is explored, and further, roots of the historic shift in prosperity from overland Silk Road to maritime Silk Road since the mid-to-late period of Tang Dynasty are investigated. Secondly, international trade on the ancient Silk Road is discussed from the perspectives of commodity and currency, which provides a historical coordinate for understanding the trade and economic cooperation on the modern Silk Road and the "Belt and Road" between China and the Middle Eastern countries. Thirdly, the historical course of Islamization of the ancient Silk Road is reviewed; on the basis of this, complicated interactions between the religious and political landscapes that may emerge on the modern Silk Road are discussed.

1.1 Land–Sea Relations

The ancient Silk Road, consisting of multiple trade routes, connected Asia, Europe and Africa through ocean and land. In different historical periods, the land and maritime trade routes have witnessed their own ups and downs.

1.1.1 *Transnational Communication via Land and Sea Routes*

Since the 2nd century BC, the Han Dynasty began to strengthen its business connection with the Western Regions and establish direct or indirect communication of personnel and trade with the Empires of Kushan, Parthia and Rome. Compared with the grassland route in the North and sea route in the South, the oasis route through the central plains played a more important and dominant role in the communication between the East and the West in the Han Dynasty. This route, the Silk Road in the narrow sense, started from Chang'an in the East, going through Hexi Corridor to Yumen and Dunhuang, and then traversing from Kashgar, across Pamir Mountains, through Yuezhi and Parthia, arriving at the East coast of the Mediterranean. Later, a similar arterial route on the Eurasian inland emerged, connecting the Sui/Tang Dynasties, Sassanid, Byzantium and its neighboring nomadic nations such as the Turkic people.[1]

---

[1] Zhang Guangda, "The Inland Transportation of Eurasia in Ancient Times— Influences of Mountains, Deserts and Oasis on Culture Exchanges between the West and the East", in Zhang Guangda, *Collection of Papers on History and Historical Geography of the Western Regions,* Shanghai: Shanghai Classical Publishing House, 1995, pp. 373–391. (张广达:《古代欧亚的内陆交通——兼论山脉、沙漠、绿洲对

Despite its short period of reign, the Sui Dynasty made great efforts in exploring the Western Regions, which laid the foundation for the prosperity of the Silk Road in the Tang Dynasty. As is recorded in *A Map of the Western Regions* by Pei Ju:

> From Dunhuang to the "Western Sea", there are three routes which traverse through mountains and across rivers. The north route: starting from Yiwu in Xinjiang, through Barkol Lake, Tiele Tribe and Turkic Khanates, across the Beiliuhe River (Yili river and Chu River), to the Byzantine Empire, arriving at the Mediterranean Sea. The central route: starting from Gaochang in Xinjiang, through Karasahr, Kucha (or Qiuci), Shule (in Kashgar), across Pamir Mountains, then passing Ferghana, Sutrushana, Samarkand, Ishtika, Kushanika, to Persia, arriving at the Persian Gulf. The south route: Starting from Shanshan in Xinjiang, passing Khotan, Karghalik, Taxkorgan, over Pamir Mountains, then through Wakhan, Tocharian, Balkh, Bamiyana, Ghazni, to North Brahman (North India), arriving at the Indian Ocean. Countries and regions along the three routes all have their own road networks.[2]

That is to say, there are three routes extending outward from Dunhuang that arrived at the Byzantine Empire in the North, Persia (the Sasanian Dynasty) in the middle, and North Brahman (North India) in the South, reaching the Mediterranean, the Persian Gulf and the Indian Ocean, respectively. As in the Han Dynasty, there existed similar trunk routes in the Sui Dynasty. As a result, Sui enjoyed deepened knowledge of the West. It can be clearly seen that the communications between the East and the West at the time was quite intensive.

At the western end of the Silk Road, the Arabians had been expanding their territory since the rise of Islam, which profoundly changed the geopolitical landscape in Western Asia, Northern Africa, Central Asia and Southern Europe. Through wars, they

---

东西文化交流的影响》，收入氏著：《西域史地丛稿初编》，上海：上海古籍出版社 1995 年版，第 373–391 页。)

[2] (Tang Dynasty) Wei Zheng et al., *Book of Sui*, Volume 67, Beijing: Zhonghua Book Company, 1973, pp. 1579–1580. [(唐)魏征等《隋书》卷六十七，北京：中华书局 1973 年版，第 1579–1580 页。]

conquered the Sasanian Dynasty within a very short period of time and occupied vast territories of the Byzantine Empire — along the eastern coast of the Mediterranean Sea and in Northern Africa, cutting off the trade route from Byzantine to the East. Since the Umayyad Empire and the Abbasid Empire, which had been successively built by the Arabians, were both powerful empires across the Afro-Eurasian continent, the Arab Empire became the de facto dominant power at the western end of the Silk Road.

In 651, the third Khalifa Osman sent envoys to Chang'an, establishing the official relation between the Tang Dynasty and the Arab Empire. This is also China's first contact with the Islamic world.[3] At that time, the Arab Empire was the most powerful country in the western world within sight of China. In 787, Li Mi, Chancellor of the Tang Dynasty, advocated for alliance with the Arab Empire against the Tibetan Empire. In his memorial to the throne, he said, "The Arab Empire is the most powerful country in the western world. Its territory, extending from Pamir to the Western Sea (the Mediterranean), almost covers half of the world. Its people held a long feud against the Tibetans. Therefore, we can build alliance with them".[4] Professor Chen Yuan, an outstanding historian, also pointed out in 1930s that the relationship between the Arab Empire and China in the Tang and Song Dynasties resembles that between Britain and America today, and that of China with Portugal in the Ming Dynasty. At that time, most foreign ships to China came from Persia and Arab.[5]

In records by Jia Dan, the prime minister of Zhenyuan Period (785–805), the transportation between China and Arab Empire in

---

[3] (Later Jin Dynasty) Liu Xu et al., *Old Book of Tang*, Volume 198, Beijing: Zhonghua Book Company, 2000, p. 3313. [(后晋)刘昫等:《旧唐书》卷一百九十八, 北京: 中华书局 2000 年版, 第 3313 页。]

[4] (Ming Dynasty) Yan Yan, *History As a Mirror (Supplement)*, Volume 233, Shanghai: Shanghai Classical Publishing House, 2007, p. 636. [(明)严衍:《资治通鉴补》卷二百三十三,上海古籍出版社 2007 年版, 第 636 页。]

[5] Chen Yuan, "History of Islamism Coming to China", in *Chen Yuan's Historiography Anthology*, Shanghai: Shanghai People's Publishing House, 1981, p. 220. (陈垣:《回回教入中国史略》, 收入氏著:《陈垣史学论著选》, 上海: 上海人民出版社 1981 年版, 第 220 页。)

the Tang Dynasty mainly relied on the land route, which extended from Anxi Protectorate to the Western Regions, and the sea route, whose starting point was Guangzhou — the two constituting the main ateries of the ancient Silk Road.[6] Specifically, the land route started from Chang'an, going through Hexi Corridor, along the southern foot of Tianshan Mountain, westward over Pamir Mountains, and then passing Talas in central Asia and Persia, and finally arrived at the capital of Arab—Bagdad. As is recorded in the famous Arabian geographical work *Book of Roads and Kingdoms* in late 9th century, the land route connecting China and the Arabian world, namely the well-known Great Khurasan Road, stretched from Bagdad to its northeast going through such famous posthouses as Hamadan, Merv, Bukhara, Samarkand, and Syr Darya towards the Chinese border.[7] The Sea route started from Guangzhou and extended westward along the coast, across the South China Sea, the Strait of Malacca, the Bay of Bengal, the Arabian Sea and the Persian Gulf, then going upstream from Tigris-Euphrates Basin towards Bagdad.[8] The Arab merchant Suleiman who once visited Guangzhou in mid-9th century took down his sailing experience. His voyage started from Siraf, passing Muscat of Oman, Sohar, Quilon of India, Island of Langabalous, Champa, and ultimately arriving in Guangzhou.[9] It took him 120 days, which is much the same as that in Jia Dan's records.

---

[6](Song Dynasty) Ouyang Xiu and Song Qi, *New Book of Tang, Volume 43*, Beijing: Zhonghua Book Company, 1975, pp. 1149–1155. [(宋) 欧阳修、宋祁:《新唐书》卷四十三, 北京: 中华书局 1975 年版, 第 1149–1155页。]

[7]Ibn Khordadbeh, *The Book of Roads and Kingdoms*, translated by Song Xian, Beijing: Zhonghua Book Company, 2001. (伊本•胡尔达兹比赫:《道里邦国志》, 宋岘译注, 中华书局 2001 年版。)

[8]The Shipping Line between China and Arab in Tang dynasty, See Li Jinming, "*Research on the Maritime Transportation Routes between China and the Arabian Countries in Tang Dynasty*", Social Sciences in Guangdong, no. 2, 2011, pp. 114–121. (李金明:《唐代中国与阿拉伯海上交通航线考释》, 载 《广东社会科学》 2011 年第 2 期, 第 114–121 页。)

[9]*Ancient Accounts of India and China*, translated by Mu Genlai, et al., Beijing: Zhonghua Book Company, 1983, pp. 7–9. [穆根来等译:《中国印度见闻录》, 北京: 中华书局 1983 年版, 第 7–9 页。]

In the Tang Dynasty, Chang'an and Bagdad were both prestigious international metropolises. The two megacities at the time connected up an array of posthouses and cities located on the vast land between the two empires of Tang and Arab. In the most prosperous age of the Tang Dynasty, markets thrived in the oasis cities and towns on both sides of the Tianshan Mountain. Merchants shared residence with the Hu people (Northern barbarian tribes in ancient China) in Xizhou, Yizhou and Tingzhou, and trade flourished. The four garrisons of Anxi Protectorate became important commercial towns. Cities like Dunhuang, Turpan, Kashgar, Fergana, Samarkand, Bukhara, etc. boomed as important transit cities on the land route. People from central Asian countries including Samarkand, Parthia, Maimargh, Koshana, Kesh, Chach and Khebud (the so-called Nine Surnames in Zhaowu) came to Tang. These people, being well-known for their business skills, contributed a lot to the communication between China and the West, both economically and culturally. A large number of traveling merchants from Arab, Persia and other central Asian ethnic groups flooded eastward into China, thus promoting the spread of material and spiritual civilization from the Middle East and Central Asia into the central plains of China.

A number of plants whose names containing the Chinese character "胡" in ancient Chinese documents, such as "胡桃" (walnut), "胡瓜" (cucumber), "胡椒" (pepper), "胡萝卜" (carrot) etc., were also mostly introduced to China through the Silk Road on the land by merchants from the West and Central Asia during this period. Likewise, a variety of exotic animals, spices, drugs, jewelry, currency, music, dance, food and costume were introduced to China in bulk. Thanks to the unimpeded land route of the Silk Road, so to speak, the Chinese civilization was able to extensively absorb elements from foreign civilization, and formed a unique multicultural landscape.[10] Meanwhile, Chinese products and techniques

---

[10] Rong Sinkiang, *Medieval China and Foreign Civilizations*, Beijing: SDX Joint Publishing Company, 2001; Edward H. Schafer, *The Golden Peaches of Samarkand: A Study of Tang Exotics*, translated by Wu Yugui, Xi'an: Shaanxi Normal University General Publishing House, 2005; Xiang Da, *Changan and the Civilization of the Western Regions in Tang Dynasty*, Shijiazhuang:Hebei Education Press, 2007. (荣新

were also spread to Central and West Asia as well as Europe. According to the study of French scholar Aly Mazaheri, Chinese millet, sorghum, cinnamon, turmeric, ginger, rice, musk, rheum officinale, etc. were spread westward through Persia along the Silk Road.[11] Besides, Chinese technological inventions such as paper-making, printing, lacquer, porcelain, gunpowder and compass were also introduced to Europe by Arabians, making significant contri-bution to world civilization.

Likewise, the rapid development of the sea route in mid-to-late Tang, Song and Yuan Dynasties was closely related to the prosperity of the international ports in China, Southeast Asia, South Asia and West Asia. As to China, cities like Guangzhou and Yangzhou had become highly internationalized trade centers even since the Tang Dynasty, in which a large number of Arabian and Persian merchants swarmed in, selling jewelry, rhinoceros horn and ivory, spice and drug. It was recorded that there were innumerable ships from Brahman, Persia and Dvipatala lining up along the rivers in Guangzhou in 750, carrying mountains of spices and jewelry. The ships were about six to seven zhangs (1 zhang ≈ 3.33 m) in depth, and it was recorded that "people from various places like Simhala, Arab, Baiman and Nanman traveled or resided here".[12] In *Ancient Accounts of India and China*, the famous Arabian work completed in mid-to-late 9th century, it is recorded that "Guangfu is a commercial port and a distributing center of Arabian and Chinese goods", and that Guangzhou is "a place where Arabian merchants gather together".[13]

江:《中古中国与外来文明》, 三联书店 2001 年版; [美]谢弗:《唐代的外来文明》, 吴玉贵译, 西安: 陕西师范大学出版社 2005 年版; 向达:《唐代长安与西域文明》, 石家庄: 河北教育出版社 2007 年版。)

[11] Aly Mazaheri, *La Route De La Soie*, translated by Geng Sheng, Beijing: Zhonghua Book Company, 1993, pp. 439–522. (阿里•玛扎海里:《丝绸之路:中国-波斯文化交流史》, 耿昇译, 中华书局 1993 年版, 第 439–552 页。)

[12] *Ōmi no Mifune, An Account of the Chinese Monk Jianzhen's Work in Japan* (Collated and annotated by Wang Xiangrong), Beijing: Zhonghua Book Company, 1993, p. 74. (真人元开:《唐大和上东征传》, 汪向荣校注, 北京: 中华书局 2000 年版, 第 74 页。)

[13] *Ancient Accounts of India and China*, p. 7 and 96. (穆根来等译:《中国印度见闻录》, 第 7、96 页。)

Since the Grand Canal was dredged in the Sui Dynasty, Yangzhou, a city sitting at the junction of the canal and the estuary of Yangtze River, became, in Tang Dynasty, an important transit port in water transport and a distributing center of goods between North and South China, and also a hub that connected the sea route of the Silk Road and vast areas of inland China. It is documented that when Tian Shengong led armed forces to suppress Liu Zhan in 760, "thousands of travelling merchants from Arab and Persia were killed" in Yangzhou,[14] which also serves as an evidence of the big number of West Asian merchants living in Yangzhou in the Tang Dynasty.

In Song Dynasty, seaborne trade had become an important source of national finance, and the authorities intensified their management of the trade ports. Since the establishment of the Bureau for Foreign Shipping in Guangzhou in Tang Dynasty, the imperial court of Song Dynasty set up nine such bureaus successively in Hangzhou, Mingzhou (now Ningbo), Quanzhou, Mizhou (now Jiaozhou), Wenzhou, Xiuzhou (now Songjiang in Shanghai), Jiangyin, and Shanghai. The most important among them were the two bureaus in Guangzhou and Quanzhou, due to the fact that overseas trade in the Song Dynasty were mainly conducted with Southeast and West Asia. Generally speaking, Guangzhou topped all the other trade ports in the Northern Song Dynasty.[15] Zhu Yu wrote in his *Pingzhou Ketan,* "at the beginning of the reign of Chongning (1102–1106), the three provinces of Zhejiang, Fujian and Guangdong respectively set their own bureaus for foreign shipping, and the one in Guangdong was the

---

[14] (Later Jin) Liu Xu et al., *Old Book of Tang,* Volume 110, Beijing: Zhonghua Book Company, 2000, p. 3313. [(后晋)刘昫等:《旧唐书》卷一百一十, 北京: 中华书局 2000 年版, 第 3313 页。]

[15] As for the trade situation of Guangzhou in Song Dynasty, see Guan Lvquan, *Overseas Trade of Guangzhou in Song Dynasty, Guangzhou:* Guangdong People's Publishing House, 1994; Quan Hansheng, "Domestic and Foreign Trade of Guangzhou in Song Dynasty", in Quan Hansheng, ed. *Researches in Chinese Economic History, Volume 2,* Beijing: Zhonghua Book Company, 2011, pp. 1–63. (关于宋代广州的贸易状况, 参阅关履权:《宋代广州的海外贸易》, 广州:广东人民出版社 1994 年版。全汉昇:《宋代广州的国内外贸易》, 收入氏著:《中国经济史研究. 2》, 北京: 中华书局 2011 年版, 第 1–63 页。)

most prosperous among the three."[16] After the Southern Song Dynasty settled its capital in Lin'an, Quanzhou, which was closer to the political center, developed rapidly and replaced Guangzhou as the biggest trade port in China in the last years of the Southern Song Dynasty, and the biggest in the Orient as well.[17] It is documented that Quanzhou at that time was already "a place where exotic goods and rare treasures can be found, and home to wealthy foreign merchants and business tycoons. It was second to none in the world."[18] Till the end of the Yuan Dynasty, Quanzhou had always been the biggest commercial port for China's foreign trade. The Italian traveler Marco Polo witnessed the spectacular view of Quanzhou Port, "a multitude of merchants gathered here, and goods were piled up like mountains. It was incredible."[19]

In the Song Dynasty when seaborne trade prospered, Srivijaya (nowadays Sumatra of Indonesia) and Quilon (in India) were the two most important transit centers for trade between China and Arab regions on the South China Sea Route. According to *Lingwai Daida* by Zhou Qufei in the Southern Song Dynasty, "the kingdom of Srivijaya is a center of waterways in the South China Sea. Countries within a vast geographical area from the Indonesian islands in the East to the Middle East in the West have to go past Srivijaya to arrive at China."[20] In Zhao Rushi's *Chu Fan Chi (Records of Foreign*

[16] (Song Dynasty) Zhu Yu, *Pingzhou Ketan,* Volume 2, Beijing: Zhonghua Book Company, 1985, p. 17. [(宋)朱彧:《萍洲可谈》(卷二), 北京: 中华书局 1985 年版, 第 17 页。]

[17] As for the reason for the rising of the Quanzhou Port in Southern Song Dynasty, See Chen Gaohua and Wu Tai, *Overseas Trade During Song and Yuan Dynasties,* Tianjin: Tianjin People's Publishing House, 1981, pp. 143–148. (陈高华、吴泰:《宋元时期的海外贸易》, 天津: 天津人民出版社 1981 年版, 第 143–148 页。)

[18] Li Xinghua, *History of Islam in China,* Beijing: China Social Sciences Press, p. 69. (李兴华:《中国伊斯兰教史》, 北京: 中国社会科学出版社 1998 年版, 第 69 页。)

[19] Marco Polo, *The Travels of Marco Polo,* Volume 2, translated and annotated by Yu Qianfan, Beijing: China Books Press, 2009, p. 367.(马可•波罗:《马可•波罗游记》(下册), 余前帆译注, 中国书籍出版社 2009 年版, 第 367 页。)

[20] (Song Dynasty) Zhou Qufei, *The Book of Collation and Annotation of Lingwai Daida,* Collated and annotated by Yang Wuquan, Beijing: Zhonghua Book

Countries), it was described as "gripping the throat of transportation."[21] Besides, "Chinese merchants heading for the Arabian countries must change for small boats in Quilon."[22] So to speak, serving as important transfer stations on the sea route connecting China with Southeast, South and West Asia and even Africa, Quilon and Srivijaya contributed a lot to the prosperity of the maritime Silk Road in the Song and Yuan Dynasties. Quilon, in particular, not only linked up China with the Arabian countries commerically, but also situated on the only route from Srivijaya to Arab.

While Chinese authorities in Song and Yuan Dynasties took initiative to conduct foreign trade, the Arabic states also showed great enthusiasm for trade with Oriental countries such as China. This is not only closely related to the acute business sense of Muslims, but also to the social turbulence and financial difficulty in West Asia caused by the Crusades and the rise of Seljuk Turks. Whether for China or Arabic states, in a sense, Silk Road trade on the sea was an essential approach to alleviate the domestic financial pressure at the time.

As a result, at the other end of the sea route, some well-known trade ports maintained long-term prosperity. Arabian merchant Suleiman observed that goods were delivered to Siraf from Basra, Oman and other places, and most Chinese vessels were loaded there.[23] Siraf is "Djerrarah" in the so-called "South China Sea Route" recorded by Jia Dan. It was destroyed in an earthquake in 977. According to Japanese historian Kuwabara Jistuzo's study, Siraf was the most prosperous among the trade ports in the Persian Gulf that conducted trade with the East Asia after mid-Tang Dynasty. Inhabitants there

---

Company, 1999, p. 367. [(宋)周去非:《岭外代答校注》, 杨武泉校注, 北京: 中华书局 1999 年版, 第 86 页。]

[21] (Song Dynasty) Zhao Rushi, *The Book of Collation and Annotation of Chu Fan Zhi (Records of Foreign Countries)*, Collated and annotated by Yang Bowen, Beijing: Zhonghua Book Company, 2000, p. 36. [(宋)赵汝适:《诸番志校释》"三佛齐"条, 杨博文校释, 北京: 中华书局 2000 年版, 第 36 页。]

[22] (Song Dynasty) Zhou Qufei, The Book of Collation and Annotation of *Lingwai Daida*, p. 91. [(宋)周去非:《岭外代答校注》, 第 91 页。]

[23] *Ancient Accounts of India and China*, p. 7. (穆根来等译:《中国印度见闻录》, 第 7 页。)

accumulated great wealth through foreign trade, and such situation was quite common across Islamic states".[24] Later, the international trade port in the Persian Gulf shifted to Kishma at the Strait of Hormuz. It was on this island port that Marco Polo landed on his voyage from Quanzhou to Persia in Yuan Dynasty, and that Ming's navy led by Zheng He on his expedition to the West traded with Persians and Arabians.[25] Meanwhile, cities like Basra of Iraq, Aden of Yemen and Sohar of Oman were also important seaborne trade centers in the Persian Gulf. *Book of Roads and Kingdoms* described "the sea lane towards the Orient starts from Basra and extends eastward along the Persian coast".[26] Obviously, Basra was viewed as the starting point of the eastward sea route to China and India. At port of Sohar in Omen, merchants from various countries gathered together, bringing a rich variety of commodities. An Arabian geographer in 10th century even held the opinion that "not a single city in the Persian Gulf and the whole Islamic world could be compared with Sohar in terms of magnificent architecture and rich foreign goods".[27] The flourishing Arab cities, whose wealth mainly came from seaborne trade, demonstrated the importance of the maritime Silk Road to the West Asia.

1.1.2 *Rise of the Sea Route and Decline of the Land Route*

The development of the ancient Silk Road is characterized by a historic shift in prosperity from the land route to the sea route, with

---

[24] Kuwabara Jitsuzo: *Study of Trading Ports during Tang and Song Dynasties*, translated by Yang Lian, Shanghai: The Commercial Press, 1935, pp. 32–33. (桑原骘藏:《唐宋贸易港研究》, 杨鍊译, 上海: 商务印书馆 1935 年版, 第 32–33 页。)

[25] Lin Meicun, *Fifteen Lectures on the Silk Road*, Beijing: Peking University Press, 2006, p. 354. (林梅村:《丝绸之路十五讲》, 北京:北京大学出版社 2006 年版, 第 354 页。)

[26] Ibn Khordadbeh, *The Book of Roads and Kingdoms*, translated by Song Xian, Beijing: Zhonghua Book Company, 2001, p. 64. (伊本•胡尔达兹比赫:《道里邦国志》, 宋岘译注, 北京: 中华书局 2001 年版, 第 64 页。)

[27] Tim Severin, *The Sindbad Voyage*, translated by Shi *Chunyong and Guming*, Beijing: World Affairs Press, 1988, p. 35. (赛弗林:《现代辛伯达航海记》, 史春永、古明译, 北京: 世界知识出版社 1988 年, 第 35 页。)

the An-Shi Rebellion (755–763) in the mid-Tang Dynasty as a dividing line. Before the rebellion, the Silk Road on the land had gradually stepped into a period of unprecedented prosperity since the Han Dynasty. Chang'an and Baghdad became the most important cosmopolitan cities at the two ends of the Silk Road in the flourishing period of the Tang Dynasty. The land route, from Arab and Persia to the central plains of China through Central Asia and the Western Regions, became an international trade corridor with greatest vitality. After that, however, the sea route gained increasing importance due to the long-term obstruction of the northwest land route and the southward shift of Chinese economic center, and maintained prosperity in the Song, Yuan and early Ming Dynasties. The land route, which extended westward from China to Central and West Asia and Europe, though revived once after the establishment of the Mongo Empire, began to wane along with the collapse of the Yuan Dynasty ruled by the Mongolians. The land route fell into complete decline since the Yongle period of the Ming Dynasty (1403–1424), when China took the defensive posture in the northwest and withdrew behind Jiayuguan.[28]

Historically, the thriving of the overland Silk Road in early-to-mid Tang Dynasty is closely related to the particular political situation at the time. Specifically, Tang gradually achieved effective rule over the Western Regions and maintained considerable influence over central Asian areas by means of long-term battles, placation, and mollification. In 629, Tang assaulted Eastern Turkic Khanate and destroyed it the next year (630). In 647, Yanran Frontier Command was set up, and was renamed as Anbei Frontier Command in 669, having jurisdiction over the tribes in the North of the Gobi Desert. Hanhai Frontier Command set up in 650 was renamed as Chanyu Frontier Command in 779, having jurisdiction over the tribes in the South of the Gobi Desert. As a result, Tang gradually took the North and South areas of Tianshan Mountain from the hands of Western Turkic

---

[28] He Fangchuan, *A History of Culture Exchanges between China and Foreign Countries*, Volume 1, Beijing: China International Culture Press, 2008, p. 62. [何芳川:《中外文化交流史》(上册), 北京: 国际文化出版公司 2008 年, 第 62 页。]

Khaganate. In 640, Tang occupied Gaochang (nowadays Turpan), and set up the Anxi Protectorate, then captured Kucha in 648 where Anxi Protectorate was resettled, ruling over the Four Garrisons of Anxi: Kucha, Khotan Kashgar and Karashahr. In 659, the rebellion in Western Turkic Khaganate was completely pacified. In 702, Anxi Frontier Command was divided into two. The Beiting Frontier Command was set up to rule over Tingzhou and nomadic minorities in the grassland areas to the North of Tianshan Mountain and Syr Darya, and Anxi Frontier Command ruled over the oasis nations to the South. The establishment of the four frontier commands — Anbei, Chanyu, Beiting and Anxi — enabled the political influence of Tang Dynasty to successfully expand westward to Central Asia. The nations in Central Asia, originally under the rule of Western Turk, came to pledge allegiance to China in succession, and tribal leaders in the northwest revered Emperor Taizong of Tang as "Tian (meaning the highest or heavenly) Khan", and Tang Dynasty as the "Celestial Empire". In 658, Emperor Gaozong sent military officer Dong Jisheng to Transoxiana to set up an Area Command, a prefecture, giving Tang nominal sovereignty over Central Asian areas.[29] The ruling over the Western Regions in early-to-mid Tang eliminated security threat from nomadic states in the northwest, ensuring an unobstructed land route from China to Central and West Asia. This served as the political foundation for the thriving of the overland Silk Road at the time. After Tang, no dynasties on the central plains, except Yuan, had the ability to regain the influence to the extent that the Tang Dynasty had reached.

Accordingly, the obstruction of the land route after mid-Tang Dynasty was due to Tang's gradual loss of dominancy over the political order in the Western Regions and Central Asia. As the political power of the Arab Empire expanded eastward, places such as Khorasan and Tokharistan became subject to the rule of the Arabs. In 751, a

---

[29] Wu Yugui, "The Year of Jimifuzhou Being Adopted in Serindia in Tang Dynasty and Its Relations with Tang Dynasty", *Journal of Xinjiang University*, no. 1, 1986, pp. 55–61. (吴玉贵：《唐代西域羁縻府州建置年代及其与唐朝的关系》, 载《新疆大学学报》1986 年第 1 期, 第 55–61 页。)

fight broke out between Tang and Arab in Talas of Central Asia. Although the defeat in the Battle of Talas did not completely elimi- nate the influence of Tang in Central Asia, it exposed its limit of strength in the region.[30] After the outbreak of An-Shi Rebellion in 755, Tibet availed itself of the opportunity to get in and take the area of Hexi and Longyou, and built its rule over the southern part of Tianshan Mountain, cutting off land transport between Tang and Central Asia. Towards the end of the Tang and during the Five Dynasties, the central plains maintained contact only with certain parts of the Western Regions — specifically, areas extending to Khotan, and completely cut off diplomatic relations with the vast regions to the west of Pamir.[31] Since then, the land transport connect- ing Tang with Central and West Asia had been disrupted by the con- stant battles and confrontations among Liao, Jin, Western Xia, Uyghur and Tibet in the northwest of China. Although the minority regimes in the northwest maintained personnel and trade exchanges with the Abbasid Empire, the land Silk Road fell into decline due to changes in the political landscape.

In this context, the maritime Silk Road picked up its momentum after mid-Tang Dynasty, and underwent unprecedented development in Song, Yuan and early Ming Dynasty. Mr. Chen Yan, an authorita- tive expert on the maritime Silk Road, pointed out that the decline of the land route and the rise of the sea route was closely related; they supplemented and alternated with each other.[32] Due to constant

---

[30] Lu Wei, "The Development and Changes of Struggles between China and Tazi in Central Asia during the Tang Dynasty", in Lu Wei, *Research on the History of Sino-foreign Relations*, Lanzhou: Lanzhou University Press, 2000, pp. 221–240; Wang Xiaofu, *History of the Political Relationship between the Tang, Tibet, and Arabic Empires*, Beijing: Peking University Press, 1992. (卢苇:《唐代中国和大食在中亚地区斗争的发展和变化》, 载卢苇:《中外关系史研究》, 兰州: 兰州大学出版社 2000 年版, 第 221–240 页; 王小甫:《唐、吐蕃、大食政治关系史》, 北京: 北京大学出版社 1992 年版。)

[31] Zhang Weihua, *History of Foreign Relations of Ancient China*, Beijing: Higher Education Press, 1993, p. 94. (张维华:《中国古代对外关系史》, 北京: 高等教育出版社 1993 年版, 第 94 页。)

[32] Chen Yan, *Maritime Silk Road and Cultural Exchanges between China and Foreign Countries*, Beijing: Peking University Press, 1996, p. 19. (陈炎:《海上丝绸之路与中

unrest in the northeast frontiers, people in Northern Song Dynasty preferred the sea route in connecting with the western countries over the land route. In 1013, an imperial decree to the Arabians wrote that "Thou shall take the sea route, from Guangzhou to the capital city."[33] In the Southern Song Dynasty, the land route to the western regions was completely obstructed, "only merchant ships could go to the minority regimes at the western frontier."[34] Later, Gu Yanwu also noted that in the early Southern Song Dynasty, the economy was in a difficult situation and everything depended on seaborne trade.[35] That is, foreign relations (specifically trade relations) of the Southern Song Dynasty were almost completely dependent on the sea route. In the Yuan Dynasty, the land route in the northwest and the sea route in the southeast coexisted all along. Nevertheless, the land route lost its magnificence as compared with the Tang Dynasty, while the sea route built up its status as a waterway connecting China with West Asia. Meanwhile, as the revenue from the Bureau for Foreign Shipping had gradually became an important source of national finance in the Song and Yuan Dynasties, the maritime Silk Road enjoyed an elevated status since it helped to attract foreign investors and conduct foreign trade. For example, Emperor Gaozong of the Song Dynasty said, "the merchant ships contribute heavily to national economy, so we should follow the old practice to attract people from faraway

外文化交流》, 北京大学出版社 1996 年版, 第 19 页。)

[33] (Yuan Dynasty) Toqto'a *et al.*, *The History of Song*, Volume 490, Beijing: Zhonghua Book Company, 1977, p. 14121. [(元)脱脱等:《宋史》卷四百九十, 北京:中华书局 1977 年版, 第 14121 页。]

[34] (Qing Dynasty) Yong Rong et al., *SikuQuanshu: The Complete Library in Four Sections*, Volume 71 (*Zhu Fan Zhi—A Description of Barbarian Nations in the Geography Section*), Beijing: Zhonghua Book Company, 1965, p. 631. [(清)永瑢等:《四库全书总书目》卷七一史部地理类四《诸蕃志》提要, 北京: 中华书局 1965 年版, 第 631 页。]

[35] (Qing Dynasty) Gu Yanwu, *Merits and Drawbacks of All the Provinces and Counties in China*, Shanghai: Shanghai Scientific and Technological Literature Press, 2003, p. 2742. [(清)顾炎武:《天下郡国利病书》, 上海: 上海科学技术文献出版社 2003 年版, 第 2742 页。]

countries."[36] As some scholars pointed out, the Abbasid Empire spared no effort in strengthening its sea transportation since its establishment in 750, and the capital Baghdad has shifted from the transportation center at the West end of the overland Silk Road to the one on the maritime Silk Road. Such transformation also accords with the historical trend of sea route replacing land route after mid-Tang Dynasty in China.[37]

Along with long-term political turbulence in the northwest after mid-Tang Dynasty, China's center of economic gravity gradually shifted to the South. Taxes levied on coastal provinces became a major source of the national tax revenue. To a certain degree, the profound changes in Chinese economic and geographical landscape were the domestic roots for the decline of the Silk Road on the land and rise of that on the sea. Before the Song Dynasty, Guanzhong and Luoyang long remained China's politcal center of gravity, and the nation's economic center of gravity also lied in the North. This led to the concentration of production base and consumer market for Silk Road trade in the North as well. Nevertheless, the economic center of gravity shifted to the South after the Song Dynasty, thus separating itself from the political center of gravity. As an important manifestation for that, production bases for Chinese export commodities in bulk (e.g. silk, china, etc.) were mostly located in the coastal areas of the southeast, providing natural geo-economic advantages to the Silk Road on the sea.

Meanwhile, the ancient Silk Road on the land has insurmountable inherent limitations, apart from structural constraints. On the one hand, it was vulnerable to political changes in the countries along the route. Domestic unrest within one country could affect the traffic on the overland Silk Road. In fact, such occurrences were quite common in northwest China and the Central Asia. On the other hand, the land

---

[36] (Qing Dynasty) Xu Song, *The Song Huiyao Jigao—Song Dynasty Manuscript Compendium*, Beijing: Zhonghua Book Company, 1957 (reprinted in 2006), p. 3375. [(清)徐松：《宋会要辑稿》职官四四之二十四, 北京: 中华书局 1957 年版(2006 年印刷), 第 3375 页。]

[37] Chen Yan, *Maritime Silk Road and Cultural Exchanges between China and Foreign Countries*, pp. 25–26. (陈炎：《海上丝绸之路与中外文化交流》, 第 25–26 页。)

route was greatly susceptible to natural conditions. People had to arduously tramp over mountains, through ravines and across the Gobi Desert. As a result, long-distance land trade possessed inherent disadvantages, such as lower volume, longer time, higher cost, and lower level of security, and thus giving rise to strong demands for cross-border infrastructure. However, even great empires like Rome, Abbasid, Tang, or Mongolia did not have the capacity to provide such large-scale regional public facilities under the condition of the time, not to mention vassal states locked in confrontation for ages.

In contrast, the sea route has evident advantages. On the one hand, although the water passage was bothered by pirates from time to time, there was no political or military power that could seriously interfere with maritime transportation. On the other hand, unlike the land route, the sea route was not subject to the spillover effect of political situation in countries along the route, and the merchant ships could choose to navigate away from turbulent countries or regions. More importantly, ocean shipping had merits like shorter traveling time, heavier loads, lower cost and greater security, compared with camel teams. It has been estimated that a desert caravan composed of 30 camels can only be loaded with 9,000 kg goods, while a ship can carry 600,000 to 700,000 kg of freight, almost equivalent to 2,000 camels.[38] Therefore, ships are more suitable for large-scale trade, and in a way, the decline of the Silk Road on the land was due to the fact that it could no longer support a skyrocketing rise in the China-West Asian trade at the time. It is worth mentioning that the large-scale export of pottery since the mid-and-later periods of Tang Dynasty, especially after Song Dynasty, further reinforced the significance of the sea route. Since pottery is heavy and brittle, its delivery was required to meet stricter transportation conditions. Generally speaking, as compared to land transportation, maritime transportation was more convenient, secure, and thus cost-saving. That's why the boom in trade of pottery often went hand in hand with development of ship manufacturing technology.

---

[38] He Fangchuan, *A History of Culture Exchanges Between China and Foreign Countries*, Volume 1, p. 62. [何芳川：《中外文化交流史》(上册), 第 62 页。]

As is recorded in *Pingzhou Ketan* by Zhu Yu, about shipping of pottery, "the ships are several dozens of zhangs (1 zhang ≈ 3.33 m) in width and depth; Each merchant has his share of storage space, which is about several chi (1 chi ≈ 0.33 m) in length. And merchants sleep on the top of their own piles of goods. The goods are mostly pottery, densely packed, with small ones wrapped in big ones."[39]

More or less, it also implied the correlation between the prosperity of the sea route and China's status as a great sea power at the time. As is recorded in *Ancient accounts of India and China*, there were reefs in the waters between Siraf and Muscat, "only small boats can go through the narrow channel between two reefs, while Chinese ships are too big to pass". At Port of Quilon, each Chinese ship paid 1000 dirhams of tax, while other ships only paid 10–20 dinars (1000 dirhams = 50 dinars).[40] Such disparity in tax is sufficient to demonstrate the immense tonnage of Chinese ships, even if the factor of differentiated tax rates is eliminated. In *Lingwai Daida*, the author Zhou Qufei from the Song Dynasty depicted the giant Chinese ships sailing through the South China Sea, "the ships are like enormous buildings, the sails are like clouds hanging from the sky, and the rudders are several zhangs in length. Each ship can be loaded with 100 men and food sufficient to feed them for a year".[41] Moroccan traveler Ibn Battuta in late Yuan Dynasty observed that Chinese ships at that time could be divided into three types: the largest ones had 3–10 sails and 1000 men working on board (600 sailors and 400 guards), with each being accompanied by three smaller ships (half, one third and a quarter in size, respectively).[42] In seaborne trade, Chinese ships had incomparable advantages. This, in fact, also reflected the changes in balance of powers on the sea route: while Western Asian merchants were

---

[39] Zhu Yu, *Pingzhou Ketan,* Volume 2, p. 18. [(宋)朱彧:《萍洲可谈》(卷二),第18页。]
[40] *Ancient Accounts of India and China,* p. 8. (穆根来等译:《中国印度见闻录》, 第 8 页。)
[41] Zhou Qufei, *The Book of Collation and Annotation of Lingwai Daida,* p. 217.(周去非:《岭外代答校注》, 第 217 页。)
[42] Ibn Battuta, *The Travels of Ibn Battuta*, translated by Ma Jinpeng, Yinchuan: Ningxia People's Publishing House, 1985, p. 490. (伊本•白图泰:《伊本•白图泰游记》, 马金鹏译, 银川: 宁夏人民出版社 1985 年版, 第 490 页。)

dominant on the sea in the early and middle periods of the Tang Dynasty, Chinese ships gradually surpassed and replaced those from Persia, Arab, India and Dvipatala in late Song times, and became the ruler of orders on the Indian Ocean. Louise Levathes once pointed out that Zheng He's seven expeditions to the West showed China's unchallengeable superiority in maritive activities in the early 15th century.[43] As a matter of fact, this superiority has been gradually established as early as the Song and Yuan Dynasties.

Later, due to limited opening up of overseas trade in mid-and-later periods of the Ming and Qing Dynasties, the long-term turbulence within the Islamic world, the domination of the sea by the western world and the global expansion of colonialism, the Silk Road on the sea that used to connect China and Southeast Asia, India, West Asia and Africa fell in decline and ultimately disappeared from history.

In short, the historic rise and decline of the Silk Road on the land and at sea is closely related to a series of factors, including changes in political situation, the southward shift of Chinese economic center of gravity, inherent limitations of land trade and China's superiority at sea. Historical experience has shown that the prosperity of the land Silk Road often depends on China's administration of its northwest borders and political stability of the Middle and West Asian regions. The revival of the Silk Road at the time of Mongol Empire was based on great political and military power; although it is no longer politically legitimate to push for regional integration through means that were adopted by ancient empires, history can offer some enlightments on how to revitalize the land Silk Road under the guidance of political cooperation.

1.2 International Trade

International trade was the central theme around which the ancient Silk Road evolved, and was also the fundamental force to sustain

---

[43] Louis Levathes, *When China Ruled the Seas: The Treasure Fleet of the Dragon Throne*, 1405–1433, New York: Oxford University Press, 1996.

long-term relations among Eurasian countries. Meanwhile, trade is mainly underpinned by a combination of commodity and currency.

1.2.1 *Commodity Composition*

Silk was China's major export during the Qin and Han Dynasties as well as the Wei Jin Southern and Northern Dynasties. At the time, the Parthian Empire and the rising Sassanid Empire monopolized silk trade on the land route between the East and the West. Thanks to merchants from Persia and Central Asia, a silk trading route running through Eurasia between China and the Roman-Byzantine Empire came into being. In order to gain predominance in silk trade, wars broke out among the Byzantine Empire, the Sassanid Empire and the Western Turkic Khaganate, which also reflected high popularity of China's silk in regions along the route.[44] Since the mid-7th century, with the rise of Islam in the Arabian Peninsula, the trade route running from the Byzantine Empire to the East was largely cut off due to military pressure from the Arab Empire. Meanwhile, the Arab Empire vigorously developed and maintained trading relations with Oriental countries through both the sea route and the land route, and thus becoming a major trading partner of China.

Gaafar Karrar Ahmed, a Sudan scholar, found out that in the Tang Dynasty, the commodities China imported from the Arab Empire mainly included frankincense, round timber, gum, Arab gum, myrrh, coffee, ivory, tortoise shell, rhinoceros horn, camphor, ambergris, spice, medical material, cane sugar, cotton, jewelry, pearl, amber, carpet, gold and silver; while China mainly exported silk, porcelain and glass — at the request of the Abbasid Empire — to the Arab Empire.[45] His findings were consistent with those of many other observers. In the 7th and 8th centuries, Al-Jahiz, a scholar from

---

[44] Zhang Yiping, *The Silk Road*, Beijing: China Intercontinental Press, 2005, p. 62. (张一平:《丝绸之路》, 北京: 五洲传播出版社 2005 年版, 第 62 页。)

[45] Gaafar Karrar Ahmed, *Sino-Arab Relations during the Tang Dynasty*, translated by Jin Bo and Yu Yan, *Journal of Xinjiang Normal University* (Social Sciences edition), 2004(3), p. 57. [加法尔•卡拉尔•阿赫默德:《唐代中国与阿拉伯世界的关系》, 金波、俞燕译, 载《新疆师范大学学报》(哲学社会科学版) 2004 年第 3 期, 第 57 页。]

Basra, kept an account of imported goods that were sold on the market of Baghdad in his *Shang Wu De Guan Cha* (Observations on Business). On his list, commodities from China included silk, porcelain, paper, Chinese ink, saddle, sword and cinnamon. In *Ru Zhong Guo Dao Li Xu Zhi* (sequels of roads of China), one chapter in his *Book of Roads and Kingdoms*, Ibn Khordadbeh also listed commodities China exported to the Arab world, including varieties of silk, porcelain, anaesthetic, musk, saddle, marten and cinnamon.[46] Besides the land route, merchants from West Asia also imported silk from China through the sea route in the Tang Dynasty.[47] Hyecho, a Buddhist monk from Silla, once noticed that Persians and Arabs "often sailed from the Western Sea (the Mediterranean Sea) to the South Sea to buy varieties of goods from Sri Lanka — a country was known for its richness in treasures, and to obtain gold from the country of Kunlun. They also sailed to Guangzhou in China to import ghatpot, thin tough silk, silk and silk floss."[48] In the Tang Dynasty, ceramic became a new product for export. Large quantities of celadon wares and ceramic whitewares were sold to Southeast Asia, India, Arab and East Africa via Guangzhou and other ports.[49] Meanwhile, in Chang'an, the capital of China in the Tang dynasty, Arabian and Persian merchants running jewelry businesses were the symbol of affluence and extravagance. *Extensive Records of the*

---

[46] Zhang Guangda, "Looking Back on the Relations between China and Arabia", in Zhang Guangda, *Collection of Papers on the History and Historical Geography of the Western Regions*, Shanghai: Shanghai Classical Publishing House, 1995, p. 426. (张广达：《海舶连天方丝路通大食——中国与阿拉伯世界的历史联系的回顾》，收入氏著：《西域史地丛稿初编》，上海：上海古籍出版社 1995 年版，第 426 页。)

[47] Zhao Feng, *Silk in Tang Dynasty and the Silk Road*, Xi'an: San Qin Press, 1992, pp. 183–236. (赵丰：《唐代丝绸与丝绸之路》，西安：三秦出版社 1992 年版，第 183–236 页。)

[48] Wang Zhongluo, *On Hermeneutics to the Remnant Volume of Chorography of Dunhuang Grottoes*, Shanghai: Shanghai Classical Publishing House, 1993, pp. 276–277. (王仲荦：《敦煌石室地志残卷考释》，上海：上海古籍出版社 1993 年版，第 276–277 页。)

[49] Li Qingxin, *Seaside World: Studies on the History of South China Sea Trade and Sino-Foreign Relations*, Beijing: Zhonghua Book Company, 2010, p. 89. (李庆新：《濒海之地：南海贸易与中外关系史研究》，北京：中华书局 2010 年版，第 89 页。)

Taiping Era recorded a lot of anecdotes of foreign merchants from West Asia in Chang'an, Luoyang, Guangzhou and Yangzhou, most of which were related with jewelry trade. Sometimes the value of trade could reach tens of millions of Guan (one Guan equals to 1000 copper cash).[50] In general, silk, ceramic, jewelry and spice were major international commodities on both the land Silk Road and the maritime Silk Road in the Tang Dynasty, among wich, silk and jewelry were the most popular items at the time.

In the Song Dynasty, the land Silk Road had long been obstructed. As a result, the Song Dynasty resorted to the sea route to trade with Arab regions. Such a seaborne trade route was known as the maritime Silk Road and was extremely prosperous after mid-Tang Dynasty. *Song Shi Shi Huo Zhi* (The Economic History of the Song Dynasty) depicted a picture of the international trade at the time,

> In 971, Emperor Taizu established a Bureau for Foreign Shipping in Guangzhou and then two more in Hangzhou and Mingzhou (now Ningbo) respectively, taking charge of trading with Arab, Guluo, Dupo, Champa, Boni (now Brunei), Mait and Srivijaya (now Sumatra of Indonesia). The commodities included gold, silver, min-qian (strings of copper coins), lead, variegated silk, porcelain, spice, medicine, rhinoceros horn, ivory, coral, amber, strings of pearls, bintie (a kind of steel in ancient times), turtle scale, tortoiseshell, agate, tridacnidae, crystal, ramie cloth, ceylon persimmon sawdust and hematoxylon.[51]

Like the Tang Dynasty, the Song Dynasty majorly exported hand-made goods, such as hardware, silk and porcelain, and imported precious resource products including spices and medicinal materials, rhinoceros horn, ivory and jewelry from Arab and other countries.

[50]Ye Delu, "Hu Merchants in Tang Dynasty and Jewelry", *Journal of Fujen University*, vol. 15, no. 1 and 2, 1947. (叶德禄:《唐代胡商与珠宝》, 载《辅仁学志》第 15 卷第 1、2 合期, 1947 年。)
[51]Toqto'a, *The History of Song*, Volume 186, pp. 4558–4559. (脱脱等:《宋史》卷一百八十六, 第 4558–4559 页。)

It is worth pointing out that compared with the Tang Dynasty, the Song Dynasty saw some changes in its commodity composition in trade with the Arab Empire and other countries. On the one hand, due to advancement in ship manufacturing and seamanship skills, the trade of porcelain in the Song Dynasty was so thriving that it eclipsed that in the Tang Dynasty. Porcelain was tied with silk as the most important bulk commodity that the Song Dynasty exported to the outside world. The technique of silk weaving had been incessantly spread from China to the West for centuries. As a result, countries in Central, West, and Southeast Asia successively mastered such a skill and even exported cloth to China in turn, imperceptibly reducing overseas needs for Chinese silk.[52] Mikami Tsugio, a Japanese scholar, held the opinion that considering the importance of ceramic in marine trade, the sea route — the predominant trade route between the East and the West since mid-Tang Dynasty, should be named "the Ceramic Road".[53] On the other hand, surging imports of spices and drugs made them primary bulk commodity from Arab countries and almost the synonym of "imported goods" in the Song Dynasty. As Bai Shouyi pointed out, in the Tang Dynasty, jewelry was the most famous goods brought in by Arabian merchants. Yet in the Song Dynasty, people valued rhinoceros horn and ivory, especially spices and drugs.[54] Quan Hansheng found in his study of the international trade in Guangzhou — the biggest trading port — that pearl, rhinoceros horn

---

[52] Indeed, we have to point out that even in Yuan and Ming dynasties, silk remained to be the most competitive export commodity in China. For example, Wang Dayuan wrote in *DaoYi ZhiLue—A Brief Account of Island Barbarians* that the main commodity, which had been transported from Vietnam to the west coast of India and to Mecca through maritime route, was silk. By the time Zheng He made his voyages to the South Sea, silk was still the main commodity in the trading with South China Sea and West Asian countries.

[53] Mikami Tsugio, *Tao Ci Zhi Lu (The China Road)*, translated by Li Xijing and GaoShanmei, Beijing: Culture Relics Press, 1984. (三上次男:《陶瓷之路》, 李锡经、高善美译, 北京:文物出版社 1984 年版。)

[54] Bai Shouyi, "Tazi Merchants' Activities in China during Song Dynasty", in Bai Shouyi, ed., *The History of Islam in China*, Yinchuan: Ningxia People's Publishing House, 1983, p. 134. (白寿彝:《宋时大食商人在中国的活动》, 收入氏著:《中国伊斯兰史存稿》, 银川: 宁夏人民出版社 1983 年版, 第 134 页。)

and ivory were the most famous of all luxuries imported from abroad to Guangzhou. Compared with other foreign commodities, Guangzhou imported more spices and drugs.[55] As Zhao Rushi, an official of a Bureau for Foreign Trade in the Southern Song Dynasty, wrote in *Chu Fan Chi* (Records of Foreign Countries), the Bureau adopted the amount of spices as a measure to rank foreign merchants.[56] Hence, there are also scholars who thought that considering the large amount of imports of spices and drugs (particularly spices) the sea route might be termed as "the Spice Road". As a matter of fact, the maritime Silk Road in the Song Dynasty genuinely was actually "the Spice and Ceramic Road".[57]

In the Song Dynasty, Arabian countries were collectively known as Tazi. According to Lingwai Daida (a geography book in the southern Song Dynasty) by Zhou Qufei, thousands of countries were collectively called Tazi. Among all of them, famous ones are just a few.[58] Among others, spices from the Arab Empire were superior in both quantity and quality.[59] According to *Chu Fan Chi* (Records of Foreign Countries), Tazi produced pearl, ivory, rhinoceros horn, frankincense, ambergris, costustoot, clove, nutmeg, benzoin, aloe, myrrh, ferula

---

[55] Quan Hansheng, *Chinese Economic History*, pp. 15–16. Also see Lin Tianwei, *A History of Spice Trade in the Song Dynasty*, Taipei City: Taiwan Chinese Culture University Press, 1986.(全汉昇:《中国经济史研究.2》, 第 15–16 页。迄今为止, 关于宋代香药贸易最详细而深入的研究, 参阅林天蔚:《宋代香药贸易史》, 台北: 台湾中国文化大学出版部 1986 年版。)

[56] Zhao Rushi, *The Book of Collation and Annotation of Zhu Fan Zhi: A Description of Barbarian Nation*, p. 163. (赵汝适:《诸蕃志校释》, "乳香条", 第 163 页。)

[57] Chen Jiarong, *"On the Ancient 'Spice-China Route'"*, UNESCO in Quanzhou International Symposium on Comprehensive Inspection of the Maritime Silk Road, *China and the Maritime Silk Road*, Fuzhou: Fujian People's Publishing House, 1991, pp. 17–19. (陈佳荣:《古代香瓷之路刍议》, 收入联合国教科文组织海上丝绸之路综合考察泉州国际学术讨论会组织委员会编:《中国与海上丝绸之路》, 福州: 福建人民出版社 1991 年版, 第 17–19 页。)

[58] Zhou Qufei, *The Book of Collation and Annotation of Lingwai Daida*, p. 99. (周去非:《岭外代答校注》, 第 99 页。)

[59] Lin Tianwei, *A History of Spice Trade in the Song Dynasty*, p. 81; Zhao Rushi, *The Book of Collation and Annotation of Zhu Fan Zhi: A Description of Barbarian Nation*, pp. 161–200. (林天蔚:《宋代香药贸易史》, 第 81 页; 赵汝适:《诸蕃志校释》, "卷下志物", 第 161–200 页。)

asafoetida, wanaqi (penis and testicle of eared seal and spotted seal), borax, colored glaze, glass, coral, gardenia, rose water, nutgall, beeswax, gold cloth, silk floss, colored satin and so on.[60] Precious spices such as frankincense, ambergris, costustoot, nutmeg, gardenia, rose water and benzoin were sold extremely well in the Song Dynasty. Spice was closely related to life both in the imperial court and of the literati and officialdom. Frankincense was the most popular of all spices. Therefore, spices, especially frankincense, were subjected to "jin que" and "bo mai". "Jin que" means the trade of certain goods under the counter is legally banned, and the right was exclusive to the government. "Bo mai" means the government makes direct purchase of the shipped goods from foreign merchants. On July 1, 1138, Emperor Gaozong of the Southern Song Dynasty gave orders to officials of Bureau for Foreign Trade in Guangzhou,

> We must restore the old system of our forbears, making direct purchase of the useful things such as frankincense and other spices and drugs. Since the frankincense is sold well, the related officials should keep it in mind and try to establish contact with more foreign merchants and make more purchase of it.[61]

In fact, the amount of frankincense purchased in accordance with the old system was quite staggering. In Guangdong Customs Records, a quotation from Zhong Shu Bei Dui (a population statistics book authored by Bi Yan in the Song Dynasty) said that, from 1076 to 1078, "the three bureaus for Foreign Trade in Mingzhou (now Ningbo), Hangzhou and Guangzhou purchased 354,449 jin (1 jin = 0.5 kg) frankincense. The sales revenue reached 894,719,350 copper."[62] The figures here tell us how thriving the spice trade was in the song Dynasty.

---

[60] Zhao Rushi: *The Book of Collation and Annotation of Zhu Fan Zhi: A Description of Barbarian Nation*, p. 90. (赵汝适:《诸藩志校释》, "大食国" 条, 第 90 页。)

[61] Xu Song, *Song Dynasty Manuscript Compendium*, p. 3372. [徐松:《宋会要辑稿》职官四四之十六, 第 3372 页。]

[62] Liang Tingnan, *Guangdong Customs Records*, Volume 3, Taipei: Taiwan Wenhai Press, 1975, pp. 145–147. (梁廷枏:《粤海关志》卷三•前代事实二, 台北: 台湾文海出版社 1975 年版, 第 145–147 页。)

It was obvious that the spice trade made a sizable contribution to national finance in the Song Dynasty. Other than tea, salt and alumen, the Song Dynasty made the most profit from spices.[63] According to Bai Shouyi's statistics, the national finance of the Song Dynasty was increasingly reliant on trades of spices, drugs, rhinoceros horns, ivories and jewels. In the early Northern Song Dynasty, foreign trade accounted for 1/50 of the annual revenue. Yet the ratio rose to 1/5 in the early Southern Song Dynasty. Needless to say, the maritime Silk Road, especially spice, drug, rhinoceros horn, ivory and jewelry in trade, was of great significance in the Song Dynasty.[64]

Except silk, the Song Dynasty exported the largest quantities of ceramic in its international trade. The prosperity of ceramic trading continued into the Yuan and Ming Dynasties. In his *Concise Book of Lands*, Ibn al-Faqih, an Arabian geographer, listed ceramic, silk and lamp as the three famous products of China.[65] Islamic scholar Al-Thaalibi, who lived in the 10th and 11th centuries, said that Arabians tended to view all delicate or exquisite vessels as Chinese products, regardless of their place of origin.[66] In order to cater to the large-scale needs overseas, there emerged hundreds of kilns in China's southeast coastal areas.[67] Today, archaeological evidences have clearly revealed the prosperity of trade of ceramic between China and Southeast Asia, West Asia and North Africa and the international sales network of Chinese ceramic since the Tang Dynasty.[68]

---

[63] Toqto'a, *The History of Song*, Volume 185, p. 4537. (脱脱等:《宋史》卷一百八十五, 第 4537 页。)

[64] Bai Shouyi, "*Tazi Merchants' Activities in China during Song Dynasty*", in Bai Shouyi, ed., *The History of Islam in China*, Yinchuan: Ningxia People's Publishing House, 1983, p. 160.

[65] Shen Fuwei, *Study on Culture Exchanges between China and West Asia*, Urumqi: Xinjiang People's Publishing House, 2010, p. 205. (沈福伟:《中国与西亚文化交流研究》, 乌鲁木齐: 新疆人民出版社 2010 年版, 第 205 页。)

[66] Du Yu, *A Brief History of the Maritime Silk Road*, Beijing: Social Sciences Academic Press, 2011, p. 93. (杜瑜:《海上丝路史话》, 北京: 社会科学文献出版社 2011 年版, 第 93 页。)

[67] Feng Xianming, *Chinese Ceramics*, Shanghai: Shanghai Classic Publishing House, 2001, p. 401. (冯先铭:《中国陶瓷》, 上海:上海古籍出版社 2001 年版, 第 401 页。)

[68] Yan WenRu, "See the Friendly Relationship between Arab and China from Archaeological Discovery", *Cultural Relics*, 1958(9); Ma Wenkuan and Meng

Ceramics of Yue Kiln in the 9th and 10th centuries were unearthed in Sarawak, Sabah, Indonesia. A large number of ceramic fragments from the Tang Dynasty, including tri-colored glazed potteries, ceramic whitewares of Xingzhou, tawny vitreous enamels of Yuezhou (now Shaoxing), and ceramics of Changsha Kiln, were found in the southern suburb of Fustat, Cairo, Egypt. At the Nishapur site in Iran, ceramics produced in Xing Kiln, Changsha Kiln and Yuezhou Kiln from the latter half of the 9th century to the first half of the 10th century in Tang Dynasty were unearthed. At the Banbhore site in Karachi, Pakistan, archaeologists excavated ceramics of Yue Kiln from the late Tang Dynasty and fragments of tawny glazed bowls with patterns of green grass and colored flowers produced in Changsha Kiln. Ceramics of Yue Kiln in the 9th and 10th centuries as well as fragments of celadon wares of Longquan Kiln in the 12th and 13th centuries were discovered in today's Iraq. Fragments of ceramic whitewares of Dehua Kiln in the Song Dynasty and celadon bowls with embossing peony of official kiln in the Southern Song Dynasty were unearthed in Hama, Syria. Fragments of celadons and blue and white porcelains from the Song and Yuan Dynasties were also found in Bahrain on the Arabian Peninsula, Abidjan in northeast Aden, Yemen and Sohar in Oman. Hence, the large quantities of Chinese ceramic for exportation and the scale of the trade back then were much in evidence.[69] Chinese ceramic was first introduced to Africa in the Tang Dynasty, and the export of large quantities of procelein to Africa did not happen until the Song and Yuan Dynasty. Chinese ceramic relics, which can be traced back to the late Tang Dynasty and early Ming Dynasty, are found everywhere along the 2-km-coastline of port Aydhab between

---

Fanren, *Chinese Ancient Ceramics Found in Africa*, Beijing: The Forbidden City Publishing House, 1987; Chinese Ceramics Association and Ancient China Ceramic Export Research Institute, *Ceramic Export in Ancient China*, Beijing: The Forbidden City Publishing House, 1988. (阎文儒：《从考古发现上看阿剌伯国家与中国的友好关系》，载《文物参考资料》1958 年第 9 期；马文宽、孟凡人：《中国古瓷在非洲的发现》，北京：紫禁城出版社 1987 年版；中国古陶瓷研究会、中国古外销陶瓷研究会：《中国古代陶瓷的外销》，北京：紫禁城出版社 1988 年版。)
[69] Du Yu, *A Brief History of Maritime Silk Road*, pp. 99–112. (杜瑜：《海上丝路史话》，第 99–112 页。)

Egypt and Sultan.[70] As Mikami Tsugio noticed, Chinese style swept the porcelain industry across the Middle East.[71]

It can be said that during the long history of the Silk Road, China as well as countries and regions along the Silk Road had seen stability in the commodity composition of their bilateral trade. China mainly exported hand-made goods such as silk and porcelain and imported precious resource commodities in bulk from West Asia and the South China Sea, such as spice, drug, rhinoceros horn, ivory and jewelry. The stability stemmed from considerable profits of the trade, strong complementarity of the two sides and lack of outside competition. American historian Stavros Stavrianos believed that disparities between China and countries along the Silk Road in their commodity structure of export and import was a manifestation of China's dominance in international trade at that time.[72] French scholar Mazaheri pointed out that the Islamic world had sent more envoy-trade caravans to China because the Iran-Islamic world was much more dependent on Chinese products, not vice versa.[73]

Although silk, porcelain, spice, drug, rhinoceros horn, ivory and jewelry gained enormous popularity at that time, they mainly catered to upper classes and barely affected the livelihood of ordinary people. Ancient China's demand for these goods is much less than the current world's reliance on "Made in China" commodities, or modern China's dependence on bulk commodities such as oil and minerals. In fact, such a fundamental shift reflected the essential difference between ancient and current international trade.

---

[70] Xia Nai, "Porcelain-Evidence of the Relationship between Ancient China and Africa", originally incorporated into *Cultural Relics*, 1963(1), then incorporated into the *Collection of Xia Nai*, Beijing: China Social Sciences Press, 2008, pp. 418–427. (夏鼐:《作为古代中非交通关系证据的瓷器》,收入氏著:《夏鼐集》,北京:中国社会科学出版社2008年版,第418–427页。)

[71] Mikami Tsugio, *The China Road*, p. 152.(三上次男:《陶瓷之路》,第 152 页。)

[72] Leften Stavros Stavrianos, *A Global History*, translated by Wu Xiangying et al., Shanghai: Shanghai Academy of Social Sciences Press, 1992, p. 438.(斯塔夫里阿诺斯:《全球通史》,吴象婴等译,上海:上海社会科学院出版社 1992 年版, 第 438 页。)

[73] Aly Mazaheri, Silk Road: *A History of Sino-Persian Cultural Exchanges*, p. 25. (阿里•玛扎海里:《丝绸之路: 中国-波斯文化交流史》, 第 25 页。)

1.2.2 *Currency Circulation*

Trade on the Silk Road primarily centered on barter at an early stage. Yet with the volume, scope and frequencey of trade growing, there emerged currencies for valuation and settlement. Since the 20th century, archaeologists constantly discovered Chinese and foreign coins, which vividly showed coexistence and mutual promotion between trade and currency circulation on the Silk Road. According to incomplete statistics, foreign coins unearthed in China mainly include Roman-Byzantine gold coin, Sassanian silver coin, Arabian gold coin, Kushan copper coin, Turgesh copper coin, Qara Khanid copper coin and Chagatai silver coin. While most of China's outflowed coins were Wuzhu coin, Kaiyuan Tongbao in Tang Dynasty and Song coin.[74]

Prior to the rise of the Arab Empire, the Byzantine Empire and the Sassanid Empire were the most powerful countries in the western part of the Silk Road. Frequent trade led to the wide spread of such major international coins as Byzantine gold coin and Persian silver coin in West Asia and Central Asia. Then they flowed into China along the Silk Road. A succession of archaeological discoveries have fully confimed it. Persian silver coins were in the largest quantity and the widest distribution (see Table 1.1) In this regard, from the 4th to the 7th centuries, the Eurasian trade route was not only the Silk Road running from the East to the West, but also a "Silver Road" running from the West to the East.[75]

Researches show that, the Byzantine gold coins discovered so far in China are mainly distributed in Xinjiang (Khotan and Turpan), Gansu (Wuwei, Tianshui and Longxi), Ningxia (Guyuan), Shaanxi (Xianyang, Xi'an, Shangzhou and Dingbian), Hebei (Zanhuang County, Cixian County) and Henan (Luoyang), all of which are

---

[74] Kang Liushuo, "See the Exchanges and Integration of the Monetary Culture of the East and the West from Ancient Foreign Coins Unearthed in China", *Gansu Finance*, no. 2, 2002, pp. 9–18. (康柳硕:《从中国境内出土发现的古代外国钱币看丝绸之路上东西方钱币文化的交流与融合》, 载《甘肃金融》2002 年第 2 期, 第 9–18 页。)
[75] Jiang Boqin, *Dunhuang and Turpan Instruments and the Silk Road*, Beijing: Culture Relics Press, 1994, p. 30. (姜伯勤:《敦煌吐鲁番文书与丝绸之路》, 北京: 文物出版社 1994 年版, 第 30 页。)

Table 1.1   Incomplete Statistics of Unearthed Gold and Silver Coins Circulated Along the Silk Road in Wei, Jin, Northern and Southern Dynasties as well as Sui and Tang Dynasties

Category	Location	Amount
Sassanian silver coin	Xinjiang, Qinghai, Shaanxi, Henan, Hebei, Inner Mongolia, Guangdong	1598
Byzantine gold coin	Xinjiang, Gansu, Ningxia, Shaanxi, Hebei, Henan	54

Source: Sun Li, "The Distribution of Sassanian Silver in China and its Functions", *ActaArchaeologica Sinica*, no. 1, 2004, pp. 35–54; Zhang Xushan, *A Study on Relationship between China and the Byzantine Empire*, Beijing: Zhonghua Book Company, 2012, pp. 202–213. (孙莉:《萨珊银币在中国的分布及其功能》, 载《考古学报》2004 年第 1 期, 第 35–54 页; 张绪山:《中国与拜占庭帝国关系研究》, 北京: 中华书局 2012 年版, 第 202–213 页。)

located along the land Silk Road.[76] The Sassanian silver coins were mainly discovered in Xinjiang (Wuqia County, Turpan, Kuqa), Qinghai (Xining), Shaanxi (Xi'an and Yaozhou District), Henan (Luoyang), Hebei (Dingxian County) and Guangdong (Yingde and Qujiang) — locations on both the land route and the sea route.[77] Connecting the foresaid locations, we can roughly outline the routes along which Byzantine gold coins and Sassanian silver coins flowed into China. Such routes are highly consistent with those of the Silk Road. Judging from the period when they were made, the quantities of the two coins unearthed in China are also a reflection of the fates of their respective empires at the time.

---

[76] Zhang Xushan, *A Study on Relationship Between China and the Byzantine Empire*, Beijing: Zhonghua Book Company, 2012, p. 216. (张绪山:《中国与拜占庭帝国关系研究》, 北京: 中华书局 2012 年版, 第 216 页。)

[77] Xia Nai, "Summary on Sassanian Persian Coins Unearthed in China", *Acta Archaeologica Sinica*, no. 1, 1974, p. 105; Sun Li, "The Distribution of Sassanian Silver Coins in China and Its Functions", *Acta Archaeologica Sinica*, no. 1, 2004, pp. 35–43. (夏鼐:《综述中国出土的波斯萨珊朝银币》, 载《考古学报》1974 年第 1 期, 第 105 页; 孙莉:《萨珊银币在中国的分布及其功能》, 载《考古学报》2004 年第 1 期, 第 35–43 页。)

Specializing in intermediary trade between the East and the West, Sogdians from Central Asia played an important role in the circulation of Sassanian silver coin. Each Sassanian coin was made of fine silver at the same weight. It is easy to be carried around. Therefore, the Sassanian silver coins gained enormous popularity in the Sogdian community in Qiuci, Gaochang and Hexi. In Wei, Jin and Southern and Northern Dynasties, Qiuci also casted copper coins that was similar to those of Central China, which ended up as fractional currency which was used in trade of small items or as the change. Trade was settled mainly in Sassanian silver coins and a small quantity of Byzantine gold coins.[78] According to *Sui Shu Shi Huo Zhi* (The Economic History of the Sui Dynasty), at the beginning of the Latter Zhou Dynasty, officials allowed foreign gold and silver coins to be circulated in prefectures of Hexi.[79]

With the rise of Islam in the mid-7th century, the Arab Empire conquered Sassanid and captured parts of Byzantine's territories. In this background, Byzantine gold coins and Persian silver coins gradually diminished and eventually disappeared in China, and were then replaced by a growing number of Arabian gold coins. In 1964, three gold coins inscribed in Arabic and with a mark of "Dinar" were unearthed in a tomb in Yaotou Village, Xi'an, Shaanxi Province, each of which weighed 4.2 to 4.3 g.[80]

In addition to the land route, Arabian and Persian merchants who frequently commuted between China and the Persian Gulf through the sea route, also promoted the circulation of gold and silver of West Asia in Lingnan Region. Yuan Zhen, a poet in the Tang Dynasty, noticed that "gold and silver were used as currencies in

---

[78] Zhang Zhongshan, *The Silk Road and Currency*, Lanzhou: Lanzhou University Press, 1999, p. 27. (张忠山:《中国丝绸之路货币》, 兰州: 兰州大学出版社 1999 年版, 第 27 页。)

[79] (Tang Dynasty) Wei Zheng et al., *The Book of Sui*, Volume 24, Beijing: Zhonghua Book Company, 1973, p. 691. [(唐)魏征等:《隋书》卷二十四, 北京: 中华书局 1973 年版, 第 691 页。]

[80] Zhang Zhongshan, *The Silk Road and Currency*, p. 59. (张忠山:《中国丝绸之路货币》, 第 59 页。)

Lingnan region."[81] Yet in 621, the imperial court of the Tang Dynasty started to cast "Kaiyuan Tongbao" copper coins, which were widely circulated in domestic market. According to *Ancient Accounts of India and China*, kings of other countries didn't own copper coin while copper coins were national currency in China and India. Kings of these two countries also possessed gold, silver, pearl, brocade and silk. These treasures, though in abundance, were merely commodities while copper coin served as currency.[82] Hence there were obvious disparities between the trade in Lingnan Region, which was conducted in gold and silver coins, and the currency circulation in other parts of China. Researchers found that extensive production of gold and silver in Lingnan Region underpinned the circulation of gold and silver in this area. However, marine trade with Arab and Persia also played an important role in facilitating the circulation.[83] *Guang Zhou Ji* (monograph on Guangzhou) of the Tang Dynasty said that "Gold scrape is produced in Arab. The Arab Empire is the biggest producer of gold and all of its trade is conducted in gold".[84] Poet Wang Jian wrote that "foreign shipping brought down the gold price."[85] Thus it can be seen that merchants from West Asia brought such a large

---

[81] (Tang Dynasty) Yuan Zhen, "About Currency", in Yuan Zhen, ed., *Yuan Shi Chang Qing Ji*, Shanghai: Shanghai Classical Publishing House, 1994, p. 180. [(唐) 元稹:《钱货议状》,收入氏著:《元氏长庆集》,上海:上海古籍出版社 1994 年版, 第 180页。]

[82] It is estimated that One Guan copper coins roughly equals to a Gold Dinar weighing 4.25 g. See *Ancient Accounts of India and China*, p. 15 and 69.

[83] Wang Chengwen, "Research on Silver and Gold Production in Lingnan Area during Tang Dynasty and Its Impact", *Journal of Chinese Historical Studies*, 2008(3), pp. 45–66. (王承文:《论唐代岭南地区的金银生产及其影响》, 载《中国史研究》2008 年第 3 期,第 45–66 页。)

[84] Wang Chengwen, *"Research on Silver and Gold Production in Lingnan Area during Tang Dynasty and its Impact"*, p. 45. (王承文:《论唐代岭南地区的金银生产及其影响》, 第 45 页。)

[85] Wang Jian, *"Seeing Shangshu Zheng Quan Off for South China Sea"*, in *The Collection of Wang Jian's Poems*, Beijing: Zhonghua Book Company, 1959, p. 51. (王建:《送郑权尚书南海》,收入氏著:《王建诗集》,北京: 中华书局 1959 年版, 第 51 页。)

quantity of gold to China through marine trade that gold price in Lingnan region was unavoidably affected.

As gold and silver of Byzantine, Persia and Arab flowed to China through the land and the sea route, the thriving trade on the Silk Road also promoted the outflow of Chinese copper coins. According to *Ancient Accounts of India and China*, "copper coins inscribed with Chinese" gained enormous popularity in the renowned Persian port Siraf.[86] *Song Shi Shi Huo Zhi* (The Economic History of the Song Dynasty) said that, "*Copper coin, which is exclusive to China, is now widely used in foreign countries.*"[87] In early Southern Song Dynasty, annual revenues from foreign trade were handsome, but foreign trade led to the outflow of large quantities of gold, silver, cooper and iron coins, especially copper coins.[88] In the Ming Dynasty, Ma Huan wrote in his *Vision in Triumph in a Boundless Sea*, "*There are numerous wealthy men in foreign countries and they resort to Chinese copper coin as a way to trade.*"[89] Such descriptions evidently showed the role of copper coin in the Tang and Song Dynasties as the most important currency in circulation. Chinese copper coins were not only circulated in Japan and Southeast Asia, but also found in abundance in Southeast Asia, West Asia and Africa. Coins of the Tang Dynasty including "Kaiyuan Tongbao", "Qianyuan Zhongbao" and "Dali Yuanbao" were unearthed in the city site at Ak-Beshim in south Tokmok.[90] 176 Chinese copper coins were found in Zanzibar, Tanzania in Africa,

---

[86] *Ancient Accounts of India and China*, p. 99. (穆根来等译：《中国印度见闻录》，第 99 页。)

[87] Toqto'a, *The History of Song*, Volume 180, p. 4384. (脱脱等：《宋史》卷一百八十，第 4384 页。)

[88] Toqto'a, *The History of Song*, Volume 186, p. 4566. (脱脱等：《宋史》卷一百八十六，第 4566 页。)

[89] Ma Huan, *Collation and Annotation of Vision in Triumph in a Boundless Sea*, collated and annotated by Feng Chengjun, Beijing: Zhonghua Book Company, 1955, p. 14. [(明)马欢：《瀛涯胜览校注》，冯承钧校注，北京：中华书局 1955 年版，第 14 页。]

[90] Wen Jiang, "The Open-up Policy and the Development of Foreign Trade in the Tang Dynasty", *Maritime History Studies*, no. 2, 1988, p. 2. (汶江：《唐代开放政策与海外贸易的发展》，载《海交史研究》1988 年第 2 期，第 2 页。)

including 4 "Kaiyuan Tongbao", 108 copper coins of the Northern Song Dynasty and 55 coins of the Southern Song Dynasty.[91]

As a matter of fact, copper coin was not only the currency of settlement for international trade but also treasured up by foreign countries. As is recorded in the Song Huiyao Jigao, "Foreign countries stored up Chinese currencies as treasures. Foreign trade was conducted exclusively in copper coin. People were flocking to copper coin in hopes of obtaining handsome profits."[92] This shows that copper coins had become one of the currencies circulated in countries in West Asia and Southeast Asia.

The long-term massive outflow of copper coin not only promoted the prosperity of international trade on the Silk Road, but also led to domestic deflation. The huge outflow of copper coins disrupted China's economic order. Therefore, since 714, the Tang Dynasty had not allowed gold, iron and copper coins to be used in foreign trade. The imperial court issued a ban in the early Song Dynasty and then repeatedly legislated against the outflow of copper coin. Yet these bans were actually unenforceable.[93] As is recorded in *Song Shi Shi Huo Zhi* (The Economic History of the Song Dynasty),

> Bureaus for Foreign Trade were set up in provinces of Zhejiang, Fujian and Guangdong to take charge of the marine trade, through which, copper coins outflowed in great quantities from China to foreign countries. A ban was issued on copper coins that were carried out of the capital city of Lin'an (now Hangzhou), or were used in foreign trade. In 1182, officials of Guangzhou, Quanzhou,

---

[91] Ma Wenkuan, "Chinese Coins Unearthed in Africa and its Significance", *Maritime History Studies*, no. 2, 1988, pp. 36–42; Tian Shumao, "Chinese Culture Relics Found in East Africa", *Academic Journal of Jinyang*, no. 6, 1982, pp. 12–14. (马文宽:《非洲出土的中国钱币及其意义》, 载《海交史研究》1988 年第 2 期, 第 36–42 页; 田树茂:《东非发现的我国文物》, 载《晋阳学刊》1982 年第 6 期, 第 12–14 页。)

[92] Xu Song, *Song Huiyao Jigao (Punishment 2)*, p. 6567. (徐松:《宋会要辑稿》(刑法二), 第 6567 页。)

[93] Kuwabara Jitsuzo, *History of Maritime Transportation between China and Arab*, translated by Feng You, Shanghai: The Commercial Press, 1934, pp. 41–46. (桑原骘藏:《中国阿剌伯海上交通史》, 冯攸译, 上海: 商务印书馆 1934 年版, 第 41–46 页。)

and Xiuzhou were punished for the loss of copper coins. In 1208, these three provinces claimed since the setting up of the Bureaus for Foreign Trade, merchant ships dispatched should obtain authorization. At the end of the period of Emperor Gaozong, it was widely discussed among officials that ships sent out by Bureaus for Foreign Trade in Quanzhou and Guangzhou as well as the other two in the southwest were loaded with cooper coins. Who could punish them for breaking the law?[94]

Such an account shed light on the importance of copper coin in overseas trade in the Song Dynasty, and also, bans on copper coins reflected the severity of the loss. Hence, government encouraged the use of silk and porcelain in exchange for foreign goods, which, objectively speaking, helped to promote the exportation of silk and porcelain. Silk, the most popular export commodity of ancient China, was widely used as a currency in international trade settlement. Some scholars pointed out that in Tang Dynasty silk was used in bulk as money on the Silk Road. It played a role as a currency, rather than a commodity.[95] Unlike copper coin, massive outflows of silk could neither harm domestic economy nor lead to currency devaluation or credit crisis. Given a huge inflow of gold and silver from West Asia, an enormous outflow of Chinese copper coin, as well as a lack of gold and silver reserve, silk, used as money, played an important role of a "buffer". In fact, it was not only in Tang Dynasty, but also during Zheng He's voyages to the West, that silk was widely accepted as a currency for settlement and pricing.

In short, during the heyday of the Silk Road between China and Southeast Asia, Central Asia and West Asia, gold and silver coins from Roman-Byzantine, Persia and Arab and copper coins from China were the major currencies for valuation in international trade. Meanwhile, China also occasionally used silk as an auxiliary commodity currency in foreign trade. It is worth mentioning that China

---

[94] Toqto'a, *The History of Song*, Volume 180, pp. 4396–4397. (脱脱等:《宋史》卷一百八十, 第 4396–4397 页。)

[95] Zhao Feng, *Silk and the Silk Road in Tang Dynasty*, Xi'an: San Qin Press, 1992, p. 208. (赵丰:《唐代丝绸与丝绸之路》, 西安: 三秦出版社 1992 年版, 第 208 页。)

mainly output base metal currencies while it took in precious metal currencies from West Asia. The evident contrast showed the dominant role of ancient China in international trade on the Silk Road. Generally speaking, at the time of metallic currency, precious metal was more likely to be used as a credible currency of settlement in international trade. Although base metals could circulate as money domestically through government enforcement, it was less competitive in international trade. Therefore, the significance of copper coin in international trade in the Tang and Song Dynasties stemmed from the comprehensive national strength of China. National power and credit of the country ensured the large overseas demands for copper coin and the enormous circulation of such a base metal. However, in essence, the circulation of various metallic coins on the Silk Road mainly depended on their convenience in transaction. None of the involved parties had ever bundled currency with the valuation and settlement of commodities such as silk, porcelain, and spice nor tried to gain trade advantage or political–economic power by asserting currency dominance. Therefore, there is a fundamental difference between the foresaid coins and today's world currencies such as USD and British pound.

1.3 Islamization

As a trade route connecting Europe and Asia in ancient times, the Silk Road genuinely served as the road of faith.[96] For an extended period,

---

[96] Susan Whitfield and Ursula Sims-Williams, The Silk Road: *Trade, Travel, War and Faith,* Chicago: Serindia Publications, 2004; Richard C. Foltz, *Religions of the Silk Road: Overland Trade and Cultural Exchange from Antiquity to the Fifteenth Century,* New York: St. Martin's Press, 1999; Richard Foltz, Religions of the Silk Road: *Pre-modern Patterns of Globalization,* New York: Palgrave Macmillan, 2010; Ma Tong, *The Muslim Culture on the Silk Road,* Yinchuan: Ningxia People's Publishing House, 2003. (马通:《丝绸之路上的穆斯林文化》, 银川: 宁夏人民出版社2003年版。); Zhou Jingbao, *Research on the Buddhist Culture on the Silk Road,* Urumqi: Xinjiang People's Publishing House, 2010.(周菁葆:《丝绸之路佛教文化研究》,乌鲁木齐:新疆人民出版社2010年版。); Li Jinxin, *Religions on the Silk Road,* Urumqi:Xinjiang People's Publishing House, 2010. (李进新:《丝绸之路宗教研究》, 乌鲁木齐:新疆人民出版社 2010 年版。)

with frequent population mobility and commercial intercourse, various Eastern and Western religions including Zoroastrianism, Buddhism, Manichaeism and Nestorianism spread along the Silk Road and coexisted peacefully with each other. However, since the mid-7th century AD, Islam evolved as the leading religion on the Silk Road, which put an end to the multireligious ecological culture. From the perspectives of geo-religion and historical geography, the rise of the Islamic world and the Islamization of the ancient land and maritime Silk Road embodied two dimensions of the same course of history.

1.3.1 *Historical Process*

The spread of Islam on the land Silk Road and on the maritime Silk Road took on different approaches. Along the sea route, this religion was spread and strengthened by trade and marriage. In contrast, the Islamization of the land route was always facilitated by a close combination of political expansion and military conquest by certain ethnic groups.

We shall start with the land route. The military expansion of the Arab Empire played a leading role in the initial expansion of Islam. At the time of the Umayyad Empire, the Arab Empire established a great empire that stretched from North Africa, Spain and Southern France in the West, to Northern and Northwestern India as well as the border of Northwest China in the East by waging wars. Since faith itself is persistent and transcending, regions far from the capital city were able to maintain multireligious despite that the Arab forcefully promoted Islam within the empire.

The historical course of Islamization in Central Asia was complicated. Other than trade and intermarriage, the primary driving forces were expansion of political power and military conquest.[97] Following the Arabs, people from Persia, Turk and Mongolia successively

---

[97] Richard C. Foltz, *Religions of the Silk Road: Overland Trade and Cultural Exchange from Antiquity to the Fifteenth Century*, New York: St. Martin's Press, 1999, pp. 95–97.

promoted Islam in Central Asia. The Turkic people and the Mongolians, in particular, should take the greatest credit. With the Turkic people going South, ethnic groups in Central Asia gradually adopted the language and lifestyle of the Turks. Turkic people also embraced Islamism and advocated Islamic faith through forceful political and military means. Then the Mongolians came to conquer, further strengthening the trend. As a matter of fact, while establishing dominance in Central and West Asia, the Mongolians themselves were undergoing Turkification and Islamization.[98] As a result, today's Islamic Corridor that stretches from North Africa to Xinjiang, China is mainly composed of three ethnic groups: Arabs, Persians and Turks. In 1258, the Abbasid Empire, the successor to the Umayyad Empire, was destroyed by the Mongolian troops. Rulers of Ilkhanate that governed Persia and its surrounding areas, of Chagatai Khanate that governed the Western Regions and of Qipchaq ulisi that governed the prairie regions successively accepted Islam, the religion of the ruled. The Turkification and Islamization of the Mongolians led to tremendous changes in the political and religious ecology of the land Silk Road. That is to say, Central Asia, Northern India and some areas in Xinjiang, China were trending towards Islamization. Buddhism, the religion used to have an important bearing on Central Asia as a whole and in Xinjiang, China, was on the decline due to prolonged attacks from the Islamic states. The decline of Buddhism and the rise of Islam revealed exactly how religious landscape changed on the land Silk Road.[99] Meanwhile, with agressive expansion of Islam in Central Asia, the once-thriving land route was on the wane. That is

---

[98] Min Xianlin, *The Intersection of Mongolian Nomadic Civilization and Islamic Civilization*, Beijing: China Religious Culture Publisher, 2010. (敏贤麟:《蒙古游牧文明与伊斯兰文明的交汇》, 北京: 宗教文化出版社 2010 年版。)

[99] Liu Xinru, "The Spread of Buddhism and Islam Along the Silk Road", in Yu Taishan and Li Jinxiu, *Silk and Porcelain Road I: Study on Sino-Foreign Relations in Ancient Times*, Beijing: The Commercial Press, 2011, pp. 67–91.(刘欣如:《丝绸之路上佛教和伊斯兰教的传播》, 载余太山、李锦绣:《丝瓷之路I: 古代中外关系史研究》, 北京:商务印书馆 2011 年版, 第 67–91 页。); Johan Elverskog, *Buddhism and Islam on the Silk Road*, Philadelphia: University of Pennsylvania Press, 2010.

where people should begin with if they want to understand the inter-action between religion and trade on the ancient Silk Road.

After the dissolution of Ilkhanate, there emerged regional empires of the Persians and the Turkic people, spliting the continent. The Turkic people that had moved from Central Asia at the end of the 13th century established the Ottoman Empire in Asia Minor and captured Constantinople (now Istanbul), the capital of the Byzantine Empire, in 1453. As a result, the whole Asia Minor Peninsula was completely Turkized and Islamized. In 1502, the Persians established the Safavid Empire (1502–1736). In 1526, the Mongols who had already been Turkized and Islamized established the Mughal Empire (1526–1857) in India. "Mughal" evolved from "Moghol". The Mughal Empire was exactly the Moghol Empire, the continuation of the Timurid Dynasty (1370–1507). Therefore, at the dawn of the 16th century, there emerged a situation of tripartite confrontation concerning the Ottoman Empire, the Safavid Empire and the Mughal Empire in the Islamic world. In other words, the Islamic zone that stretched from North Africa, West Asia in the West to Xinjiang, China in the East took shape around the year 1500. The land Silk Road finally finished its course of Islamization.

Now we shall shift to the sea route. The Islamization of the mari-time Silk Road, that is, the spread of Islam in Southeast Asia, mainly stemmed from trade instead of wars.[100] The Islamization in Indonesia and Malaysia was closely linked to their special geographical locations as transfer hubs on the maritime Silk Road. In fact, never before in world history had a religion been so keen on trade like Islam.[101] With Arab merchants coming to the East by the sea route, Islam was ini-tially scattered in some coastal trading ports. After the 8th century, as a number of Islamic merchants settled down in coastal regions in North Sumatra, Islamism gradually spread in local areas through intermarriage, assimilation and missionary work. In the early 16th century, Islam swept across most of the coastal cities along the

---

[100] Malise Ruthven and Azim Nanji, *Historical Atlas of the Islamic World,* Cambridge, MA: Harvard University Press, 2004, p. 106.
[101] Richard C. Foltz, *Religions of the Silk Road,* p. 89.

maritime Silk Road, and it continued to spread into inland spaces in Indonesia and Malaysia thereafter. These areas were completely Islamized around the year 1800.

For China, Islam was a "branch" instead of a "source". The propagation process of Islam in China mainly included three significant historical periods: In Tang and Song Dynasties, Islam followed the Islamic merchants from Arab and Persia as they came to eastern coastal areas in China along the maritime Silk Road. In the Yuan Dynasty, Mongolia's expedition to the West forced Muslims of various ethnicities to move from Central Asia to Shaanxi, Gansu, Qinghai and Ningxia through the land route, enabling a significant expansion of Islam. In the Ming Dynasty, Islam gradually penetrated into Xinjiang till the Islamization there was basically completed.[102] Specifically, the spread of Islam takes on different looks in different regions at different times.

In the Tang dynasty, there emerged Islamic communities named "Fan Fang" (蕃坊) in Guangzhou. "Fan Fang" was not only the administrative unit of Arabs in China, but also the earliest Islamic organization in China whose officer-in-charge was appointed by the Chinese emperor. French scholar Zhang Riming even asserted with exaggeration that China's politics once fell under the influence of the Islamic merchants' economic interests in the Tang Dynasty.[103] In the Song Dynasty, Muslims in China were almost entirely composed of "foreign merchants" who settled in China's Southeast coastal cities such as Guangzhou, Quanzhou and Yangzhou, and descendants of the "foreign merchants" that came to China during the Tang Dynasty. In the Southern and Northern Song Dynasties, the prosperous international trade on the maritime Silk Road brought up a wealthy Islamic stratum. Japanese scholar Jitsuzo Kuwabara's research on Pu

---

[102] China Islamic Association, *An Overview of Islam in China*, Beijing: China Religious Culture Publisher, 2011, p. 7. (中国伊斯兰教协会编:《中国伊斯兰教简志》, 北京: 宗教文化出版社 2011 年版, 第 7 页。)

[103] Zhang Riming, *China and Tazi Muslim in Tang Dynasty*, translated by Yao Jide and ShaDezhen, Yinchuan: Ningxia People's Publishing House, 2002, p. 119. (张日铭:《唐代中国与大食穆斯林》, 姚继德、沙德珍译, 宁夏人民出版社 2002 年版, 第119 页。)

Shougeng, an Arabian merchant who lived in Quanzhou in the Song and Yuan Dynasties, revealed tight trade relations between China and the Arabic world as well as Islamic merchants' strong impact on Chinese society.[104] In fact, it also vividly mirrored the interaction between religion and trade on the Silk Road. However, unlike the Islamization of Indonesia and Malaysia, Islam promoted through trade in eastern coastal areas was mainly limited within the communities of foreign merchants and not even close to penetrating into the vast Chinese society. The influence of Islam in the eastern coastal areas gradually wore off with the decline of the maritime Silk Road.

The Yuan Dynasty saw the boom of Islam in China and how Shaanxi, Gansu, Qinghai and Ningxia gradually became home to Muslims. Over the course of half a century of its western expedition, the Mongolian troops brought people from various ethnic groups in Central Asia and West Asia to China, and most of them were Muslims. The soldiers, gunners, craftsmen, doctors and missionaries were organized into the "Tamaci Army" and were forced to fight against Central Plain for Mongolia. When the wars were over, the survivors settled down in wastelands in various regions, especially in the northwest region. In the Yuan Dynasty, there were over a million Muslims in China. The imperial court set up a specific institution governing Islamic affairs — Bureau for Hui people and hadjis. In the process of Zheng He's voyages to the West, Muslims played an important part in communication with Islamic regions in Southeast Asia and West Asia.

The Islamization of Xinjiang, which was quite different from that of Shaanxi, Gansu, Qinghai and Ningxia, shared more similarities with that of Central Asia as a whole. Since the beginning of the 1st century AD, Zoroastrianism, Buddhism, Manicheism and Nestorianism were successively introduced to Xinjiang along the land Silk Road. Prior to the introduction of Islam, Buddhism, which centered in Khotan, Qiuci and Gaochang, had the longest history, the largest

---

[104] Kuwabara Jitsuzo, *A Book about PuShougeng, translated by Chen Yujing*, Beijing: Zhonghua Book Company, 1954. (桑原骘藏:《蒲寿庚考》, 陈裕菁译, 中华书局 1954 年版。)

number of believers, the most solid social foundation and the most far-reaching influence in Xinjiang. Accordingly, the spread of Islam in Xinjiang had been accompanied by wars between Islam and Buddhism.[105] The most famous war was the so-called "jihad" that started by Qara-Khanid Khanate and Moghulistan. Islam was introduced to Xinjiang at the time of the Qara-Khanid Khanate, with Sutug Bughraxan accepting and promoting Islam as a defining mark. In 960, Arslan Khan, the son of Bughraxan, declared Islam the national religion and made Kashgar the capital of the empire. Therefore, Kashgar evolved to be the center of politics, economy, culture and religion. The Islamization of Qara-Khanid Khanate brought profound changes to geopolitical situation and geo-religious reality in Xinjiang and even in Central Asia as a whole. The Samanid dynasty, located to the west of the Qara-Khanid Khanate, was its political opponent. However, shared belief in Islam eased the political tension between the two empires. Yet Gaochang and Khotan, Buddhist centers respectively located to the east and south of Qara-Khanid Khanate, turned from friendly neighbors into enemies in the aftermath of the "jihad". Therefore, Xinjiang once saw a situation of tripartite confrontation concerning three political forces (Qara-Khanid Khanate, Gaochang and Khotan) and the confrontation between Buddhism and Islam. Qara-Khanid Khanate's "jihad" against Khotan was the first large-scale war against Buddhism since the introduction of Islam to Xinjiang. Never before in history had Xinjiang witnessed such a large-scale and protracted war with far-reaching consequences. The war broke out in 960. In 1024, Qara-Khanid Khanate captured Khotan as a whole. Since then, Buddhism pulled out of the western and southern regions of Tarim Basin.[106] Moghulistan

---

[105] Hatani Ryōtai, *Buddhism in Western Regions,* translated by He Changqun, Beijing: The Commercial Press, 1999.(羽溪了谛:《西域之佛教》, 贺昌群译, 北京: 商务印书馆 1999 年版。); CaiWu Jia Fu, *Research on Sinkiang Ancient Buddhism,* Beijing: Social Sciences Academic Press, 2011. (才吾加甫:《新疆古代佛教研究》, 北京: 社会科学文献出版社 2011 年版。)

[106] Wei Liangtao: *History of QaraKhanid Dynasty,* Urumqi: Xinjiang People's Publishing House, 1986.(魏良弢:《喀喇汗王朝史稿》, 乌鲁木齐: 新疆人民出版社 1986年版。); Li Jinxin, *History of Sinkiang Islam and QaraKhanid,* Beijing: China

was founded in the early 14th century and its founder Tughlugh Timur Khan converted to Islam. With the Islamization and Turkification of the Mongols, Islam continued to spread into the eastern part of the areas at the south of Tianshan Mountain at the time of Moghulistan. Moghulistan captured Kucha (i.e. Qiuci) through "jihad" around the year 1392 and forced the local Buddhists to convert to Islam. Till late-15th century and early-16th century, Buddhism completely disappeared from Kucha. Hence, the three Buddhists' holy lands, Khotan, Qiuci and Gaochang, were successively lost to Islam. The Islamized Kucha assimilated Turpan, the last Buddhist center in Xinjiang. Since Turpan was home to Uighurs, its Islamization eventually put an end to the religious pluralism among Uighurs in Southern Xinjiang. In the 16th century, the ruler of Kumul converted to Islam and called himself "Sultan". In this case, Islam reached the eastern edge of Xinjiang. Except for the Oirat people that adhered to Tibetan Buddhism, various minority nationalities in Xinjiang took Islam as their major religion.[107] From the mid-10th century when Islam was introduced to Kashgar to the 16th century when the Kumul region embraced Islam, it took 600 years for Xinjiang to complete the Islamization.

In short, motivated by such factors as trade, intermarriage, missionary activities, political expansion and military conquest, the ancient Silk Road both on the land and on the sea were largely Islamized around the 16th century. The unique process of Islamization

Religious Culture Publisher, 1999. (李进新:《新疆伊斯兰汗朝史略》, 北京: 宗教文化出版社1999年版。); Yu Zhengui, *The Central Governments of All Dynasties in China and Islam*, Yinchuan: Ningxia People's Publishing House, 1996. (余振贵:《中国历代政权与伊斯兰教》,宁夏人民出版社 1996 年版;)

[107] Tian Weijiang, *Research on The Silk Road and the History of the Eastern Chagatai Khanate*, Urumqi: Xinjiang People's Publishing House, 1997. (田卫疆:《丝绸之路与东察合台汗国史研究》, 乌鲁木齐: 新疆人民出版社 1997 年版。); Liu Yingsheng: *Study on the History of Chagatai Khanate*, Shanghai: Shanghai Classical Publishing House, 2006. (刘迎胜:《察合台汗国史研究》, 上海: 上海古籍出版社 2006 年版。); Chen Huisheng, *History of Islam in Xinjiang*, Volume 1, Urumqi: Xinjiang People's Publishing House, 1999. (陈慧生:《中国新疆地区伊斯兰教史》(第一册), 乌鲁木齐: 新疆人民出版社 1999 年版。)

of different regions and peoples also gave rise to regional differences and complex genealogies within the Islamic world.

1.3.2 *Modern-Day Legacies*

At present, the religious map of the Islamic world stretches from North Africa and the Middle East in the West to Central Asia and northwestern China along the land route, and to Malaysia, Indonesia and Brunei in Southeast Asia along the sea route, constituting the Islamic Corridor running from East to West.[108] Statistics showed that there were about 1.6 billion Muslims across the world up to 2010. Yet, the number is expected to rise to 2.2 billion by 2030, which will make up approximately a quarter of the world population.[109]

The Islamization of the maritime Silk Road resulted in the fact that countries along the Straits of Malacca such as Indonesia, Malaysia and Brunei successively accepted Islam as their major religion. As of 2010, Indonesia, with 205 million Muslims, had the largest Muslim population in the world, which made up approximately one-eighth of the world's total.[110] In contrast, the spread of religion through trade on the maritiem Silk Road failed to realize the Islamization of China's eastern coastal areas. Moreover, with the decline of the maritime Silk Road, the Islamic merchants gradually lost their impact in Guangzhou and other trading ports. People of today can only relish the powerful influence once enjoyed by the Persian and Arabian merchants through four historical relics: Huaisheng Mosque in Guangzhou, Qilin Mosque in Quanzhou, Fenghuang Mosque in Hangzhou and Xianhe Mosque in Yangzhou.

The land Silk Road, as compared to the maritime Silk Road, left more historical heritages and seemed to be more intricate due to multi-dimensions of history embedded in it. The vast areas between

---

[108] Xu Yihua and Zou Lei, "Geo-religion and China's Foreign Policy", *International Studies*, no. 1, 2013, p. 35. (徐以骅、邹磊：《地缘宗教与中国对外战略》, 载《国际问题研究》2013 年第1期, 第 35 页。)

[109] Pew Research Center's Forum on Religion & Public Life, *The Future of the Global Muslim Population: Projections for 2010–2030*, January 2011, p. 13.

[110] *Ibid.*, p. 11.

the Middle East and Central Asia have been seeing the most intensified clashes among ethnic groups and the fiercest competition between external great powers, for they occupy a vital strategic position in global geopolitics and energy landscape. Since modern times, amid the global expansion of imperialism and colonialism, almost the whole Islamic world had fallen into the hands of the Western countries or under their sphere of influence.[111] After World War I, the collapse of the Ottoman Empire and the abolition of the Caliphate utterly disrupted the political order in the Middle East. Yet political arrangements made by the western powers in accordance with their own interests increased the threat of regional conflicts for the future. At the time of the Cold War, the Middle East became the contested frontier between the United States and the Soviet Union. The sharp confrontations between the Arabic countries and Israel, and between Sunnite and Shiah evolved to be a prolonged war amid the game of the super powers.

Since the Westphalian Peace Conference in 1648, religion, deprived of its legitimacy at the level of international relation, retreated to the realm of individual belief and domestic affair. In other words, it was expelled from the Westphalian system. However, to the Islamic world and Islamic countries, religion must be given top priority in political, social and diplomatic affairs, and the conviction to rejuvenate the Islamic world never faded. Moreover, the strong rise of political Islam since 1970s was viewed as one of the major events that marked the global revival of religion.[112] Political Islam was not only a conservative religious ideology, but also an extremely aggressive political view, whose central aim was to rebuild political order and

---

[111] Specifically, Egypt, Sudan and India became British colonies; Algeria and Tunisia became French Colonies; Morocco became a colony of France and Spain; Libya became an Italian colony; Syria and Lebanon were subordinated to France; Indonesia and Malaysia became colonies of Netherlands and Britain; Iran and Afghanistan were subordinated to Britain and Russia.

[112] Peter L. Berger, *The Desecularization of the World: Resurgent Religion and World Politics,* translated by Li Junkang, Shanghai: Shanghai Classical Publishing House, 2005, pp. 9–11. (彼得•伯格等:《世界的非世俗化: 复兴的宗教及全球政治》, 李骏康译, 上海: 上海古籍出版社 2005 年版, 第 9–11 页。)

secular life compliant with Sharia. It combined ideals with reality and utilized a strategy involving both tough and soft means. As a result, political Islam could go beyond geographical limitations to impact on international relations and global governance. Aided by a shared belief in Islam, it is also capable of activating cross-boundary interactions and global mobilization. Since modern times, political Islam, against the current international system dominated by the West, has attempted not only to restore caesaropapism Islamic countries used to adopt, but also to rebuild an international political order in accordance with Islamic spirit. This further intensified the tension between the religious landscape of Islam and the political landscape of the nation-state. The former actively tried to restructure the latter according to its own laws which partly resulted in the fact that the political order and state-building in North Africa, the Middle East and Central Asia were assaulted by transnational network of religious fundamentalists after the Cold War. The pattern of "weak state vs. strong religion" often meant the inability of external the country to address severe challenges. The continuous infiltration and intervention of external great powers greatly exacerbated the political turmoil in North Africa, the Middle East and Central Asia.

It can be said that against the background of global religious revivalism and the great power shift, the intertwining of the religious heritages of the Islamization of the ancient Silk Road, the political heritages of the colonization of the Islamic world in modern times, and the contemporary international political and economic structure will have an impact on the political order of the land Silk Road. To a large extent, these structural challenges were embedded in the multi-layered historical heritages. From North Africa, the Middle East and Central Asia to South Asia, political turmoil triggered by the strong rise of political Islam or Islamic caesaropapism is becoming the structural crisis that many Islamic countries along the Silk Road are facing.

The religious heritages left from the Islamization in northwest China include numerous mosques, an abundance of philosophical books, a complicated variety of religious denominations and sects, as well as a large number of Muslim population. It is estimated that there were about 23 million Muslims in China by the end of 2010, some

17.69 million of whom were in Xinjiang, Ningxia, Gansu and Qinghai, making up three-quarters of the Muslim population in China.[113] The foresaid four provinces and regions have beome home to Chinese Muslims, which has profoundly changed China's political, ethnic, and religious ecosystems, and thus greatly strengthening the aspect of "diversity" proposed in the policy of "Pattern of Diversity in Unity of the Chinese Nation".

In terms of state-building, the relationship between the Muslim communities in northwest China and China's political landscape involves the relationships not only between the central authorities and the local authorities, but also between politics and religion. Under different historical conditions and within specific regions, the two sides may be able to achieve a benign interaction. But chances are better that there will be considerable tension or even conflict inbetween.

To be more specific, on the one hand, the Muslim communities in northwest China serve as a bond and a channel of communication between China and the Islamic world. With China's policy of "going global" and the globalization of its national interest, it is important for China to go beyond the limit of the nation-state, particularly to consider its national interest in the context of the "Islamic world" and other global religious landscapes.[114] The communication between the Muslim communities in northwest China and other Islamic countries/ regions can be understood as the interregional interaction within the religious world (or religious landscape). That means in rejuvenating the land Silk Road, chances are that the Chinese Muslim communities will play a key role in connecting China with the Islamic world. Meanwhile, given the unique religious and cultural advantages, the Muslim communities in northwest China have the potential to re-attract Islamic merchants and investment from the Middle East and

---

[113] According to the report of Pew Research Center, there were about 16.839 million Muslims in China in 1990, accounting for about 1.5% of the total population. In 2010, there were 23.308 million Muslims in China, accounting for 1.8% of the total population. By 2030, the population of Muslim in China is expected to reach 29.949 million, accounting for 2.1% of the total population.

[114] Xu Yihua and Zou Lei, "Believing China", *International Studies*, no. 1, 2012, p. 47. (徐以骅、邹磊:《信仰中国》, 载《国际问题研究》2012 年第 1 期, 第 47 页。)

Central Asia or to promote China's policy of "opening to the west" and "going global".

On the other hand, that the religious bond can aid in China's overall diplomatic strategy is more of a theory. In the unified multi-ethnic country, it's more likely that religion will have obviously negative effect on China's political landscape and state-building. In the Qing Dynasty, for instance, the imperial court had to devote huge efforts and resources in military operations in the northwest and southwest so as to suppress the uprising/rebellion of the Moslems.[115] According to statistics, of nearly 50 historical strategy books on how to suppress internal rebellion and counter foreign aggression in the Qing Dynasty, 11 were related to Islam—more than one-fifth of the total.[116] Since the founding of the PRC, the central government has greatly improved the relations with Islamic communities in the northwest and southwest China. What is more, never before in history have Islamic communities in Gansu, Qinghai and Ningxia maintained such long-term stability. However, Xinjiang (especially southern Xinjiang) has been under constant threat from "the Three Forces". In pursuit of their own interest, some Middle Eastern countries not only export

---

[115] Li Fanwen and Yu Zhengui, *Compilation of Researches on the Northwest Hui People's Uprising*, Yinchuan: Ningxia People's Publishing House, 1988. (李范文、余振贵:《西北回民起义研究资料汇编》, 银川: 宁夏人民出版社 1988 年版。); Ma Changshou, *Research on the Uprising of the Hui in Shaanxi during the Reign of Emperor Tongzhi*, Xi'an: Shaanxi People's Publishing House, 1993. (马长寿:《同治年间陕西回民起义历史调查记录》, 西安: 陕西人民出版社 1993 年版。); Zhang Zhongfu, *The Uprising of the Hui people in Northwest China in Qing Dynasty: Reflect on Acculturation and National Identity*, Taipei: Taipei Linking Publishing, 2001.(张中复:《清代西北回民事变——社会文化适应与民族认同的省思》, 台北:台北联经出版事业公司 2001 年版。); Pan Xiangming, *A Study of the Khojas Rebellion in Sinkiang in the Qing Dynasty*, Beijing: China Renmin University Press, 2011(潘向明:《清代新疆和卓叛乱研究》, 北京: 中国人民大学出版社 2011 年版。); Wen-Djang Chu, *The Moslem Rebellion in Northwest China 1862–1878*, Hague: Mouton & Co., 1966; Hodong Kim, *Holy War in China: The Muslim Rebellion and State in Chinese Central Asia*, 1864–1877, Stanford, California: Stanford University Press, 2004.

[116] It includes *Strategies of Quelling the Islam Uprising in Yunnan*, *Strategies of Quelling the Uprising in Shaanxi, Gansu and Sinkiang*, *Strategies of Quelling Hui Jiang Bandits*.

ideas of pan-Islamism and pan-Turkism, but also provide financial aid through various means, facilitating the cross-boundary networking of ideology, organization, mobilization and support for "the Three Forces". Islam, as compared to other religions, has more awareness of a transnational religious landscape, and developed a Mecca-centric identity. Since the Turkic people once established a transnational empire covering Central Asia and some areas in Xinjiang, the revival of a transnational ethnic landscape with Turkey in the Middle East as the object of identification has been the main theme in spreading the idea of Pan-Turkism. "The Three Forces" reveals that the intertwining of universal religion and trans-border nationalism has posed a serious challenge to the political unity and political identity of China.

The Muslim communities in northwest China, which have long been at the converging point of specific political territory and certain religous landscape, not only lie on the inland frontier the territory of contemporary China, but also serve as the eastern border of the Islamic world. The long-term existence of this dual identity/identification makes religion a potential resource to promote transnational exchanges, and a negative force to split the political landscape as well.

2

The "Modern Silk Road" between China and the Middle East

As the routes of trade, civilization and faith connecting China and Eurasian countries, the ancient land and maritime Silk Road were once the most important geo-economic integration and cultural-religious bond before the rise of the West. While western countries embarked on the road of modernization and developed their sea power, the maritime Silk Road between China and the Middle East sank into idleness for centuries. Since the 21st century, however, various signs indicate that, with the two-way flow of Chinese-made products and Middle Eastern oil, a "Modern Silk Road" joining China's eastern coastal provinces to the Persian Gulf has been emerging, rejuvenating the long-lost economic bond between them. In the 21st century, the connectivity between the world's major manufacturing base and oil-exporting region gives profound geo-economic and geo-political meaning to the "Modern Silk Road". Accordingly, western political elites are increasingly paying attention to the political implications of such a trade relation (especially its implications to the West).

Against the background that Chinese government officially proposed the initiative of the Silk Road Economic Belt and the 21st-century Maritime Silk Road in 2013, how should we understand the "Modern Silk Road" that spontaneously arises between China and the Middle East? To answer this question, this chapter is divided into three parts. The first part depicts a macroscopic picture as well as microscopic images of the so-called "Modern Silk Road". The second part analyzes its origin, with an emphasis on the structural conditions for its rise. The third part analyzes the nature and predicament of the "Modern Silk Road" in the macrostructure of contemporary international political economy.

2.1 Rise of the "Modern Silk Road"

The rise of "Modern Silk Road" between China and the Middle East can be studied from macro and micro perspectives. From the macro perspective, the "Modern Silk Road" is presented as a rapid and large-scale flow of commodity, funds, and people between the two regions, as reflected in statistics. From the micro perspective, it reveals the trading, religious, and societal life of a unique community, as reflected in individuals' lives and experiences. The city of Yiwu in Zhejiang Province is a typical example.

2.1.1 *A Macroscopic Perspective*

Currently, the Middle East market is full of "Made in China" products, such as mechanical and electrical products, apparels and attires, transportation equipment, steel and building materials, and furniture. For the past 10 years, Chinese products have been a feature in department stores across the Middle East. In Mecca, the holiest city of Islamism, religious souvenirs made in China, such as electronic Koran, Muslim apparels, and praying mattress, can be seen everywhere, which also shows China's ever-increasing commercial presence in the Middle East.[1] Australian observer Ben Simpfendorfer, in

---

[1] Alshin Molavi, "The New Silk Road, 'Chindia,' and the Geo-Economic Ties That Bind the Middle East and Asia", in Bryce Wakefield and Susan L. Levenstein, eds.,

his field investigation, found that electronic Koran was overwhelmingly popular in Syria before the civil war.[2] The Chinese products, with low price, fine quality, and rich variety, are especially attractive to middle or lower class in the Middle East. In the wake of the Iraq War, over 1.5 million Iraqi refugees rushed into Syria in 2003. Almost all the daily necessities they consumed were imported from China by over 1000 Iraqi merchants in Yiwu of Zhejiang Province.[3] As for Iran, a nation suffered severely from Western sanctions, Chinese commodities were extremely important for its people to maintain daily life.

In fact, not only can middle- and low-end Chinese products offer competitive price, but also some high-end products, especially in equipment manufacture, are showing great market potential. In November 2010, the Mecca Light Rail, built by China Railway Construction Corporation Limited (CRCC), was put into operation, offering transport services for Muslim pilgrims from all over the world. During the 2013 Hajj, the Mecca Light Rail was running for 162 consecutive hours in 7 days and 6 nights, carrying 3,800,000 pilgrims to the holy sites, successfully fulfilling its mission in the Mecca pilgrimage.[4] On March 3, 2014, the first batch of Lifan sedans came off the assembly line in Iraq, signaling that the Lifan Motor, a Chinese independent auto brand, officially launched its knocked-down (KD) assembly plant in Iraq. As estimated, the new assembly

---

China and the Persian Gulf: Implications for the United States, Washington, DC: Woodrow Wilson International Center for Scholars, 2011, p. 45.

[2] Ben Simpfendorfer, *The New Silk Road: How a Rising Arab World Is Turning Away from the West and Rediscovering China*, translated by Cheng Rentao, Beijing: The Oriental Press, 2011, p. 11. (贝哲民：《新丝绸之路:阿拉伯世界如何重新发现中国》，程仁桃译, 北京:东方出版社 2011 年版, 第 11 页。)

[3] Zhang Yan, "Yiwu—*A City Being Changed by Arabian, Reuters China*", March 7, 2008, http://cn.reuters.com/article/oddlyEnoughNews/idCNChina-75272008030 7? sp=true, log-in time: February 1, 2013 (张研：《被阿拉伯人改变着的义乌》, 2008 年 3 月 7 日。)

[4] China Railway Construction Corporation Limited, "*Mission in Mecca Pilgrimage Accomplished*", October 22, 2013, http://www.crcc.cn/g282/s962/t38748.aspx, log-in time: March 11, 2014. (中国铁建股份有限公司:《中国铁建圆满完成今年沙特麦加朝觐运营任务》, 2013 年 10 月 22 日。)

Table 2.1   Crude oil import into China and the United States from Saudi Arabia 2008–2013 (1000 bbl/d)

	2008	2009	2010	2011	2012	2013
United States	1529	1004	1096	1195	1361	1328
China	731	843	896	1010	1083	1083

Source: Tian Chunrong, "Analysis on China's Import and Export of Petroleum and Natural Gas in 2013," *International Petroleum Economics*, no. 3, 2014, p. 33; US Energy Information Administration, http://www.eia.gov/dnav/pet/pet_move_impcus_a2_nus_ep00_im0_mbblpd_a.htm
Note: The original measurement unit was 10,000 tons. The data in the table have been converted by the author.

plant, with annual production capacity of 10,000 units, will help Lifan occupy 15% of Iraqi imported auto market.[5]

While Chinese products swarm into the Middle East market, Middle East oil is flowing into China at an amazing pace. In recent years, as the energy demand explodes, China has increased its annual oil import from the world's largest oil exporter, Saudi Arabia. The gap between China and the United States in terms of oil import from Saudi Arabia is shrinking rapidly. In 2008, the oil imported by China from Saudi Arabia was less than half of that of the United States. But in 2011, the import volumes of the two countries are similar (see Table 2.1). In 2009, the crude oil import of the United States from the Saudi Arabia dropped to the lowest point since 1989. In November and December of the same year, China surpassed the United States as the biggest oil importer for Saudi Arabia. Such a breakthrough, though a temporary phenomenon, evoked concern and anxiety among American mainstream media and political elites.[6]

---

[5] Guancha.cn, "*Chinese Home-grown Auto Brand Makes Its Debut in Iraq; Lifan Invests ¥120 Million in the New Plant*", http://www.guancha.cn/economy/2014_03_05_211008.shtml, log-time: March 11, 2014. (观察者网:《中国自主汽车品牌首次在伊拉克生产 力帆斥资 1.2 亿新厂启动》, 2014 年 3 月 5 日。)
[6] Jad Mouawad, "China's Growth Shifts the Geopolitics of Oil", *The New York Times*, March 19, 2010, http://www.nytimes.com/2010/03/20/business/energy-environment/20saudi.html, log-time: March 20, 2013.

Propelled by oil trade, China gradually surpassed the United States as the top trading partner with Saudi Arabia, which is the largest economy in the Middle East. According to the Census Bureau of the US Department of Commerce, in 2011, US export to Saudi Arabia reached $13.830 billion and its import from Saudi Arabia reached 47.476 billion, totaling $61.306 billion.[7] In the same year, bilateral trade between Saudi Arabia and Japan, South Korea, and Singapore, respectively, reached $57.1 billion, $43.9 billion, and $18.5 billion, all lower than China–Saudi Arabia trade of $64.318 billion.[8] This means that in 2011, China made a historic breakthrough in surpassing the United States as the largest trading partner with Saudi Arabia.[9] At the same time, according to annual import and export statistics of Saudi Customs, in 2010, China replaced the United Arab Emirates as the largest non-oil export destination country of Saudi Arabia; in 2011, China replaced the United States as the largest exporter to Saudi Arabia (see Table 2.2). According to indexes of total import and export, export, oil import, and non-oil import, China has become Saudi Arabia's top trading partner.

Iran, as China's second largest trading partner in the region, has a growing dependence on China in recent years. In fact, since 2008, China has become the top trading partner of Iran, which can be largely attributed to China's oil import. Statistics have shown that Iran's oil export in 2012, under Western sanctions, went almost exclusively to four Asian countries of China, Republic of Korea,

---

[7] United States Census Bureau, "*2011: U.S. Trade in Goods with Saudi Arabia*", http://www.census.gov/foreign-trade/balance/c5170.html, log-time: February 1, 2013.

[8] The Economic and Commercial Counselor's Office of the Embassy of the People's Republic of China in the Kingdom of Saudi Arabia, "*China Emerges as Saudi Arabia's Top Trading Partner*", April 16, 2012, http://sa.mofcom.gov.cn/article/sqfb/e/201204/20120408071718.shtml, log-in time: March 11, 2014. (中国驻沙特阿拉伯大使馆经济商务参赞处:《中国跃居沙特外贸首位》, 2012 年 4 月 16 日。)

[9] The Economic and Commercial Counselor's Office of the Embassy of the People's Republic of China in the Kingdom of Saudi Arabia, "*China-Saudi Arabia Trade Hits Record High in 2012*", January 8, 2013, http://sa.mofcom.gov.cn/article/jmxw/201301/20130108517347.shtml, log-time: February 1, 2013. (中国驻沙特阿拉伯大使馆经济商务参赞处:《2012 年中沙贸易额创历史新高》, 2013 年 1 月 8 日。)

Table 2.2 Import and Export between Saudi Arabia and its Main Trading Partners 2009–2011 (One Hundred Million Saudi Riyal)

	Import				Non-Oil Product Export		
Country	2009	2010	2011	Country	2009	2010	2011
China	405.9	486.6	649.9	China	86.6	134	221.8
America	509.9	527.5	619.3	UAE	127.6	131.2	173.1
Germany	286.6	309.3	339.5	Singapore	41.4	79.1	117.5
Japan	271.4	298.4	314.5	India	49	64	82.6
Total	3584.3	4007.7	4955.7	Total	879.9	1177.2	1575

Source: Saudi Customs, *Annual Report*, 2010–2011.

Japan, and India, with half of the oil export going to China. Therefore, although China's oil import from Iran dropped by 23% in 2012, it still consumed half of Iran's oil export.[10]

Meanwhile, according to the General Administration of Customs of People's Republic of China (PRC), China's oil import from Iraq in 2013 increased by a whopping 49.9%, reaching 23.51 million tons. Iraq became the fastest growing oil supplier in that year.[11] The explosive growth of cooperation in energy and trade between China and Iraq, as perceived by some Western scholars, shows that China, a country having nothing to do with the Iraqi War, has become the biggest beneficiary of the post-Saddam oil boom in Iraq.[12] As estimated

---

[10] Li Liang, "*Nearly All of Iran's Oil Exports Are Going to Asia with China Buying a Half According to a British Report*", January 6, 2013, http://finance.huanqiu.com/view/2013-01/3453303.html, log-in time: February 1, 2013. 李亮:《英报告称2012 伊朗石油出口全流往亚洲中国占五成》，2013 年 1 月 6 日。)

[11] Tian Chunrong, "Analysis on China's Import and Export of Petroleum and Natural Gas in 2013", *International Petroleum Economics*, no. 3, 2014, p. 34. (田春荣:《2013 年中国石油和天然气进出口状况分析》，载《国际石油经济》2014 年第 3 期，第 34 页。)

[12] Naser Al-Tamimi, "*China in Iraq: Winning without a War*", March 16, 2013, http://english.alarabiya.net/en/views/2013/03/16/China-in-Iraq-Winning-Without-a-War.html, log-in time: March 20, 2013; Tim Arango and Clifford Krauss, "*China Is Reaping Biggest Benefits of Iraq Oil Boom*", *The New York Times*, June 2, 2013.

by the International Energy Agency, by 2035 oil produced by Iraq will exceed 8 million barrels a day, 25% of which (about 2 million barrels) will be exported to China. That is why one scholar dubbed the China–Iraq relationship as "the Beijing–Baghdad Oil Axis".[13]

The exchanges of "Made in China" commodities and Middle Eastern oil were accompanied by an ever-increasing flow of funds. In June 2010, the Kuwait Investment Authority invested $2.8 billion in Agricultural Bank of China, and then added its investment to $6 billion. In August 2012, Qatari Sovereignty Wealth Fund bought 22% stake of Chinese International Trust and Investment Corporation.[14] JL McGregor & Company estimated that from 2008 to 2013, the capital flow from the Middle East to China totaled $250 billion. In contrast, after 911, Middle East countries reduced their investments in the United States by $200 billion during the ensuing period from 2003 to 2008.[15] McKinsey & Company predicted that robust and consistent oil demand of Asian countries, including China and India, would drive the trade volume between China and the Middle East to $350–$500 billion by 2020 — a six-time increase over the year 2005. Meanwhile, by 2020, the cross-border capital flow between the Gulf Cooperation Council (GCC) and Asian countries such as China and India will possibly grow from a yearly $15 billion in 2005 to $300 billion by 2020.[16] Similarly, government-backed investment institutions in Kuwait believe that if the international oil price remains at $80 per barrel, the capital flow from GCC countries to Asian countries (Japan excluded) will exceed $360 billion by 2020.[17] A report released by Merrill Lynch predicts that by 2020, GCC countries and

---

[13] Javier Blas, "The Beijing-Baghdad Oil Axis", *The Financial Times*, October 11, 2012.
[14] Fu Bilian, "RMB Settlement Business Continue to Rise", *International Finance News*, July 25, 2013, p. 6. (付碧莲:《人民币结算业务将持续增加》, 载《国际金融报》2013 年 7 月 25 日, 第 6 版。)
[15] Fred Bergsten et al., *China's Rise: Challenges and Opportunities*, Washington, DC: Center for Strategic and International Studies, 2008, pp. 222 and 333, note 36.
[16] Dominic Barton and Kito de Boer, "Tread Lightly along the New Silk Road", *The McKinsey Quarterly*, March 2007.
[17] Andrew England, "Chinese Trade Flows along New Silk Road", *Financial Times*, December 14, 2009.

other Middle East investors will invest a whopping $300 billion in Chinese stock market.[18]

Based on the economic links — both substantial and symbolic — between China and the Middle East, McKinsey & Company's senior board member Dominic Barton and others pointed out that since the new century, oil-rich Gulf countries and fast growing Asian countries like China have accelerated the exchanges of commodities, people, and capital. The "Silk Road" between East Asia (China) and the Middle East, which had been idle for hundreds of years, is showing signs of rejuvenation.[19] A *Newsweek* article titled "The Modern Silk Road" (May 26/June 2, 2008) predicts that the connectivity between the Middle East and East Asia (China) — both regions are with the highest degree of mobility — is reshaping the global economy, shifting the world's economic center of gravity from the United States and the Europe to the Middle East and East Asia.[20]

2.1.2 *A Microscopic Perspective*

The trade statistics only depict a macroscopic picture of the efflux of "Made in China" goods and influx of Middle East oil. Nevertheless, the frequent exchanges of people between China and the Middle East, especially the growth in Muslim population and the revival of "Fan Fang" (蕃坊, i.e. foreign quarters that once accommodated numerous non-Han sojourners or settlers) — phenomena resulting from active international trading activities in Yiwu, draw the most vivid and symbolic microscopic images of a rising "Modern Silk Road".

Historically, Yiwu was not a port or manufacturing base on the maritime Silk Road, and remained unknown to the public until 2000. However, within a very short span of time, Yiwu has become the

---

[18] Zhu Yiming, "Petro-dollar Seeks Dominance in Global Finance", *21st Century Business Herald*, December 31, 2007, p. 54. (朱益民:《中东石油美元图谋全球金融权力中心》,载《21 世纪经济报道》2007 年 12 月 31 日,第 54 版。)

[19] Dominic Barton, Kito de Boer, and Gregory P. Wilson, "The New Silk Road: Opportunities for Asia and the Gulf", *The McKinsey Quarterly*, July 2006.

[20] Stephen Glain, "The Modern Silk Road", *Newsweek*, May 26/June 2, 2008, pp. 32–33.

world's largest small commodity collection and distribution center, with export taking up 65% of its overall trade volume. In this sense, Yiwu can be viewed as a highly internationalized municipal actor.[21] Yiwu small commodity wholesale market sells 4,202 categories, altogether 1.7 million goods, to 219 countries and regions.[22] Almost all kinds of daily use articles can be found here, such as accessories, hardware, rain gears, electrical appliances, gimcrack toys, cosmetics, stationery and sporting goods, nonstaple food, and textiles (the production and sales volumes of accessories, socks, and toys account for one third of the Chinese market). Just as China is dubbed "factory of the world", Yiwu can be called a "showcase" of Chinese-made goods which are rapidly going global.

The Middle East, buying one third of Yiwu's export, is the most important consumer for Yiwu's small commodities.[23] Against the backdrop of the shrinking European and American markets, as a result from international financial crisis and European debt crisis, the trade between Yiwu and the Middle East is steadily on the rise. An increasing number of Middle East merchants are coming to Yiwu for inexpensive and fine-quality "Made in China" commodities. By attracting Middle Eastern merchants to its market, Yiwu is selling goods to Middle Eastern Markets. It highly resembles a historical scene that a large number of Arabian and Persian merchants traveled between port cities such as Guangzhou, Quanzhou, and Mingzhou and shipped silk and porcelain back to the Middle East in Tang and Song dynasties. Nowadays, since oil businesses are monopolized by local authorities

---

[21] As for the internationalization of Yiwu small commodity city, See Gao Shangtao *et al.*, *Municipal Actors in International Relations*, Beijing: World Affairs Press, 2010, pp. 203–207. (高尚涛等：《国际关系中的城市行为体》，北京:世界知识出版社2010 年版，第 203–207 页。)

[22] Shi Xiaofei, "Yiwu Becomes the 10th 'New Special Zone' in China", *Consumption Daily*, April 6, 2011, p. A01. (史晓菲：《义乌成我国第十个"新特区"》，载《消费日报》2011 年 4 月 6 日，第 A01 版。)

[23] Hong Xinnian and He Wenshuai, Yiwu Customs, "Foreign Trade Prospect Remains Grim This Year", *Yiwu Business News*, February 3, 2012, p. 13. (洪新年、何文帅：《义乌海关:今年外贸形势依然严峻》，载《义乌商报》2012 年 2 月 3 日，第 13 版。)

and large transnational corporations, individual merchants of the Middle East are no comparison to their historical counterparts who dominated the trade of spices and jewelry. In contrast to government-backed or state-owned enterprises (SOEs)-backed oil businesses, the production of Chinese commodities in the Yangtze River Delta and Pearl River Delta and their sales in Dubai, Damascus, Teheran, Mecca, Cairo, and Istanbul are usually conducted by private enterprises or individual merchants. Such a trade relation, which is driven by numerous individuals, is obviously unbalanced, as compared to that on the ancient maritime Silk Road. While China's huge oil import from the Middle East is grabbing wide attention, the personal stories happening on the new Silk Road go unnoticed. However, hundreds of thousands of people are working in the same direction to reopen the giant trade corridor, and that is exactly where the Modern Silk Road draws vitality.

After 911, Islamophobia has been pervading western societies, especially the United States, as a result of which, the United States has tightened visa rules in the Middle East. Statistics show about 250 thousand Arabians traveled to the United States in 2000, while the figure decreased to 170 thousand in 2007.[24] By contrast, China relaxed visas restrictions for the Middle East after joining the World Trade Organization (WTO). According to the statistics, there are 145 flights between China and Arab countries each week and over 830 thousand people traveling between the two regions each year.[25] In fact, Dubai alone is accommodating 200 thousand Chinese, and it is home to the largest overseas nonpermanent Chinese community so far.[26] Moreover, over 200 thousand Middle Eastern people travel to

---

[24] Ben Simpfendorfer, *The New Silk Road: How a Rising Arab World Is Turning Away from the West and Rediscovering China*, New York: Palgrave Macmillan, 2009, p. 10.
[25] Wang Yi, "To Strengthen Forum Construction and Build an 'Upgraded Version' of China-Arab Relations", *People's Daily*, June 4, 2014, p. 21. (王毅:《加强论坛建设, 打造中阿关系"升级版"》, 载《人民日报》2014 年 6 月 4 日, 第 21 版。)
[26] Ben Simpfendorfer, "China's Historic Return to the Gulf", *Foreign Policy*, April 2, 2010, http://mideast.foreignpolicy.com/posts/2010/04/02/china_s_historic_return_to_the_gulf, log-in time: March 20, 2013.

Yiwu each year — a bigger number than that of the Middle Easterners going to the United States (180 thousand people per year).[27]

In a field trip to Yiwu, the author found that, with an influx of Middle Eastern merchants, Yiwu has seen great changes in its social ecosystem. Arabian culture has permeated the city. A large Muslim community is gradually taking shape along the street down North Chouzhou Road where Yiwu International Trade City is located. Viewed from historic perspective, it is the revival of "*Fan Fang*" of the ancient Silk Road. Arabic language has become an important spoken and written language, besides Chinese and English. Arabic billboards and doorplates can be seen everywhere, signaling the importance of the Arabian merchants. The author also found that streets in Yiwu are lined up with import and export corporations, translation companies, language schools, and Muslim restaurants, which are set up by either Arabian or Chinese (see Figures 2.1 and 2.2). Middle Eastern merchants in Yiwu are generally well-educated, wealthy young men with acute business senses. Al Jazeera is the main channel for Arabs in Yiwu to keep track of political, social, and economic news in the Middle East. Numerous Arabian restaurants in Yiwu can accommodate the needs of people from different Arabian countries. For example, Al-Aqsa restaurants accommodate Palestinians while Damascus restaurants mainly serve Syrians.

Meanwhile, Middle Eastern merchants have generated huge business opportunities in Yiwu, which in turn attract Muslim populations from all over China, especially Hui people from Ningxia, Henan, and Yunnan, and Uyghur people from Xinjiang. At the beginning of the new century, a small number of Muslim people from Northwest China went to Yiwu in search of business opportunities in small commodities. And today's Muslim influx can be largely attributed to the flock of Middle Eastern merchants in Yiwu. At present, Chinese Muslims in Yiwu mainly engage in catering service, trade, and translation, because the Muslim identity works to their advantage in such occupations. Ben Simpfendorfer believes the Arabic language translators play an important role in linking the Arab world with China from

---

[27] Alshin Molavi, "The New Silk Road", p. 46.

Figure 2.1   Streetside Arab Shops in Yiwu
Photographed by ZOU Lei (the author), April 14, 2012.

bottom to top.[28] Muslim populations from the Middle East and from Northwestern China have created a unique social ecosystem in Yiwu, in which Muslims from both China and abroad coexist in the same community. To some extent, it is a revival and reorganization of the faith legacy inherited from the ancient Silk Road.

During the heyday of the ancient maritime Silk Road, a large number of Arabian and Persian merchants from the Middle East traveled frequently between China's eastern coastal regions and the Persian Gulf. There emerged unique Muslim communities "*Fan Fang*", which often centered around the local mosque, in important port cities such as Guangzhou, Yangzhou, Quanzhou, and Hangzhou.

---

[28] Ben Simpfendorfer, *The New Silk Road: How a Rising Arab World Is Turning Away from the West and Rediscovering China*, p. 116. (贝哲民:《新丝绸之路:阿拉伯世界如何重新发现中国》, 第 116 页。)

Figure 2.2 Recruitment Advertisement in a Yiwu Store
Photographed by ZOU Lei (the author), April 14, 2012.

The influx of Muslim populations from both China and abroad, especially over 20 thousand Arab Muslims among them, has turned Yiwu,
a county-level city used to have no Islamic mosques, cemeteries, or
religious practices, into a large Muslim community in China's eastern
coastal region. Only in a few years, Yiwu, with a skyrocketing Muslim
population, has built one mosque and five worship sites. In a sense,
the interaction and mutual promotion between trade and faith in
Yiwu help to reveal a historical picture of what Middle Eastern merchants' lives were like in China when ancient Silk Road was prosperous, and also provides a glimpse of the Islamization of the ancient Silk
Road.

In 2001, the authorities approved of setting up a temporary worship site in Hong Lou Hotel which accommodated foreign merchants
from Pakistan and Afghanistan. It is the first time for Zhejiang province to establish such a religious site for foreign Muslims, marking the

official entry of Islam into Yiwu. In 2002, the Yiwu municipal government rented a hall at the second floor of 200 Nanmen Rd to set up an Islamic worship site. This hall, covering 500 square meters, can accommodate more than 500 people at one time. In August 2004, the worship site was moved to the former Yiwu Silk Factory — a place of 2,500 square meters, big enough to hold up to 5,000 people. In 2007, due to rapid growth in Muslim population, Yiwu municipal government extended the mosque on Jiangbin West Road, which is called "Yiwu Mosque" or "Grand Mosque" by local Muslims (see Figures 2.3 and 2.4). Meanwhile, the worship site in Hong Lou Hotel has been preserved.[29] In the field trip in April 2012, the author learned that over 7,000 Muslims gathered in Yiwu Mosque each week

Figure 2.3   Grand Mosque in Yiwu

Photographed by ZOU Lei (the author), April 14, 2012.

---

[29] Zhou Zhizhong and Li Huimin, "Life and Work in Yiwu" (no. 1), *China Ethnic News*, February 15, 2011, p. 7. (周志忠、李辉民:《安居乐业在义乌 (上)》, 载《中国民族报》2011 年 2 月 15 日, 第 7 版。)

Figure 2.4   Grand Mosque in Yiwu
Photographed by ZOU Lei (the author), April 14, 2012.

(60% of whom were foreign Muslims), which beat Id Kah Mosque in Kashgar, Xinjiang, which, with a weekly attendance of 5,000–6,000, is known as the largest mosque in China.

It can be said that the growth of Muslim population spurred by Yiwu–Middle East trade relation, the revival of "*Fan Fang*", and the expansion of the mosque are creating an unprecedented religious landscape and social ecosystem in China's Eastern coastal cities since the decline of the ancient Silk Road. Such a phenomenon is symbolically significant, considering Western suspicions toward Islam and mosques after the 9/11. Ben Simpfendorfer even regarded it as "epitome showing how China and the West split up since 2011".[30]

---

[30] Ben Simpfendorfer, *The New Silk Road: How a Rising Arab World Is Turning Away from the West and Rediscovering China*, p. 8. (贝哲民:《新丝绸之路: 阿拉伯世界如何重新发现中国》, 第 8 页。)

In summary, since the new century, growth in trade volume between China and the Middle East has accelerated the flow of commodity, oil, personnel, and capital, reestablishing the long-lost geo-economic bond between the two regions. The spreading of Islam and the changing social ecosystem in Yiwu, driven by international trading activities, have symbolic significance and are evoking historical memories of the ancient Silk Road.

2.2 Origins of the "Modern Silk Road"

The rise of the "Modern Silk Road" between China and the Middle East is not an isolated or accidental event, but a product of multiple structural conditions.

2.2.1 *The Globalization of China's Manufacturing Industry*

Since the reform and opening up, in order to attract foreign direct investment (FDI) and earn more foreign exchange through the expansion of export to the best of its ability, a national development strategy of giving priority to eastern coastal development and export-oriented manufacturing industry has been adopted by China. Specifically, supported by resources input and preferential policies, a series of special economic zones and economic and technological development zones were established in Eastern coastal areas. Since Western countries, Japan and the Chinese communities in Hong Kong, Taiwan, and Southeast Asia have become major trading partners of China, and international trade is relying heavily on sea transportation, the Eastern coastal areas undoubtedly enjoys geographic advantages. In particular, it is worth noting that Guangdong and Fujian have become key investment destinations for a significant number of overseas Chinese, thanks to the flesh-and-blood bond. In virtue of low-cost and high-quality labor force, rich natural resources, complete industrial systems, and efficient governments, China seized the opportunity as Western developed countries transferred the medium-end and low-end manufacturing industries overseas and quickly became one of the largest manufacturing powers in the world.

In the 21st century, the rise of China's manufacturing industry not only gives momentum to the miracle of China's economy, but also drives the growth of the whole world. From 2002 to 2011, the industrial added value of enterprises above designated size grew at an average annual rate of 15.4%, the industry sector as a proportion of gross domestic product (GDP) maintained around 40% and the contribution of China's manufacturing toward national economic growth exceeded 45%.[31] As the global financial crisis and European debt crisis worsen, China's manufacturing-oriented economy has become the stabilizer and engine of the world economy.

It is estimated by IHS Global Insight, a US economic advisory agency, that in 2010, the output of China's manufacturing accounted for 19.8% of the total output worldwide, a little higher than that of the United States at 19.4%. Therefore, China surpassed the United States as the largest manufacturing nation in the world, which put an end to the US monopolization of the position as the largest commodity producing country for as long as 110 years. According to the historical statistics, it was in approximately 1830 when China occupied this position for the last time. At that time, the output of China's manufacturing accounted for 30% of the total output worldwide; however, the figure dropped to about 6% in 1900 and went further down to about 3% in 1990.[32] The authoritative data from the Ministry of Industry and Information Technology shows that China ranks the first in seven of the 22 major categories of manufacturing industry; China's outputs of 220 products in 500 major industrial products of the world rank the top globally; in 2011, China's output of crude steel ranked the first in the world and accounted for 44.7%

---

[31] Huang Xin, "To Win the Battle of China's Industrial Transformation and Upgrading: Interview with Miao Wei, the Minister and Party Secretary of Ministry of Industry and Information", *Economic Daily*, October 17, 2012, p. 7. (黄鑫:《打好工业转型升级攻坚战——访工业和信息化部党组书记、部长苗圩》, 载《经济日报》2012 年 10 月 17 日, 第 7 版。)

[32] Peter Marsh, "China Noses Back Ahead as Top Goods Producer to Halt 110-year US Run", *Financial Times*, March 14, 2011.

of the world's total; in 2011, China's output of electrolytic aluminum ranked the first globally and accounted for 40% of the total output; also in 2011, the output of China's color TVs, mobile phones, computers, and integrated circuits ranked the first globally, respectively, accounting for 48.8%, 70.6%, and 90.6% of the global output.[33]

In the equipment manufacturing sector, China's manufacturing also takes on a swift and violent growth momentum. According to the statistics of the Ministry of Industry and Information Technology, the production value of China's equipment manufacturing industry in 2013 exceeded 20 trillion Yuan, accounting for more than one third of the global equipment manufacturing industry, which ensured its champion place. Only the United States and the United Kingdom once achieved or exceeded that proportion in history. In the same year, China's electricity generation output reached 120 million kilowatt, accounting for 60% of the world's total; the Chinese shipbuilding industry completed ships with a combined gross tonnage (gt) of 45.34 million, accounting for 41% of the world's total; Chinese output of automobiles reached 22.117 million, accounting for 25% of the world's total; and the output of machine tools achieved 959 thousand, accounting for 38% of the world's total.[34] It can be concluded that China has already become a "world factory" in a real sense.

The transformation of China's export commodity composition provides an evident clue for the decisive role played by Chinese-made products. From 1980 to 1990, the manufactured goods surpassed primary commodities to become the major export commodities; from 1990 to 2000, China's manufacturing industry successfully shifted its

---

[33] General Office of the Ministry of Industry and Information Technology, "China Will Become the World's Largest Manufacturing Country", December 27, 2012, http://www.miit.gov.cn/n11293472/n11293832/n11293907/n11368223/15089301.html, log-in time: February 1, 2013. (工信部办公厅:《工作会专稿: 我国成为全球制造业第一大国》, 2012 年 12 月 27 日。)

[34] Pang Geping and Wang Yunna, "China Tops World in Equipment Manufacturing Output", *People's Daily*, April 3, 2014, p. 10. (庞革平、王云娜:《我装备制造业产值居世界首位》, 载《人民日报》2014 年 4 月 3 日, 第 10 版。)

focus from textiles and other light industrial goods to mechanical and electrical products which accounted for 42.3% of China's total export. In the first decade of the 21st century, the proportion of mechanical and electrical products exceeded 50% of the total export, and that of high-tech products represented by electronics and information technology kept growing and reached 31.2% in 2010. It is reported that new breakthroughs have been made in the export of large-scale mechanical and electrical products and complete sets of equipments, including automobiles, ships, planes, railway equipment, and communication products.[35]

The 21st century is the era of "Made in China". Through large-scale export, Chinese-made goods have swept across the globe. The period between 1978 and 2010 has witnessed an explosive growth in the export of Chinese goods (see Figure 2.5).

In 2009, China surpassed Germany to become the world's top goods exporter, with Chinese-made commodities accounting for

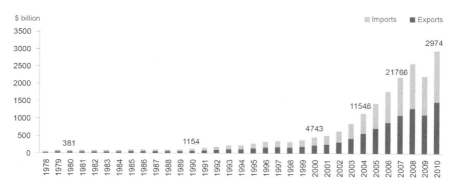

Figure 2.5   Total Value of China's Imports and Exports (1978–2010)

Source: The State Council Information Office of the PRC, *China's Foreign Trade, People's Daily,* December 8, 2011, p. 14.

---

[35] Guan Peili, "Opening Wider to the Outside World—Structure of Foreign Trade Is Improving", *Economic Daily,* September 6, 2012, p. 5. (管培利:《扩大开放——外贸结构在优化》, 载《经济日报》2012 年 9 月 6 日, 第 5 版。)

9.6% of world's total exports.[36] In 2012, China remained the world's largest manufacturer with a 20% share of world's manufacturing activities. Meanwhile, China's export of manufactured goods occupied one seventh of global trade in the category.[37] Institute of International Trade of Korea International Trade Association released a report entitled *A Comparison of the Export Competitiveness of Foreign Countries through Their Products with the Largest Market Shares*. According to the report, on the worldwide list of the exporting products with the largest market share in 2012, China took the first place with 1485 kinds of products ranking top — a figure bigger than the combined number of Germany (703) and the United States (603).[38] According to statistics from the WTO Secretariat, in 2013, China's total volume of foreign trade amounted to $4.16 trillion (with export reaching $2.21 trillion and import reaching $1.95 trillion), surpassing the United States as the world's largest trading nation.[39] Meanwhile, China has become the largest trading partner of over two-thirds of the countries and regions in the world, indicating that the global trade landscape has been undergoing drastic changes. For this, statistics showed that the United States was the largest trading partner of 127 countries while China was the largest partner of 70 countries in 2006. Yet by the end of 2011, the situation was totally reversed. China became the largest trading partner of 126 countries while the United States only had 76 countries that took it as the largest trade partner.[40]

---

[36] Lu Zheng, "Treating 'Export No.1' with Calm, *China Securities Journal*, February 11, 2010, p. A02. (卢铮:《冷静看待"出口全球第一"》, 载《中国证券报》2010 年 2 月 11 日, 第 A02 版。)

[37] Miao Wei, "Building a Strong Manufacturing Country While Deepening Reform Comprehensively", *Qiushi*, no. 5, 2014, p. 15. (苗圩:《在全面深化改革中打造制造业强国》, 载《求是》2014 年第 5 期, 第 15 页。)

[38] "China Ranks Top in World's Top Exports", *Reference News*, January 24, 2014, p. 4. (《中国"全球第一产品"世界居首》, 载《参考消息》2014 年 1 月 24 日, 第 4 版。)

[39] Wang Ke, "China Becomes the Biggest Goods Trading Country", *People's Daily*, March 2, 2014, p. 1. (王珂:《中国成为第一货物贸易大国》, 载《人民日报》2014 年 3 月 2 日, 第 1 版。)

[40] Chu Mo, "*China Overtakes the United States as the Largest Trading Partner of Most Countries*", December 3, 2012, http://finance.sina.com.cn/world/20121203/

It can be concluded that the globalization of China's manufacturing has already become a fundamental characteristic of international political economy. From an island country in the South Pacific Ocean to African continent, from the East end of Eurasia to Atlantic coasts, the "Made in China" label is ubiquitous. The whole world is benefiting from low-cost, high-quality Chinese-made goods. In this sense, the appearance of large quantities of Chinese goods in the Middle East is a local manifestation of a global phenomenon. Chinese and Middle Eastern merchants have been playing a role of intermediaries to propel this process.

2.2.2 The Middle Easternization of China's Oil Import

The globalization of Chinese-made goods promotes China's export of manufactured goods to global markets. At the same time, China (especially the Eastern coastal areas) is becoming more dependent on global markets for staple commodities like resources, energy, and even food. In fact, the two tendencies are just different forms of the same economic logic.

Undoubtedly, petroleum is an important strategic resource in the international market of staple commodity, and thus becomes China's top priority of energy strategy. According to the statistics, since 1978, coal has been remaining around 70% of the total energy consumption in China while petroleum has been constantly taking up around 20%.[41] It can be said that coal is still China's most important energy source. However, under current conditions, petroleum has an irreplaceable influence on Chinese products, national economy, and people's daily lives. Therefore, China's economic miracle as well as the globalization of Chinese-made products also means that China is highly dependent on international oil market. In 1993, China became a net importer of petroleum products, and then in 1996, China

---

155413878413.shtml, log-in time: March 11, 2014. (楚墨编译:《中国超过美国成为多数国家最大贸易伙伴》, 2012 年 12 月 3 日。)

[41] National Bureau of Statistics of the People's Republic of China, *China Statistical Yearbook* 2012, Beijing: China Statistics Press, 2012, p. 273. (中国国家统计局:《中国统计年鉴. 2012》, 北京:中国统计出版社 2012 年版, 第 273 页。)

turned from a net exporter of crude oil to a net importer. BP's statistics show that China's net daily petroleum import in 2013 amounted to 7 million barrels, once beyond that of the United States at 6.5 million barrels (the lowest since 1988), and leapt to the world's largest net petroleum importer.[42] With the expansion of China's oil import, its dependence on crude oil import (the ratio of net petroleum import to total volume needed in refinery plants) rose from 34.6% in 2003 to 58.6% in 2013. Accordingly, its dependence on oil import (the ratio of net oil import volume to total consumption) skyrocketed from 39.1% in 2003 to 61.7% in 2013.[43]

In the light of its increasingly heavy dependence on foreign oil, China enacted a national energy strategy in 2001. In 2003, the central government put forward the strategy of "going global" in the hope of solving the problem of oil shortage by using "two markets" and developing "two resources". It can be said that expanding the oil sources in global market to guarantee supply is the dominant issue in China's energy security strategy. Petroleum has gradually become a significant variable with a significant impact on China's foreign policy.[44]

As to the source of China's import of crude oil, since the beginning of the new century, a strategic oil import zone, mainly including the former Soviet Union region (Central Asia and Russia), Africa and the Middle East, has gradually taken shape.[45] In 2013, China imported 281.2 million tons of crude oil in total, of which the oil import from Russia and Kazakhstan accounted for around 13%, oil import from Africa accounted for 23% (oil import from Angola was about 14%), oil import from the Middle East took up around 52%,

---

[42] BP, *BP Statistical Review of World Energy*, June 2014, p. 3.

[43] Tian Chunrong, "Analysis on China's Import and Export", pp. 30–31.

[44] David Zweig and Bi Jianhai, "China's Global Hunt for Energy", *Foreign Affairs* 84, no. 5, Sep.–Oct. 2005, pp. 25–38; Charles E. Ziegler, "The Energy Factor in China's Foreign Policy", *Journal of Chinese Political Science* 11, no. 1, Spring 2006, pp. 1–23; Aaron L. Friedberg, "'Going Out': China's Pursuit of Natural Resources and Implications for the PRC's Grand Strategy", *NBR Analysis* 17, no. 3, Sep. 2006, pp. 5–34.

[45] Shi Dan, "*International Environment of China's Energy Security*", Beijing: Social Sciences Academic Press, 2013. (史丹:《中国能源安全的国际环境》,北京: 社会科学文献出版社 2013 年版。)

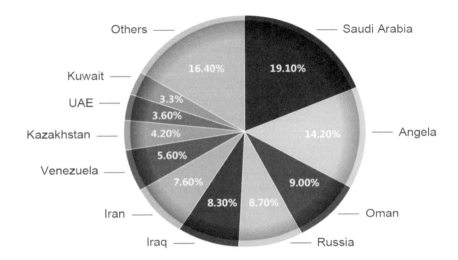

Figure 2.6   China Oil Imports by Country of Origin 2013

Source: Tian Chunrong, "Analysis of the Status of China's Import and Export of Petroleum and Natural Gas in 2013," *International Petroleum Economics*, no. 3, 2014, pp. 34–35.

with Saudi Arabia, Oman, Iraq, Iran, the United Arab Emirates, and Kuwait, respectively, ranking the first (19.1%), the third (9%), the fifth (8.3%), the sixth (7.3%), the ninth (3.6%), and the tenth (3.3%) largest exporters (see Figure 2.6).

Obviously, China is heavily dependent on petroleum import from the Middle East, especially the petroleum-producing countries like Saudi Arabia, Iran, Oman, and Iraq. In fact, since China became a net oil importer in 1996, Middle Eastern crude oil has taken up half of China's import. In the same year, China's import of crude oil amounted to 22.6169 million tons, of which 52.9% — 11.96 million tons — was from the Middle East with Oman, Yemen, and Iran as the biggest exporters.[46] Since the 21st century, Middle Eastern oil has

---

[46] "China's Crude Oil Import Sources and Its Export from 1996 to 2001", *Energy Policy Research*, no. 1, 2002, pp. 88–89. (《中国 1996–2001 年原油进口来源和出口去向》, 载《能源政策研究》2002 年第 1 期, 第 88–89 页。)

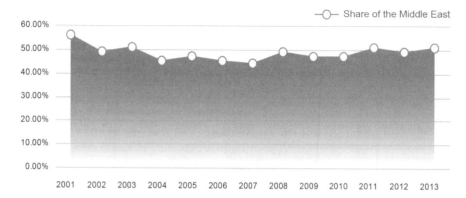

Figure 2.7   Share of Middle Eastern Oil in China's Crude Oil Import from 2001 to 2013

Source: Tian Chunrong, "Analysis on China's Import and Export of Petroleum and Natural Gas in 2005," *International Petroleum Economics,* no. 3, 2006, p. 4; Tian Chunrong, "Analysis on China's Import and Export of Petroleum and Natural Gas in 2013," *International Petroleum Economics,* no. 3, 2014, p. 34.

remained around 50% of China's total crude oil import. Therefore, China's oil import shows a clear "Middle East" Characteristic (see Figure 2.7). Such a situation is reflected in China's trade structure: on the one hand, China has a trade deficit with Middle East oil-producing countries; on the other hand, crude oil remains Middle East's dominant export to China.

It can be said that the giant ships sailing from the Persian Gulf and Strait of Hormuz to China's East coast are now filled with petroleum, instead of spices, rhino horns, elephant's tusks, and jewelry in ancient times. But oil has a much bigger influence on China's society, politics, economy, and foreign policy than the abovementioned products. Thus, guaranteed oil supply from the Middle East has become top concern of China's Middle East policy.[47]

---

[47] Jin Liangxiang, "China and the Middle East: Energy First", *Middle East Quarterly,* Spring 2005, pp. 3–10; Henry Lee and Dan Shalmon, "*Searching for Petroleum: China's Petroleum Initiatives in the Middle East*", Discussion Paper, Belfer Center for Science and International Affairs, John F. Kennedy School of Government, Harvard

From a more macro view, China's heavy dependence on the Middle Eastern oil reflects the tendency of East Asia's mounting oil import from the Middle East, which stands in sharp contrast to Western countries' decreasing appetite for Middle Eastern oil. After the first oil crisis in the 1970s, the developed countries have adopted a diversification strategy to expand petroleum sources, with the aim to reduce dependence on Middle Eastern oil, and thus to decrease energy security risks caused by the political situation in the Middle East. It now appears that the Western developed countries have basically gotten rid of energy dependence on the Middle East.

In American continent, the United States and other American countries are the largest oil partners of each other. In 2013, the United States' biggest oil import (crude oil and oil products) was from it's home continent, reaching 58.7% of the total, with Canada and Mexico accounting for 41.4% and Central and South America 17.3%. Meanwhile, the Middle East was downgraded to the second largest supplier (about 20.7%) for the United States. Import from West Africa and North Africa combined accounted for 8.4%. Obviously, the oil import pattern of the US is featuring American countries as the main suppliers and the Middle Eastern and African countries as supplement providers. It is worth noting that, with shale gas in the United States, petroleum sand in Canada, and deepwater petroleum in Brazil being exploited, America will possibly become the "New Middle East", fundamentally altering the global energy landscape, and even the world's geo-political and geo-economic structure in decades to come.

As for Europe, the European Union (EU) and the former Soviet Union region are the largest oil partners with each other. In 2013, the former Soviet Union area was the largest oil exporter for EU countries, accounting for 47.4% of EU's total import. Africa (West Africa and North Africa) was the second largest exporter, accounting for

---

University, January 2007; Gang Chen and Ryan Clarke, *China's Intensified Energy Engagement in the Middle East*, Singapore: National University of Singapore, 2010; Christina Lin, *The New Silk Road: China's Energy Strategy in the Greater Middle East*, Washington, DC: Washington Institute for Near East Policy, 2011.

23.6%. The Middle East only occupied 16.5%. Accordingly, the EU bought 66% of the total export from the former Soviet Union area in 2013.

In terms of Asia, China, Japan, India, and other Asian countries are the largest oil partners with the Middle East. In 2013, Middle East petroleum (crude petroleum and petroleum products) accounted for 43%, 61%, and 73% in the total import of China, India, and Japan, with the ratios of crude petroleum even higher. Accordingly, in 2013, Asia took 76% share of Middle Eastern oil export (see Figure 2.8).

In short, the current global oil supply and demand have shown the characteristic of "regionalization". With the United States gradually returning to the American continent and Europe becoming more dependent on former Soviet Union area for oil import, the Middle East has become the primary oil supplier for Asia.[48] As a result, the Middle East increasingly relies on the Asian consumers for its oil export. The situation in the Middle East, however, exhibits varying degrees of spillover effects on Asia, Europe, and America. It is of particular note that in recent years, the "shale gas revolution" has turned the United States into the fastest growing producer of petroleum and gas. The United States surpassed Russia in 2009 to become the largest producer of natural gas. Moreover, it became a net exporter of petroleum products for the first time over the last 60 years. According to the World Energy Outlook 2012 released by the International Energy Agency, the United States will overtake Saudi Arabia to become the largest petroleum producer in the world by 2020. And North America is expected to become a net petroleum export area around 2030. By then, the United States, a country whose current import occupies around 20% of its energy consumption, will become self-sufficient in energy.[49] In this sense, the fact that China replaces the United States as the largest buyer of Middle Eastern oil (especially from Saudi Arabia) epitomizes the significant changes in the global

---

[48] Mikkal E. Herberg *et al.*, *The New Energy Silk Road: The Growing Asia-Middle East Energy Nexus*, Washington, DC: The National Bureau of Asian Research, 2009.

[49] Bai Yang *et al.*, "Global Energy Distribution Presents Major Changes", *People's Daily*, November 14, 2012, p. 3. (白阳等:《全球能源分布格局呈现重大变化》,载《人民日报》2012 年 11 月 14 日, 第 3 版。)

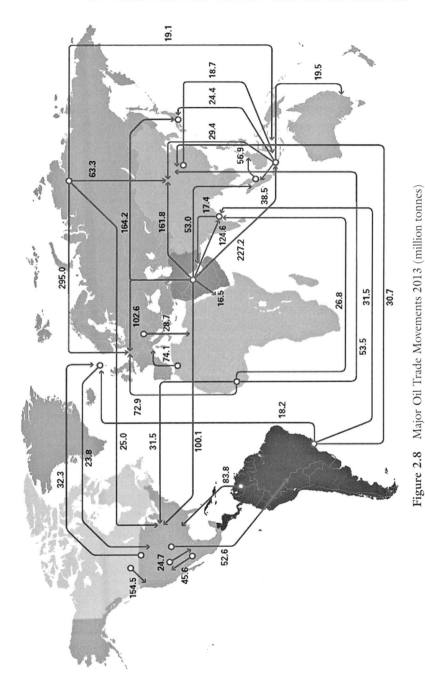

Figure 2.8 Major Oil Trade Movements 2013 (million tonnes)

Source: BP, BP Statistical Review of World Energy, June 2014, p. 19.

landscape of oil supply and demand. What lies behind is the tremendous risks and ongoing challenges in energy security and even in national security for China (East Asia).

2.2.3 *China's Coast-Oriented Economy*

Along with the globalization of Chinese-made products and the dependence on the Middle East for petroleum import, China's economic center of gravity has been shifting to the coastal areas. From a historical point of view, China's economic center of gravity has been gradually transferring to the South since the Song Dynasty. The eastern coastal areas became the main source of tax revenue and the platform for foreign trade, which, among other factors, led to the thriving of ancient Silk Road. The rise of the western countries in modern times has enhanced maritime trade to be the dominant form of international trade. With domestic and international factors reinforcing each other, the unique position of eastern coastal areas has been further strengthened.

Since the founding of the People's Republic of China, enormous efforts, especially the "Third-Front Movement" from 1964 to 1980, were made by the central government to promote balanced-development in different regions.[50] However, after the adoption of the reform and opening-up policy, the advantages of the Eastern coastal areas have quickly become salient. China's eastern coastal regions occupy a predominant position in the country's economic geographical landscape, considering all the favorable factors, such as natural resource endowment, the national development strategy of giving priority to Eastern coastal areas, export-oriented industrial policy, as well as the geographical advantages for maritime trade geared to the western developed countries, Japan, Chinese Taiwan, Chinese Hongkong, and the Southeast Asia. During the time, the human resources and natural

---

[50] Chen Donglin, *The Third-Front Movement—Western Development during the Period of Preparation for the War*, Beijing: Party School of the Central Committee of C.P.C Press, 2003. (陈东林：《三线建设——备战时期的西部开发》, 北京:中共中央党校出版社 2003 年版。)

resources have been quickly flowing from western China to the eastern areas on a large scale. Driven by policy and market, the existing East–West imbalance in China has become more serious. As a result, the Pearl River Delta, the Yangtze River Delta, Beijing–Tianjin–Hebei Region have become city clusters where resources, labors, capitals, products, and industries are assembled. Coastal area is a feature of China's regional economic landscape. China's eastern coastal provinces are both the production bases for "Made in China" goods and major consumers of Middle Eastern oil.

These provinces are leading the country in economic development, which is reflected in industrial distributions and statistical indexes. In 2012, the Eastern regions (*Note:* including such 10 provinces as Beijing, Tianjin, Hebei, Liaoning, Shanghai, Jiangsu, Zhejiang, Fujian, Shandong, and Guangdong) covering 9.5% of China's total land area, have 38.2% of China's total population and 47.4% of the total labor force, and contribute 51.3% of total GDP and 84.6% of the country's import and export[51]. In terms of the layout of export processing zones, China had approved the establishment of 102 special customs oversight areas, such as export processing zones, in 25 provinces by the end of 2011, 76 of which were located in the eastern coastal areas, 11 in central China, and only 15 in western China.[52] In terms of the distribution of high-tech zones, as of 2012, of 105 national high-tech zones, 46 (43.4%) were in the eastern region, 23 (21.7%) in the central region, and 24 (22.6%) in the western region.[53] In terms of the National Economic and Technical Development Zones, in 2011, the regional GDP and volume of foreign trade of the

---

[51] National Bureau of Statistics of the People's Republic of China, *China Statistical Yearbook* 2013, Beijing: China Statistics Press, 2013, pp. 18–19. (中华人民共和国国家统计局:《中国统计年鉴. 2013》, 北京:中国统计出版社 2013 年版, 第 18–19 页。)

[52] Huo Jianguo, "To Consolidate and Improve China's Position as Global Manufacturing Center", July 12, 2012, http://www.caitec.org.cn/c/cn/news/2012-07/13/news_3404.html, log-in time: February 1, 2013. (霍建国:《巩固提升中国"全球制造业中心"地位》, 2012 年 7 月 12 日)

[53] Zhao Yongxin, "National High-Tech Zones Have an Eye-catching Performance", *People's Daily*, December 18, 2012, p. 1. (赵永新:《国家高新区表现抢眼》, 载《人民日报》2012 年 12 月 18 日, 第 1 版。)

66 state-level Economic and Technical Development Zones in the eastern region reached 2862.35 billion Yuan and 590.87 billion dollars, respectively, which accounted for 69.2% and 89.6% of China's total in their own categories. In 2011, the number of FDI enterprises in the Eastern region amounted to 616,000 which accounted for 83.4% of the total in China. The accumulated actual use of foreign capital reached $1 trillion, which accounted for 81.7% the total foreign capital. In 2011, enterprises with over $100 million FDI amounted to 362, an increase of 205 over the year of 2002.[54] It can be said that since the new century, China has become the world's manufacturing center, and China's eastern coastal areas have become the country's manufacturing center. As a consequence, China's eastern coastal areas have always been highly dependent on foreign trade. In 2012, the GDP of the 10 provinces in East China region amounted to 29,589.2 billion Yuan and the total import–export volume reached $3271.08 billion. With the central parity rate of the RMB against the US dollar (USD) reaching 6.2855 by the end of 2011, East China's reliance on foreign trade was around 70%.[55]

It is worth pointing out that such an economic geography is also reflected in crude petroleum import of each province. For instance, China's crude petroleum import totaled 282,140,000 tons in 2013 and the import volume of 10 provinces and cities in the Eastern coastal region reached 237,843,000 tons, valued at $184.09 billion, accounting for 84% of China's total import volume and the total value. In recent years, China, together with Saudi Arabia and Kuwait, had set up joint ventures of petroleum refining and petrochemical enterprises

---

[54] Ministry of Commerce of PRC, "Summary on the Business Accomplishments since the 16th CPC National Congress 6: Opening-up of the East Reached a New Stage", November 1, 2012, http://www.mofcom.gov.cn/article/ae/ai/201211/20121108414144. shtml, log-in time: November 3, 2012. (中国商务部:《十六大以来商务成就综述之六:东部地区对外开放迈上新台阶》, 2012 年 11 月 1 日。)

[55] National Bureau of Statistics of the People's Republic of China, *China Statistical Yearbook*. 2012, p. 19; State Administration of Foreign Exchange of PRC, *Annual Report of the State Administration of Foreign Exchange* (2012), 2013, p. 23. (中华人民共和国国家统计局:《中国统计年鉴. 2012》, 北京:中国统计出版社 2012 年版, 第 19 页; 中国国家外汇管理局:《国家外汇管理局年报 (2012)》, 2013 年, 第 23 页。)

in Shandong, Fujian, Tianjin, Zhejiang, and Hainan. Geographically, all of them are located in China's eastern coastal region. As a result, in addition to very large crude carriers (VLCCs) moving between China and the Middle East, China's eastern coastal region has become an "unmovable station" to receive oil flowing from the Middle East.

With China's economic center of gravity being transferred to coastal areas, China's eastern coastal regions have gained a dominant position in international trade. Meanwhile, China's foreign trade has become highly reliant on maritime transportation. After the middle and late Tang Dynasty, the maritime Silk Road gradually triumphed over the land Silk Road. Thus, silk and porcelain from China and spices, rhinoceros horn, and ivory from the Middle East were shipped between the two regions. Today, sea transport is a main mode of trade transactions between China and its major trading partners, and it is dominant in large-scale exports of "Made in China" products as well as imports of Middle Eastern oil and other bulk commodities. Before Sino-Russia and Sino-Myanmar Oil and Gas Pipelines being put into operation, nearly 95% of China's petroleum import was carried out by sea transportation. China's imports of petroleum accounts for about one third of global seaborne trade of oil. It is estimated that China, as the biggest consumer of bulk commodities, imports 99% of iron ore through sea routes and 93% of its total foreign trade volume is realized by sea transportation.[56] As a matter of fact, maritime transportation will remain the dominant support of China's foreign trade for a long time. China's import and export will take up over 60% of the annual increase in global seaborne trade volume.[57] Therefore, the

---

[56] Chen Yuan *et al.*, *Study on Modern and Comprehensive Transportation System*, Beijing: Yanjiu Press, 2008, pp. 251 and 257. Quoted from Wang Xiangsui, "Lean on the Land and Face to the Sea: Rebalance of China's Strategic Emphasis", *Contemporary International Relations*, 2010 Celebration Special Issue, p. 55 (陈元等:《现代综合交通体系建设研究》,研究出版社 2008 年版,第 251、257 页。转引自王湘穗:《倚陆向海:中国战略重心的再平衡》,载《现代国际关系》2010 年庆典特刊,第 55 页。)

[57] Rong Xinchun, "Road to a Great Maritime Power", *People's Daily*, February 21, 2014, p. 23. (彤新春:《通往海运强国之路》,载《人民日报》 2014 年 2 月 21 日,第 23 版。)

fact that Yiwu and Guangzhou could re-attract a large number of Middle Eastern merchants, and the revitalization of the maritime Silk Road between China's eastern coastal regions and the Persian Gulf in the Middle East, to some extent, are both the logical outcomes and vivid manifestation of the coast orientation of China's economy.

To put it in a nutshell, the global flow of Chinese manufactured goods, China's demand for Middle Eastern oil and the coast orientation of China's economic geography, jointly reveal the roots of the rising "Modern Silk Road" between China and the Middle East since the 21st century.

2.3 Essence of the "Modern Silk Road"

The rise of the "Modern Silk Road" between China and the Middle East is by no means a simple reproduction of the ancient Silk Road. Rather, it is deeply rooted in the macro structure of contemporary international political economy.

2.3.1 *A Derived Product of Contemporary International System*

With the prosperity and development of the ancient Silk Road, the flow of silk and porcelain from China and spices, rhinoceros horn, and ivory from the Middle East constituted the basic form of international trade back then. Nowadays, the "Modern Silk Road" between China and the Middle East is based on a similar pattern that characterizes the two-way flow of "Made in China" goods and Middle Eastern oil, which are the most influential and symbolic commodities in contemporary international political economy. In ancient times, Arabian and Persian merchants brought to China a large amount of luxury products such as spices, medicines, jewelries, rhinoceros horns, and ivories by sea or camels. Today, commodities transported from the Middle East to China via tankers are mostly petroleum and other mineral products. In ancient times, Chins first exported great quantities of silk to the Middle East through the land and maritime Silk Road and then sold handmade silk and porcelain products to the Middle East via sea route. Nowadays, Chinese goods (bulk commodities including mechanical and electrical products, textile and garment, transportation equipment) produced in Eastern coastal regions in Pearl River Delta and the Yangtze River Delta are transported to the Middle East by sea. It can be found that the commodity composition of international trade on both the ancient and modern Silk Road has been maintaining a high degree of stability — that is to say, the Middle East has always been exporting resource products while China has always been exporting manufactured commodities. However, profound changes have been taking place underneath the surface. The contemporary international political and economic structure is deeply embedded in the "Modern Silk Road".

In ancient times, the Middle East was more dependent on China's silk and porcelain than China on its spices and jewelry. But today, the situation is reversed. China has become more heavily dependent on Middle Eastern oil than the Middle East on "Made in China" goods. Petroleum, as a strategic commodity, also bears political and economic significance. It has a widespread and deep impact on China's economy and people's livelihood, which is unparalleled by commodities such as spices, rhinoceros horn, ivory, and jewelry. Under the global division of labor system, the international bulk commodities are indispensable necessities, which embodies the essential differences between ancient and modern international trade.

International trade in ancient times evolved around excessive products of natural economy in various regions. All economies were on a fairly equal footing to conduct exchanges of goods. International trade, at the time, did not carry enough weight to affect a nation's economy, society or people's livelihood, let alone help a nation gain dominance over others. However, with the rise of the West, international trade evolved into a coercive exchange between manufactured goods and raw materials. Its corresponding phenomenon was the "center-periphery" structure between the western developed countries and developing countries in Africa, Asia, and Latin America. The looseness and equality in international trade relations gradually gave way to the dominant-subordinate structure. Under this dual structure, developed countries were dominant in rules formulating, currency, and price setting in international trade while developing countries degenerate to raw material producers and industrial products consumers.

Since the Reform and Opening-up, China has made unprecedented efforts to participate in the international division of labor system and trade system. In accordance to an international trade system dominated by maritime trade, China attaches great importance to the development of eastern coastal areas. The booming manufacturing industry in eastern China has not only created an economic miracle, but also has been gradually changing the "center-periphery" dual structure created by the West.

To be more specific, rapid economic growth of China (East Asia) is transforming the traditional dual structure of international trade into a brand new triangular structure. In the old days, the term "triangular trade" was used to describe the trade circulation, in which the European colonists transported textiles, fruit wine, and groceries to Africa in exchange for slaves, then sold slaves in America to buy raw materials such as gold and silver, cotton and minerals, and finally traded finished products for more slaves in Africa. Such trading activities were named "triangular trade" because three continents — Europe, America, and Africa — were involved. However, main actors in the new triangular trade are consumers — North America and West Europe, producers — East Asian countries like China, and resource suppliers — oil-producing countries in the Middle East. The mechanism of the new triangular circulation works as follows: producing countries import raw materials from resource countries and export finished products to the consuming countries, while consuming countries provide capital, technologies, and services to other countries, and absorb trade surplus and foreign currency reserve from them. Thus, the three parties have a clear division of function: financing (currency, capital), commodities (manufactured goods), and raw materials (bulk commodities). Compared to the dual structure of "center-periphery", the triangular trade structure presents some new characteristics: on the one hand, consuming countries are now exploiting other countries in a more profound and covert way, since the negative balance on the current account is offset by the active balance on capital and financial account; On the other hand, the direct exchange of manufactured goods and raw materials between developed countries and developing countries is being gradually substituted by China's import of raw materials and export of manufactured goods. Therefore, the trade between consuming countries and resource suppliers is becoming less direct. As a result, China becomes desperately eager for bulk commodities and has to pay high price for that on political, economic, and moral level. According to the report of 2012 from Great Wall Strategy Consultants Company, by the end of 2011, in the surveyed 25 kinds of bulk commodities, China ranked the first globally in the consumption of 19 kinds. China's total amount of bulk commodity consumption claimed about 18.7% in the total consumption globally. China's consumption of eight items of bulk commodities exceeded 40% of their total consumption globally. They were iron ore (68%), rare earth (67%), purified terephthalic acid (PTA) (52%), coal (48%), methyl alcohol (45%), refined copper (41%), primary aluminum (41%), and cotton (40%). Meanwhile, after becoming a net oil importer in 1993, China has changed from a net exporter to a net importer of soybean (1996), copper (1998), iron ore (2000), nickel (2003), zinc (2004), silver (2007), refined lead (2009), corn (2009), and coal (2009). During the process, each turning point came with a rise in commodity prices.[58] In this sense, the ultimate reason behind China's mounting demand and America's decreasing demand for Middle Eastern oil is that China now bears the cost shifted from developed countries' consumption of resources under the framework of the new triangular trade.

Therefore, though China has become the pivot to connect consuming countries with resource countries, it is the United States and the US-dominated trading rules, price system, transaction settlement system, and the political security order thereon, that are the preconditions for the functioning of the new triangular trade. The economic relations between China and a vast number of developing countries is

---

[58] Great Wall Strategy Consultants Company, Commodities in China: Research Report on Commodity Industry in 2010, 2012. (长城战略咨询：《大宗商品中国时刻—2010年大宗商品产业研究报告》, 2012年。)

still subject to the United States and the basic structure of today's international politics and economy has never changed fundamentally. That is to say, the "Modern Silk Road" connecting China and the Middle East is exactly an outcome of the US global hegemony.

First, the West, particularly the United States, is in possession of the pricing power in international commodity trade. The supplier, consumer, and price maker of bulk commodities are separate nations. Take the international crude oil trade as an example. The Organization of Petroleum Exporting Countries (OPEC), composed mainly of oil-producing countries in the Middle East, is crude oil supplier while East Asian countries including China and Japan are major oil consumers, but neither of them has the pricing power. For a long time, different pricing formulas have been adopted when Middle Eastern oil is exported to different regions. Premium is charged or discount is offered according to different benchmark prices. Usually, the United States and European customers are offered discount, while Asian buyers are charged premium. In oil pricing, America mainly uses West Texas Intermediate (WTI) as a benchmark while Western Europe goes with the Brent Crude. Although the Asian market uses the average price of Dubai and Oman crudes, Dubai/Oman benchmark is heavily influenced by the Brent Crude futures. Therefore, Asian countries have to pay higher price than the United States and Europe do (about one dollar more for per barrel). That is called "Asian Premium". Under such a pricing system, China (East Asia), as a major oil-importing country, does not have a say in crude oil pricing and has to accept whatever is offered as well as the Asian Premium.

Second, the USD is a dominant currency in the international economic, trade, and financial systems. It has three major functions: medium of global exchange, store of value, and unit of account. A survey conducted by the Bank for International Settlements on the trading volume of the global foreign exchange market reveals that the proportion of the USD has always been maintained around 87% in the global foreign exchange market from 2001 to 2013.[59] In terms of currency reserve, the USD has occupied 61% of currency composition

---

[59] Bank for International Settlements, *Triennial Central Bank Survey 2013*, September 2013, p. 10.

of official foreign exchange reserves (COFER) globally by the end of 2013, according to the statistics of International Monetary Fund (IMF).[60] From the perspective of valuation, the bulk commodity trade in today's global market — including petroleum, gold, nonferrous metals, and food — are almost exclusively priced in USDs. It is the same with the spot market, futures market, and their derivatives markets, as well as WTI and Brent crude. The US' monopoly of the pricing and settlement of strategic resources like petroleum and food, especially the USD as the settlement currency in Middle Eastern oil trade, ensures a dominant role in international trade. On the ancient Silk Road, a quasi-local currency settlement system was adopted, in which copper cash and gold and silver were the dominant settlement currencies in the trading activities between China and the Middle East. Therefore, copper coins and gold and silver, as forms of metal currency, were widely stored in each other's countries. The historic shift from local currency to a third currency (also the world's dominant currency) in trade settlement is a revolutionary change on the "Modern Silk Road".

Third, the ocean trade dominated by the West since the modern times remains central to today's international trade. Marine transportation is still the support of modern trading activities. It is estimated that more than 90% of the global trade volume are transported by sea.[61] In virtue of strong marine military power and global power projection capabilities, the West, especially the United States, has all major trade routes and passages under its control. The Strait of Malacca, the Suez Canal, and the Strait of Hormuz are all within America's military reach. Thus, a vast number of non-Western countries including China have always been living under the threat of damaged and destroyed trade routes. Today's trade route connecting China and the Middle East resembles the sea way of the ancient maritime Silk Road — a route starting from China's Eastern coastal regions and moving along South China Sea, the Strait of Malacca, the

---

[60] IMF, "Currency Composition of Official Foreign Exchange Reserves" (Last updated: March 31, 2014), http://www.imf.org/External/np/sta/cofer/eng/index.htm, log-in time: May 5, 2014.
[61] Rong Xinchun, "Becoming a Great Maritime Power".

Arabian Sea-the Strait of Hormuz, and the Gulf of Aden. Nevertheless, the situation that China faces has changed a lot.

Fourth, the US' control over the pricing of bulk commodities, settlement currency, and trade routes is undergirded by the US-dominated international political security architecture. The country's political and military power serves as the credit basis for a series of trade, financial, and geo-political arrangements. Politics and economy are closely interlinked. The petrodollar system, to a large extent, is an outward manifestation of the Middle East political security architecture led by the United States. Just as petrodollar is dependent on the US financial hegemony, the Persian oil-producing countries depend on the US politically and militarily. They are two sides of one coin, or the latter constitutes the basis of the former. The reason why the Iran nuclear issue has evoked strong reactions from the United States and has involved all major countries in the world is because it poses an existential threat to the Middle East security architecture and the dollar standard system. Although the United States is getting rid of dependence on Middle Eastern oil and moving its strategic focus eastward, it will never weaken its political and military dominance in the region. As a result, today's global energy map does not match the international political structure. On the one hand, the United States and European countries have diversified their oil supply channels, but have been maintaining political and military dominance on oil-producing countries in the Middle East; on the other hand, China is increasingly relying on the turbulent Middle East for oil import, but still trails the West in political and military influence and overseas power projection capabilities. Meanwhile, China, with its huge investments in Iran, Sudan, and other countries, has to face up to the political pressure from the West, and has already suffered economic losses caused by political risks.

In this sense, although China's economic growth is bringing radical changes to the international trade structure which has been dominated by the West since the modern times, it is far from revolutionizing the global trade system in a real sense. The "Modern Silk Road" between China and the Middle East remains a derived product of today's international political and economic architecture. From the perspective of the triangular trade structure in today's international political economy, a closer observation can be made on the interaction between Middle Eastern petroleum, the USD, and China's manufacturing industry, and thus the predicament facing China at the moment.

2.3.2 *The Triangular Cycle of Oil, US Dollar, and "Made in China" Products*

In the current international trade and financial system, oil, as an important strategic resource, is a commodity bearing political and financial significance. The USD is an international currency dominating the contemporary international political economy. The exports of East Asian goods including those made in China, and international commodity trade are basically denominated and settled in USD. "Made in China" goods, as the engine driving China's economic miracle of 30 years' reform and opening up, have become one of the most important and popular genres of commodity in the world. Thus, the triangular cycle of oil, dollar, and "Made in China" can be seen as the most concentrated and vivid reflection of the triangular trade structure in the contemporary international political economy. Also, it reveals a true picture of the "Modern Silk Road" between China and the Middle East.

First of all, due to large-scale export of Chinese-made products and oil, both China and the Middle East have a huge current account surplus which takes the form of "commodity dollars" and petrodollars respectively. While the proportion of current account surplus to China's foreign exchange reserves has been declining year by year, the ratio of capital account surplus has been rising. But in the long run, the "commodity dollars" generated by exports of Chinese-made commodities will take up the biggest share in China's huge foreign exchange reserve. In fact, the rapid accumulation of "commodity dollars" and petrodollars in China/East Asian countries and in the Middle Eastern oil-producing countries is reconstructing the global capital markets at an unprecedented pace. According to a report released by the McKinsey Global Institute in 2007, since the new century, the petrodollars, Asian central banks, hedge funds, and private equity firms having been rising rapidly to become the world's new financial power brokers.[62] As of the end of 2013, China's foreign exchange reserves rose to 3.82 trillion in US dollars.[63] Correspondingly, as of the end of 2012, the sovereign wealth fund assets of the six GCC countries totaled $1.6 trillion, equivalent to 107% of their GDP and more than 32.6% as a share of the global sovereign wealth funds of $5.2 trillion. Specifically, Saudi Arabia topped the list with $641 billion in its sovereign wealth fund assets. The UAE and Kuwait, ranking the second and the third, reported a total of $397 billion and $395 billion, respectively.[64] According to the International Monetary Fund, the overseas assets of the six GCC countries will reach 3 trillion in US dollars by 2017.[65] It can be said that the "commodity dollars" of China and other East Asian countries and the petrodollars of the Middle Eastern oil-producing countries have become the two most important forces in the international capital markets. For that, the essence of the "Modern Silk Road" lies in the monetization of the East Asian/"Made in China" goods and the Middle Eastern oil — to be more specific, the dollarization of them. In recent years, the well-funded sovereign wealth funds have become extremely active and attention-grabbing institutional investors in the international financial

---

[62] McKinsey Global Institute, *The New Power Brokers: How Oil, Asia, Hedge Funds, and Private Equity Are Shaping Global Capital Markets*, October 2007.

[63] National Bureau of Statistics of the People's Republic of China, "Statistical Bulletin on the 2013 National Economic and Social Development of the People's Republic of China", *People's Daily*, February 24, 2014, p. 10. (中国国家统计局:《中华人民共和国 2013 年国民经济和社会发展统计公报》, 载《人民日报》2014 年 2 月 24 日, 第 10 版。)

[64] Wang Junpeng, "Gulf Countries' Sovereign Wealth Funds Are Well-financed", *Economic Daily*, August 20, 2013, p. 4. (王俊鹏:《海湾国家主权财富基金充裕》, 载《经济日报》2013 年 8 月 20 日, 第 4 版。)

[65] Economic and Commercial Counselor's Office of the Embassy of the People's Republic of China in the Kingdom of Bahrain, "GCC's Overseas Assets Will Reach 3 Trillion USD by 2017", November 14, 2012, http://www.mofcom.gov.cn/article/i/jyjl/k/201211/20121108435237.shtml, log-in time: March 10, 2013. (中国驻巴林大使馆经商处:《到 2017 年海合会国家的境外资产将达 3 万亿美元》, 2012年 11 月 14 日。)

markets. There are two kinds of sovereign wealth fund owners: (1) oil-producing countries with huge amounts of petrodollars, such as the UAE, Saudi Arabia, Kuwait, Russia, Norway, Kazakhstan, Brunei, Iran, and so on; (2) East Asian countries with huge trade surplus and foreign exchange reserves, such as China, South Korea, Malaysia, and so on. Therefore, the so-called sovereign wealth fund is only a new face of petrodollars and "commodity dollars".

Second, the oil-producing countries in the Middle East pay dollars to China for various "Made in China" goods, so as to convert part of their petrodollars to commodity dollars; meanwhile, when China buys Middle Eastern oil, commodity dollars are turning into petrodollars. It can be said that the essence of the two-way flow of "Made in China" products and Middle Eastern oil on the new Silk Road is the continuous exchange of petrodollars and commodity dollars. The United States and the dollar, as the third party, are involved in the whole trading process. In this sense, the flow rate of oil, dollar, and "Made in China" products is a reflection of the close economic ties between China and the Middle East.

In recent years, a large number of Middle Eastern merchants are coming to Yiwu, Guangzhou, and other cities in China, while a great number of Chinese merchants and enterprises can be seen in Dubai and other places in the Middle East. The dominant logic behind it is that petrodollars flow into China either overtly or covertly. In such a process, religious factors (whether it is Chinese-made Islamic goods, Yiwu's newly built Muslim mosque or the rejuvenation and remoulding of the Islamic heritage of the ancient Silk Road) and individual activities are important, but in essence, what really matters is the triangular relation of oil, dollar, and "Made in China" which is embedded in the "Modern Silk Road".

The primary destination for the outflow of the Middle East petrodollars and the Chinese/East Asian commodity dollars is still the United States. Since the oil-exporting countries cannot absorb a large number of petrodollars domestically, the petrodollars will flow back to the United States — a country with the most mature financial market in the world — as bank deposits, stocks, bonds, and other financial assets. Therefore, the United States can maintain a long-term balance between current account deficit and capital account surplus. Data released by the US Department of Treasury show that as of June 30, 2009, the major oil-exporting countries directly held $512.1 billion in US financial assets including stocks, bonds, corporate bonds, and institutional debt, accounting for 4% of the total. The US financial derivatives purchased by those countries — either directly or indirectly through offshore financial centers like London and Singapore — were greater at value. From 2002 to 2008, the funds repatriated to the United States by major oil exporters through commodity purchase accumulated up to $243.7 billion.[66] The International Monetary Fund estimates that, from the 1970s to the 1980s, more than 80% of the petrodollars flowing into the international market were financial assets such as deposits, bonds, and equities stored in the West.[67] After the 9/11 terrorist attack, the United States suspicion over Middle East funds led to some petrodollars fleeing from the United States. However, according to a McKinsey report, from 2002 to 2006, capital export of the six GCC countries totaled $542 billion, among which, 55% went to the United States, 18% to Europe, and only 11% to Asia (see Figure 2.9). The annual report of the Abu Dhabi Investment Authority also shows that in 2012, 35%–50% of its investment went to North America, 20%–35% to Europe, and 10%–20% to developed Asia. Emerging market countries only took up a share of 15%–25% (see Figure 2.10). To summarize, the United States is still the primary destination for Middle East petrodollars. Correspondingly, China and other East Asian countries mainly invest their foreign exchange reserves in US Treasury bonds. East Asian countries including China and OPEC member countries including the Middle East oil-producing countries constitute the most important group of foreign holders of US financial assets. Take the US bonds for an example, as of 2013, of the $5,802 billion of US bonds issued, the mainland of China, Japan, OPEC oil-producing countries

---

[66]Wang Zhen, "Understanding Petrodollar as an Important Bargain Chip", *China Business News*, December 30, 2011, p. T40. (王震:《掌握石油美元重要砝码》,载《第一财经日报》2011 年 12 月 30 日,第 T40 版。)

[67]Mei Xinyu, "To Grasp the Opportunity of the New Petrodollars Surge", *Xin LiCai*, no. 4, 2006, p. 13. (梅新育:《抓住石油美元新高潮的机遇》,载《新理财》2006 年第 4 期,第 13 页。)

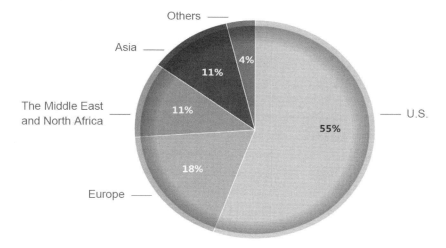

Figure 2.9 The Global Distribution of Outbound Investment of the GCC Countries from 2002 to 2006

Source: McKinsey Global Institute, The New Power Brokers: How Oil, Asia, Hedge Funds, and Private Equity Are Shaping Global Capital Markets, October 2007, p. 62.

were the first, second and fifth largest US creditors, holding $1270 billion, $1,285.5 billion, and $238.3 billion, respectively. To some extent, it is the monetization of East Asian goods/"Made in China" products and the Middle Eastern oil that underpins the US economy and further consolidates the dollar's position as the global currency.

Therefore, the functioning of the dynamic triangular cycle of oil, dollar, and "Made in China" was made possible because the United States maintains a long-term balance in international payments between current account deficit and capital account surplus. In fact, only when the US maintains a long-term current account deficit — that is, the United States keeps importing great quantities of physical goods (including "Made in China" products and oil) and pays with dollar — can other countries get a constant flow of USDs to fill their foreign exchange reserves, so as to ensure the smooth proceeding of international trades which are denominated and settled in USD. Meanwhile, only by maintaining a long-term capital account surplus — that is, the United States attracts the foreign-held dollars back with

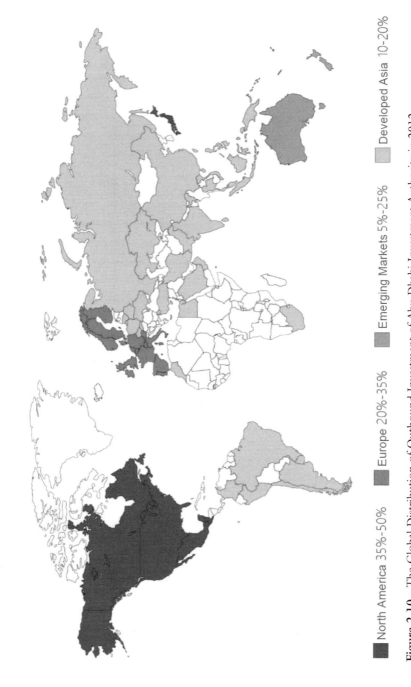

Figure 2.10 The Global Distribution of Outbound Investment of Abu Dhabi Investment Authority in 2012

Source: Abu Dhabi Investment Authority, *ADIA Review 2012*, p. 21.

various financial asset vouchers — can the country offset its current account deficit, thus maintaining the balance in international payments and the credibility of dollars internationally. In short, the United States exchanges dollars with foreign physical goods in the current account and exchanges virtual financial asset vouchers with foreign-held dollars in the capital account, thus achieving the circulation between US financial products and foreign physical goods. In such a process, oil and "Made in China" products and their derivative forms (petrodollars and commodity dollars) play a key role.

This also means that the triangular relationship of oil, dollar, and the "Made in China" is not equal and the flow between the three is uneven. This is also where the structural dilemma of the "Modern Silk Road" between China and the Middle East originates. Unlike the international trade on the ancient Silk Road, China's dependence on the Middle Eastern oil nowadays is much greater than the Middle East's demands for "Made in China" products. In fact, such a reversal is a clear manifestation of the "price scissors" phenomenon in the contemporary international trade — that means, since industrial products are becoming cheaper and raw materials more and more expensive, industrial countries have to use more industrial products to trade for less raw material. Therefore, the global flow of "Made in China" products is achieved at the expense of China's swelling demands for oil and other international bulk commodities. In this sense, that exchange between the Middle Eastern crude oil and China's/East Asian industrial products reflects the covert exploitation of industrial countries by resource-rich countries in the contemporary international trade system.

At the same time, China, Japan, South Korea, Singapore, and other East Asian countries are not only the world's most important manufacturing countries and exporters, but also the major importers of the Middle Eastern oil. Therefore, the rapid rise in international oil prices forces China and other manufacturing countries to pay more for the Middle Eastern oil. This means that more commodity dollars are converted to petrodollars, and in turn more petrodollars go back to the United States to offset its capital account deficit, which will further strengthen the "(China/East Asia) commodity dollars — (the

Middle East) petrodollars — the US dollar" triangular cycle. For the United States, rise in international oil prices widens its current account deficit, but it also means a swelling demand of oil-importing countries for USDs, as well as more petrodollars flowing back to the US financial market. Therefore, when international trade (especially in oil and other bulk commodity) is denominated and settled in dollar, oil price increases will lead to a petrodollar surge and the acceleration of petrodollar recycling. In the triangular relationship among oil, US dollar and "Made in China" products, China suffers the greatest losses and risks, while the United States and oil-producing countries are undoubtedly the biggest beneficiaries. In this sense, the United States and the Middle East oil producers lack initiative to make adjustments, and are even willing to maintain the status quo.

To conclude, the so-called "Modern Silk Road", with USD as the settlement currency, is of benefit to the United States. While cementing the economic ties between China and the Middle East, the "Modern Silk Road" increased their dependence on the US financial hegemony. It can be said that under the current international political and economic power structure, the "Modern Silk Road", which features only the two-way flow of "Made in China" products and Middle Eastern oil (or commodity dollars and petrodollars), is "old wine in a new bottle", and bears no strategic significance for changing the inherent structure of the international political economy.

3

Understanding China's Belt and Road Initiative in the New Era

In September and October 2013, when Chinese President Xi Jinping visited Central and Southeast Asia, he officially proposed a Silk Road Economic Belt and a 21st-century Maritime Silk Road, now together referred to as the Belt and Road Initiative. This is another major national development strategy raised by Xi's Administration, besides the construction of several China Pilot Free Trade Zones, the coordinated development of Beijing-Tianjin-Hebei region and the development of Yangtze River Economic Belt. It is also the first time that the Chinese government has unveiled the top-level design of the economic cooperation among neighboring and Eurasian countries in the name of "Silk Road", which embodies the spirit of a new era and is of unique historical significances.

In order to have a thorough understanding of the Chinese Belt and Road Initiative, this chapter is divided into three sections. The first section elaborates the multiple historical conditions under which the B&R Initiative is put forward; the second section explores a series of important practical considerations behind the B&R Initiative; and finally, the third section describes the long-term visions of the B&R Initiative from both domestic and international perspectives.

3.1 Historical Background

The Belt and Road Initiative is not a vague Silk Road revival plan in an isolated time–space setting. On the contrary, it is closely related to various domestic and international political, economic and technological factors since the beginning of the 21st century. Specifically, progresses such as the revival of China's comprehensive national strength, the improvement of Eurasian geopolitical environment, the enhancement of economic ties along the Belt and Road and the innovation in transportation technology, constitute the historical conditions of the New Silk Road Initiative.

3.1.1 *The Revival of China's National Strength*

As the most important country on the East end of the Silk Road, the rise and fall of China's national power directly affects the rise and fall of the Silk Road. The primary historical condition of the Belt and Road Initiative lies in the overall revival of China's comprehensive national strength.

First of all, based on solid foundation established within the first 30 years since the founding of People's Republic of China (PRC) in 1949, China's national strength, especially its economic strength, has reached an unprecedented stage since the adoption of the Reform and Opening-up policy in 1978. For the industrial system, at present, China has 39 industrial categories, 191 classes and 525 subclasses. It is the only country in the world that has all the industrial categories as classified by the United Nations. It has formed the world's most completed national economy and industrial system.[1] As for the main economic indicators, according to the National Bureau of Statistics, from 1979 to 2012, China's annual gross domestic product (GDP)

---

[1] Mei Xinyu, *Where Do China's Manufacturing Industries Head*, Kunming: Yunnan Education Publishing House, 2013, p. 29. (梅新育:《中国制造业向何处去》,昆明:云南教育出版社 2013 年版,第 29 页。)

grew by an average rate of 9.8%, as compared with 2.8% of the world economy; China's share of the world's total economy surged from 1.8% in 1978 to 11.5% in 2012; its national fiscal revenue also soared from 113.2 billion yuan in 1978 to 11,730 billion yuan in 2012, an increase of more than 103 times with an average annual growth of 14.6%.[2] During the same period, China's foreign exchange reserves were only $167 million in 1978, ranking thirty-eighth in the world, but the reserves hiked up to $3,820 billion in 2013, ranking first in the world.[3] In the same year China surpassed the United States, becoming the world's largest trading country of tangible goods, and the largest trading partner for more than two-thirds of all the countries and regions in the world. In 1978, China's economy ranked only tenth in the world, but in 2008 and 2010, China successively surpassed Germany and Japan, thus becoming the world's second largest economy, only next to the United States. According to a World Bank report released on April 30, 2014, taking purchasing power parity into consideration, China's economy might exceed the United States in 2014, becoming the world's largest economy.[4] It seems to be a safe conclusion that China already has the material conditions in palce for the revival of the Silk Road.

Second, since the founding of the People's Republic of China in 1949, China's governance of the western frontier has reached an unprecedented level in depth and breadth. From the historical point

---

[2] National Bureau of Statistics of the People's Republic of China, "The Reform and Opening-up Policy Composes a New Chapter of Brilliant Economic Development—Great Social and Economic Changes in China since 1978", *People's Daily*, November 6, 2013, p. 10. (国家统计局:《改革开放铸辉煌经济发展谱新篇——1978 年以来我国经济社会发展的巨大变化》, 载《人民日报》2013 年 11 月 6 日, 第 10 版。)

[3] National Bureau of Statistics of the People's Republic of China, "Statistical Bulletin of the People's Republic of China on the 2013 National Economic and Social Development", *People's Daily*, February 24, 2014, p. 10. (中国国家统计局:《中华人民共和国 2013 年国民经济和社会发展统计公报》, 载《人民日报》2014 年 2 月 24 日, 第 10 版); International Balance of Payments Analysis Unit of the State Administration of Foreign Exchange, *China's Balance of Payments Report in 2013*, April 4, 2014, p. 11. (中国国家外汇管理局国际收支分析小组:《2013 年中国国际收支报告》, 2014 年 4 月 4 日, 第 11 页。)

[4] World Bank, *Purchasing Power Parities and Real Expenditures of World Economies*, March 30, 2014.

of view, except the Yuan Dynasty (1271–1368), virtually all the dynasties in the Chinese history were facing long-term political and security threats at the western frontier. The defensive postures taken by ancient Chinese dynasties determined that the relationship with the ethnic minorities was always the central concern in their strategic considerations. However, the Western Region's affinity with the central government was in a state of constant instability for a long time. Even in the powerful Tang Dynasty (618–907), the governance of the Western Region could only be realized by ways of mollification and conciliation. The Battle of Talas between Tang Dynasty and the Arabs fully exposed China's strength limit in its west. In fact, China's effective governance in Xinjiang, Tibet and Mongolian areas was quite recent. Although still facing challenges from separatist in Xinjiang and Tibet, the PRC has basically eliminated the risk of internal armed rebellions that the ancient dynasties had always been dealing with at the western frontier. Only in this way can China maximize the mobilization and integration of domestic resources, and make outward expansions along the Silk Road.

Historical experience shows that the rise and fall of the ancient Silk Road was not only closely related to the specific political and economic conditions of the Eurasian continent, but also depended on the Chinese government's control over its western frontier. Although located in the middle of the Eurasian continent, the Central Asia has been weak in its economic strength. Therefore, the revival of the Silk Road on land will ultimately depend on whether China, especially the western China including Xinjiang, can provide enough domestic support. Before the Tang Dynasty, Chinese political and economic center was located in the Guanzhong Area (currently the central area of Shannxi Province) for a very long time. Big cities such as Chang'an (today's Xi'an), Luoyang were international cities which were swarmed with Arabian and Persian merchants. With overall improvement in national economy and frontier governance, China's ability to manage its west has been greatly enhanced, so that the revival of the Silk Road has attained the domestic basis.

It may well be said that with the overall revival of comprehensive national strength, China has so far accumulated the preliminary ability to revive the Silk Road, both on the land and sea.

3.1.2 *Improvement of the Eurasian Geopolitical Environment*

The rise and fall of the Silk Road is always closely related to the specific geopolitical conditions. With the rise of the western world and the expansion of colonialism, areas along the maritime and land Silk Road became an arena for external forces to compete. The debate on "Land Defense vs. Sea Defense" inside the Late Qing Empire showed that, for the first time in history, China faced serious security threats from two directions: land and sea, and the dynasty must priortize one over the other. In the Eurasian continent, fierce competitions between Britain and Russia in Central Asia even gave rise to a classic international political term — "the Great Game in Central Asia". During the Cold War, China was once faced with double security threats: one from the eastern ocean by the United States and the other from the North and West land by the Soviet Union. Constant political turmoils and military confrontations made it impossible to revive the Silk Road at the time. Considering such a background, it is easily understood that the proposal of the Belt and Road Initiative, especially the Silk Road Economic Belt must be based on the right political and security conditions.

First of all, the normalization of Sino–Soviet relations in 1989 led to the termination of the political and military confrontations with the Soviet Union and the Soviet military siege in the West and North of China. If we say that the Sino–US reconciliation in 1972 made China break the political, economic and military blockades imposed by the United States and its Western allies, thus laying the political foundation for China's integration into the Western-led international economic system, it may also be well concluded that the normalization of Sino–Soviet relations helped China strike a balance between its national development strategy of Reform and Opening-up and its independent foreign policy of peace, thus bidding farewell to the Cold War and its mentality ahead of time.[5]

---

[5] Niu Jun, "A Farewell to the Cold War: Historical Implications of the Normalization of Sino-Soviet Relations for China", *Historical Research*, no. 1, 2008, pp. 126–140.

Second, in the 1990s, China effectively set up friendly relations and mechanisms of mutual trust with Russia and Central Asian countries, and successfully resolved the border disputes with those countries. In history, the northwest was always a hidden danger for the Chinese dynasties, and in light of the serious military threat once posed by the Soviet Union's deployment of millions of troops at the northwest and northern borders, the importance of mutual trust should be more highly valued. So far, except India and Bhutan, China has completely solved the land border disputes with 12 neighboring countries.[6]

It is a safe conclusion that since the normalization of Sino–Soviet relations, the security threat at the land border in west China which had been a long-term problem bothering ancient China through consecutive dynasties has been greatly alleviated. The likelihood of China suffering a massive military threat or an organized challenge from a certain nation at the western borer has been greatly decreased, in spite of nontraditional security threats such as "the Three Forces" and strategically competitive relations of China with Russia and with India. In contrast, from the Yellow Sea, the East China Sea to the South China Sea, and from the Diaoyu Islands to the Huangyan Island, China has territorial disputes, to varying extents, with Japan, South Korea, Vietnam, the Philippines and other neighboring East Asian countries. Driven by the dual factors of competitions for economic resources and the intervention of external powers, especially against the background of the U.S. pivoting to Asia, the complexity of territorial disputes in East Asia has dramatically increased, constituting a dilemma that directly affects the political relations between China and its neighbors in East Asia. It can be said that China's geopolitical situation has undergone a profound reversal both at land and sea. That is, traditional security threats from the west are greatly reduced, while

---

(牛军:《"告别冷战": 中国实现中苏关系正常化的历史含义》, 载《历史研究》2008 年第 1 期, 第 126–140 页。)

[6]Yang Jiechi, "Unswervingly Following the Path of Peaceful Development", *People's Daily*, December 14, 2012, p. 6. (杨洁篪:《始终不渝走和平发展道路》, 载《人民日报》2012 年 12 月 14 日, 第 6 版。)

military challenges from the east(sea) drastically increased. Therefore, the institutional guarantees of border security between China and the Central Asian countries in the 1990s have not only eased off military pressure in west China, but also made it possible for China to divert more economic and military resources to deal with challenges from the East.

Since the decline of the ancient Silk Road and the shift of China's economic center of gravity to eastern coastal areas were directly related to the deterioration of the Eurasian geopolitical environment, the improvement of China's political security situation in its west is undoubtedly of special historical significances. In fact, this is the most favorable geopolitical situation that China has ever enjoyed since the collapse of the Mongolian Empire.

This fundamental shift means a lot. On the one hand, more possibilities of economic construction, rather than a mere combat-readiness economy, is open to China in the western region. This is also the external political condition set for the national strategy of large-scale development of the western region in the new century. On the other hand, the improvement of the geopolitical environment has made it possible for the Eurasian continent to build its new geoeconomic potentials, and this is the very political basis for the international cooperation in cross-border infrastructure constructions after the Cold War. In this context, it is likely for China to gradually expand its geo-political and geo-economic space, which has been compressed and blocked for a long time, on the Eurasian continent. What the national strategy of "Opening to the West" and the Belt and Road Initiative (especially the Silk Road Economic Belt) intend is to unleash their great potentials.

3.1.3 *Enhancement of the Eurasian Economic Tie*

Historically, economic exchanges were crucial to the development of the ancient Silk Road. The prosperity of trade led to the flow and integration of population, nationality, religion, ideology and culture. Hundreds of years later, now China and the European Union (EU), the world's most developed market on the west end of the Silk Road, recognize each other as the most important trading partners. What's more, China interacts much more frequently with other B&R developing countries in term of trading, investment, and personnel exchange, while the latter has been gaining an increasingly prominent status in China's foreign economic cooperation.

The historical significance of this profound change lies in the following two aspects. On one hand, the economic ties between China and Europe, which disintegrated due to Osman Empire's monopoly of the East–West trade channel, have been re-established, and the unequal political and economic relations dominated by the West is undergoing a change gradually. On the other hand, China and other developing countries have restrengthened their economic ties which were once seriously impaired by the impact of the western world, and have gradually established a new mode of cooperative relationship among themselves. China has become the largest trading partner, the largest export market and an important funding source for many countries along the Silk Road. It can be inferred that since the beginning of the new century, with the strengthening of economic ties between China and other developing as well as developed countries along the Belt and Road, the revival of the Silk Road has gained a thorough historical foundation.

Different from the ancient Silk Road trade or the so-called "Tributary Trade" in history, the current economic and trade exchanges between China and the countries along the Silk Road are carried out under the framework of the global economic and trade system. For each country, economic and trade exchanges are not a privileged or accidental behavior of a few businessmen or the upper class, but rather a national, structural activity closely related to the national economy. In this context, the decline of the ancient Silk Road or "Tributary Trade" had a relatively limited impact on China and the countries along the Belt and Road. And the majority of the ancient Chinese Dynasties lacked a strong national will to expand the foreign trade. However, the situation has been totally tumbled upside down today. China's economic ties with countries along the Silk Road have reached an unprecedented level of tightness. It's a "symbiotic relationship" as they are so closely bound together, for good or ill.

Specifically, in 2013, the trade between China and ASEAN amounted to $443.6 billion, with an average annual growth rate above 20% over the previous decade. At the end of June 2014, the total volume of two-way cumulative investment between China and ASEAN reached nearly $120 billion, of which ASEAN countries invested more than $80 billion in China, and Chinese total investment in ASEAN countries reached nearly $40 billion. At the same time, Chinese enterprises signed contracted projects with ASEAN countries worth more than $180 billion, and had a turnover of more than $125 billion.[7] ASEAN has become China's third largest trading partner, the top fourth export market and the second largest source of imports. Meanwhile, China has become ASEAN's largest trading partner. The China–ASEAN Free Trade Area which was established in 2010 is the largest FTA among developing countries, with a GDP of approximately $6 trillion and trade volume of about $4.5 trillion. As a vivid reflection of the increasingly close economic ties, personnel exchanges between China and ASEAN countries each year have reached 18 million person-times, with more than one thousand flights between China and ASEAN countries per week.[8]

In 2012, trade among the member states and observers of Shanghai Cooperation Organization reached more than $310 billion, of which trade volume between China and the member states and observer countries amounted to $246.2 billion, accounting for about 80% of the total.[9] China's trade with Central Asian countries

---

[7] State Council Information Office of PRC, "Press Conference of the 11th China-ASEAN EXPO (July 22, 2014)", http://www.scio.gov.cn/xwfbh/xwbfbh/wqfbh/2014/20140722/index.htm, log-in time: July 29, 2014. (中国国务院新闻办公室:《国新办举行第 11 届中国-东盟博览会等情况新闻发布会》, 2014 年 7 月 22日。)

[8] Zhang Gaoli, "Jointly Building the Maritime Silk Road in the 21st Century and Creating a Beautiful Future for China and ASEAN—Speech at the 11th China-ASEAN EXPO and Business and Investment Summit", *People's Daily*, September 17, 2014, p. 4. (张高丽:《携手共建 21 世纪海上丝绸之路共创中国—东盟友好合作美好未来——在第十一届中国—东盟博览会和中国—东盟商务与投资峰会上的致辞》(2014 年 9 月 16 日, 广西南宁), 载《人民日报》2014 年 9 月 17 日, 第 4 版。)

[9] Wang Yang, "Inheriting the Spirit of the Silk Road and Promoting Common Prosperity—Keynote Speech at Euro-Asia Economic Forum", *Xi'an Daily*, September

increased from $460 million at the beginning of diplomatic relations to $46 billion in 2012, 100 times what it was 21 years ago.[10] At present, China has become the largest trading partner of Russia, Kazakhstan and Turkmenistan, the second largest trading partner of Kyrgyzstan and Uzbekistan, and the third largest trading partner of Tajikistan.

To the west, the bilateral trade between China and Arabia amounted to $238.9 billion in 2013, compared to only $25.5 billion in 2004, an increase of about 8.4 times with an average annual growth of more than 25% over the previous 10 years. The newly signed project contracts by Chinese companies in Arabia soared from $2.6 billion in 2004 to $29.1 billion in 2013, with an average annual growth of 27%. At present, Arabia is China's seventh largest trading partner, while China is the second largest trading partner of Arabia as a whole and the largest trading partner of nine Arabian countries.[11] Over the same period, China's trade with 16 Central and Eastern European countries reached $55.1 billion, a record high, and an increase of 5.3 times compared with 10 years ago.[12] According to statistics from Grison's Peak, a London-based commercial bank, since

26, 2013, p. 1. [汪洋:《传承丝路精神促进共同繁荣——在 2013 欧亚经济论坛上的主旨演讲》(2013 年 9 月 26 日, 西安), 载《西安日报》2013 年 9 月 27 日, 第 1 版]; National Bureau of Statistics of PRC, *China Statistical Yearbook* of 2013, Beijing: China Statistics Press, 2013, p. 233. (国家统计局:《中国统计年鉴. 2013》, 中国统计出版社 2013 年版, 第 233 页。)

[10] Du Shangze, "Dream, Coming from the Depths of the History—President Xi Jinping's Visits of Four Countries of Central Asia and the Jointly-built Silk Road Economic Belt", *People's Daily*, September 13, 2013, p. 2. (杜尚泽:《梦想, 从历史深处走来——记习近平主席访问中亚四国和共建 "丝绸之路经济带"》, 载《人民日报》2013 年 9 月 13 日, 第 2 版。)

[11] Wang Yi, "To Strengthen Forum Construction and Build An 'Upgraded Version' of China-Arab Relations", *People's Daily*, June 4, 2014, p. 21. (王毅:《加强论坛建设, 打造中阿关系"升级版"》, 载《人民日报》2014 年 6 月 4 日, 第 21 版。)

[12] Zhang Qizhi *et al.*, "Ministerial Conference of China and Central and Eastern European Countries on Promoting Trade and Economic Cooperation", *People's Daily*, June 9, 2014, p. 22. (张奇志等:《中国—中东欧国家经贸促进部长级会议召开》, 载《人民日报》2014 年 6 月 9 日, 第 22 版。)

the establishment of cooperation mechanism between China and Central and Eastern European countries, China had signed loans and investment agreements with 16 Central and Eastern European countries from 2011 to 2013 with a total value of $52 billion, of which $22.2 billion were signed in 2013 alone.[13]

It is particularly worth pointing out that the bilateral trade between China and the EU surged from $125.2 billion to $559.1 billion from 2003 to 2013, with an increase of about four times over the previous 10 years. (See Figure 3.1) EU has been China's largest trading partner for 10 consecutive years. And China has become the second largest trading partner of the EU, only next to the United States, for 11 consecutive years.[14] By the end of 2013, EU investment in China had totaled more than $90 billion, and China's cumulative direct investment in the EU had exceeded $35 billion.[15] At present, China–EU economic and trade relation has become one of the largest and most dynamic relations in the world.

In other words, the economic ties between China and countries along the Belt and Road have received a historic reinforcement since the beginning of the 21st century. While actively developing trade with countries along the Belt and Road, China has gradually embarked on a series of economic cooperation platforms such as the Shanghai Cooperation Organization (SCO), Central America Free Trade Agreement (CAFTA), China — Central and Eastern European Countries Cooperation Forum, China–Arabia Cooperation Forum, China–Eurasia Expo, China–South Asia Expo and so on. In the

---

[13] James Kynge, "Ukraine a setback in China's eastern Europe strategy", *Financial Times*, February 27, 2014. http://blogs.ft.com/beyond-brics/2014/02/27/ukraine-a-setback-in-chinas-eastern-europe-strategy/ (log-in time: March 11, 2014)

[14] Chen Jian, "Investment Will Become the New Engine of Sino-Europe Cooperation", *Economic Daily*, April 10, 2014, p. 4. (陈建:《投资将成中欧合作新引擎》, 载《经济日报》2014 年 4 月 10 日, 第 4 版。)

[15] The Ministry of Commerce of PRC, "Regular Press Conference Held by Ministry of Commerce (February 18, 2014)", http://www.mofcom.gov.cn/article/ae/ah/diaocd/201402/20140200491167.shtml, log-in time: March 11, 2014. (中国商务部:《商务部召开例行新闻发布会, 2014 年 2 月 18 日。)

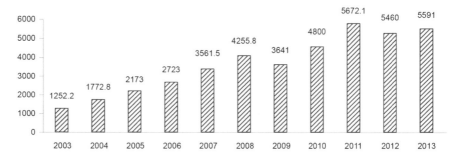

Figure 3.1   Bilateral trade volume between China and the EU in 2003–2013 (unit: $100 million)

Source: The Ministry of Commerce of PRC, "Regular Press Conference (January 16, 2014)", http://www.mofcom.gov.cn/xwfbh/20140116.shtml, login time: July 15, 2014; National Bureau of Statistics, *China Statistical Yearbook* (2003–2013), Beijing: China Statistics Press 2003–2013.

meantime, China is also working with relevant parties to carry out consultations, negotiations and research on a series of major economic cooperation mechanisms, such as the Asian Infrastructure Investment Bank, the SCO Development Bank, China–Pakistan Economic Corridor, Bangladesh–China–Burma–India Economic Corridor, upgraded version of the CAFTA, the Regional Comprehensive Economic Partnership (RCEP), China–Gulf Cooperation Council (GCC) Free Trade Agreement (FTA), China–EU Investment Agreement, China–EU FTA, and so on. It is just in this sense that the Belt and Road Initiative is not a brand new Eurasian cooperation program, but rather, a further integration and upgradation of the existing economic cooperation mechanisms, platforms and networks among China and B&R countries.

3.1.4 *Innovation in Transportation Technology*

In addition to the specific political and economic conditions, the emergence of the B&R Initiative is inseparable from the innovation in modern transportation technology. On one side, with the development of modern marine transport technology, the traditional ocean trade has been greatly improved, which was once constrained by climate, ocean current, logistic supply and communication. And on the other side, with the rise of aviation, highways, railways, pipelines and other cross-border modes of transportation, the modern trade and transportation system, which is dominated by shipping, has been effectively supplemented.

Throughout the history of the ancient Silk Road, there is a general rise of the sea route and fall of the land route, and the inherent weakness of land transportation is an important reason for this shift. Compared with sea transportation, land transportation was more directly subjected to geographical environment, climatic conditions as well as political, military and ethinic situations in regimes along the route. At the same time, compared to large ships, ancient land transportation modes, such as those by camels or manpower, inevitably had problems of a smaller volume, higher cost, and lower safety. Besides, the fragility of ceramic products made it difficult for land transport to meet the actual needs of the growing trade. With the emerging of ocean trade era dominated by the west, the maritime transport were further strengthened, thus becoming the most important form of logistics in international trade, which still prevails till now.

The problems of land transportation and the high costs thus incurred directly resulted in the lag of land trade between Asia and Europe. A study shows that the transport cost of a typical landlocked country is 50% higher than that of a coastal country, and the trade volume is 60% lower; while a 10% reduction in transport costs will increase the trade volume by 25%.[16] Therefore, compared with the elimination of tariff and non-tariff barriers, the improvement of land transport infrastructure will be more conducive to reducing the cost and increasing volume of trade between Asia and Europe.

Since the beginning of the 21st century, the construction of onshore oil and gas pipelines offers a new way for China's energy import besides shipping. At the same time, with the rapid

---

[16] Asian Development Bank and Asian Development Bank Institute, *Infrastructure for a Seamless Asia*, Tokyo: Asian Development Bank Institute, 2009, p. 42.

development of modern railway and highway transportation technology, especially the rise of high-speed rail and heavy rail, land transport costs have been significantly reduced. The problem of insufficient carrying capacity of the ancient Silk Road has been greatly alleviated. Compared with ocean transportation, railway transportation enjoys a time-saving advantage; compared to air transport, rail transport boasts a cost-saving advantage. More importantly, it has brought a new opportunity for trade contacts between the European and Asian continents, and in particular, the trade flows in Central Asia.

In recent years, optimists represented by Professor Gao Bai at Duke University fully affirm the strategic significance of high-speed railway technology in the promotion of economic integration in Europe and Asia. They believe that the construction of the Eurasian high-speed rail network will help to ease the challenges that China is facing from the ocean, and realize a strategic hedging with the "Blue Ocean Strategy" through the geostrategic adjustment from the sea to land.[17] This proposition was subjected to sharp criticism since it directly linked the high-speed rail with China's strategic shift from sea to land, while significantly underestimated its potential political risks, such as the deterioration of Sino–Russian relations.[18] However, it's an indisputable fact that the high-speed railway, as the representative of the land transportation technology innovation, is to awaken the land trade channel in Eurasian continent that has been in a long silence. Behind, it is precisely that China's domestic railway especially high-speed rail technology has made significant progress since the

---

[17] Gao Bai, *The High Speed Rail and China's Grand Strategy in the 21st Century*, Beijing: The Social Sciences Academic Press, 2012. (高柏:《高铁与中国 21 世纪大战略》, 北京: 社会科学文献出版社, 2012 年。)

[18] Wu Zhengyu, "Land or Ocean—Re-reflections on High Speed Rail and China in the 21st Century", *21st Century*, February, 2013, pp. 105–113. (吴征宇:《向"陆"还是向"洋"——对<高铁与中国 21 世纪大战略>的再思考》, 载《二十一世纪》2013 年 2 月号, 第 105–113 页); Zhang Wenmu, "The Silk Road and Security of China's Western Regions—Historical Conditions, Law and Coping Strategies of the Rise of Central Asia", *World Economics and Politics*, no. 3, 2014, pp. 22–24. (张文木:《丝绸之路与中国西域安全——兼论中亚地区力量崛起的历史条件、规律及其因应战略》, 载《世界政治与经济》2014 年第 3 期, 第 22–24 页。)

beginning of the new century. In this sense, the high-speed rail's success in reducing both time and cost of transport within China provides a golden reference for the promotion of interconnectivity on the Eurasian land.

At present, China has become the country that enjoys the fastest development in high-speed rail, the longest operating mileage, the highest operational speed, the largest construction scale, and the most comprehensive technology. With the development of Chinese high-speed rail, China has been gradually completing its "Four Vertical and Four Horizontal High-speed Railway Network" and six intercity express systems. It can be said that since the beginning of the new century, the rapid development of railway, especially high-speed railway, has been reshaping the economic and personnel exchanges between China and other countries in an unprecedented way. Meanwhile, related Chinese enterprises have obtained obvious advantages in the field of technology research and development, design and construction, operation management and equipment manufacture. With advantages in technology, equipment, construction experience and low project cost, Premier Li Keqiang has been able to promote Chinese railway infrastructure and equipment when he visited Thailand, Eastern Europe, Africa, Britain, Russia and other countries and regions since 2013. In this sense, the high-speed rail, as a representative of the "Going Out" of Chinese high-end equipment manufacturing, has not only become a new business card of China's diplomacy, but also an important symbol of China's "Export Upgrading". In this context, China's capital, technology, equipment, infrastructure construction and labor service are expected to comprehensively promote interconnectivity — a promising development trend in the Eurasian continent.

In short, since the beginning of the 21st century, the combination of various political, economic and technological conditions, both domestic and international, has offered an hitherto unprecedented historic opportunity for the revival of the Silk Road, which also makes it highly likely that the Belt and Road Initiative will transcend all the vague and general Silk Road revival plans before, and have a solid foundation for actual realization.

3.2 Practical Considerations

At present, there are various interpretations of the strategic considerations regarding the B&R Initiative, both at home and abroad. In order to facilitate understanding, this part will summarize and elaborate on them from two perspectives. On the one hand, the Belt and Road is China's response to as well as planning for the changing regional and international order since its rise; on the other hand, the Belt and Road reflects China's structural adjustments to many existing modes of economic development.

3.2.1 *In the Perspective of China's Rise*

3.2.1.1 *Contributing to Global Governance with the "Chinese Proposal"*

Since the beginning of the new century, Chinese comprehensive national strength has increased rapidly. As a result, China is becoming more confident in making greater contributions to regional and global governance; and there is an urgent need for China to claim an international position and the discourse power that correspond to its strength.

At the beginning of the Reform and Opening-up, due to the limitation of national strength, China's main focus was on domestic economic development; the main tone of foreign relations was "keeping a low profile and taking a proactive role", with more emphasis on the former part. In recent years, with an obvious rise in China's comprehensive national strength and international status, China's relations with the world have undergone great changes. The international community's expectations of China have been raised; the resources and means are more abundant for China to mobilize and manage foreign relations; and China's ability to shape the external environment has also been significantly improved. Based on national strength, China's "major-power diplomacy" is characterized by an adherence to "keeping a low profile" but with an increasing emphasis on "taking a proactive role" at the same time. Specifically, China's participation in international and regional affairs has greatly increased; China is more active in strategic issues, trying to offer a Chinese voice, Chinese wisdom and Chinese proposal that fully reflects the role of China, so as to solve various hot issues, promote regional and global cooperation and development. China emphasizes on the provision of more public goods for the international community, just as what President Xi Jinping announced at the opening ceremony of the Asia–Pacific Economic Cooperation (APEC) CEO Summit in November 2014,

> As its overall national strength grows, China will be both capable and willing to provide more public goods for the Asia-Pacific and the world, especially new initiatives and visions for enhancing regional cooperation. China is ready to work with other countries in promoting the building of the 'Silk Road Economic Belt' and the '21st-century Maritime Silk Road', getting more engaged with regional cooperation, and making new contributions to the connectivity, development and prosperity of the Asia-Pacific area.[19]

Currently, the global governance system and rules are subject to major adjustments. From a global perspective, the global governance pattern is facing a rapid shift: the influence of developing and emerging economies has been evidently greater than before; the competition among countries on rule-making power and discourse power over international regimes is getting fierce; with the progress of economic globalization, global challenges are emerging in an endless stream that require the joint efforts of all the countries; although the overall Eurasian political security environment has improved, and the possibility of direct military conflicts between major powers is greatly reduced, the geopolitical risks in certain regions are intertwined with nontraditional security risks; global economic recovery is weak with plummeting prices of major commodities so that trade and investment protectionism is on the rise; the gap between the North and South is further widening; regional interconnectivity faces many

---

[19] Xi Jinping, "Seek Sustained Development and Fulfill the Asia-Pacific Dream—Keynote Speech at the APEC CEO Summit", *People's Daily*, November 10, 2014, p. 2. (习近平: 《谋求持久发展共筑亚太梦想——在亚太经合组织工商领导人峰会开幕式上的演讲》(2014 年 11 月 9 日, 北京), 载 《人民日报》2014 年 11 月 10 日, 第 2 版。)

bottlenecks; the process of industrialization in developing countries urgently needs financial and technical support; China's overall national strength and international status have undergone historic changes; China has further strengthened the bond with other countries, and the international community has higher expectations of the Chinese Proposal.

In this context, China has the responsibility to put forward its own solution for promoting global development cooperation and improving global governance system. As the general guideline of China's opening-up to and cooperation with foreign countries for now and the future, the Belt and Road Initiative offers an inclusive development platform that will combine the rapid development of China's economy with the interests of countries along the Belt and Road, just as what President Xi Jinping stressed on several occasions,

> China will continue to contribute to global development and will continue to pursue an opening up strategy of mutual benefit. The door of China's opening up will never shut and China welcomes all countries to ride on its development.[20]

In the meantime, at the turning point of global governance transformation, China is also facing a great opportunity to increase its say in global economic governance. On October 12, 2015, the Political Bureau of Communist Party of China (CPC) Central Committee carried out the twenty-seventh collective learning on the subject of global governance pattern and global governance system. General Secretary Xi Jinping stressed,

---

[20] Xi Jinping, "Address at AIIB Inauguration Ceremony", *People's Daily*, January 17, 2016, p. 2. (习近平:《在亚洲基础设施投资银行开业仪式上的致辞》(2016 年 1 月 16 日, 钓鱼台国宾馆),《人民日报》2016 年 1 月 17 日, 第 2 版。); Xi Jinping, "Open Up New Horizons for China-Mongolia Relations through Mutual Assistance— Speech at the State Great Khural of Mongolia", *People's Daily*, August 23, 2014, p. 2. (习近平:《守望相助, 共创中蒙关系发展新时代——在蒙古国国家大呼拉尔的演讲》(2014 年 8 月 22 日, 乌兰巴托), 载《人民日报》2014 年 8 月 23 日, 第 2版。)

With increasing global challenges, it is a general trend to strengthen global governance and promote the reform of global governance system. This is not only a response to global challenges, but is also related to setting rules and directions of international order and system; it is not only related to the competition for the high ground of development, but also related to the status and role of all the countries in the international order and system. We put forward ideas and measures such as the Belt and Road Initiative, the establishment of a new type of international relations featuring win-win cooperation, adherence to the principle of upholding justice while pursuing shared interests, and the building of a community with a shared future for mankind. All these conform to the trend of the times, being in line with the interests of all countries, and expanding convergence of interests between China and other countries.[21]

In this sense, the Belt and Road Initiative reflects a major strategic decision made by China at the key moment of global governance transformation. It is not only the "Chinese Proposal" and "public goods" to promote global development and cooperation in the new era, but also the active planning of China to further enhance its international status and increase its say over international regimes.

3.2.1.2 *Responses to Doubts and Expectations of the International Community*

The second direct consequence of China's rise is that the outside world has different opinions towards China's international behavior and its consequences, which has resulted in different policy responses. Therefore, China needs to clearly express its ideas and propositions to the outside world, especially the neighboring countries.

Some neighboring countries are confused about how China will deal with them since China has become the most powerful country in

---

[21] Xinhua News Agency, "To Promote a More Just and Reasonable Global Governance System and Create Favorable Conditions for China's Development and World Peace", *People's Daily*, October 14, 2015, p. 1. (新华社:《推动全球治理体制更加公正更加合理为我国发展和世界和平创造有利条件》, 载《人民日报》2015 年 10 月 14 日, 第 1 版。)

the region. Will it bring peace and development or conflict and hegemony to the region and the international community? Some developing countries are expecting China, the world's second most powerful country, to continue its focus on South–South cooperation, and share the fruits of development with other countries. But some extra-regional powers are taking China's rise as a threat, carrying out the so-called "Strategic Rebalancing" and provoking confrontations between China and the neighboring countries.

The Belt and Road Initiative is China's strong response to the doubts and expectations of the outside, especially to the neighboring countries. As Fu Ying, director of the Foreign Affairs Committee of the National People's Congress (NPC), said at a press conference of the third session of the twelfth NPC:

> Our top leader puts forward the Belt and Road initiative, whose central aim is to develop the region better. There is a very important idea in our policies, that is, to make the fruits of China's development better benefit our neighbors. The outside world often asks: since China has been strong, how will it influence the world? How will it affect the surrounding regions? I think that the Belt and Road is an important initiative. It shows China's intention to use its own development advantages to build a new cooperation framework in the region.[22]

Therefore, the Belt and Road Initiative aims to express to the outside world with practical actions that China's rise is not a threat in the region at all. Instead, it provides an important opportunity to promote common development and win–win cooperation. In November 2014, President Xi Jinping made it clear at the dialogue on Strengthening Connectivity Partnership,

---

[22] Zhou Xiaolu and Guo Lei, "Fu Ying: The Belt and Road Initiative Brings Benefits to neighboring Countries", March 4, 2015, http://news.xinhuanet.com/politics/2015-03/04/c_127543043.htm (周小璐、郭蕾:《傅莹:"一带一路"让中国发展成果更好惠及周边》, 新华网, 2015 年 3 月 4 日)

The "Belt and Road" initiative represents a joint undertaking by China and its Asian neighbors. China gives top priority to countries in the neighborhood in its foreign policy and pursues amity, sincerity, mutual-benefit and inclusiveness in growing relations with them. China is ready to provide more public goods to its Asian neighbors through connectivity development and welcomes them to get on board the train of China's development.[23]

In this sense, the Belt and Road Initiative is China's commitment to win-win cooperation with the world, especially the neighboring countries. Objectively, it also helps to create a favorable environment for the development of China.

3.2.2 *In the Perspective of China's Development Mode Adjustment*

3.2.2.1 *Facilitating China's Economic Transformation*

At present, China's economy has entered a phase called the "New Normal" when multiple challenges are present, such as the declining growth rate, and the shrinking foreign trade coupled with excess capacity. The pressure to safeguard national economic security is at unprecedentedly high level. The Belt and Road Initiative, as the top-level design of China's economic diplomacy in the new era, reflects China's efforts to promote economic transformation and upgrade through strengthening international cooperation (especially a full range of Going-out).

For a long time, external demand has been vital for China to actualize sustainable economic growth. However, due to the pressures from domestic economic downturn, the weak global economic recovery and plummeting prices of major commodities, China's foreign trade situation is deteriorating. According to the statistics of the

---

[23]Xi Jinping, "Connectivity Spearheads Development and Partnership Enables Cooperation—Address at Dialogue on Strengthening Connectivity Partnership", *People's Daily*, November 9, 2014, p. 2. [习近平:《联通引领发展伙伴聚焦合作——在"加强互联互通伙伴关系"东道主伙伴对话会上的讲话》(2014 年 11 月 8 日, 钓鱼台国宾馆), 载《人民日报》2014 年 11 月 9 日, 第 2 版。]

General Administration of Customs, China's total import and export of goods fell by 7% in 2015 compared with 2014, with a respective decrease of 13.2% and 1.8% for import and export; the bilateral trade volumes fell by 7.2% and 0.6%, respectively, with the first and third largest trading partner, namely the EU and ASEAN; the import and export of foreign-invested enterprises and the state-owned enterprises fell by 6.5% and 12.1%, respectively; the import and export volume of processing trade fell by 10.6%; the export value of mechanical and electrical products only increased by 1.2%, a decrease of 1.4 percentage compared with the previous year; the export value of traditional labor-intensive products decreased by 1.7%.[24] Such a harsh situation is rare in recent years. Against this background, it has become a pressing matter as how to tap the potentials of foreign trade, especially how to revitalize the economic and trade cooperation with countries along the Belt and Road.

In addition to the shrinking foreign trade, China is also facing a serious problem — excess capacity. According to an investigation by the Ministry of Industry and the National Development and Reform Commission, China's capacity utilization rates of steel, cement, electrolytic aluminum, flat glass and shipping were only 72%, 73.7%, 71.9%, 73.1% and 75%, respectively, by the end of 2012, significantly lower than the international level.[25] At the same time, China's utilization rates of wind-power equipment manufacturing, photovoltaic cells, polysilicon and other emerging industries were only 67%, 57% and 35%, respectively.[26] Of the 39 products surveyed by their

---

[24] General Administration of Customs of PRC, "China's Total Foreign Trade Value Reaches 24.59 Trillion Yuan in 2015", January 13, 2016 http://www.customs.gov.cn/publish/portal0/tab65602/info784205.htm (海关总署:《2015 年我国进出口总值 24.59 万亿元》, 2016 年 1 月 13 日。)

[25] State Council of PRC, *Guiding Opinions of the State Council on Resolving Serious Production Overcapacity* (No. 41 Document of State Council, 2013), October 6, 2013. (中国国务院:《关于化解产能严重过剩矛盾的指导意见》(国发〔2013〕41号), 2013 年 10 月 6 日。)

[26] Li Yizhong, "Excess Capacity of Some Industries is the Main Cause of Economic Downturn", 21CN Finance, July 31, 2013, http://finance.21cn.com/webfocus/a/2013/0731/13/23146570.shtml (李毅中:《部分行业产能严重过剩是经济下行主因》, 21CN 财经网, 2013 年 7 月 31 日。)

cooresponding industry associations, 21 had a capacity utilization rate that was lower than 75%, which could be defined as "serious excess of production capacity" according to world-acknowledged standards.[27] Therefore, compared with previous ones, the current round of excess capacity is a general surplus of the industrial sector, involving both traditional industries and emerging industries. This problem is much more difficult and complex to be solved. The serious excess capacity leads to a series of problems, such as difficulties in business operation, less financial revenue and the accumulation of financial risks.

At the same time, the scale and speed of China's direct investment in foreign countries have been on the rise: the "going-out" of enterprises and equipments takes on a great momentum and the aggregate number of overseas contracted projects has reached a new level. The experience of developed countries shows that it is a necessary stage of economic transformation and upgrade that the "capital going-out" promotes the going-out of competitive industries, excess capacity, and high-end equipment so as for China to be actively engaged in the layout of global industrial chain and value chain. It's also an upgrade of the opening-up and going-out strategy. Xi Jinping, General Secretary of the CPC Central Commission, pointed out in a Standing Committee meeting of the Political Bureau in September 2013: *"Excess capacity is a burden on us, but it is a wealth to neighboring countries and other developing countries. Besides expecting us to increase imports from them, many countries also expect us to invest more."*[28]

---

[27] The National Development and Reform Commission of PRC, "Steel Industry Held a Meeting about the Implementation of the State Council's Guidance on Resolving Serious Overcapacity", November 20, 2013, http://gys.ndrc.gov.cn/gzdt/201311/t20131120_567428.html （中国国家发改委：《钢铁行业召开贯彻落实国务院关于化解产能严重过剩矛盾的指导意见会议》，2013 年 11 月 20 日。）

[28] Xi Jinping, "Address about Solving Overcapacity at a Standing Committee meeting of the Political Bureau of the CPC Central Committee", September 22, 2013, quoted from Dong Xiaojun, "Selecting the Path for China's Next Phase of Industrial Transfer—Based on the Japanese and US Models for International Transfer of Production Capacity", *People's Forum: Frontiers*, no. 2, December 2013, p. 74. (习近平：《在中央政治局常委会会议上关于化解产能过剩的讲话》，2013 年 9 月 22日。转引自董小君：《中国下阶段产业转移的道路选择——基于产能国际转移日美两种模式的创新探索》，《人民论坛•学术前沿》2013 年 12 月下，第 74 页。)

Under this background it has become an important consideration of the Belt and Road Initiative to encourage Chinese competitive enterprises to invest in the B&R countries and carry out integrations of resources and value chains on a global scale.

3.2.2.2 *Promoting Coordinated Regional Development and Opening-up*

China covers massive sea and land territory. However, the country's regional development and opening-up has long been imbalanced. That is, China's economic development is fast in the East but slow in the West; strong along the coast but weak on the inner land. There are multiple factors accounting for it, such as geographical location, natural resource reserves, national policies, international environment, etc. The Belt and Road Initiative, as a comprehensive strategy that integrates regional development with the country's opening-up, reflects the Chinese government's overall planning concerning the problem in the new period.

After the founding of the People's Republic of China in 1949, the state once consciously promoted the coordinated development among regions through various institutional arrangements and industrial distribution. However, with the adoption of the Reform and Opening-up policy in 1978, China rejoined the Western-dominated international trade system. The advantage of the eastern coastal areas became salient in the export-oriented economic structure. Human resources, material resources and financial resources moved quickly from central and western regions to the eastern coastal areas. In this process, China achieved a high degree of coordination among its industrial advantage (export-oriented, labor-intensive manufacturing industry), regional strategy (giving priority to the development of the eastern coastal areas) and opening-up strategy (coastal opening). In 1992 and 1999, China successively implemented the strategies of "opening border areas to the outside world" and "large-scale development of the western region." Although the result is quite fruitful, there still exists imbalanced development between east and west China. According to statistics, the coastal areas still account for more than 80% of China's total imports and exports; over the past 20 years, the average annual growth rate of foreign trade in the border area is only half that of the coastal areas.[29]

The western region and Eurasian continent provide vast strategic space to ensure China's sustainable development. And how China will manage its west determines the breadth of strategic space. As Premier Li Keqiang stressed, "*the greatest potential for future opening-up and room for maneuver is in the Middle and West regions.*"[30] In the meantime, amid a climate of global economic stagnation, it is also in an urgent need for the eastern region to realize transformation and upgrade, and to deepen opening-up. These are the important considerations behind the proposal of the Belt and Road Initiative. Aiming to adjust and transcend the existing structure of economic development, namely "being fast in the East but slow in the West; strong along the coast but weak on the inner land", the Silk Road Economic Belt Initiative can better reflect China's active, positive and long-term strategic planning in the new era.

3.2.23 *Diversifying Energy Imports and Trade Routes*

For a long time, as the world's largest consumer of raw materials and commodity producing country, China's energy import and foreign trade are highly reliant on maritime transport. The Belt and the Road, as two strategic channels that complement each other geographically, reflect China's efforts to diversify its trade routes.

As the world's biggest provider of industrial products China relies heavily on foreign markets to fill its energy and resource demand, and such a situation will remain unchanged, if not worse, in the forseeable future. Take oil import for example, China surpassed the United States to become the world's largest oil importer and consumer in

---

[29] The National Development and Reform Commission of PRC, "To Pace Up the Development and Opening-up of Key Border Areas and Promote the Construction of the Belt and Road Initiative", January 11, 2016, http://www.sdpc.gov.cn/xwzx/xwfb/201601/t20160111_771029.html (中国国家发改委：《推进沿边重点地区开发开放步伐构筑推进"一带一路"建设重要支撑》, 2016 年 1 月 11 日。)

[30] Li Keqiang, "On Deepening Economic System Reform", *Qiushi*, no. 9, 2014, p. 9.(李克强：《关于深化经济体制改革的若干问题》, 载《求是》2014 年第 9 期, 第 9 页。)

2011; China's dependence on foreign oil (i.e., the ratio of net oil imports to domestic oil consumption) exceeded 60% in 2015 for the first time. In terms of source of import, the proportion of Middle East oil has remained at around 50% since 1996 when China became a net importer of crude oil. However, in the world's geopolitical map, the Middle East is known to be the region with the most complex ethnic and religious relations, the fiercest competition between great powers, and the highest frequency of hot conflicts. In a sharp contrast with China, America's dependence on Middle East oil has fallen to around 20%, with Canada, Mexico and other countries becoming its main source of oil imports.

On June 13, 2014, the Central Leading Group for Economic and Financial Affairs held its sixth meeting, which specifically analyzed China's energy security strategy under the new situation. Xi Jinping stressed: "*strengthening international cooperation in an all-round way to achieve energy security under open conditions. Pushing for energy cooperation along the Belt and Road, and practically enhancing oil and gas cooperation with Central Asian, Middle Eastern, South American and African countries.*"[31] This is the first time that China's top decision-makers officially linked the Belt and Road Initiative with the national energy security strategy. In the future, the construction of the Belt and Road will promote the diversification of energy imports from three aspects, namely the source, the mode of transport and the currency settlement. First, in the context that the Middle East remains the primary source of oil, China will actively expand oil and gas cooperation with countries and regions such as Russia, Central Asia and Africa to promote the diversification of energy sources. Second, although maritime transport still plays a major role, China will cooperate with neighboring countries on the construction of oil and gas pipelines on land. Third, in the context that the US dollar still remains the main currency for evalution and settlement of bulk commodity

---

[31] Xinhua News Agency, "To Promote China's Energy Production and Consumption Revolution, Speed Up the Implementation of Major Tasks in Energy Industry", *People's Daily*, June 14, 2014, p. 1. (新华社:《积极推动我国能源生产和消费革命加快实施能源领域重点任务重大举措》, 载《人民日报》2014 年 6 月 14 日, 第 1 版。)

and energy trade, China should take resource and energy cooperation as a breakthrough, advocating the use of local currency or RMB for trade settlement so as to diversify the currencies used in energy import.

Similar to energy imports, China's foreign trade is also highly dependent on maritime transport. In 2013 alone, more than 90% of China's imports of goods were transported by sea; and trade in goods accounted for about 65% of the total foreign trade. Due to limitation in transportation and logistics, the proportion of land trade was very low. Therefore, taking infrastructure connectivity and facilitation of investment and trade as the breakthrough point, it is a vital for the Belt and Road Initiative to take the first step by opening up the land trade corridors between China and Eurasian countries while continuing to tap into the potentials of maritime trade. In this sense, the construction of the Silk Road Economic Belt has a far-reaching historical and strategic significance. It would not only help to reactivate the land trade routes which had been in idleness for several centuries, but also make up for the deficiency of sea route to some extent.

3.3 Future Vision

The Belt and Road Initiative reflects China's thinking of and response to some realistic problems. At the same time, the Initiative also incorporates the strategic planning of Xi's Administration regarding the future regional development and opening-up pattern as well as the new international political and economic order. To some extent, this is also the key reason why the Belt and Road is a strategic initiative for a new era that truly transcends the ancient Silk Road and the "Modern Silk Road" between China and the Middle East.

3.3.1 *New Pattern of Opening-up to the Outside World*

The Belt and Road Initiative, on one hand, is based on the coordinated development of domestic regions, and on the other hand, focuses on the opening-up of both land and sea to the outside world. It is a comprehensive strategy that coordinates China's development with that of B&R countries. From a long-term perspective, the Initiative is expected to redress the long-existing regional imbalance in economic development, so as to create a new opening-up pattern characterized by sea–land interaction, and overall opening-up of both East and West regions.

First of all, the Initiative aims to establish the market mechanism to realize the smooth flow of elements and the coordinated development between east and west China, and form a unified national market. In fact, this is also the most important foundation and premise to link and coordinate between the East and West, sea and land along the Belt and Road. No matter whether it was in the past dynasties or since the founding of the People's Republic of China in 1949, state power and relevant policies and institutional arrangements have always been the fundamental driving forces for regional resource reallocation. Take China's western development strategy for example, on one hand, the central government has implemented various special policies and preferential measures to divert resources into the western region, and use the tool of financial transfer payments to aid the construction of the western region; on the other hand, the State adopts political mobilization to encourage the eastern provinces to provide one-for-one aid for the western region. It should be admitted that since the western region is weak in terms of self-development capacity, external support and state-led regional coordination are fairly beneficial for the western region to promote its capacity building and realize a leap-forward development. The rapid economic growth of the western region in recent years is a sound proof of the positive effects of these measures. However, the flow of resources between the East and West guided by state policies is mainly a redistribution of resources, which fails to maximize the initiatives of the eastern region, and a big gap still exists for the western region to achieve effective self-development. Therefore, in addition to preferential policies, what is more important is the formation of a market-oriented mechanism for coordinating and balancing interregional interests. On April 23, 2014, the National Development and Reform Commission held a press conference on the launch of the 13th 5-Year Plan. Xu Lin, the then director of the Department of Development Planning in DNRC pointed out, "*the coordinated development of different regions can not only rely on regional planning and favorable policy. What we may need more is to establish a system and mechanism of coordinated regional development, that is, within the framework of a unified national market, we need to further promote the free flow of all elements, so that the market will play a decisive role in the allocation of resources.*"[32] Therefore, against the background that the eastern area is under the pressure for transformation and upgrade, national strategies and policies, such as the Belt and Road Initiative, the new round of western development, the national new mode of urbanization, the Yangtze River Economic Belt and so on, have offered a gold oppertunity to transfer industries from eastern regions to middle and western areas and thus enable them to improve self-development capacity, so as to achieve coordinated regional development in the new era.

Second, it aims to promote the comprehensive opening-up of both land and sea, and to achieve the integration of domestic regional development with in-depth opening-up to the outside world. The Belt and the Road are not only international trade routes between China and Asian, European and African countries, but rather, channels that connect east and west China with B&R countries via sea and land. Specifically, along the northern, central and southern routes of the Silk Road Economic Belt, the western region of China extends into the Eurasian continent, all the way to Southeast Asia, South Asia, Central Asia, Russia, Mongolia, West Asia, Southern Europe, Central and Eastern Europe and Western Europe. With the promotion of infrastructure connectivity, the land trade channel that once connected Chang'an, Luoyang, Samarkand, Baghdad, Damascus, Byzantium and Rome in history is likely to rise again, and will surpass the ancient Silk Road both in depth and width. Similarly, along the 21st-Century Maritime Silk Road, China's eastern coastal areas can

---

[32] State Council Information Office, "National Development and Reform Commission Held a Press Conference about Planning of the 13th Five-Year Plan", April 24, 2014, http://www. scio.gov.cn/xwfbh/gbwxwfbh/xwfbh/fzggw/Document/1368872/1368872.htm (log-in time: July 11, 2014) (中国国务院新闻办公室:《发改委就启动 "十三五" 规划编制工作举行新闻发布会》, 2014 年 4 月 24 日。)

be closely connected with the Pacific Ocean and the Indian Ocean, all the way to the South China Sea, the Strait of Malacca, the Bay of Bengal, the Arabia Sea, the Persian Gulf, the Gulf of Aden and even the Mediterranean countries. Through port cooperation network and maritime connectivity construction, the once prosperous maritime trade routes in history may be activated again between Chinese ports like Guangzhou, Quanzhou, Yangzhou, Ningbo and harbors like Sumatra, Java, Malacca, Quilon, Aden, Basra and so on. This will be a new picture of maritime connectivity in modern history when the West has been dominant in setting up the maritime order. Therefore, the Belt and Road Initiative undoubtedly incorporates China's eastern and western areas into a broader development landscape. The Silk Road Economic Belt Initiative means that the future western development and westward opening will be launched within the framework of the entire Eurasian market, and the western region will become the bridgehead of land cooperation between China and Eurasian countries. With the proposal of the 21st-century Maritime Silk Road, China's eastern coastal areas, currently serving as a global manufacturing base and export base, will provide fundamental support for China to forge a maritime cooperation partnership with countries along the Pacific and India Oceans. In the process, port cities, with their construction of industrial zones, will take on new functions of driving industrial transfer and industrial development.

Third, the Initiative aims to coordinate regional development and opening-up of both the sea and land as a whole, so as to achieve synergy between the Belt and the Road. The Belt and the Road are not competitive and antagonistic to each other. The fact that the two were put forward at the same time just reflects Chinese overall strategic consideration of striking a balance between eastern and western regions and between sea and land in the new period. In March 2014, Premier Li Keqiang proposed in his Government Work Report: *"to design a new chess game for regional development, i.e. to promote gradient development from east to west, from the coast to the inner-land, along the major rivers and overland transportation routes."*[33] The

---

[33] Li Keqiang, "Report on the Work of the Government—Delivered at the Second Session of the Twelfth National People's Congress", *People's Daily*, March 5, 2014,

construction of a unified domestic market and internally-circulated economy contributes to the gradual shift of elements, resources and industries from the eastern areas to the central and western regions of China. On basis of it, China's western regions can serve as a bridgehead of industrial transfer from eastern coastal regions to the developing countries along the route, so that the transformation and upgrade of China's eastern region can be carried out in the macro-framework of the entire Eurasian market. Furthermore, in the future, goods, personnels and industries of the eastern region can move to not only countries of the Pacific Ocean and Indian Ocean along the 21st century Maritime Silk Road but also the land countries via the western region along the Silk Road Economic Belt. Similarly, the western region of China, apart from being a bridge connecting inland Eurasian countries with the Pacific will also act as a "transfer station" for the transit of energy from Africa, Middle East, Central Asia, Russia and Mongolia to China, especially the eastern coastal area of China. It is worth noting that, as another national strategy proposed by Xi's Administration, the Yangtze River Economic Belt will become a link between the Belt and the Road. *The Guiding Opinions on Promoting the Development of the Yangtze River Economic Belt on the Basis of the Golden Waterway* issued by the State Council in September 2014 clearly stated, "to make the best use of the local resources that are open to both sea and land, to innovate the opening-up mode and complement each other's advantages, to cultivate a high ground for inner-land opening-up, to accelerate infrastructure interconnectivity with neighboring countries and regions, and to strengthen interactions with the Silk Road Economic Belt and Maritime Silk Road."[34] In the future, if the Belt, the Road and the Yangtze River Economic Belt forge an effective linkage among

---

p. 1. (李克强:《政府工作报告——二〇一四年三月五日在第十二届全国人民代表大会第二次会议上》, 载《人民日报》2014 年 3 月 15 日, 第 1 版。)

[34] State Council of PRC, *Guiding Opinions of the State Council on Promoting the Development of the Yangtze River Economic Belt by Relying on the Golden Waterway* (No. 39 Document of State Council, 2014), September 25, 2014. (中国国务院:《关于依托黄金水道推动长江经济带发展的指导意见》(国发〔2014〕39 号), 2014 年 9 月 25 日。)

themselves, a new landscape of coordinated development and comprehensive opening-up will emerge.

In short, the Belt and Road Initiative is not a temporary solution that tries to hedge against the sea power with land power, or to counter the US' "Pivot to Asia" with China's "Marching Westwards." In the long run, the Belt and Road Initiative aims to redress the long-existing imbalance in China's regional development and opening up, and to bring about a new phase of all-around, two-way opening up with links running eastward and westward, over land and sea.

3.3.2 *New Mode of Economic Cooperation*

It is estimated that the total population along the Belt and Road is about 4.4 billion, with a total economy of about $21 trillion, accounting for 63% and 29% of the world, respectively; most B&R countries are emerging economies and developing countries.[35] *Asian Development Outlook 2014* released by the Asian Development Bank showed that the annual economic growth of 45 Asian developing economies would reach 6.2% and 6.4% in 2014 and 2015, respectively, more than two times higher than those of the developed countries.[36] Against the background of a weak economic recovery in developed countries in Europe and North America, developing countries in Asia have shown bright prospects for development, and this lays a firm foundation for the Belt and Road construction.

However, as mentioned in the discussion of the "Modern Silk Road" between China and the Middle East, under the existing international political and economic system, a new triangular trade structure has taken form among China, the Middle East and the United States. They represent Asian manufacturing, Asia-Africa-Latin America resource-exporting and western consuming countries respectively. As

---

[35] Gao Hucheng, "To Deepen Economic and Trade Cooperation, Create New Success", *People's Daily*, July 2, 2014, p. 11. (高虎城：《深化经贸合作共创新的辉煌》, 载《人民日报》2014 年 7 月 2 日, 第 11 版。)

[36] Asian Development Bank, *Asian Development Outlook 2014*. Manila, Philippines: Asian Development Bank, 2014.

the world's largest importer of raw materials and the largest exporter of manufactured goods, China has become the hub of the triangular circulation. However, the United States or the West has always been in the dominant position in the triangle by control of international trade rules, currencies, pricing right and many other elements. Correspondingly, although China and some developing countries have made great progress, they have been heavily restricted by the internal logic of this system. For most developing countries, due to the notable lack of industrial, transportation and livelihood infrastructures, the pace of industrialization is extremely slow. It is difficult for them to accept industries transferred from the western developed countries or emerging market countries, and then an economic development mode is formed that is highly dependent on the export of energy resources. At the same time, due to the "Reverse Price Scissors" in the modern international trade, industrial products are getting cheaper while raw materials are becoming more and more expensive, which forces China and other producers to trade more industrial goods for fewer raw materials.

Therefore, it is necessary for manufacturing countries and resource-producing countries to make adjustments to the pattern of international trade and economic cooperation in the dollar standard system, such as "industrial products for raw materials" or "commodity for energy", and seek new ways for developing South–South cooperation so as to promote the establishment of a more equal international economic structure. In fact, this is the very strategic meaning that the Belt and Road Initiative entails. China and B&R countries have a high degree of complementarity in various fields, which forms a practical basis for developing an optimal economic relations.

1. Capital. China has the largest foreign exchange reserves in the world. Most B&R countries face a shortage of funds except for a few oil-producing countries in the Middle East. In the context of the global commodity price slump, the situation is even worse for countries that mainly rely on the export of resources and energy. Therefore, there is a high degree of complementarity

between China and those countries in terms of capital supply and demand. China's foreign investment will exceed $650 billion in the next 5 years. With capital advantage, China is likely to provide financing support for infrastructure construction, resource and energy development in developing countries through a variety of bilateral and multilateral financial arrangements. In the past, China used a considerable portion of its foreign exchange reserves to buy US treasury bonds. Therefore, investing hugely in B&R countries will undoubtedly lead to a more balanced capital outflow.

2. Industrialization. China has become the manufacturing superpower by having the most complete industrial system and categories all over the world. In contrast, many B&R countries are still in their early stage of industrialization, with very weak industrial base. Out of the world's 500 major industrial products, China ranks first in the production of 220 kinds, especially in the field of equipment manufacturing, where China has developed a complete industrial system with all different type of categories, at a considerably high technical standard and the ability to finish the complete sets. Such a manufacturing scale comprises one-third of the world's total production. China's high-speed rail, nuclear power, ultrahigh voltage (UHV), communications and port machinery are enjoying a world-wide good reputation. With low cost and promising market prospects, these products are ideal choices for international transfer. Correspondingly, since many B&R countries are still weak industrial bases, foreign investment is highly needed to assist them in developing their own industries. Therefore, the international cooperation in production capacity and equipment manufacturing, as well as overseas economic and trade cooperation zones and industry cluster zones, will enable China to lend its support to B&R countries in their industrialization.

3. Infrastructure construction. By having the strongest infrastructure construction ability over the world, and armed with extensive experience as being contractor, "China Infrastructure" has established its status internationally. At present, the offshore

business of China's infrastructure construction companies begin to penetrate high value added areas, including but not limited to general contracting, project financing, design consulting, operation and maintenance management. A World Bank report shows that the cost of China's high-speed rail per kilometer is about two-thirds that of the developed countries in Europe and America, and the project completion time is about three-fourths that of other countries.[37] In addition, Chinese enterprises have already been active in the construction of ports, electricity and communications facilities, and industrial parks in the countries along the routes. Accordingly, in order to speed up the process of industrialization and, to improve the level of national economy and the people's living standard and employment, B&R countries have enormous and burning needs for infrastructure construction in transportation, electricity, communications, energy, education, agriculture, medical care, and so on. But for a long time, the infrastructure construction in many developing countries has been retarded by the shortage of funds and the backwardness of engineering capacity, which not only hinders the economic development, but also causes inconvenience for their people. On the other hand, a number of developed countries are facing the problems of aging infrastructures and their upgrade. What's more, the lack of cross-border infrastructure has also led to difficulties in the exchanges of commodity, capital and personnel among different countries. In this context, many countries have introduced a variety of infrastructure investment plans, showing great interests in strengthening cross-border infrastructure connectivity.

4. Resource and energy. China is currently the world's largest consumer of resources, energy and other commodities, and its import demand is expected to be enduring and on the rise. B&R countries are mostly rich in resource reserves and their main export commodities are primary products such as raw materials.

---

[37] Gerald Ollivier *et al*. High-speed Railways in China: A Look at Construction Costs, Washington, DC: World Bank Group, 2014.

Therefore, there is a high degree of complementarity between the two sides in the field of resources and energy. The trade between China and Southeast Asia, Central Asia, West Asia, Russia, Mongolia and other areas along the Belt and Road mainly involves the exchange of manufactured goods and raw materials at the expense of a large trade deficit on the China side. Currently, with global demand for commodities shrinking and prices plummeting, the Chinese market as a export destination has been gaining importance. Meanwhile, against the background of the Belt and Road Initiative, cooperation in resources and energies will promote cooperation in the whole industry chain. These countries will be strengthened in their development of a industrial system of resources and energies, so as to improve their local processing and intensive processing capacity.

Complementarity in these aspects makes it possible for China to transform its traditional trading style, which is characterized by inexpensive Chinese-made products and "Commodity for Resource" with other developing countries, into a new type of economic cooperation with B&R countries based on "going global", especially in industries, production capacities, equipment, infrastructure construction and labor service, which are driven by the go-global of Chinese capitals. Along the process, the "3 in 1" cooperation mode — namely, the integration of financial cooperation, resources and energy development, and infrastructure construction — should serve as a breakthrough point that enable a virtuous cycle to be formed among capital, commodity, equipment, technology, standard, production capacity, labor service on the China side and resource, energy and market in B&R countries.

The underlying logic behind is as follows: China (sometimes together with other countries or financial institutions) firstly provides project financing for major infrastructure construction to B&R countries, by means of setting up development financial institutions, cooperative investment funds and special loans, while B&R countries put up resources and energies as a guarantee or equivalent compensation. Secondly, Chinese construction companies will be the contractor for those projects and B&R countries will pay with financing they received earlier for all relevant materials, products, equipment and labor. By collaborating with B&R countries, along with executing its predominance in fields of equipment and engineering, China will likely make a gradual transition from exporting physical goods to technical standards instead. Thirdly, the development of energies and resources is expected to meet the needs of both China and the global market, promote the export of Chinese energy equipment, as well as accelerate the accumulation of capitals needed to develop domestic economy in countries along the routes. Fourthly, enhancement in infrastructure in B&R countries will lead to improvements in their domestic market, employment, and investment environment, which will not only lay the foundation for China's industrial transformation, but also cultivate the market for the export of more Chinese goods and company's investment. Fifthly, through cross-border infra-structure connectivity, China will be closely connected with other Asian, European and African countries. This will further promote interregional exchanges and mutual complementarity, establish and enhance an in-depth cooperation in Eurasia supply chain, industrial chain and value chain, and develop mutually-complemented indus-trial network and economic system.

Therefore, taking the building of the Belt and Road as an oppor-tunity, China and B&R countries are likely to advance the trading pattern of "Commodity for Resource" within the framework of the international triangular trade. Instead, China can gradually connect its capital, technology, equipment, commodities, construction, capac-ity, labor service, even its currency (RMB) with resources, energy and market in other B&R countries, especially ASEAN and central Asia. Therefore, a brand new type of economic collaboration among Asian developing countries, featuring equality, mutual benefit and a win-win partnership can be established. With such prospect in mind, the Belt and Road Initiative is likely to create a new aspect of South-South cooperation. Thus the Initiative contains strategic potentials of transforming the unequal international political and economic order, which was shaped after the World War II and has been strengthened in the age of globalization.

However, it must be made clear that the strategic intention of the Belt and Road Initiative is by no means to counter the United States by creating of a Chinese version of COMECON, nor is it to establish a new international economic system in which China and RMB will take the place of the US and USD. Such a prospect is neither realistic nor desirable, and is surely to arouse deep suspicion in B&R countries and strong resistance from the United States. China alone is not capable of shouldering the responsibility of realizing common development for dozens of B&R countries. It can be predicted that the triangle trade structure, which is dominated by the United States, will continue to exist for a fairly long period of time.

Chapter

4

Cooperation Framework of Building the Belt and Road

Since the Belt and Road Initiative was proposed in September 2013, the Chinese central government has crafted the top-level design of its construction after more than one year's repeated deliberation.

In terms of organizational structure, the leading group for the Belt and Road Initiative has been put into operation. On February 1, 2015, the first working conference on the Belt and Road Initiative was held in Beijing, in which a leading group, led by Zhang Gaoli, member of the Politburo Standing Committee of the Communist Party of China and Vice Premier, made its debut. Other members of the group include Wang Huning (CPC Politburo member, Director of the Central Policy Research Office, and Director of the Office of Central Leading Group for Comprehensively Deepening Reforms), Wang Yang (CPC Politburo member and Vice Premier), and Yang Jiechi (State Councilor and Director of the Office of the Central Leading Group for Foreign Affairs). As indicated in publicized information, the leading group office, which takes charge of daily routine and coordination work, was set up under the National Development and Reform Commission.

In terms of policy planning, the National Development and Reform Commission, Ministry of Foreign Affairs and Ministry of Commerce of the People's Republic of China issued the *Vision and Actions on Jointly Building Silk Road Economic Belt and 21st-Century Maritime Silk Road* (hereinafter referred to as "*Vision and Actions*") on March 28, 2015, which explicitly elaborated the vision, principles, framework, key routes, main content, cooperation mechanisms and positioning of domestic regions in the Belt and Road construction.

According to *Vision and Actions*, the Belt and Road Initiative aims to set up all-dimensional, multitiered and composite connectivity networks, realize diversified, independent, balanced and sustainable development in B&R countries, enhance cultural and people-to-people exchanges as well as mutual learning among the peoples of these countries and build a community of shared interests, destiny and responsibility featuring mutual political trust, economic integration and cultural inclusiveness.

4.1 Principles and Strategies

4.1.1 *Principles*

4.1.1.1 *Open for Cooperation*

The Belt and Road Initiative is open for cooperation. It doesn't limit itself to the area of the ancient Silk Road, nor does it put a cap on the number of participating countries. It is not an exclusive plan against specific countries, nor is it designed to weaken the influence of other countries. It is open to all countries, international and regional organizations for engagement. In September 2015, President Xi Jinping, during his visit to the United States, stated that "the China-proposed initiatives, such as Belt and Road and Asian Infrastructure Investment Bank, are open, transparent and inclusive, so all parties including the United States are welcome to take an active part."[1] In October, President Xi reiterated, in his visit to the United Kingdom, that the

---

[1] Du Shangze and Chen Lidan, "President Xi Jinping and President Obama Held a Joint Press Conference", *People's Daily*, September 26, 2015, p. 2.(杜尚泽、陈丽丹:《习近平同美国总统奥巴马共同会见记者》, 载《人民日报》2015 年 9 月 26 日, 第2 版。)

Belt and Road originated from, but was not limited to, the ancient Silk Road. It is actually a broad "circle of friends" that runs through Africa and connects Asia with Europe. All interested countries could be a part of it.[2] In addition, the Belt and Road construction is a cooperative project. It is by no means an investment plan led exclusively by China. Without understanding, support or engagement of other countries, the Belt and Road Initiative will remain an oral or written plan.

4.1.1.2 *Market Operation*

Although the Belt and Road is a large-scale cooperation initiative promoted by the national government, it is the enterprises that play the primary role in its construction. Such a practice abides by international norms, and also reflects the different roles of government and market. The governments do not possess all related information, funds or resources in the Belt and Road construction, nor can they take the place of the enterprises in the actual implementation of various cooperative projects. Against the backdrop of Chinese enterprises going global, the governments should play an increasingly important role in providing macro guidance and facilitating services; in the meanwhile, the governments should set up platforms for cooperation, eliminate policy barriers and ensure security for transnational investment and operation via intergovernmental consultation and coordination.

4.1.1.3 *Mutual Benefits*

The Belt and Road Initiative is by no means just for the benefits of China or Chinese enterprises. Only when the interests and comfort level of all involved parties are sufficiently considered can the Initiative attract cooperation partners. Accordingly, only when other countries fully understand that their engagement in the Initiative can bring benefits, will they show willingness to participate. This requires China to keep an open mind and seek a conjunction of interests for different

---

[2] Du Shangze and Huang Peizhao, "Xi Jinping Attends and Addresses the China–UK Business Summit", *People's Daily*, October 22, 2015, p. 1. (杜尚泽、黄培昭:《习近平出席中英工商峰会并致辞》,载《人民日报》2015 年 10 月 22 日,第 1 版。)

parties in promoting the Initiative, especially in the implementation of major projects.

4.1.2 *Strategies*

4.1.2.1 *From Point to Area*

The Belt and Road Initiative, involving numerous countries and fields, also faces unprecedented challenges. Therefore, special attention should be paid to the breakthroughs at key points while comprehensively promoting the Initiative. Generally speaking, the success of a major landmark project will enhance the development of a city. And the prosperity of a hub city will have a demonstration effect on the whole country and even the neighboring regions. Thus, we should focus on "key points" in a country or a region, and give priority to strategic nodes in promoting the Initiative.

As mentioned in *Vision and Actions*, on land, the Initiative will focus on jointly building a new Eurasian Land Bridge and developing China–Mongolia–Russia, China–Central Asia–West Asia, China–Indochina Peninsula, China–Pakistan and Bangladesh–China–India–Myanmar economic corridors by taking advantage of international transport routes, relying on hub cities along the Belt and Road and using key economic and trade industrial parks as cooperation platforms. At sea, the Initiative will focus on jointly building smooth, secure and efficient transport routes connecting major seaports along the Belt and Road. This shows that both the "Belt" and the "Road" give full play to the role of "nodes" (core cities, major seaports, key economic and trade industrial parks), forming a construction approach of from point to area, from line to surface.

In fact, at the second and third working conferences for advancing the Belt and Road in July 2015 and January 2016, the leaders laid repeated emphasis on key directions, countries, fields and projects.

4.1.2.2 *Step by Step*

Since China's national strength is limited and countries along the routes can hardly reach a consensus in regard to the Belt and Road

Initiative, China should take caution to avoid being hasty and over-stretched in building the B&R.

With regard to B&R partners, China should prioritize cooperation with neighboring countries, especially those with solid industrial foundation, key geographical position, non-negligible political influence and high willingness in participating the Initiative. By this standard, Kazakhstan, Indonesia, Pakistan and Russia are potential partners that China should work more with.

With regard to cooperation fields, major flagship projects should be launched and completed as demonstrative models as soon as possible. Early fruits yielded in building the BRI will increase its appeal to countries along the routes and boost confidence of Chinese people. For this reason, infrastructure construction (especially energy, transport and communications projects that are directly related to people's livelihood) will be priorities in the early construction of B&R because of its visible, apparent and rapid effects. In respect of industrial cooperation, the establishment of overseas or cross-border industrial parks that act as gathering places and platforms would be the first choice. Correspondingly, in respect of financial cooperation, the investment and financing for infrastructure construction and industrial cooperation are the most urgent issues to be settled.

4.2 Key Routes and Economic Corridors

According to *Vision and Actions*, the Belt and Road runs through the continents of Asia, Europe and Africa, connecting the vibrant East Asia economic circle at one end and developed European economic circle at the other, and encompassing vast developing countries in the middle.

The Silk Road Economic Belt focuses on three key routes, namely (1) north route, from China to Europe (the Baltic) through Central Asia and Russia; (2) central route, from China to the Persian Gulf and the Mediterranean Sea through Central Asia and West Asia; and (3) south route, from China to Southeast Asia, South Asia and the Indian Ocean.

The 21st-century Maritime Silk Road is designed for two key routes, respectively (1) from China's coast to Europe through the South China Sea and the Indian Ocean and (2) from China's coast through the South China Sea to the South Pacific.

Along these key routes, China will enhance the construction of a new Eurasian Land Bridge, as well as China–Mongolia–Russia, China–Central Asia–West Asia, China–Indochina Peninsula, China–Pakistan and Bangladesh–China–India–Myanmar economic corridors.

4.2.1 *New Eurasian Land Bridge Economic Corridor*

The New Eurasian Land Bridge, also called the Second Eurasian Continental Bridge, extends from China's port cities Lianyungang and Rizhao, goes along the Longhai Railway and Lanzhou–Xinjiang Railway and across the border via Alashankou and Khorgas in Xinjiang, and then runs through Kazakhstan, Russia, Belarus, Poland and Germany to Netherlands' Rotterdam and Belgium's Antwerp. It is an international passageway for land–ocean transportation with a length of more than 10,000 km. Compared with the original Siberian Land Bridge, the New Eurasian Land Bridge enjoys advantageous geographic conditions, climate conditions, throughput and economic costs. Connecting the East Asia economic circle with the West European economic circle, the corridor possesses massive potential for cooperation and is expected to reshape the economic and geographic patterns of Eurasia. What's worth mentioning is that countries along the New Eurasian Land Bridge have been generally enjoying political stability, sound economic foundation and low security risks, which makes them ideal destinations for trade, investment, industries and capitals. At the current stage, infrastructure connectivity and investment and trade facilitation are the top priorities in building the New Eurasian Land Bridge Economic Corridor.

4.2.2 *China–Mongolia–Russia Economic Corridor*

At his meeting on September 11, 2014 with the leaders of Russia and Mongolia, President Xi Jinping put forward the idea of dovetailing the Silk Road Economic Belt with Russia's Eurasian Railway and Mongolia's Prairie Road program, to build the China–Mongolia–Russia Economic Corridor. It is reported that Mongolian President Elbegdorj proposed the Prairie Road program in 2014 to give full play to its advantageous geographic location between Europe and Asia. With an investment totaling 50 billion USD, this initiative includes railways linking China and Russia, highways connecting Asia and Europe, outbound power transmission channels to China, and oil and gas pipelines running through Mongolia. In the meantime, the Russian government also proposed the establishment of development zones in the Far East region, which, drawing on experiences from China's building of special economic zones, would attract foreign investment into new businesses and factories via preferential policies such as tax exemption.[3] It is reported that the China–Mongolia–Russia Economic Corridor is composed of two routes: one starting from the Beijing-Tianjin–Hebei Region, through Hohhot in the North China, to Mongolia and Russia; the other one starting from Dalian, Shenyang, Changchun and Harbin to Manzhouli in the Northeast China, and then to Chita in Russia.[4] With stable political environment and abundant mineral, oil and gas resources, both Mongolia and Russia are promising emerging markets, which can play a big complementary role to China's industries. The construction of the China–Mongolia–Russia Economic Corridor will also enhance the economic development and opening-up of North China and Northeast China. At present, the construction of this corridor is impeded by backward infrastructure, insufficient investment and trade barriers, as well as various constraints in hardware and software. Such issues should be promptly addressed.

4.2.3 *China–Central Asia–West Asia Economic Corridor*

The China–Central Asia–West Asia Economic Corridor extends westward from Xinjiang via five Central Asian countries (Kazakhstan, Kyrgyzstan, Tajikistan, Uzbekistan and Turkmenistan), Iran, Iraq,

---

[3] Lin Xuedan and Huo Wen, "China, Russia and Mongolia to Jointly Draw a Blueprint", *People's Daily*, July 7, 2015, p. 3. (林雪丹、霍文:《中俄蒙共绘发展蓝图》,载《人民日报》2015 年 7 月 7 日, 第 3 版。)
[4] Shi Yanjun and Wu Jing, "How Long Are the Six Economic Corridors", *International Financial News*, June 1, 2015, p. 6. (史燕君、吴婧:《六大经济走廊有多长》,载《国际金融报》2015 年 6 月 1 日, 第 6 版。)

Saudi Arabia and Turkey, to the Persian Gulf and the Mediterranean coast. The corridor links numerous countries with rich resources and energy reserves, large Islamic populations, complex ethnic and religious issues, and relatively backward infrastructure. The building of the corridor will face bright prospect for economic development and international cooperation, and considerable challenges and constraints as well.

4.2.4 *China–Indochina Peninsula Economic Corridor*

The China–Indochina Peninsula Economic Corridor starts from hub cities like Nanning in Guangxi Zhuang Autonomous Region and Kunming in Yunnan Province, across Vietnam, Laos, Cambodia, Thailand and Malaysia of Indochina Peninsula, to Singapore, and further to Indonesia. With abundant natural and human resources, the countries along this route neighbor China across mountains or seas and share plentiful cultural similarities with China. Under the framework of existing mechanisms, such as China–ASEAN Free Trade Area and Great Mekong Subregion Cooperation, bilateral economic and trade ties have been strengthening. China and countries along the route will have great potential to expand cooperation in key areas of industrial investment and connectivity.

4.2.5 *China–Pakistan Economic Corridor*

Premier Li Keqiang first brought up the China–Pakistan Economic Corridor project during his visit to Pakistan in May 2013. As an integral part of the Belt and Road, this corridor links Kashgar, Xinjiang on the north end and Gwadar, Pakistan on the south end, stretching for a distance of over 3,000 km across plateau, valleys, basins and deserts. Governments of the two countries have set up the Joint Cooperation Committee on the long-term plan for the China–Pakistan Economic Corridor, led respectively by the National Development and Reform Commission of China and the Ministry of Planning and Development of Pakistan, to take charge of the design, implementation and supervision of the corridor. Gwadar port, energy, transport infrastructure and industrial park are the four key areas at current and future phases of building the corridor. According to Pakistani Ambassador to China Masood Khalid, the Pakistani government will establish "China-Pakistan investment zones" and "industrial parks" along the corridor, offering industrial land, communication network, dry port facilities, tax abatement and customs duty exemption to enterprises investing in these regions.[5] As an all-weather strategic partner of China, Pakistan holds a significant strategic position. The rock-solid relationship between the two countries makes huge room for future cooperation. However, intricate ethnic groups and religious forces in Pakistan will pose security challenges which China cannot afford to neglect.

4.2.6 *Bangladesh–China–India–Myanmar Economic Corridor*

Premier Li Keqiang first proposed the Bangladesh–China–India–Myanmar Economic Corridor project during his visit to India in May 2013. The corridor, connecting four countries of China, Myanmar, Bangladesh and India, starts from Yunnan and covers important hub cities of Kunming, Mandalay, Dhaka and Kolkata. It is located at the junction of the "Belt" and the "Road". To advance its construction, the four countries have set up the Joint Working Group for the Bangladesh–China–India–Myanmar Economic Corridor, which has convened two meetings: one held in China in December 2013 and the other held in Bangladesh in December 2014. Countries along the corridor have large populations, rich products and high economic complementarity. However, constrained by the political transformation in Myanmar, ambiguous attitude of India and poor connectivity in subregions, the construction of the corridor faces many difficulties.

---

[5] Lu Yao, Yao Yibo and Wang Ziyi, "A Clearer Picture of the New Maritime Silk Road", *Oriental Outlook*, June 5, 2014.(芦垚、姚亿博、汪子怡:《新"海上丝绸之路"轮廓渐清》, 载《瞭望东方周刊》, 2014 年 6 月 5 日。)

4.3 Cooperation Priorities

The construction of B&R contains five major parts, namely policy coordination, connectivity of infrastructure and facilities, unimpeded trade, financial integration and people-to-people bonds.

4.3.1 *Policy Coordination*

Policy coordination is the premise and guarantee for implementing the Belt and Road Initiative. As a mega transcontinental economic cooperation initiative, the Belt and Road involves vast areas and various countries with diversified interest appeals and different development paces. China alone cannot shoulder the responsibility of implementing the Initiative. Therefore, understanding, support and engagement of major powers and B&R countries are needed. Only by multilevel and multiform intergovernmental communication and exchange can these countries enhance trust and clarify doubts, eliminating misunderstandings such as China using "westward strategy" to counter the United States' "strategic eastward shift", exerting land power to hedge sea power, "the Chinese version of Marshall Plan", "the Asian version of the Monroe Doctrine", and "the Chinese version of Council for Mutual Economic Assistance". Only by policy coordination and seeking the conjunction of interests between the Initiative and the development strategies of the countries and international organizations along the Belt and Road, can we work out well-targeted win-win strategies and roadmaps for joint building of the Initiative, thus converting the parties involved into actual stakeholders and increasing their sense of identity and level of participation. It is based on this idea that President Xi Jinping pointed out, "The Belt and Road will be a real chorus comprising all countries along the routes, not a solo for China itself."[6]

---

[6]Xi Jinping, "Towards a Community of Common Destiny and a New Future for Asia—Keynote Speech at the Boao Forum for Asia Annual Conference 2015", *People's Daily*, March 29, 2015, p. 2. 习近平:《迈向命运共同体开创亚洲新未来——在博鳌亚洲论坛 2015 年年会上的主旨演讲》(2015 年 3 月 28 日, 海南博鳌), 载《人民日报》2015 年 3 月 29 日, 第 2 版。

4.3.2 *Connectivity of Infrastructure and Facilities*

Building the road is the first step to become rich. That is the success experience drawn by People's Republic of China from more than 60 years' history. Thus infrastructure connectivity, a field most likely to yield fruits in a short span of time, should be a priority in building the B&R. Connectivity in infrastructure can eliminate the geographic barriers between China and B&R countries, facilitate the cluster and exchange of people, goods, funds and resources, boost people's livelihood, industrial development and economic growth in relevant countries (especially developing countries), and increase the appeal of the B&R Initiative.

Mu Hong, Standing Vice Minister of the Office of the Central Leading Group for Comprehensively Deepening Reforms and Vice Minister with the National Development and Reform Commission, said that one of the priority tasks of B&R during the 13th Five-Year Plan Period was the construction of "six means of communication and multiple ports". "Six means of communication" refers to railways, highways, seagoing transport, aviation, pipelines and aerospace integrated information network; "Multiple ports" refer to a number of ports that ensure safe and smooth sea passages.[7] It means that infrastructure cooperation in transport, energy and communications should be the top priorities in achieving facilities connectivity. **With regard to transport,** China will make breakthroughs in key passageways, junctions and projects, to strengthen construction and cooperation in highways, railways, waterways, ports and aviation and build a unified coordination mechanism for whole-course transportation, so as to facilitate land, sea, water and air transport. **With regard to energy**, China will work in concert with B&R countries to ensure security of cross-border oil and gas pipelines, build cross-border power supply networks and power transmission routes, and cooperate in regional power grid upgrading and transformation. **With regard to communications**, China will advance the

---

[7] Mu Hong, "Advancing the Belt and Road Initiative", *People's Daily*, December 11, 2015, p. 7. (穆虹:《推进"一带一路"建设》, 载《人民日报》2015 年 12 月 11 日, 第 7 版。)

construction of cross-border optical cables, transcontinental submarine optical cables and other communications trunk line networks, to create an "Information Silk Road".

4.3.3 Unimpeded Trade

Investment and trade cooperation is an important area in building B&R. It is also the key to accelerate the industrialization of B&R countries and realize balanced development for global economy. At the present stage, economic and trade cooperation is enhanced in three respects: investment and trade facilitation, international capacity and equipment manufacturing cooperation and resources and energy cooperation.

(1) *Investment and trade facilitation.* At the Boao Forum for Asia held in March 2015, President Xi Jinping held talks with representatives of entrepreneurs from China and foreign countries and he said that the Chinese government hoped the annual trade volume of China with B&R countries would exceed 2.5 trillion USD in about 10 years.[8] Nevertheless, there still exist investment and trade barriers, a lack of coordination in customs clearance, logistics, certification and standard, and trade protectionism and the so-called "national security review". For these reasons, China should push forward negotiations with B&R countries on free trade zones, investment protection agreements and double taxation avoidance agreements; boost bilateral and multilateral cooperation in the fields of customs, inspection and quarantine, certification and accreditation, standard measurement and statistical information; establish a "single-window" in border ports; facilitate mutual recognition of Authorized Economic Operators; and develop modern business models like cross-border e-commerce.

---

[8] Du Shangze and Zhao Minghao, "Chinese President Xi Jinping Holds Talks with Representatives of Chinese and Foreign Entrepreneur Attending the BFA Annual Conference 2015", *People's Daily*, March 30, 2015, p. 1.(杜尚泽、赵明昊:《习近平同出席博鳌亚洲论坛年会的中外企业家代表座谈》,载《人民日报》2015 年 3 月 30 日,第 1 版。)

(2) *International capacity and equipment manufacturing cooperation.* As Premier Li Keqiang have stated on many occasions, China is currently positioned in the middle of the global industrial chain, with a large amount of competitive industries and spare production capacity which are low in price. While a majority of developing countries are still in their initial stage of industrialization, aspiring for modern equipments in its infrastructure construction, some developed countries have entered the late stage of industrialization or the phase of postindustrialization, longing for export expansion for their high-end equipments. Enhancing the international capacity and equipment manufacturing cooperation not only contributes to the enlargement of the international market share of China's competitive industries and elevates the industrialization level of developing countries, but also spurs the export of core technologies and components from developed countries. It is indeed a new approach to achieve a triple-win situation in the South–South and the South–North cooperation. According to the *Guiding Opinions of the State Council of the People's Republic of China, on Promoting International Capacity and Equipment Manufacturing Cooperation* released in May 2015, China will work with developing countries with great equipment and capacity compatibility, strong desire for cooperation and good cooperation conditions and foundation, to promote cooperation in key industries, including steel, nonferrous metals, building materials, railways, electric power, chemical, textile, automobile, communications, construction machinery, aerospace, shipbuilding and marine engineering. Various cooperation modes—trade, contract project and investment—will be adopted, based on different characteristics of partner countries and industries. Facts show that industrial parks and industry cluster areas like overseas economic and trade cooperation zones and cross-border economic cooperation zones are precious experiences accumulated from China's reform and opening-up and full participation in economic globalization. They are also crucial platforms for Chinese enterprises to "go global" in recent years. Joint building of industrial parks helps B&R countries to develop much-needed production lines,

industrial systems and workers training program. It is also expected to increase taxes revenue and raise employment rate. Meanwhile, Chinese enterprises will have access to a broader overseas market and enjoy more guarantee and convenience in personnel security, tax preference, visa processing, infrastructure, transport and logistics.

(3) *Resources and energy cooperation.* China will deepen cooperation in the exploration and development of coal, oil, gas, metal, minerals and other conventional energy sources; advance cooperation in hydropower, nuclear power, wind power, solar power and other renewable, clean energy sources; and strengthen cooperation with key countries in the processing and conversion of energy and resources at or near places where they are exploited, so as to create an integrated industrial chain of energy and resource cooperation. The upstream industrial chain focuses on the oil and gas cooperation mainly in regions like Central Asia, Russia, the Middle East and Africa; the midstream cooperation centers around the connectivity construction of oil and gas pipeline networks; the downstream cooperation emphasizes the establishment, in both the resource-rich countries and resource-importing countries, of a series of environment-friendly overseas production bases, technology research and development bases and equipment manufacturing bases that give full play to the resource superiority in oil and gas chemical, coal chemical, potash fertilizer, steel and nonferrous metals, so as to develop six industrial parks in west China, Kazakhstan in Central Asia, Gwadar of Pakistan, the Middle East, the Far East region of Russia and Southeast Asia. In addition, we will set up and perfect oil and gas trading centers and develop a number of world-class transnational oil and gas companies to accelerate the "going global" process of energy equipment manufacturing and energy service enterprises.[9]

---

[9] Mu Hong, "Advancing the Belt and Road Initiative"; Wang Lu and Zhao Jing, "The Belt and Road Initiative Oil and Gas Cooperation Focuses on Six Fields", *China Energy News*, November 30, 2015, p. 13. (王璐、赵晶:《一带一路油气合作瞄准六大领域》, 载《中国能源报》2015 年 11 月 30 日, 第 13 版。)

4.3.4 *Financial Integration*

Financial integration is an important underpinning for implementing the Belt and Road Initiative. Without financial support, any cooperation can be a mission impossible. Specifically, the financial integration will be achieved in terms of investment and financing, currency circulation and financial security.

With regard to investment and financing, China will set up and put into operation new cooperation platforms such as the Asian Infrastructure Investment Bank, BRICS New Development Bank and the Silk Road Fund and conduct negotiation among related parties on establishing Shanghai Cooperation Organization (SCO) development bank and development fund; give full play to China–ASEAN Investment Cooperation Fund, China–CEE Investment Cooperation Fund and China-Eurasia Economic Cooperation Fund, strengthen practical cooperation of China-ASEAN Interbank Association and SCO Interbank Association and encourage China Development Bank and the Export–Import Bank of China to carry out bilateral and multilateral financial cooperation in the form of syndicated loans and bank credit; open and develop the bond market in Asia; and further expand the cooperation with policy banks, commercial banks and sovereign wealth funds in countries where the projects are located, and deepen the cooperation with other international financial institutions, sovereign wealth funds, industrial investment funds, insurance companies and risk capitals, to ensure financial guarantee for the construction of the Belt and Road.

With regard to currency circulation, China will enlarge the scope and scale of bilateral currency swap, settlement and direct trading with B&R countries; accelerate the development of Cross-border Inter-bank Payment System and further perfect the global RMB settlement system; use RMB as the main currency in foreign-related economic management, accounting and statistics and encourage the usage of RMB in outbound loans and investment; support the efforts of B&R countries and their companies and financial institutions to issue RMB bonds in China, and qualified Chinese financial institutions and companies to issue bonds in both Renminbi and foreign currencies abroad; advocate innovations in RMB-denominated offshore financial products, speed up the construction of offshore RMB market, and expand the RMB circulation in foreign countries; and encourage bank card clearing institutions and payment institutions to offer cross-border settlement service and cross-border payment service respectively, aiding developing countries along the Belt and Road in their financial infrastructure construction.

With regard to financial security, more efforts will be devoted in building a currency stability system and credit information system in Asia, improving the system of risk response and crisis management, building a regional financial risk early warning system, creating an exchange and cooperation mechanism of addressing cross-border risks and crises, and increasing cross-border exchange and cooperation between credit investigation regulators, credit investigation institutions and credit rating institutions.

4.3.5 *Closer People-to-People Ties*

People-to-people ties provide the public support for implementing the Belt and Road Initiative. History has proven that the people-to-people and cultural exchanges were the most important driving force for the growth of the ancient Silk Road. With communication and promotion only at the government level, the Initiative can by no means be carried out in a real sense in B&R countries, nor can it win long-term understanding and support from these countries. Previous lessons have shown that China put too much stake in high-level consultations and governmental relations for building its major cooperation projects abroad. A lack of grassroots support made it harder to protect China's overseas interests. Working on the grassroots may be slow to take effect. Nevertheless, it is the genuine "centennial project." Only when the general public in the relevant countries get involved and harvest benefits from the Initiative will it be possible to build the most extensive and solid mass foundation.

In terms of actors in people-to-people exchange, overseas students, volunteers, youth, women, the general public, nongovernmental organizations, legislative bodies, major political parties, political organizations, sister cities and think tanks are all involved in cementing the ties between China and relevant countries. What deserves mentioning is that the Chinese government is planning to expand the scale of student exchange with B&R countries, to promote cooperation in jointly running schools and provide 10,000 government scholarships to these countries every year.

In terms of exchange fields, the people-to-people bond will include cooperation and exchange in culture, academia, media, art, film and television, books, tourism, sports, health care, medicine, sci-tech innovation, environmental protection, talent cultivation, entrepreneurship training, vocational skills, social security and public welfare and charity. In the key cooperation field on sci-tech innovation, China will establish joint labs or research centers, international technology transfer centers and maritime cooperation centers with B&R countries, promote sci-tech personnel exchanges and cooperate in tackling key sci-tech problems.

In a word, the overall framework for jointly building the Belt and Road has been basically determined and a grand blueprint has been outlined. The fact that the Belt and Road Initiative is a universal, comprehensive cooperation initiative does not mean China will rush forward in all directions. Instead, abiding by the cooperation framework of "from point to area" and "step by step", China will further focus on the key routes (the six international economic corridors), key countries (friendly countries with solid industrial foundation, key geographical position and non-negligible political influence), key fields (infrastructure connectivity, international capacity and equipment manufacturing cooperation, resources and energy cooperation and people-to-people and cultural exchanges) and key projects (flagship projects with iconic demonstration effects), so as to actively and prudently promote the practical cooperation on the Belt and Road Initiative in an orderly manner.

5

Development Opportunities of the Belt and Road Initiative

As a major national development strategy and international coopera-tion proposal in the new era, the Belt and Road Initiative will bring multifaceted opportunities. As the cooperation framework gets clear, especially after the publication of *Vision and Actions on Jointly Building Silk Road Economic Belt and 21st-Century Maritime Silk Road*, the BRI will promote the development of the international community and China itself, benefiting governments, markets and ordinary people concurrently.

5.1 Opportunities for Global Development

The opportunities brought about by the Belt and Road Initiative lies in the fact that it will not only inject new energies into the sluggish global economy, but also effectively promote the connectivity and industrialization for all countries along the routes.

5.1.1 *Promoting Connectivity among B&R Countries*

Connectivity is an important precondition for B&R countries to promote economic development and international exchanges. That is why it is treated as a priority in building the Belt and Road. In November 2014, President Xi Jinping said at Dialogue on Strengthening Connectivity Partnership,

> The Belt and Road Initiative and the connectivity endeavor are compatible and mutually reinforcing. If the "Belt and Road" are likened to the two wings of a soaring Asia, then connectivity is like their arteries and veins.

How does China interpret the Belt and Road Initiative? President Xi Jinping pointed out,

> The connectivity we talk about today is not merely about building roads and bridges or making linear connection of different places on surface. More importantly, it should be a three-way combination of infrastructure, institutions and people-to-people exchanges. It is a wide-ranging and multi-dimensional connectivity network.[1]

Among the three elements, infrastructure connectivity is the most urgent task. For a long time, the outdated infrastructure hindered the economic take-off for countries along the routes. The landlocked countries far away from the sea and developing countries without convenient communications are not favored by capitals or industries. The five Central Asian countries at the junction of Asia and Europe have abundant natural resources. In total, they have a population of more than 60 million. However, Kyrgyzstan has only more than 400 km of railway, and what makes it even worse, it falls into two

---

[1] Xi Jinping, "Connectivity Spearheads Development and Partnership Enables Cooperation — Address at Dialogue on Strengthening Connectivity Partnership", *People's Daily*, November 9, 2014, p. 2. [习近平:《联通引领发展伙伴聚焦合作——在"加强互联互通伙伴关系"东道主伙伴对话会上的讲话》, 载《人民日报》2014 年 11 月 9 日, 第 2 版。]

Figure 5.1   Thanaleng Railway Station in Laos
Photographed by Mr. WANG Zhe, October 2015.

geographically disconnected parts: the North part and the South part. Without sea gates or railway network, the transportation in Kyrgyzstan mainly depends on its highway system. As the largest landlocked country, Kazakhstan still has many places where the hard-surfaced road is less than 60%. Before the China–Laos railway, Thanaleng is the only railway station in Laos and the railway starting from Nong Khai only covers 3.5 km in Laos (See Figure 5.1). Due to inefficient transportation, the logistics costs account for 25%–30% of Indonesian's gross domestic product (GDP). Domestic mango sells at more than 40 RMB per kg in Jakarta, almost the same as that of Vietnam mango sold in Shanghai. As an important shipping and logistic hub, Sri Lanka had an annual throughput capacity of only 4 million standard containers before China Merchants Port Holdings Company Limited helped to establish and operate the South Container Terminal at the Port of Colombo.

Inconvenient transportation, especially the land transportation, and high costs have always been the crucial problems plaguing trade and people-to-people exchange in Eurasia. At present, the majority of the trunk roads connecting China and B&R countries have unconnected sections, and many roads are inferior in quality and in poor conditions. According to statistics, the trade volume between Europe and Asia only takes up to 10% of the total trade volume of the two continents. The trade potential is far from being tapped. Relevant research also shows that the transportation cost and trade volume of a typical landlocked country is 50% higher and 60% lower than that of a coastal country. A 10% reduction in transportation cost means 25% increase in trade volume.[2] However, financing is a common issue for B&R countries. The existing international financing institutes cannot fill the huge capital gap.

In this sense, China's Belt and Road Initiative will provide invaluable opportunities for improving connectivity among countries along the route. China enjoys the largest foreign reserve, and the Asian Infrastructure Investment Bank (AIIB), the New Development Bank, Silk Road Fund and other infrastructure concessionary loans are set up with the aim of providing new financing channels for countries along the route. In the meantime, China, with rich experiences in infrastructure development, labor contracting, project management and others, is willing to share them with other developing countries.

China's first step, as planned, is to coordinate the BRI with the development strategies of relevant countries, establish financing platforms, and build cooperative relations with hub cities. The joint building of the Belt and Road will prioritize "six means of communication and multiple ports" — that is, enhancing the connectivity of rail, highways, seagoing transport, aviation, pipelines and aerospace integrated information network, and developing several pivotal ports — to build safe, convenient, green and effective international channels connecting China with B&R countries, and thus to develop six international economic corridors.[3] In the meantime, China will sign agreements with B&R countries to facilitate communication, trade and investment, unify various regulations and rules, so as to

---

[2] Asian Development Bank and Asian Development Bank Institute, *Infrastructure for a Seamless Asia*, Tokyo: Asian Development Bank Institute, 2009, p. 42.

[3] Mu Hong, "Advancing the Construction of the Belt and Road", *People's Daily*, December 11, 2015, p. 7. (穆虹:《推进"一带一路"建设》,载《人民日报》2015 年 12 月 11 日, 第 7 版。)

reduce the cost and time of cross-border flow of people, commodities and capitals.

The positive effects of connectivity are self-evident. According to Moody's report, the implementation of the BRI will probably have a revolutionary impact on South Asian and Southeast Asian countries with poor infrastructure. Among these countries, Bangladesh, Cambodia, Pakistan and Vietnam will probably benefit the most from infrastructure development. In the meantime, improved infrastructure will advance trade activities in Kazakhstan, Mongolia and other Central Asian countries.[4] The BRI will not only link landlocked countries with the sea, turning Central Asia into a convenient corridor between Asia and Europe, but also transform Central and East European countries, Thailand, Indonesia, Sri Lanka, Greece and other countries into regional and international trading and logistics hubs, reshaping the economic landscape in Eurasia or even of the world. In Africa, the "three networks and industrialization", namely African high-speed rail network, expressway network, regional airline network and industrialization in infrastructure, will vigorously promote local connectivity and lay a solid foundation for economic development. From April to May 2015, JoongAng Ilbo and Korea International Trade Association (KITA) conducted a field trip along the Silk Road Economic Belt, finding that the BRI will offer a great opportunity to improve the logistic environment for South Korea. A large amount of Korean goods can be transported from Chinese ports to Central Asia and Europe through the new Asian–European Land Bridge, and the China Railway Express to Europe will be the shortest logistic route between Korea and Europe.[5] At present, the practice of sea–rail combined transportation has been adopted in many Chinese ports, significantly simplifying custom clearance procedure. As a result, seamless transit between ships

---

[4] Wang Zichen, "Mu Di: The Belt and Road Initiative Has Positive Credit Impact on Emerging Market Economics and China", July 29, 2015, http://news.xinhuanet.com/politics/2015-07/29/c_1116075476.htm, log-in time: September 8, 2015. (王子辰:《穆迪: "一带一路"对新兴市场国家及中国具有正面信用影响》, 2015 年 7 月 29 日。)

[5] Chen Shangwen, "The Belt and Road Initiative Brings Opportunities to South Korea", *People's Daily*, June 4, 2015, p. 3. (陈尚文:《"一带一路"建设带给韩国机遇》, 载《人民日报》2015 年 6 月 4 日, 第 3 版。)

and rails can be achieved, greatly reducing business cost for import and export traders.

With the improved infrastructure and connectivity, developing countries along the routes are expected to attract more capitals and industries, whereas the developed countries will find more investing and trading opportunities. This is exactly the significance of the BRI as a public good offered by China to the whole world.

5.1.2 *Promoting the Industrialization in B&R Countries*

Industrialization is a shared dream for a majority of developing countries. At present, most of the countries along the routes are at the initial stage of industrialization. For these countries, the industrial value-added output accounts for about 30% of their GDP, and in most African countries, the manufacturing only contributes less than 15% to their GDP.[6] In the meantime, a report from the United Nations Conference on Trade and Development suggests that two-thirds of developing countries rely heavily on primary commodity export, and almost 50% of developing countries are increasingly dependent on the primary commodity export.[7] In recent years, due to the price slump of raw materials such as oil, metal and primary commodities like grains, some developing countries are experiencing severe fiscal and monetary downturns, and the North-South gap keeps widening.

Against such a background, developing countries are seeking economic transformation in an effort to change the old economic development model which is heavily oriented towards primary commodity export, and promoting industrialization as a national development strategy. For example, the African Union made it clear in *Agenda 2063* that the manufacturing will contribute at least 50% to GDP and employ more than 50% of newly added labor force. South Africa and

---

[6] Xu Huixi, "Good Time to Promote Sino-Africa Production Capacity Cooperation", *Economic Daily*, December 5, 2015, p. 6. (徐惠喜:《推进中非产能合作正当时》, 载《经济日报》2015 年 12 月 5 日, 第 6 版。)

[7] Chen Jian, "Most Developing Countries are Over Dependent on the Import of Primary Commodities", *Economic Daily*, July 10, 2015, p. 12. (陈建:《多数发展中国家过度依赖初级产品出口》, 载《经济日报》2015 年 7 月 10 日, 第 12 版。)

Ethiopia set industrialization as one of the major directions for its economic diversification. Many countries in Southeast Asia, Central Asia, South Asia and Latin America have listed industrialization as their middle and long-term development targets.

However, the global economic history after World War II showed that only very few developing countries, like China, have achieved industrialization painstakingly and moved towards the middle and high end of industrial value chain. The existing modes of North–South cooperation and South–South cooperation have failed to promote the comprehensive development for developing countries. Therefore, a large number of developing countries have long been trapped in the low end of industrial value chain. In fact, suffering from a weak industrial basis and a lack of professional talents, and backward infrastructure, most developing countries had no choice but to take the low value-added and high-polluting industries which have been abandoned by the developed countries.

As a highlight of China's economic diplomacy, international production capacity and equipment manufacturing cooperation tops the agenda of the BRI, which, as is expected by B&R countries, will bring about precious opportunities for them to achieve industrialization. Just as Ibraev Danil Tursunbekovich, deputy Minister of Economy of Kyrgyzstan at the time, said,

> We hope not only to revive the glory of ancient Silk Road, but also to absorb advanced production techniques, bringing long-term prosperity to the region. For a long time, we were just one segment of the industrial chain of former Soviet Union. After independence, we suffered a disconnect in the phases of raw material supply, production and consumption. Although we have engaged in global integration and Eurasian Union, we should establish a relatively complete industrial system, sending Kyrgyzstan products to the world. Meanwhile, we hope the Silk Road corridor will bring us and neighboring countries more low-price and fine-quality products.[8]

---

[8] Zhao Yining, "Vice Minister of Economy of Kirgizia: 'The Belt and Road Initiative' is an Important Opportunity", *21st Century Business Herald*, May 11, 2015, p. 6. (赵忆宁:《吉尔吉斯经济部副部长:"一带一路"战略是一次重要机遇》, 载《21 世纪经济报道》2015 年 5 月 11 日, 第 6 版。)

Since 1980s, production capacity transfered from western developed countries has played an important role for China's economic development. At present, China has entered the middle and late stage of industrialization, with complete industrial system, substantial advantageous industries and surplus capacity, cost-effective equipments and competence in comprehensive support service and engineering construction. In contrast to developed countries' strategy of industrial transfer and outbound investment, the international cooperation on industrial capacity and manufacturing production, advocated by China, lays emphasis on cultivating the development ability and industrial system for developing countries. In the meantime, such cooperation focuses on building a complete industrial chain in B&R countries, which is quite different from the "going global" or internationalized operation of China's enterprises in the past. Mr. Gu Dawei, director of Department of Foreign Capital and Overseas Investment in National Development and Reform Commission (NDRC), clearly stated at a regular press conference on May 20, 2015,

> The purpose of the production capacity cooperation is the export of industries and capacities. To export industries involves not only selling our products to other countries, but exporting our industries as a whole to different countries and helping them build more comprehensive industrial systems and production capacities. Therefore the key for international cooperation on industrial capacity and manufacturing production is to shift from the export of trade and products to that of industries and capacities.[9]

Based on "from point to area" strategy, China will direct its capitals and enterprises to countries along the six major international economic corridors, cooperate with them in building badly needed assembly lines, foreign industrial parks and industrial clusters, so as to

---

[9] The National Development and Reform Commission of PRC, "National Development and Reform Commission Introduces *'Guiding Opinions of the State Council on Promoting International Cooperation on Production Capacity and Equipment Manufacturing'* at Regular Press Conference", May 21, 2015, http://www.sdpc.gov.cn/xwzx/xwfb/201505/t20150520_692690.html, log-in time: May 21, 2015.(中国国家发改委:《国家发展改革委举行例行新闻发布会介绍<国务院关于推进国际产能和装备制造合作的指导意见>有关情况》, 2015 年 5 月 21 日。)

help establish local industrial systems and promote employment. China will comprehensively advance the "going global" strategy for its capitals, technologies, projects, standards, equipments and management experience with emphasis on key cooperation projects and high-end equipments such as high-speed rails and nuclear power. With technology transfer, joint operation, talents training, and others, China will help B&R countries cultivate their own industrial development capacities and industry professionals, and promote the development of relevant enterprises and supporting industries. In the meantime, the abundant resources and energy in countries along the route can be used as advantages to promote cooperation in energy processing and conversion at or near places where they are exploited, and formulate integrated industrial chains, helping host countries improve the added value of resources and turn the resources advantage into development impetus.

Such a cooperation mode, with its focus on cultivating development ability and establishing industrial system, will bring opportunities for developing countries along the routes to achieve industrialization. Different from the trade mode of "industrial products for raw materials", or the intergovernmental assistance programs, the international cooperation on industrial capacity and manufacturing production will have a deeper, wider and stronger influence. The developed countries will also find more investment opportunities in trilateral international production capacity cooperation advocated by China.

5.2 Opportunities for China

While promoting global development and win-win cooperation, the Belt and Road Initiative will bring multifaceted opportunities for China.

5.2.1 *Cultivating New Advantages for International Cooperation*

Most countries along the routes are developing countries with huge populations, large economic aggregates, considerable economic scales, and great potential. For a long time, trade has been the major driving force in bilateral cooperation between China and countries along the routes. Based on its strong industrial manufacturing capability and low-cost labor, China has been able to export Chinese-made products in great quantities to foreign countries, and in return, receives huge trade surplus, substantial resources and energy, and invaluable advanced technologies. Nevertheless, China remains in the middle and low end of global industry value chains. Although Chinese enterprises, during their "going global" process, have moved into areas of high added value, an overall layout of industrial chain is far from being complete in China.

At present, China has entered a critical period for economic upgrading, transformation and structural adjustment. On the one hand, with excess production capacity in certain industries, the supply side reform represents the trend in the "New Normal" phase. On the other hand, China possesses substantial capitals and has formed a strong global competitive edge in some industries such as infrastructure construction, equipment manufacturing, information and communication, and new energies. Due to lingering effects of the financial crisis, economic recovery in developed countries has been sluggish, and developing countries have been suffering from price slump of bulk commodities such as resources and energy — another blow on their already fragile economy. Against such a backdrop, China's import and export are shrinking, and its traditional economic cooperation mode hits a bottleneck.

The implementation of the BRI is expected to bring about new opportunities for China to promote economic transformation and upgrading, especially to cultivate new advantage for outbound cooperation. With advantages in capitals and engineering and construction, China will focus on connectivity and industrial capacity cooperation, and make joint efforts with countries along the routes to build infrastructure projects, assembly lines, industrial parks and clusters. On the one hand, it will help achieve resources integration and technological upgrading and updating, accelerate the "going global" process for China's capitals, industrial capacity, equipments, technologies, products, labor service, standards, and even RMB, and help industrial surplus capacity to be absorbed and strong industries to be distributed abroad. On the other hand, it will enormously improve infrastructure, industrial structure and trading conditions for countries along the routes, and also improve employment, living standard and income. Objectively, it will provide opportunities for China to continuously expand export and move up the global industrial value chains.

5.2.2 *Accelerating RMB Globalization*

The globalization of RMB will have strategic and symbolic significance for China to have a bigger say in global economic governance. As to financial integration of the BRI, besides expanding financing channels and upholding financial security, accelerating RMB globalization is another important aspect. Through currency swap, cross-border trade settlement and offshore RMB center in recent years, RMB has been increasingly gaining ground in global financial system. With the advancement of BRI, RMB is expected to receive more attention from countries along the routes.

It is stated in the *Vision and Action* that the scope and scale of bilateral currency swap and settlement with B&R countries will be expanded. While intensifying financial cooperation with UK, France, Germany and other European Union (EU) nations, China can apply RMB settlement for bulk commodities such as resources, energy and grains experimentally in ASEAN, Russia, Central Asia, Mongolia, Africa and other countries and regions along the routes. With an edge in equipments, engineering and others fields, China can encourage its enterprises to promote RMB settlement for major equipments export in energy exploiting and development projects and infrastructure projects.

In the meantime, China may expand channels for RMB direct investments in countries along the routes. For example, it may encourage RMB or specialized RMB funds to directly invest in infrastructure, resources and energy development projects in countries along the routes, establish specialized RMB production capacity cooperation funds to facilitate international production capacity cooperation, including overseas industrial parks and clusters. In accordance, China can offer RMB loans to countries along the routes, especially developing countries, for them to procure Chinese commodities, equipments, engineering and labor. Since the debts must be paid in RMB, and B&R countries are usually major exporters of raw materials and bulk commodities, such a practice will also enhance RMB settlement in trade of bulk commodities.

The *Vision and Action* also points out, China will support the efforts of governments of B&R countries and their companies and financial institutions with good credit rating to issue RMB bonds in China, and qualified Chinese financial institutions and companies are encouraged to issue bonds in both Renminbi and foreign currencies outside China. This will reinforce RMB in cross-border financing, and accelerate the development of RMB-denominated bonds market.

5.2.3 *Generating New Dividends for Local Development*

Local authorities at various levels are the major driving force for and implementor of the Belt and Road Initiative. As a national strategy with top-level designing and large-scale influence, the BRI is expected to generate new "development dividends" for 31 provinces, municipalities, and autonomous regions plus Xinjiang Production and Construction Corps and even Hong Kong, Macao and Taiwan.

On the whole, since infrastructure connectivity stands as the priority of the Belt and Road Initiative, and infrastructure construction is an effective measure to promote economic development, enlarge employment and consume excess industrial capacities, local governments are expected to set off another upsurge of infrastructure investment. *Vision and Actions* also lays down arrangements for local authorities to accelerate infrastructure construction, including improving the railway links connecting Heilongjiang province with Russia and the regional railway network; advancing the construction of an Eurasian high-speed transport corridor linking Beijing and Moscow; building an international corridor in Guangxi opening to the ASEAN region; advancing the construction of an international transport corridor connecting Yunnan with neighboring countries; strengthening the port construction of coastal cities such as Shanghai, Tianjin,

Ningbo-Zhoushan, Guangzhou, Shenzhen, Zhanjiang, Shantou, Qingdao, Yantai, Dalian, Fuzhou, Xiamen, Quanzhou, Haikou and Sanya, and strengthening the functions of international hub airports such as Shanghai and Guangzhou; supporting inland cities such as Zhengzhou and Xi'an in building airports and international land ports. Apparently, these arrangements will serve as important basis for local authorities to scale-up investment in infrastructures.

As to specific regions, the border areas will further enhance sub-regional cooperation with neighboring countries. For example, the northeastern regions of China have been in economic slowdown in recent years and lack impetus for rejuvenating the traditional industrial base. By fully integrating itself in the construction of China–Mongolia–Russia Economic Corridor, the region is expected to embrace more development opportunities. The western regions of China, which used to lag behind in economic growth, have emerged as the frontier opening to the West since China's development of its west is a major orientation of the BRI. Judging from the fact that the Office of the Leading Group for the Belt and Road Initiative was set up under the Department of Western Region Development of the NDRC, the western regions will possibly obtain policy preferences and more investments in the future. The large-scale development of the western regions would usher in the "2.0" era. Their rich resources in cultural tourism resources are expected to be further explored. At the end of December 2015, in order to set the role of border areas in supporting the construction of the BRI into full play, the State Council issued *Opinions on Several Policies for Supporting the Development and Opening-Up of Major Border Areas*, outlining a multifaceted work arrangements. The coastal regions, especially major ports, will be pacesetters and main forces in the 21st-Century Maritime Silk Road. They will receive more support for their pilot implementation of the innovative and open economic models, besides embracing new opportunities in maritime economy, foreign trade and industrial investment.

As to specific provinces, *Vision and Actions* has identified Xinjiang and Fujian as two core areas, whose importance is self-evident. Predictably, both provinces, including Xinjiang Production and

Construction Corps, will receive far more policy and resources supports than other provinces.

Besides the two core areas, the comparative advantages of other regions will be fully leveraged. Ningxia will continue to play the role as a cultural bond between China and the Arab-Muslim world, by building the Inland Opening-up Pilot Economic Zone. Shanghai's targets of building the "four centers", namely the international economic center, financial center, shipping center and trade center, fall in line with the Belt and Road Initiative. If the Shanghai Cooperation Organization (SCO) Development Bank would locate its headquarters in Shanghai, as the new development bank of BRICS did, more weight would be added to the city as an international financial center. Hainan, as an international tourism island, will open wider to the world. Zhejiang will continue its efforts in establishing the maritime economy development demonstration zone and Zhoushan Archipelago New Area. Below the provincial level, inland and coastal node cities and development cooperation zones, such as Qianhai in Shenzhen, Nansha in Guangzhou, Hengqin in Zhuhai, Pingtan in Fujian, and famous hubs along the ancient Silk Road, will also find their opportunities.

What is worth mentioning is that the BRI will explore new space for Hong Kong, Macao, and Taiwan to be involved in global economic cooperation. With advantages in their political and financial systems, and a high level of globalization, Hong Kong and Macao are expected to contribute positively to the Belt and Road Initiative. Taiwan, with a sluggish economy, has long passed the era of so-called "Four Asian Tigers", and has lost its developing orientation in internal political rivalries. If Taiwan could have a clear understanding of itself and adjust its mentality, it is welcomed to get a free ride in the building of the Belt and Road to expand its markets in countries along the routes.

5.3 Opportunities for the Market

Enterprises are both the contributors and beneficiaries of the Belt and Road Initiative. Since the proposal of the Initiative, especially the release of *the Vision and Actions,* various industries, enterprises and stocks industries, enterprises and stocks that are related with this initiative have been gaining momentum. Opportunities are created for Chinese enterprises as well as companies in B&R countries and developed countries. For example, transportation facilitation, "single window", mutual recognition of an authorized economic operator (AEO), and reduction of non-tariff barriers will help enterprises save time and cost in international trade. In December 2015, Foreign and Commonwealth Office of UK and the China–Britain Business Council jointly released a report, *A Role for British Companies in Developing China's New Initiative,* which concluded that the BRI will provide multiple opportunities for British companies to develop third-party markets jointly with their Chinese counterparts. The British and Chinese enterprises may start cooperation in infrastructure, financial and professional services, advanced manufacturing, transportation and logistics.[10] Some industries will be taken as examples to elaborate on the market opportunities arisen from the B&R.

5.3.1 *Financial Industry*

In promoting the Belt and Road Initiative, the financial industry is indispensable for infrastructure development, financial and trade cooperation, industrial investment, resources and energy development, maritime cooperation, and cultural and people-to-people exchanges. Rising people-to-people and business exchanges between China and B&R countries have resulted in growing demands of Chinese and foreign financial institutions for cross-border currency exchange, settlement, financing and guarantee. At present, many policy-based and commercial banks have established huge project reserves for the BRI, and innovated cross-border financing modes in accordance with project requirements. The *Vision and Action* points

---

[10] Jiang Huadong, "The Belt and Road Initiative Brings New Opportunities for Sino-British Economic and Trade Cooperation", *Economic Daily*, December 11, 2015, p. 4.(蒋华栋:《"一带一路"为中英经贸合作带来新机遇》, 载《经济日报》2015 年 12 月 11 日, 第 4 版。)

out, it will "support the efforts of governments of B&R countries and their companies and financial institutions with good credit-rating to issue Renminbi bonds in China. Qualified Chinese financial institutions and companies are encouraged to issue bonds in both Renminbi and foreign currencies outside China, and use the funds thus collected in B&R countries." In addition, Chinese banks will embrace new opportunities for cross-border RMB business in the process of RMB globalization.

5.3.2 *Infrastructure Construction*

Infrastructure connectivity is a priority area of building the Belt and Road. Many countries along the routes are facing growing demands for infrastructure upgrading or construction — vast opportunities for infrastructure construction enterprises. At present, Chinese enterprises have participated in the construction of ports, airports, express ways and railways in many countries, and accumulated rich experiences in project planning, designing, construction, operation and management. At the same time, with advantage in domestic capital and the establishment of various financing platforms, infrastructure engineering enterprises will enjoy more capital support while expanding overseas business. What is worth mentioning is that infrastructure construction, as the comprehensive carrier of cargo, technology and service trade, is expected to promote the export of production capacity, equipment and labor and the development of relevant industries including transportation, communication and financing.

5.3.3 *Industries with Strong Production Capacities*

Many countries along the Belt and Road are currently at the initial stage of industrialization and urbanization. The strong desire for infrastructure upgrading and construction brings about substantial demands for industrial capacity. Strong (sometimes excess) production capabilities in China are welcomed in many developing countries. It is calculated that 100 million RMB investments in railway construction will approximately result in demand of 3,330 tons steel.

Infrastructure construction will exert enormous pulling effect on steel demand along the Belt and Road.[11] Since infrastructure connectivity and international industrial capacity cooperation are the two focuses of the BRI, both will bring new opportunities for enterprises with strong production capacities to go global.

5.3.4 *Equipment Manufacturing*

So far, a comprehensive industrial system for equipment manufacturing, with complete industrial categories, advanced technology and supporting technology, has emerged in China. Boasting apparent advantages in price, quality, construction period, and maintenance service, China's equipment manufacturing industry has established numerous overseas branches and R&D centers. High-speed rail and nuclear power, which enjoy government support and promotion, have become the typical epitome of Chinese manufacturing going global. According to authoritative surveys, railway facilities in South America, Middle and East Europe and Russian-speaking countries and territories are due for upgrading, and the demand for locomotives, freight trains and passenger trains in Africa is on the rise. Many countries have set high-speed rail as a priority in transportation development. In 2018, the global rail market will possibly be valued at 190 billion Euros.[12] Statistics also show that 25 countries along the routes have plans for developing nuclear power, with approximately 140 nuclear power units and more than 1.2 trillion dollars' investment.[13] With the

---

[11] Chong Hua, "Hebei NPC and CPPCC Discuss about the Overcapacity Going Out via the Belt and Road Initiative", January 13, 2015, http://www.yicai.com/news/4062672.html, log-in time: May 8, 2015.(重华:《河北"两会"热议"一带一路"过剩产能借势走出去》, 2015 年 1 月 13 日。)

[12] Ministry of Commerce of PRC, "Ministry of Commerce Held News Briefing about Railway Equipment Export", February 5, 2015, http://www.mofcom.gov.cn/article/ae/slfw/201502/20150200889819.shtml, log-in time: May 8, 2015. (中国商务部:《商务部举行我国铁路设备出口情况新闻吹风会》, 2015 年 2 月 5 日。)

[13] Zhu Xuerui, "China Ranks among the Countries with Best Nuclear Power", *China Energy News*, May 25, 2015, p. 17.(朱学蕊:《中国跻身世界核电第一方阵》, 载《中国能源报》2015 年 5 月 25 日, 第 17 版。)

advancement of the BRI, some top-ranking equipment manufacturing industries, including automobiles, ships, machinery, power generators, and engineering equipments, will also embrace new opportunities.

5.3.5 *Resources and Energy Industry*

Countries along the routes are rich in resources and energy, yet lacking in advanced equipments and infrastructure, which creats important opportunities for relevant Chinese enterprises. As to the oil and gas industry, being incapable of oil exploration, production, transportation and processing, many oil-producing countries along the routes have to import oil. Mr. Lu Ruquan, a scholar in energy strategy, pointed out that apart from investing in oil and gas projects, Chinese enterprises could also make a foray into oil refining and petrochemical industry, technical service, equipment manufacturing, and energy finance. In particular, the export of equipments or building of local equipment bases will help popularize Chinese petroleum industry standards — an enhancement of the initiative, voice and profiting ability for China.[14] As to the power industry, countries in Southeast Asia, South Asia and Central Asia suffer varying degrees of power shortage, and one-third of African populations are still in need of sufficient electrical lighting. In Pakistan, an electricity crisis has been severely affecting both industrial and domestic consumption. Pakistan has been slow in exploiting hydropower, wind power and solar power despite their richness. As a result, nationwide power failures occur frequently during summer peak hours. At present, Chinese enterprises, with advantages in power equipments, planning, engineering, operation and maintenance, are capable of taking more overseas power projects. In the meantime, according to the *Vision and Actions*, the BRI aims at increasing cooperation in the exploration and development of coal, oil, gas, metal minerals and other conventional energy sources, and advancing cooperation in hydropower, nuclear power, wind power,

---

[14] Lu Ruquan *et al.*, Petroleum and the Belt and Road Initiative. Beijing: Petroleum Industry Press, 2015, pp. 6–8. (陆如泉等:《"一带一路"话石油》, 北京: 石油工业出版社, 2015 年, 第6–8页。)

solar power and other clean, renewable energy sources. What is worth mentioning is that, with continuous development of solar power and wind power, China is becoming the largest renewable energy investor. Relevant enterprises are expected to become the main force in building an environment-friendly Silk Road.

5.3.6 *Information and Communication Industry*

Information and communication is a key segment of infrastructure connectivity. After decades of independent innovation and practical development, China's information and communication industry are leading the world in maturity of technical patent and industrial chains. Huawei, ZTE Corporation, CMCC, China Unicom and other excellent information and communication enterprises and optical fiber and optical cable suppliers have already made their way into the markets in countries along the routes and are providing various services ranging from equipment, technology and operation to comprehensive solutions. The *Vision and Actions* states that the Initiative will "jointly advance the construction of cross-border optical cables and other communications trunk line networks, improve international communications connectivity, and create an Information Silk Road." Also, the Initiative will "build bilateral cross-border optical cable networks at a quicker pace, plan transcontinental submarine optical cable projects, and improve spatial (satellite) information passageways to expand information exchanges and cooperation". Meanwhile, *the Infrastructure Construction Plan to Promote Connectivity with Neighboring Countries*, which was formulated under the guidance of the Ministry of Industry and Information Technology, makes further arrangements for building a "digital Silk Road". All these efforts will bring new opportunities for information and communication enterprises. What is worth mentioning is that the BRI will promote the internationalization of China's BeiDou Navigation Satellite System (BDS). So far, the BDS has established a relatively complete industrial system covering basic products, application terminals and global positioning system (GPS) service. By 2020, the BDS is projected to provide global users with geopositioning and will be valued at 400 billion RMB.

5.3.7 *Cross-Border E-Commerce*

As a new business mode for international trade, cross-border e-commerce will facilitate global exchange of goods. At present, among 110 million netizens in the West Asia and North Africa, 30 million have experiences of online shopping. Russia has 70 million internet users — the largest internet population in Europe. Chinese e-commerce platforms, represented by Alibaba, have already sped up in deploying and operating cross-border e-commerce platforms. According to statistics, the gross merchandise value (GMV) of Chinese cross-border e-commerce stood at approximately 4.2 trillion RMB in 2014, a 33.3% year-on-year growth. Export accounted for 85.4% of the total GMV, and Business-to-business (B2B) took up 93.5%.[15] With the advancement of the Belt and Road Initiative, cross-border e-commerce will step onto a bigger stage. Moreover, with the Chongqing–Xinjiang–Europe International Railway and other China–Europe freight trains being put into operation, the transportation cost and time will be reduced, and the transfer rate of import from Europe will double, which will be of great help to relevant enterprises.[16]

5.3.8 *Marine Industry*

In recent years, the gross ocean product (GOP) is growing at an average annual rate of 11% and is expected to reach 3 trillion USD by 2020. The *Vision and Actions* puts forward that it will actively promote cooperation in marine-product farming, deep-sea fishing, aquatic product processing, seawater desalination, marine biopharmacy, ocean engineering technology, environmental protection industries, marine tourism and other fields. As a key part of 21st-Century Maritime Silk Road, marine industry will have a bright future.

---

[15] Zhu Long and Han Xu, "The Belt and Road Initiative Promotes New Modes of Commodity Trading across Borders", *People's Daily Overseas Edition*, October 16, 2015, p. 9. (祝龙、韩煦:《"一带一路"助力大宗商品跨境交易新模式》, 载《人民日报海外版》2015 年 10 月 16 日, 第 9 版。)

[16] Gao Jianghong, "Chongqing-Xinjiang-Europe International Railway to Drive Cross-border E-commerce ", *21st Century Business Herald*, June 29, 2015, p. 11. (高江虹:《跨境电商首搭"渝新欧" 掘金重庆一带一路》, 载《21世纪经济报道》2015 年 6 月 29 日, 第 11 版。)

5.3.9 *Culture and Tourism*

There are very rich and diversified resources in culture and tourism in B&R countries. Constrained by transportation, visa, capital and natural environment, such resources have not been fully tapped. It is estimated that more than 150 million Chinese tourists will go to countries along the route in the next five years, driving tourism consumption to more than 200 billion USD. In the meantime, China is expected to attract 85 million visitors from B&R countries, generating 110 billion USD.[17] Due to high popularity and acceptability of the "Silk Road", the cultural and tourism industries developed under such a concept will embrace an unprecedented opportunity for future development.

5.4 Opportunities for Ordinary People

As a global and regional public good provided by China, the Belt and Road Initiative will bring about changes and benefits to people in both China and countries along the routes.

5.4.1 *Daily life*

The outdated infrastructures in transportation, energy and communication have caused daily life troubles in many countries along the routes. For example, roads in Jakarta, Indonesian capital, are in horrible conditions, causing severe traffic conjestions. It usually takes people 1 hour to drive less than 5 km. Rosita, who lives in the suburb of Jakarta, has to leave home at 5:30 am and leave office at 7:30 pm, just to avoid the peak hour in the morning and evening. In Pakistan, power shortage has been a long-term problem. During summer, the daily power failure lasts 12 hours in Islamabad, and the figure in most rural and mountain areas jumps to 20 hours. Mohammed·Han, a student living in the mountain areas in Kashmir, has to travel more than 5 km to get home after school, and the first thing he does at home is to finish the homework before sunset. The

---

[17] Qian Chunxian, "China Depicts the Belt and Road Tourism Blueprint", June 19, 2015, http://news.xinhuanet.com/politics/2015-06/19/c_1115673270.htm, log-in time: May 8, 2015. (钱春弦等:《中国描摹"一带一路"旅游发展蓝图》, 2015 年 6 月 19 日。)

photo which was awarded the World Press Photo of the year 2014 depicts a group of African migrants on the shore of Djibouti City at night, raising their phones in an attempt to catch an inexpensive signal from neighboring Somalia.

The BRI will prioritize infrastructure connectivity. In China, local authorities at different levels are launching or are about to launch a series of infrastructure projects. In B&R countries, people will be benefiting from the implementation of connectivity projects, thanks to China's strong capacity in infrastructure engineering and various financing platforms such as AIIB, the New Development Bank, Silk Road Fund and European Bank for Reconstruction and Development (EBRD). Take Pakistan as an example, the energy projects are a focus of China–Pakistan Economic Corridor. The power projects contracted by Chinese enterprises, with short construction period, can ensure early harvest, meeting the urgent needs of Pakistan people. In Africa, with the advancement of three transport networks, namely high-speed rail, express way and regional airline networks, local people will see positive changes in their daily lives.

5.4.2 *Employment*

Domestically, the Belt and Road Initiative, which involves numerous fields, projects and investments, is expected to create vast job opportunities. For B&R countries, cooperations in infrastructure, finance and trade, industrial investment, and resources and energy development will also increase local employment. Since Chinese companies are increasingly laying emphasis on social responsibilities and localized operation, they will ramp up local recruitment and employee training.

5.4.3 *Consumption*

The *Vision and Action* states that, the Initiative will devote efforts in removing investment and trade barriers, jointly opening free trade areas, and developing cross-border e-commerce. This means that in the future, people in China and B&R countries will be able to buy more diversified, fresh and inexpensive foreign goods. It is worth mentioning that the financial cooperation advocated by the BRI will also bring benefits. With the globalization of RMB, Chinese consumers are expected to make payments increasingly in RMB or with Union Pay, so as to save the surcharge caused by multiple currency exchanges.

5.4.4 *Education*

According to the *Vision and Action*, China will "send more students to each other's countries, and promote cooperation in jointly running schools. China provides 10,000 government scholarships to B&R countries every year". Students in B&R countries will have more chances to study in China — a new option besides domestic education and studying abroad in developed countries like the U.S. and European countries. Accordingly, Chinese students will have more chances to visit and study in B&R countries. But currently, they usually go to developed countries like the U.S., European countries, Japan and South Korea for higher education. In alignment with the Belt and Road Initiative, local governments have put forward their own strategies, which also involve cooperating with B&R countries to jointly launch education programs or encouraging local schools to build branch campuses in countries along the routes. Thus, more opportunities are open to ordinary students in both China and B&R countries.

5.4.5 *Academic Research*

The Belt and Road Initiative will bring unprecedentedly wide space and precious opportunities for academic research. Chinese scientists or social science scholars of international economy, international politics, country or regional study didn't have the opportunities, platforms or funds to conduct field work and academic exchanges in developing countries. In the future, guided and bolstered by the Initiative, Chinese scholars will increasingly travel to countries along the routes, especially the developing countries. Diversity and richness in their political and social norms, cultural and natural environment, economic development modes, ethnics and religion will greatly expand the horizon of Chinese scholars. Through intensified academic cooperation, scholars in China and B&R countries can make their voice better heard in the international academic circle, breaking the academic monopoly by Western scholars. What is worth mentioning is that Chinese enterprises, during their going global to the developing countries along the routes, are in urgent demand of various information of the host countries, which will offer great opportunities to relative think tanks and their researchers.

5.4.6 *Culture and Art*

According to the *Vision and Actions*, China and B&R countries "should hold culture years, arts festivals, film festivals, TV weeks and book fairs in each other's countries; cooperate on the production and translation of fine films, radio and TV programs; and jointly apply for and protect World Cultural Heritage sites". Therefore, Chinese people will have more access to foreign culture and art shows, culture relic's exhibition, TV programs and books. In the meantime, the Initiative will also bring more Chinese culture and art products to countries along the routes.

5.4.7 *Tourism*

The building of the Belt and Road expands the landscape of tourism industry. Such a prospect is welcomed by the general public. Due to constraints in transportation, climate and environment, the tourism resources in western China and B&R countries were not fully tapped. Moreover, issues like expense and visa are also possible barriers when people travel abroad. For example, Lake Issyk-Kul in the east of Kyrgyzstan, one of the largest lakes in the world, is attractive to tourists, with blue and boundless water, white and crystal clouds and snows covering the top of surrounding mountains. Unfortunately, no direct flight between Beijing and Bishkek was available in the past. An increasing number of people dream of traveling along the route that Xuan Zang had covered in his 17-year overland journey to India in the Tang dynasty. However, only a few can make it due to various constraints. Many Chinese people want to take a train to Europe, and enjoy the beautiful sceneries along the route, and so far, the only passenger train available is the one between Beijing and Moscow. The *Vision and Action* states that China will jointly create competitive international tourist routes and products with Silk Road features; and make it more convenient to apply for tourist visa in B&R countries; quicken our pace in improving aviation infrastructure; and advance the construction of an Eurasian high-speed transport corridor linking Beijing and Moscow. Predictably, tourist programs in countries along the routes will be more convenient, more diversified and less costly.

What is worth mentioning is that cruise tourism, as an emerging recreational way, is an important part of the 21st-Century Maritime Silk Road. In recent years, Shanghai, Tianjin, Xiamen, Sanya, Zhoushan, Qingdao and other port cities have successively launched the construction of cruise home ports. Shenzhen, Guangzhou, Beihai, Yantai, Haikou and Dalian will join the line soon. A series of international routes are being opened along the 21st-Century Maritime Silk Road. In the future, Chinese tourists will be able to take a cruise tour to Malaysia, Singapore, Indonesia, Sri Lanka and even the Mediterranean Sea. Accordingly, countless tourists from countries along the routes will also visit China by cruise.

The BRI will bring multifaceted opportunities. With the advancement of comprehensive and practical cooperation, potential opportunities will turn into actual results. China, B&R countries, companies, and ordinary people will be direct beneficiaries. The Initiative will manifest itself increasingly as a public good and development platform. However, such a transformation will by no means be automatic or easy. Setbacks and risks are also involved. A maximum use of opportunities and minimum damage of risks can only be achieved with wisdom, patience and cooperation of all the related parties.

Chapter

6

Government Actions on Building the Belt and Road

Ever since the Belt and Road Initiative was proposed by President Xi Jinping in 2013, it has become top agenda of the Chinese governments at all levels. From the central government to local authorities, a series of plans, arrangements and measures have been launched. The grand blueprint of the Belt and Road Initiative is turning into concrete actions.

6.1 Central Government

At the central government level, the Leading Group for the Belt and Road Initiative led by Zhang Gaoli, the standing Deputy Premier, was set up. **The National Development and Reform Commission (NDRC), the Ministry of Commerce (MOFCOM) and the Ministry of Foreign Affairs (MOFA)** take the lead and coordinate the implementation of the B&R. They jointly formulated and issued *the Vision and Actions on Jointly Building Silk Road Economic Belt and 21st-Century Maritime Silk Road*, and are active in guiding, supporting and servicing all sectors of government and local authorities in aligning their own agendas with the BRI.

Among the three government organs, the NDRC, under which the Leading Group for Advancing the Belt and Road Initiative was established, plays a bigger role in leading and coordinating. Several subgroups were set up under the Leading Group Office, namely: Comprehensive Coordination group, Silk Road group, Maritime Silk Road group and Foreign Cooperation group.[1] Currently, **the NDRC** gets involved in almost all important matters in building the B&R, and approves the docking schemes for all sectors of government and local authorities. According to Li Pumin, the NDRC's Secretary-General, the priority areas for advancing the construction of the B&R will include: (1) actively advancing the iconic projects; (2) steadily building the "six corridors and multiple harbors"; (3) advancing cooperation with key countries and creating cooperation models in the B&R construction; (4) enhancing international communication; (5) coordinating and combining domestic resources into a single driving force.[2]

What's worth mentioning is that, **the Office of Central Leading Group for Comprehensively Deepening Reforms, the Office of the Central Leading Group for Financial and Economic Affairs, the Office of the Central Leading Group for Foreign Affairs** occupy a central place in top-level decision-making respectively on political, economic and foreign affairs. Their chiefs are included in the Leading Group for the Belt and Road Initiative. Obviously, the three "super offices" will play an immeasurably important role in advancing the BRI, particularly in terms of providing macro-guidance and overall coordination.

In light of the unified deployment of the central government, the relevant central organs have generally established their leadership

---

[1] Nie Ou and Gong Wanru, "What Has the Belt and Road Initiative Already Accomplished", *Economy & Nation Weekly*, no. 26, 2015. (聂欧、龚婉茹:《"一带一路"已做了什么》, 载《财经国家周刊》2015 年第 26 期。)

[2] China.com, "National Development and Reform Commission Held Press Conference on Macro-economic Performance", October 15 2015, http://www.china.com.cn/zhibo/2015-10/15/content_36809100.html(中国网:《发改委就宏观经济运行数据举行发布会》, 2015 年 10 月 15 日。)

mechanisms, added the Belt and Road Initiative into their top priorities, and formulated policy planning for specific programs. In order to highlight the importance, comprehensiveness and synergy of the BRI, the discussion below will focus on the "Five-connectivity" (connectivity of policy, infrastructure, trade, finance and people). We will make a reference to all sorts of publicized information and summarize the deployments and actions launched by each central and state organ concerning the BRI. However, it should be pointed out that their work has overlapped in all aspects of the "five-connectivity". Such a classification is made largely for the convenience of writing and understanding.

6.1.1 *Policy Coordination*

Ministry of Foreign Affairs. The MOFA, as a specialized agency under the State Council in charge of foreign affairs and execution of foreign policies, is a major working organ to coordinate policies concerning the Belt and Road Initiative. The MOFA, via bilateral and multilateral platforms, and on numerous occasions — both at home or abroad, interpret the vision, road map and actions of the BRI to countries along the routes, international organizations and foreign ambassadors in China; clarify misunderstandings on the BRI; and promote the signing of cooperation documents and MOUs on jointly building the B&R. Meanwhile, the Chinese embassies and consulates overseas also take their share of responsibility to explain relevant policies to governments, major parties and mainstream media in countries along the routes.

International Department, Central Committee of CPC. It is the major functional organization responsible for promoting the party's external relations and inter-party communication. Its work include elaborating and interpreting the Belt and Road Initiative to major parties, foreign ambassadors and international organizations of the countries along routes; enhancing mutual trust and reduce doubt; and seeking common grounds in development strategies.

In addition, other ministries and commissions such as the NDRC and the Ministry of Commerce also play a role in policy coordinating, with governments of the B&R countries, international organizations and foreign institutions in China, as well as in promoting development strategies, shared interests and the alignment of cooperation projects.

6.1.2 *Connectivity of Infrastructure*

Ministry of Transport (MOT). The connectivity in transport is the key of infrastructure connectivity. In April of 2015, the spokesperson of the MOT stated that the Ministry would align with the Belt and Road Initiative in three aspects: (1) coordinating the 13th Five Year Plan of transport industry with the connectivity programs of neighboring countries to jointly advance the construction of major international routes; (2) focusing on key passageways, junctions and projects of transport infrastructure to create international trunk passageways featuring smoothness and interconnectivity both at home and abroad. With the priority assigning to linking up unconnected road sections and removing transport bottlenecks, the Ministry would attach great importance to the construction of China–Europe railways such as Chongqing–Xinjiang–Europe railway, Wuhan–Xinjiang–Europe railway and Yiwu–Xinjiang–Europe railway; speed up the construction of international road transportation and land–water transportation channels connecting China with Myanmar, Laos and Thailand, Vietnam, and Mogolia and Russia; identify priority areas and key projects together with countries along the routes; advance the construction of both ongoing and new infrastructure projects on railway, road, water supply and air transportation; (3) vigorously encouraging transport enterprises to go global and thus materializing the upgrading and transformation of relevant industries.[3] In June 2015, the Ministry of Transport reviewed and adopted *the Belt and Road Initiative Implementation Plan (Draft)*. Publicized information shows that the Plan includes the following aspects: overall layout of transport

---

[3] Ministry of Transport of PRC, "The Second Regular Press Conference in 2015", April 16, 2015, http://www.mot.gov.cn/zhuzhan/wangshangzhibo/2015second/index.html (中国交通运输部:《2015 年度第二次例行新闻发布会》, 2015 年 4 月 16 日。)

planning, development of major corridors, milestone projects, transport facilitation, multiplatform cooperation, bilateral relations and government guidance in the B&R. In early December, Yang Chuantang, the Minister of Transport, in his address at the Central Party School, pointed out that in order to serve the Belt and Road Initiative, the Ministry of Transport would endeavor to advance the construction of international land transport routes, improve maritime strategic passageways, promote international transport facilitation, and actively expand international aviation network and postal service network.[4] The Ministry of Transportation, representing the Chinese government, signed more than 130 bilateral, multilateral and regional transportation agreements with B&R countries, including railway, road, marine, air and postal cooperation contracts, such as the *SCO Intergovernmental Agreement on Creation of Beneficial Conditions for International Road Transportation* and the *China-ASEAN Marine Transportation Agreement.*

National Railway Administration (NRA). Its responsibilities cover the following major aspects: deepening and enhancing China's cooperation with neighboring countries on railway construction projects; strengthening communication and exchanges with institutions such as the International Organization for Standardization; promoting intergovernmental cooperation and exchanges on railway transport, providing robust support for the "going global" strategy of China's railway.

Civil Aviation Administration of China (CAAC). It is working on a construction plan of the BRI and cooperation programs with relevant countries. According to the *List of Large and Medium Civil Aviation Key Construction Projects in the Year 2015*, there are altogether 51 key projects that directly serve the BRI, with a total investment of 200 billion yuan. In the future, the CAAC will particularly enhance the construction of international airport hubs in Beijing,

---

[4] China Transport News, "Yang Chuantang Was Invited to Address the Central Party School Students, Serving the 'Three Strategies' and Building a Traffic and Transportation Power", December 2, 2015, http://www.zgjtb.com/2015-12/01/content_62620.htm (中国交通新闻网:《杨传堂应邀为中央党校学员作报告服务国家"三大战略",建设交通运输强国》, 2015 年 12 月 2 日。)

Shanghai and Guangzhou; make Xi'an, Urumqi, Nanning, Kunming and Xiamen regional hubs; and strengthen the construction of medium- and small-sized airports. Meanwhile, the CAAC, along with B&R countries, will innovate their cooperation modes in terms of expanding the opening-up of markets, ensuring transport safety, enhancing infrastructure construction and materializing transport facilitation.[5]

Maritime Safety Administration (MSA). In April 2015, China's MSA released six measures to advance the Belt and Road Initiative and maritime connectivity, which included launching maritime cooperation projects at the Strait of Malacca (Malaysia), land and maritime joint transport channel on the Indian Ocean (Myanmar), and South Indian Ocean channel (Sri Lanka), and promoting the construction of maritime strategic stronghold of the key channels mentioned above.[6]

National Energy Administration (NEA). In May 2015, the NEA held a conference on promoting international energy cooperation through the Belt and Road Initiative, which outlined key tasks for promoting the B&R energy cooperation. They include: promoting cooperation in the connectivity of energy infrastructure, working in concert to ensure the security of oil and gas pipelines, building cross-border power supply networks and power-transmission routes, and cooperating in regional power grid upgrading and transformation.[7] In May 2017, the National Energy Administration and the NDRC jointly launched the Vision and Actions on Promoting Energy Cooperation along the Silk Road Economic Belt and the 21st-Century Maritime

---

[5] Li Jiaxiang, "Taking the Opportunity of the Belt and Road Initiative to Build a New Mode of Regional Cooperation for Civil Aviation Development", *Air Transport & Business*, no. 7, 2015, pp. 11–13. (李家祥:《以推进"一带一路"战略为契机构建民航区域合作发展新模式》,载《空运商务》2015 年第 7 期,第 11–13 页。)

[6] Long Wei, "China MSA Rolled Out Measures to Promote the Belt and Road Initiative", *China Water Transport*, April 24, 2015, p. 2. (龙巍:《中国海事局公布推进"一带一路"多项举措》,载《中国水运报》2015 年 4 月 24 日,第 2 版。)

[7] The National Energy Administration of PRC, "National Energy Administration Held a Conference on Promoting International Energy Cooperation through the Belt and Road Initiative", May 14, 2015, http://www.nea.gov.cn/2015-05/14/c_134237339.html(中国国家能源局:《国家能源局召开落实"一带一路"战略推进能源国际合作会议》,2015 年 5 月 14 日。)

Silk Road, setting out arrangements for further enhancing international energy cooperation along the Belt and Road.

Ministry of Industry and Information Technology (MIIT). Publicized information shows that, the MIIT participated in the formulation of the *Infrastructure Construction Plan to Promote Connectivity with Neighboring Countries,* which aims to promote the construction of information highway between China and its neighboring countries, creating a "digital Silk Road". It would forcefully promote cross-border cable construction, encourage telecoms companies to set up overseas branches and promote the application of the new generation of ICTs and the adoption of latest standards so as to help the economic and social development in countries along the Belt and Road. In the meantime, it has accelerated the establishment of the International Communications Gateway Facilities, and put in place a network of gateway facilities comprising international business bureaus, regional bureaus, border bureaus and international communications channel bureaus.[8]

State Administration of Science, Technology and Industry for National Defense (SASTIND). It is actively advancing the B&R Space Information Corridor project, which is a 2015 new project of the B&R 3-year (2015–2017) rolling strategic plan. The project, with space-based infrastructure (such as satellite communications, remote sensing and navigation) as its main content, and terrestrial network and infrastructure connectivity as key areas, not only provides space information integrated application services to Ministries and Commissions directly under the State Council, local governments and enterprises, but also offers support to countries along the routes in terms of disaster prevention and mitigation, resources and energy development, infrastructure construction and marine emergency services.[9]

---

[8] The State Council Information Office of PRC, "The SCIO's Press Conference on Production Capacity Cooperation among Countries and Regions along the Belt and Road", May 12, 2017, http://www.scio.gov.cn/xwfbh/xwbfbh/wqfbh/35861/36661/index.htm (国务院新闻办公室:《国新办举行"一带一路"沿线国家和地区产能合作发布会》, 2017 年 5 月 12 日。)

[9] The State Administration of Science, Technology and Industry for National Defense of PRC, "State Administration of Science, Technology and Industry for National Defense Will Speed up the Construction of the Belt and Road Initiative Space

6.1.3 *Unimpeded Trade*

Ministry of Commerce (MOFCOM). According to the statements made by the Ministry's spokesperson at various occasions, the ongoing and future tasks of the MOFCOM in the construction of the B&R include: (1) in accordance with the unified arrangements of the central government, formulating a timetable and roadmap for advancing economic and trade cooperation, and making plans for the B&R key projects; (2) relying on cooperative mechanisms such as bilateral joint trade committees and mixed committees to give full play to the role of overseas trade agencies, enhance communication and coordination with countries along the routes, and promote the implementation of a series of major cooperation projects; (3) guiding and encouraging domestic enterprises to invest in countries along the routes and setting up industrial parks, to promote the internationalization of Chinese enterprises in manufacturing and service industries; (4) boosting trade with B&R countries, improving trade facilitation, and exploring new growth areas of trade; (5) deepening regional and subregional cooperation and advancing negotiations on free trade zones; (6) scaling up assistance to neighboring and B&R countries, and focusing on livelihood projects and cooperation on human resources development.[10]

National Development and Reform Commission. In terms of unimpeded trade, the key task of the NDRC to serve the BRI is to promote international cooperation in production capabilities and equipment manufacturing. Besides implementing confirmed policies, measures that need to be taken at current and next stages include: (1) working in conjunction with the MOFCOM and the MOFA in formulating the *International Production Capabilities Cooperation*

Information Corridor", July 13, 2015, http://www.sastind.gov.cn/n112/n117/ c6054430/content.html (中国国家国防科工局：《国防科工局将加快"一带一路"空间信息走廊建设》, 2015 年 7 月 13 日。)

[10] Ministry of Commerce of PRC, "The Ministry of Commerce Held a Regular Press Conference", December 16, 2014, http://www.mofcom.gov.cn/article/ae/ah/ diaocd/201412/20141200834923.shtml(中国商务部：《商务部召开例行新闻发布会, 2014 年 12 月 16 日。)

Plan, and defining key regions and countries; (2) establishing cooperative mechanisms with relevant provinces, key enterprises and major financial agencies; (3) expanding bilateral cooperation on production capabilities with B&R countries, and boosting the implementation of key cooperation projects; (4 inviting developed countries in joint development of the third-party markets.[11]

Ministry of Industry and Information Technology. It has established and improved the interdepartmental coordination mechanism with the NDRC and the Ministry of Commerce; established cooperation mechanisms with financial institutions such as China Development Bank and Export-Import Bank of China; enhanced communications and coordination with key industry associations and research institutes; directed petrochemicals, steel, nonferrous metals, construction materials and telecoms industry associations to jointly form an international capacity cooperation association; put in place an information and data platform and key projects bank for the industrial telecommunications industry, developed a platform for international capacity and equipment manufacturing cooperation and organizes overseas trips for industry associations and companies to meet their foreign counterparts and discuss cooperation. In addition, the Ministry promotes the construction of industrial parks with foreign entities, makes development guidelines and supports the industrial development and telecoms infrastructure building in cooperation zones.[12]

State-Owned Assets Supervision and Administration Commission (SASAC) of the State Council. In June 2015, the SASAC convened a working conference on promoting SOEs' participation in the BRI and international cooperation in production capabilities and equipment manufacturing. The SOEs are required to put emphasis on the

---

[11] The National Development and Reform Commission of PRC, "Cooperation in Production Capacity and Equipment Manufacturing Yields a Good Result in the First Half Year", August 11, 2015, http://www.sdpc.gov.cn/xwzx/xwfb/201508/t20150811_744978.html (中国国家发改委:《上半年国际产能和装备制造合作成效显著》, 2015 年 8 月 11 日。)

[12] The State Council Information Office of PRC, "The SCIO's Press Conference on Production Capacity Cooperation among Countries and Regions along the Belt and Road".

construction of the B&R in their 13th Five Year Plan and medium- and long-term development plan, concentrate on individual projects, formulate specific policies toward different countries, industries and enterprises, adopt flexible measures such as trade, investment, industrial parks, technological cooperation, jointly launch "going global" strategy, and improve risk management and control system.[13]

State Administration of Taxation (SAT). Taxation is a major issue faced by Chinese enterprises in going global. In April 2015, the SAT released the *Notice on Implementing the B&R Initiative and Improving Taxation Service and Management*, which introduced 10 measures in three aspects — negotiating and signing agreements to safeguard rights, improving services to boost development, enhancing cooperation to seek win–win outcome. The 10 measures are: stepping up efforts in negotiating, signing and revising taxation treaties; strengthening bilateral negotiation in taxation disputes; developing the B&R taxation service websites, releasing the B&R taxation guides for different countries, issuing taxation policy interpretation and taxation service guides; organizing "going global" workshops on taxation treaties for enterprises; setting up "12366 hotline" dedicated to taxation services; guiding intermediary service agencies such as CPA and CTA firms to go global; holding face-to-face sessions for enterprises seeking global presence; establishing taxation coordination mechanisms for B&R countries; holding forums for taxation chiefs of the B&R countries; and aiding the developing countries along the routes in taxation training.[14] Later, the State Administration of Taxation

---

[13] State-Owned Assets Supervision and Administration Commission of the State Council, "Promoting Central SOEs' Participation in the Belt and Road Initiative and International Cooperation in Production Capacity and Equipment Manufacturing", June 19, 2015. http://www.sasac.gov.cn/n1808314/n2106300/n2106312/c2106461/content.html (中国国务院国资委：《国资委召开推进中央企业参与"一带一路"建设暨国际产能和装备制造合作工作会议》, 2015 年 6 月 19 日。)

[14] State Administration of Taxation of PRC, *Notice on Implementing the B&R Initiative and Improving Taxation Service and Management*. Document Issued by State Administration of Taxation, no. 60, April 21, 2015.(中国国家税务总局：《关于落实"一带一路"发展战略要求做好税收服务与管理工作的通知》税总发〔2015〕60 号, 2015 年 4 月 21 日。)

expanded services to eight fields, including providing country-specific investment and tax consulting service, launched 40 taxation guidelines for investment in B&R countries and sent tax officials to relevant countries and international organizations. As of the end of 2016, China had signed bilateral investment agreements with 53 relevant countries and agreements on avoidance of double taxation with 54 relevant countries.[15]

General Administration of Customs. With the support of the General Administration of Customs, since May 2015, 10 cities, including Qingdao, Jinan, Zhengzhou, Taiyuan, Xi'an, Lanzhou, Yinchuan, Xining, Urumqi and Lhasa, in nine provinces (regions), namely Shandong, Henan, Shanxi, Shaanxi, Gansu, Ningxia, Qinghai, Xinjiang and Tibet, have launched regional customs clearance integration reform, which enables enterprises to "register at one place and clear Customs at multiple places". In May 2015, the General Administration of Customs released its implementation scheme of serving the BRI, introducing 16 measures in three aspects — smoothing passageways, enhancing trade and deepening cooperation. Specifically, the scheme includes planning the development and layout of ports as a whole; innovating the managing mode of ports; establishing the "single window" for international trade; promoting new ways of customs clearance such as "joint inspection, one stop release"; supporting the construction of two core regions — Xinjiang and Fujian; strengthening the institutional arrangements with Customs of countries along the routes, such as cooperation agreements; facilitating mutual recognition of Authorized Economic Operators; enhancing Customs cooperation with B&R countries in information exchange, mutual recognition of regulations, and mutual assistance in law enforcement, and setting up service sharing platforms; creating model projects for building connectivity.[16]

[15] The State Council Information Office of PRC, "The SCIO's Press Conference on Production Capacity Cooperation among Countries and Regions along the Belt and Road".

[16] China Customs, "Smoothing Passageways, Enhancing Trade and Deepening Cooperation — 16 Measures to Serve the Belt and Road Initiative", May 29, 2015, http://www.customs.gov.cn/publish/portal0/tab65602/info743890.htm(中国国

***Ministry of Land and Resources (MLR)*.** In June 2015, China Geological Survey under the MLR organized and completed the compilation of the *Atlas of Energy and Important Mineral Resources along the Belt and Road*. The main contents include: administrative division and physical geography of B&R countries; distribution of resources, which serves as a foundation for China to invest in mining industry and conduct trade cooperation with B&R countries; potentials for launching cooperation in quality production capabilities; chances of participating in the industrialization and urbanization of B&R countries; construction conditions for important infrastructure and major projects construction; major geological problems in building the Belt and Road; information channels to obtain data concerning on the geology and mineral resources in B&R countries and so on.[17]

***National Energy Administration (NEA)*.** Energy cooperation is the key to unimpeded trade. The energy plan, which was compiled under the guidance of the NEA, made it clear that, besides connectivity in oil and gas pipelines network, China will also advance the construction of "4 cooperation zones" and "6 industrial parks", establish and improve oil and gas trade center, open up new land–sea transportation routes, cultivate a batch of world-class international oil and gas companies, and encourage energy equipment manufacturing and energy service enterprises to go global.[18]

***State Oceanic Administration (SOA)*.** According to Wang Hong, the administrator of the SOA, during the 13th Five Year Plan,

家海关总署:《畅顺大通道、提升大经贸、深化大合作 — — 海关总署出台服务"一带一路"建设 16 条措施》, 2015 年 5 月 29 日。)

[17] China Geological Survey, "Most Important Work in Compiling the *Atlas of Energy and Important Mineral Resources along the Belt and Road* Accomplished", June 29, 2015. http://www.drc.cgs.gov.cn/cgkx/123246.htm (中国地质调查局:《中国地质调查局<"一带一路"能源和其他重要矿产资源图集>编制重中之重工作全面完成》, 2015 年 6 月 29 日)

[18] Wang Lu and Zhao Jing, "Oil & Gas Cooperation in the Belt and Road Initiative Focuses on Six Fields", *China Energy News*, November 30, 2015, p. 13. (王璐、赵晶:《一带一路油气合作瞄准六大领域》, 载《中国能源报》2015 年 11 月 30 日, 第 13 版。)

the SOA will conduct studies on policies and measures in support of marine-related enterprises' "going global" and cooperation in marine industry; advance the establishment of bilateral or multilateral marine industrial parks or model bases; establish transnational industrial chain; elevate the status of domestic marine industry in global value chain; promote marine connectivity; turn the geographical advantages of China's adjacency to coastal countries into practical cooperation and sustainable development.[19]

6.1.4 *Financial Integration*

Ministry of Finance (MOF). According to its work list of the year 2015, the MOF's tasks concerning the building of the B&R include taking the lead in the preparation for the Asian Infrastructure Investment Bank and New Development Bank; speeding up the preparations for financing institutions of Shanghai Cooperation Organization (SCO); improving policies and measures to promote foreign trade; advancing the implementation of major projects in infrastructure connectivity, and encouraging strong industries to go global; enhancing financial exchanges and cooperation with foreign countries, getting deeply involved in multilateral cooperation mechanisms such as G20, 10 + 3, BRICS and SCO.

People's Bank of China (PBC). Publicized information shows that measures that the PBC has taken to support the BRI mainly include taking the lead in the establishment of the Silk Road fund; expanding the scope and scale of currency swap and settlement with B&R countries, establishing efficient and secure Renminbi cross-border payment and settlement system, actively and orderly advancing the internationalization of Renminbi; encouraging the signing of MOUs on cooperation in bilateral financial regulation, improving the system of risk response and crisis management, and setting up a regional financial crisis early warning system.

---

[19] Du Fang and Shen Hui, "The Blue Engine Is Gaining Momentum: Interview with Wang Hong, Administrator of the State Oceanic Administration", *Economic Daily*, January 14, 2015, p. 11. (杜芳、沈慧:《蓝色引擎强劲发力 — — 访国家海洋局局长王宏》, 载《经济日报》2016 年 1 月 14 日, 第 11 版。)

6.1.5 *Closer People-to-People Ties*

National Health and Family Planning Commission (NHFPC). International assistance and cooperation in medicine and health care is a fine tradition of PRC's diplomacy. In October, 2015, the NHFPC released the *Three-year Implementation Plan of Promoting the B&R Initiative Health Care Cooperation and Exchanges (2015–2017)*, outlining eight key cooperation areas, namely: building cooperation mechanisms, prevention and control of infectious diseases, capacity building and talents cultivation, health emergency response and emergency medical aid, traditional medicine, health care system and policy exchanges, development assistance for health, health industry development. Key projects and events include: holding "Silk Road Forum on Health Cooperation", joint prevention and control of communicable diseases in Central Asia and Greater Mekong Subregion, China–ASEAN Plan on Training One Hundred Health Professionals, China–Central and Eastern European countries cooperation network of public hospitals, China–Russia cooperation projects on disaster medicine, construction projects of China–ASEAN traditional medicine exchanges and cooperation center, "Towards Brightness" free ophthalmic service, "Shaanxi Village" hospital construction project in Kazakhstan.

Ministry of Science and Technology (MOST). It is responsible for making plans on the B&R scientific and technological innovation cooperation and helping to build the Asia–Europe Center on Science and Technology Innovation and Cooperation. In the 2016 National Science and Technology Working Conference, Minister Wan Gang pointed out that during the 13th Five Year Plan period, the Ministry would focus on improving capabilities in allocating global innovative resources, taking an in-depth part in global innovation management, providing public goods for international technological cooperation, promoting two-way openness and flow of innovative resources, building the B&R collaborative innovation community and enhancing the opening-up of science and technology. In 2016, the main tasks of MOST were, in accordance with the development conditions and demands of the B&R countries, advancing the construction of innovation platforms and increasing technological and cultural exchanges by means of science and technology partnership programs and intergovernmental cooperation mechanism on technology innovation. Meanwhile, the MOST is also charged with responsibility of promoting joint R&D, technical transfer and innovation cooperation in key areas such as climate change and environment; jointly building featured parks; encouraging strong industries to go global; deepening the integration of international production capabilities; and building the B&R collaborative innovation community.[20] In September 2016, the Ministry of Science and Technology, together with other departments, launched the Special Planning on Promoting Cooperation on Science and Technology to build the Belt and Road. The document identified five key tasks of cooperation, including cooperation in people-to-people exchanges, technology transfer, technological resources sharing, special industrial parks and research. It also designated 12 key areas of cooperation, including agriculture, energy, transportation, information and communications, environment, ocean, advanced manufacturing, new materials, space and aeronautics, medicine and health care, and disaster prevention and relief.

State Administration of Press, Publication, Radio, Film and Television. The main tasks of the SARFT include: launching a "Literary Silk Road" project and five subprograms, which are oriented toward the B&R countries; guiding the media of radio and television to produce quality news coverage of the B&R; producing fine movies and TV programs, including several documentaries, creating a favorable international public opinion environment for the BRI.

National Tourism Administration (NTA). In 2015, the NTA launched the "Beautiful China, 2015 — Year of Silk Road Tourism" project. Working with relevant provinces, the NTA held the Silk Road International Tourism Festival, promoting the Silk Road in its overseas publicity campaign. Meanwhile, NTA formulated the *Strategic*

---

[20] Wan Gang, *Innovation-Driven and Technology-Led: A Good Start of the 13th Five-Year Plan: Report at National Sci-technology Conference 2016*, Beijing, January 11, 2016. (万钢:《坚持创新驱动强化科技引领实现"十三五"良好开局 —— 在 2016 年全国科技工作会议上的报告》, 2016 年 1 月 11 日, 北京。)

Plan of the Silk Road Economic Belt and 21st-Century Maritime Silk Road Tourism Cooperation and Development, which involves the implementation of key actions, improved guarantee mechanism and advancement of 3-year plan.[21]

Publicized information shows that **the Ministry of Education, the Ministry of Agriculture, the Ministry of Culture and the Ministry of Environmental Protection** have taken the lead in formulating a batch of specialized plans. On top of that, other central state organs have also stepped up their efforts in supporting and serving the B&R Initiative within their own sphere of responsibility.

The United Front Work Department of CPC Central Committee. In May 2015, The United Front Work Department of CPC Central Committee issued the *Opinions on the United Front Supporting the B&R Initiative*, which stated that the United Front would mobilize various forces into the construction of the B&R. Specifically, the tasks involve supporting people from non-Communist parties, the All-China Federation of Industry and Commerce, and those without party affiliation to conduct field investigations; supporting capable private enterprises in developing natural resources, contracting for projects and building sales network in the B&R countries and regions; encouraging compatriots in Hong Kong, Macau and Taiwan, overseas Chinese and students to jump on the wave of the BRI; guiding all kinds of communities and organizations to conduct extensive international exchange and cooperation with nongovernmental and international organizations along the routes; training members of the united front on how to eliminate doubts and confusions about the BRI in their contact with foreigners.[22]

---

[21] National Tourism Administration of PRC, "How to Materialize Tourism Scenario of the Belt and Road Initiative", April 7, 2015, http://dj.cnta.gov.cn/html/2015-04/1824.shtml (国家旅游局：《"一带一路"的旅游愿景如何实现》，2015 年 4 月 7 日。)

[22] Chinanews.com, "The United Front Work Department of CPC Central Committee Issued Opinions Concerning Action Plan on the Belt and Road Initiative", May 12, 2015, http://www.chinanews.com/gn/2015/05-12/7270401.shtml(中新网：《中央统战部印发意见就统一战线服务"一带一路"战略作出部署》，2015 年 5 月 12 日。)

Supreme People's Court. In July 2015, *Several Opinions of Supreme People's Court on Providing Judicial Service and Guarantee for the B&R Initiative* was released, which requires that People's Court be given full play to its role in trials to effectively serve and safeguard the smooth implementation of the BRI. Its responsibilities include enhancing judicial review on foreign-related criminal, civil, commercial, maritime and maritime commercial, international commercial arbitration as well as judicial trial of disputes related to free trade zones; promoting international judicial assistance and cooperation with B&R countries, accurately applying international treaties, conventions and foreign laws; building and perfecting diversified dispute settlement mechanisms; taking an active part in formulating relevant international judicial rules.[23]

National Bureau of Statistics. In October 2015, on the B&R National Statistics Development Conference, the National Bureau of Statistics stated that it would collect and sort out statistical information concerning relevant B&R countries, build statistics sharing platforms with countries along the routes, systematically monitor changes in goods, capital, services, technologies and trade, effectively supervise the implementation of major projects.[24]

6.2 Local Authorities

Local authorities at various levels are the major forces in building the B&R. Since the Initiative was put forward, relevant provinces, regions and cities (particularly the five north-west provinces and coastal regions) have shown great enthusiasm for participation. They came up with working mechanisms for building the B&R, and put forward their own

[23] Xu Juan, "Supreme People's Court of the PRC Issued Opinions on Providing Judicial Service and Guarantee for the B&R Initiative", *People's Daily*, July 8, 2015, p. 11. (徐隽：《最高法发布意见为"一带一路"建设提供司法服务保障》，载《人民日报》2015 年 7 月 8 日，第 11 版。)

[24] Wang Yichen, "National Conference on Statistics and Development of the Belt and Road Initiative", *Economic Daily*, October 20, 2015, p. 4. (王轶辰：《"一带一路"国家统计发展会议召开》，载《经济日报》2015 年 10 月 20 日，第 4 版。)

roadmaps, work plans and project lists to be docked with the BRI. By the end of October 2015, a total of 31 provinces, regions and cities and Xinjiang Production and Construction Corps have completed formulating their plans for building the B&R, and have submitted them to the Office of the Leading Group for the Belt and Road Initiative.[25]

Based on publicized information, all the provinces and regions have come up with clear, sensible and practical ideas for advancing the BRI. At the provincial level, the implementation plans and measures adopted by the government usually center round infrastructure connectivity, unimpeded trade, financial integration, and people-to-people bonds. Altogether eight concrete aspects are involved: infrastructure construction, economic and trade cooperation, industrial investment, resources and energy, financial cooperation, ecological environment, cultural exchanges and maritime cooperation.[26]

6.2.1 *Promoting Connectivity of Infrastructure and Facilities*

Chongqing, Xinjiang, Inner Mongolia, Hunan, Hubei, Henan, Heilongjiang, Liaoning, Zhejiang, Yunnan, Sichuang, Guizhou, Shandong and Jiangsu have successively opened international freight trains toward Central Asia and Europe. **Gansu province** will focus on the "6873" traffic break-through program, enhancing the construction of passageways with strong transport capacity, speeding up the renovation of Longhai–Lanxin Railway, and improving Gansu's connectivity in the Silk Road Economic Belt. **Inner Mongolia** will accelerate the construction of highways connecting China with Russia and Mongolia, focus on advancing the construction of two sea routes, three energy transportation channels and three tourism routes. **Fujian** will concentrate its efforts on building core port districts, with two ports for container transport, two for bulk cargo transport, and two

---

[25] The National Development and Reform Commission of PRC, "Comprehensive Coordination and Orderly Promotion: The Implementation Plan of the Belt and Road Initiative Is Showing Early Results", November 20, 2015, http://www.sdpc.gov.cn/xwzx/xwfb/201511/t20151120_759151.html(中国国家发改委：《统筹协调有序推进——"一带一路"建设的地方实施方案衔接工作成效初显》, 2015 年 11 月 20 日。)
[26] All the following information comes from publicized information.

for liquid cargo transport, and accelerate the construction of Xiamen port as China's South-East International Shipping Logistics Center and Xiamen's new airports. **Ningxia** will open direct flights to Dubai, Singapore and Malaysia, gradually expand direct flights to six Gulf states, make Yinchuan–Kazakhstan cargo charter flights available on a regular basis, open cargo charter flights to European and Middle East countries step by step. **Yunnan** actively promotes the construction of seven transprovincial and five cross-border highway channels, focusing on building an interconnective transportation support system. **Shanghai** will take the opportunity of building Asia–Pacific Model E-Port to accelerate the connectivity with major ports in countries along the routes. **Hunan** will open cargo flights between Changsha and Hong Kong, and transcontinental flights from Changsha to Europe, the United States, Australia, Russia, Japan and West Asia. **Guangdong** will enhance the construction of airport cluster in the Pearl River Delta area, with Guangzhou Baiyun Airport as a leading facility, and will build a major China–ASEAN corridor featuring highway and high-speed rail transport. In **Shaanxi**, the national and international codes for Xi'an Hub have been activated, materializing the clearance mode of "one declaration, one check, one clearance", which marks its official entry into the international trade and transport system. In **Jiangsu**, the China-Kazakhstan(Lianyungang) international logistics cooperation base and SCO(Lianyungang) international logistics park have been making orderly progress. **Jilin** will accelerate the building of an intelligent information platform for dealing with international mails, and advance the construction of overseas ports in Rajin and Zarubino.

6.2.2 *Enhancing Economic and Trade Cooperation*

Shanghai will accelerate the signing of economic and trade cooperation MOUs with economic and trade departments in B&R countries or hub cities such as Singapore, Czech, Turkey and Emirates, and continue to encourage regional headquarters of transnational enterprises to expand their businesses, further implement policies and measures that promote steady growth of foreign trade, development of service trade and cross-border e-commerce. **Zhejiang**, along with the B&R countries, will establish efficient supporting systems such as customs supervision, inspection and quarantine, tax return, cross-border payment tailored to cross-border e-commerce transactions, building a cross-border e-commerce information service platform. **Guangdong** will build several import products trade centers that serve the entire province and even the whole country, and set up sales centers in the B&R countries featuring Guangdong's speciality products such as building materials and hotel supplies. **Guangxi** will accelerate building the China–ASEAN Commodity Trading Center, building a bulk commodity trading center for regional speciality products such as palm oil, rubber, nonferrous metals and cereals and oils. **Jiangsu** will further build and operate overseas economic and trade cooperation zones and industrial clusters such as Sihanoukville Special Economic Zone of Cambodia. **Shaanxi** will advance the building of Shaanxi–Korea industrial cooperation parks, China–Russia Silk Road high tech industrial parks and China–Central Asia economic cooperation industrial parks. **Gansu** has set up commercial representative offices in countries such as Belarus, Iran, Kyrgyzstan, Indonesia, and in Khorgos port in Xinjiang province, and established trading centers for speciality commodities. **Heilongjiang** province will advance setting up cross-border economic cooperation zones in Hei He, Suifenhe and Heixiazi Island, support the construction of economic and trade cooperation zone in Ussuriysk, Russia. **Anhui**'s first comprehensive bonded zone — Hefei Comprehensive Bonded Zone — has been officially in operation. And a 12-inch wafer manufacturing base, with a total investment of 2.2 billion USD, has been under construction. In addition, provinces including Fujian, Sichuan, Ningxia, Qinghai, Xinjiang and Inner Mongolia have been actively expanding their economic and trade cooperation with the B&R countries via various expos and events.

6.2.3 *Expanding Production Capacity and Investment Cooperation*

Hebei encourages photovoltaic, steel, glass and cement enterprises with excessive production capabilities and comparative advantages to set up production bases abroad, particularly in central and eastern

European countries, and has also made a more detailed "map of cooperative countries" to demonstrate the industries and their transfer regions. **Guangxi** will rely on industrial parks, both home and abroad, such as China–Malaysia "Two countries, Twin parks", China–Vietnam Cross-Border Economic Cooperation Zone, China–Indonesia Economic and Trade Cooperation Zone and Brunei–Guangxi Economic Corridor, to support domestic equipment manufacturing industries with quality capabilities in investing in ASEAN countries. **Sichuan** has formulated a "251 3-year action plan", aiming at encouraging 20 key countries, 50 major programs and 100 enterprises with willingness and capabilities to participate in the B&R Initiative. **Hunan** plans to breed about 20 industries with domestic and overseas influence to go global as well as several key international projects contracting enterprises; enhance ongoing construction projects of North Europe–Hunan agricultural industrial park, Thailand–Hunan industrial park, Vietnam commercial and trade and logistic park and China town in Ajman, UAE. In **Anhui,** enterprises in the field of building materials, automobiles, agriculture and mineral resources development will accelerate international cooperation in production capabilities; Conch Group has made progress in multiple cement projects in Indonesia, Laos, Cambodia and Myanmar. **Zhejiang** will establish a batch of overseas economic and trade cooperation zones in major hub cities and ports in countries along the routes, promote overseas industrial clusters for China's quality production capabilities. **Xinjiang Production and Construction Corps** will further speed up the pace of its agricultural enterprises' going global.

6.2.4 *Expanding Resources and Energy Cooperation*

Fujian will rely on major ports to establish logistics transfer and processing bases for imported oil, gas and minerals from the B&R countries and regions. **Shanxi** will enhance its cooperation with Central Asia regions in terms of equipment for coal excavation, washing and transport; advance the construction of a China-invested project of natural gas equipment manufacturing factory in Kazakhstan. **Shandong** will promote projects such as bauxite mining in Indonesia and gold mining in Ghana, and set up overseas resources supply bases in

Australia, Russia and Indonesia. **Jiangxi** will encourage geological exploration institutes to conduct geological surveys and explore mineral resources in the B&R countries such as Cambodia, Indonesia, the Philippines and Iran, and encourage leading enterprises to participate in developing mineral resources in the B&R countries. **Liaoning** has launched overseas resources development projects such as nickel mining in Indonesia and copper mining in Kazakhstan. **Guangdong** will focus on promoting overseas cooperation projects such as Zhenrong's 5 million-ton oil refining project in Myanmar, Yudean — Indonesia power supply cooperation, GRAM (Guangdong Rising Assets Management Co., Ltd.) — PanAust-Lao copper and gold mining, Guangxin Holdings Group Ltd's nickel and iron mining in Indonesia, Guangken Rubber Group's rubber plantation and processing bases in Southeast Asia. Besides, border provinces/areas such as **Xinjiang, Heilongjiang, Yunnan and Inner Mongolia** have expressed intentions to improve the connectivity of energy infrastructures with neighboring countries and regions, including oil and gas pipelines, cross-border power supply and power transmission channels and regional power grid.

6.2.5 *Expanding Financial Cooperation*

Shanghai will take the financial innovation of pilot free trade zone as a breakthrough point to expand functions of free trade accounts, actively explore the transition and interaction between offshore and onshore markets, innovate Renminbi financial products with international orientation, promote the building of platforms for issuing, trading and liquidating Asian bonds, advance free convertibility under capital accounts in an orderly manner, study and explore how to implement financial cooperation agreements with major financial centers of the B&R countries. **Guangdong** has set up Guangdong Silk Road fund with multiple currencies; the initial investment will go to projects such as industrial parks, major infrastructure, fishery and agriculture, manufacturing and service industries in key countries and also go to national Silk Road Fund and its sub-funds. **Tianjin** will make full use of financial instruments such as lease, factoring and bonds to promote innovation in cross-border Renminbi business, and to compete for projects financed by national investment fund. In **Heilongjiang**, Heihe and Suifenhe customs have begun to offer cross-border customs clearance service in rubles. On basis of this, Heilongjiang will set up the China–Russia cross-border e-commerce online payment settlement platform, building a regional financial service center that serves Russia and Northeast Asia. **Shaanxi** will establish cooperation development funds with Central Asian countries, with priority on Shaanxi–Kazakhstan cooperation fund. **Henan** build a B&R blanket insurance platform for policy export credit insurance, realizing financing insurance coverage for export of large set equipment. **Ningxia** will encourage financial institutions to actively establish financial cooperation with Arab countries, striving to set up a center for RMB trade settlement between China and Arab countries. **Yunnan** will rely on border financial comprehensive reform pilot areas to attract financial institutions such as banks, securities in Southeast Asian and South Asian countries to Yunnan, improving cross-border financial services. **Xinjiang** will make integrated arrangements and build Urumqi into the region's international financial center, build Kashgar into the regional financial and trade zone and subregional financial center, and Khorgos into an offshore Renminbi pilot financial harbor, forming a financial golden triangle of Xinjiang.

6.2.6 *Strengthening Cooperation on Ecological and Environmental Protection*

Gansu will make good use of its technological advantages in ecological management of continental river valley, sand control and shelter forest, rainwater harvesting and utilization, and wildlife preservation, to carry out cooperation and exchanges with Central Asian countries in terms of sandstorm prevention, ecological management of sand source areas, desertification monitoring and control, dry farming and water-saving irrigation and wetland protection. **Yunnan** has been actively promoting wetland protection and capacity building of the Great Mekong River Subregion. **Jiangxi,** via World Low-carbon and

Eco-economy Conference, International White Crane Forum and International Living Lakes Conference, will enhance cooperation in addressing climate change, develop low-carbon technology and green economy, and protect wintering white crane. **Guangdong** will advance its cooperation with the B&R countries in terms of disaster prevention and mitigation and ecological protection, establish coordination mechanism for marine pollution prevention and control, and collaboratively conduct researches in offshore marine ecosystem protection. **Shaanxi** will launch extensive cooperations and exchanges with the B&R countries in terms of joint protection and establishment of ecosystem, forest products processing and trade, forestry science and technology, forest tourism and so on, fully implementing the China project in the overall building of the Silk Road ecosystem. **Xinjiang** will constantly advance two major international cooperation projects supported by the Ministry of Science and Technology. The province has collected data on hydrologic resources, meteorological observation and climate change of the five Central Asian countries over the past century, and established the first ecosystem field inspection and research network that covers Central Asia, the first Central Asian ecological and environment database in the world, and the first Central Asian ecosystem model.

6.2.7 *Strengthening Cultural Exchanges*

Fujian has been holding Silk Road International Film Festival, building "Maritime Silk Road Digital Cultural Corridor", supporting Quanzhou in integrating museum resources, such as overseas transport history museums and overseas Chinese history museums, establishing Silk Road international cultural exchanges exhibition center. **Guangdong** will set up an overseas tourism promotion center, build international cruise homeports in Guangzhou and Shenzhen, and develop cruise tourism in cities such as Zhuhai, Shantou and Zhanjiang. **Shaanxi** will approve cultural tourism projects such as Silk Road cultural base, cultural scenic spot of ruins of Chang'an city of Han dynasty, talent exchange programs such as Xi'an Silk Road Economic Belt International Youth Exchange Center. **Gansu** will take advantage of the events such as Silk Road (Dunhuang) International Culture Expo, Lanzhou Investment and Trade Fair and Dunhuang Tour — Silk Road International Tourism Festival to boost festival and exhibition economy. **Heilongjiang** will enhance the overall protection of China Eastern railroad building cluster; develop China–Russia classic tourist routes and tourist products such as ecological sightseeing, health care vacation and winter tourism; attract Russian medical tourists to Suifen River. **Hunan** will speed up the construction of China–Italy Low-Carbon Research Center, China–UK Green Environmental Protection Center, Hunan international technology transfer center (1 + *N*) and branch institutes of Hybrid Rice R&D Center in Bangladesh, Pakistan, Indonesia, India and Thailand. **Jiangxi** will explore cultural deposits of Jingdezhen porcelain and ceramics, enhance the construction of Jingdezhen Imperial Kiln Site and Jingdezhen Ceramics Museum of China and create an international porcelain and ceramics culture exchange center. **Ningxia** will accelerate building China–Arab technology transfer center and sub-centers, and implement China–Arab Science and Technology Partnership Program. **Xinjiang** will actively advance "SCO Science and Technology Partnership Program", making full use of "China–Central Asia Science and Technology Cooperation Center" and China–Tajikistan Agricultural Science and Technology Cooperation Park to enhance science and technology cooperation.

6.2.8 *Promoting Maritime Cooperation*

Fujian will develop fishery resources in the high seas of Pacific and Indian Ocean, establish enduring and stable fishery cooperation with interested countries in Southeast Asia, South Asia, West Asia and Africa, attach importance to the construction of China–ASEAN Maritime Cooperation Center and ASEAN Fishing Boat Inspection Center, support Fuzhou in accelerating the building of China–ASEAN Marine Products Exchange, to form a marine product e-commerce platform for the B&R countries and regions. **Guangdong** will advance projects like Guangdong–Malacca Maritime Industrial Park and China–ASEAN Marine Fishery Technology Cooperation and Industrial Development Model Program. **Guangxi** will encourage Qinzhou City, Guangxi Beibu Gulf International Port Group Co., Ltd., ASEAN and prominent shipping enterprises both home and abroad to jointly develop a maritime route named "21st-Century Maritime Silk Road". **Jiangsu** has officially launched the Distant Water Fishery Cooperation Project with Malaysia, and signed cooperation MOUs with India and Punjab, Pakistan in aquaculture and technology cooperation. In the future, the province will also establish deep-sea fishery industry stock fund, provide guidance for Jiangsu enterprises and social capital to cooperate with the B&R countries in fishery projects and to coestablish two to three maritime economy innovation model parks and maritime technology cooperation parks. **Shandong** will speed up the building of East Asia maritime cooperation platform and overseas distant water fishery bases in Indonesia, Sri Lanka, Uruguay, Ghana, Solomon Islands and Fiji.

Besides governments at provincial level, some important hub cities have also put forward their own plans in alignment with the B&R Initiative. For example, **Lanzhou**, the capital city of **Gansu province**, has put forward "1851" development strategy which, aiming at making Lanzhou a national strategic platform of opening up to the west and an important hub city along the Silk Road Economic Belt, involves implementing eight major tasks and creating five major platforms, materializing 1 trillion yuan's investment within five years, and over 5 billion USD in total import and export volume from and to Central Asia and the B&R countries. **Xi'an,** the capital city of **Shaanxi province,** will build five major platforms for international cooperation, education innovation, economic and trade logistics, financial services and cultural exchanges, gradually making itself a hub for financial and commercial logistics, mechanical manufacturing, energy storage, transport and trade, culture and tourism, scientific and technological R&D and high-end talent cultivation. **Dalian** of Liaoning province will make full use of the platform of Jinpu New District to link the two markets of Northeast Asia and Europe. In **Zhejiang province**, the Ningbo Shipping Exchange has issued "Maritime Silk Road Index". The Ningbo Containerized Freight Index (NCFI) has been successfully issued on the official website of the Baltic Exchange in October 2015. It was the first time since its founding in 1744 for Baltic Exchange to issue an index for an institution other than itself, which marks that Chinese shipping index has gained international recognition. **Quanzhou** of Fujian province will implement the "ten action plans", namely port rejuvenation, bilateral trade and two-way investment, cooperation with overseas Chinese to create win–win situation, extension of the new corridor to Arab countries, green manufacturing improvement, financial innovation, integration with free trade zone, modern coastal city construction, international cultural tourism cooperation, talent cultivation and people exchanges. **Fuzhou** of Fujian province, together with Fuzhou Branch of China Development Bank and China–Africa Development Fund, has jointly established a "Maritime Silk Road Fund" with around 10 billion yuan. The city hopes to contribute to the "21st-Century Maritime Silk Road" by means of market-oriented operation of the Fund. **Sanya** of Hainan province is accelerating the second stage project of Phoenix Island international cruise port, and is planning the Maritime Silk Road cruise tourism route. **Zhanjiang** of Guangdong province will rely on its deep water port to speed up the implementation of major industrial projects such as steel, petrochemical and paper industry. **Zhuhai** of Guangdong province has established sister-city and friendly-port relationship with Gwadar city of Pakistan. Their initial cooperation will center on commercial logistics, and a future plan will involve building a "Zhuhai-Gwadar Cross-Border Economic Cooperation Zone" in the free trade zone of the Gwadar port. **Qinzhou** of Guangxi province will take the China–ASEAN port cities cooperation network as a platform to build a Maritime Silk Road cooperation mechanism that involves 47 port cities in China and ASEAN countries. In addition, the city will open new liner routes between Qinzhou and major ports in ASEAN countries, accelerate building China–ASEAN port logistics data center, and advance Maritime Silk Road port-surrounding industrial belt through the building of China–Malaysia "Two Countries, Twin parks".

The B&R implementation plans and measures of governments at all levels share common features, which we summarize as "three emphases".

First, emphasis on regional characteristics and advantages. For example, coastal provinces and major port cities have set priority on enhancing port construction, developing port-surrounding industries and expanding maritime cooperation. The border provinces have chosen neighboring countries/regions as preferred partners. With enhanced subregional cooperation, the coastal and border provinces have become main forces in building the six major economic corridors. **Ningxia,** taking advantage of their cultural bonds with Arabic countries, is building cooperation bases mainly toward Arabic–Islamic world, to offset its own disadvantages in geological economy. Provinces such as **Zhejiang, Fujian, Guangdong** and **Hainan** rely on their bonds with overseas Chinese to attract them to the B&R Initiative. **Shanghai** attaches importance to integrating the building of "four centers" with the BRI, scales up their integrating efforts in fields of economy and trade, finance and shipping, and exert the pioneering role in institutional innovation in the field of financial cooperation. As a major energy-rich province, the implementation plan of **Xinjiang** focuses on the three major energy bases: oil and gas production, processing and reserve base, coal, coal power and coal chemical industry base, and wind power and photovoltaic power base. Provinces such as **Shaanxi, Gansu** and **Fujian** actively explore historic heritage of ancient Silk Road and highlight their advantages in history, culture and tourism. **Guizhou** features ecological civilization and mega-data in its cooperation in the BRI. **Hainan** focuses on the construction of international tourism island, promoting tourism cooperation as its priority.

Second, emphasis on the role of cooperation platforms. On the one hand, all provinces and hub cities have scaled up their efforts in building overseas or cross-border economic and trade cooperation zones and industrial parks, and vigorously encouraged local enterprises to build industrial cooperation platforms in the B&R countries. On the other hand, many hub cities have made full use of various international expos, forums, trade fairs to further enhance international connections for Chinese local governments. Such platforms include China–ASEAN Expo (Nanning, Guangxi), China–Eurasia Expo (Urumqi, Xinjiang), China–Arab States Expo (Yinchuan, Ningxia),

Euro–Asia Economic Forum (Xi'an, Shaanxi), China–South Asia Expo (Kunming, Yunnan), China–Northeast Asia Expo(Changchun, Jilin), Western China International Fair (Chengdu, Sichuan), 21st-Century Maritime Silk Road International Expo (Fuzhou, Fujian), China Import and Export Fair (Guangzhou, Guangdong), China International Fair for Investment and Trade (Xiamen, Fujian), Qianhai Cooperative Forum (Shenzhen, Guangdong), China–Russia Expo (Harbin, Heilongjiang), and China–Mongolia Expo (Hohhot, Inner Mongolia) and so on. What's worth mentioning is that, in November 2015, the third government-to-government (G-to-G) project between China and Singapore chose its site in Chongqing. The project, themed on "modern connectivity and modern services", has established a three-tier cooperation mechanism — at national, ministerial and municipal levels — to coordinate its operation. In January 2016, China–Singapore (Chongqing) Demonstration Initiative on Strategic Connectivity Administrative Bureau was announced to be established in Chongqing. The city has thus obtained an important platform to contribute to the BRI.

Third, emphasis on the leading effect of major projects. For example, **Hunan** will invest over 300 billion yuan into around 80 major projects. **Gansu** has established a pool of 214 key projects, covering five categories of infrastructure, energy and resources, production capabilities, cultural exchanges and other. **Guangdong** has chosen 68 projects as its priorities, which, with a total investment of 55.4 billion USD, covering six major fields of infrastructure, energy and resources, manufacturing, and service and so on. **Jiangxi,** during the period of 2015–2017, has come up with 26 key projects covering five aspects and 26 categories, such as construction of passageways and so on. **Quanzhou** of Fujian province has selected 180 supporting projects to go with its "10 action plans", including over 50 infrastructure projects. **Ningbo** of Zhejiang has adopted the "610 action plan" which centers on six major tasks, namely port cooperation, passageway construction, economic and trade cooperation, cultural exchanges, cross-border e-commerce and system innovation, with about 10 key projects in each task and a total investment of 142 billion yuan. **Xi'an** of Shaanxi province has launched the first batch of 60 Silk Road

Economic Belt projects, with a total investment of 115.5 billion yuan, among which, four projects have a total investment of over 10 billion yuan. **Qingdao** of Shandong province, aiming at building an important gateway city in northern China, has rolled out a batch of key investment and trade projects, including 30 industrial transfer projects such as Haier going to Russia and Hisense going to Egypt, and 20 overseas resources and energy development projects such as shale oil mining in Jordan, and lead and Zinc mines in Mongolia. **Nanning** of Guangxi province has established "Major B&R Projects Pool", involving multiple fields of infrastructure, energy development, economic and trade cooperation, agriculture and tourism.

What is worth mentioning is that, besides mainland China, Macau and Hong Kong have also scaled up their involvement in the B&R Initiative. On November 17, 2015, Cui Shian, the Chief Executive of Macau SAR, has pointed out, in 2016 Policy Address, that the Macau SAR government would leverage the unique role of its own system and overseas Chinese, and grasp the precious opportunity of the BRI. It was the first time that the B&R is included in the annual policy address of Macau's chief executive. Macau plans to push for the integration of China–Portuguese service platform for trade cooperation with the BRI, give full play to its Renminbi clearing platform, boost financial cooperation between China and Portuguese-speaking countries, and invest some of its fiscal reserves in the B&R via its cooperation with China Development Bank. On December 10, 2015, Liang Zhenying, the then chief executive of HK SAR, stated that HK could serve as an investor, coordinator and supporter of the B&R Initiative. Earlier, HK Trade Development Council had launched a website on B&R news and information. In December 2017, the National Development and Reform Commission (NDRC) Chairman He Lifeng and Chief Executive of Hong Kong Special Administrative Region Carrie Lam Cheng Yuet-ngor signed an *Arrangement for Advancing Hong Kong's Full Participation in and Contribution to the Belt and Road Initiative*. The Arrangement covers a wide range of areas, which include facilitating co-operation of all key stakeholders through the platform of Hong Kong to provide for the Belt and Road Initiative the funds required as well as a diversity of financing channels; fully leveraging Hong Kong's status as the global offshore Renminbi business hub to accelerate the internationalization of RMB; supporting Hong Kong's maritime development; deepening cooperation between the Mainland and Hong Kong in infrastructure construction, such as information, highways, railways, ports and airports; supporting Hong Kong in participating in relevant regional economic cooperation mechanisms; supporting Hong Kong in holding high-level forums and international expos on building the Belt and Road.

In summary, from central government to local authorities, all government agencies, within their own responsibilities and functions, have rolled out work deployments in the BRI. As the old saying goes, all things are difficult before they are easy. While government agencies cannot shoulder all the tasks in building the BRI, the guidance they provide at the initial stage has laid a foundation and set the direction for future efforts. Their actions are concrete steps of a national strategy, and critical driving forces as well, ensuring the practical implementation of a grand concept. Aligning their own development strategies with the BRI, the local authorities at all levels not only contribute directly to the national strategy, but also earn new opportunities for development and opening up. In that sense, the BRI is also a product of win–win cooperation between the central government and local authorities.

New Developments of Building the Belt and Road

As Chinese President Xi Jinping stated, *"the Belt and Road Initiative is not meant as rhetoric. It represents real work that could be seen and felt to bring real benefits to countries in the region"*.[1] Since its proposal in 2013, the Belt and Road Initiative, which focuses on key routes, key countries, key fields and key projects, has achieved tremendous progress in terms of policy coordination, connectivity of infrastructure and facilities, unimpeded trade, financial integration and closer people-to-people ties thanks to the concerted efforts of China and B&R countries.

---

[1] Xi Jinping, "Towards a Community of Common Destiny and a New Future for Asia: Keynote Speech at the Boao Forum for Asia Annual Conference 2015", *People's Daily*, March 29, 2015, p. 2. [习近平:《迈向命运共同体开创亚洲新未来——在博鳌亚洲论坛 2015 年年会上的主旨演讲》(2015 年 3 月 28 日, 海南博鳌), 载《人民日报》2015 年 3 月 29 日, 第 2 版。]

7.1 Policy Coordination

Policy coordination is the point of departure for building the Belt and Road, which also provides basis for the implementation of the Initiative. From September 2013 to the beginning of 2015, China consciously included the BRI into its diplomatic agendas and intensified policy coordination with relevant countries. Through diversified platforms and mechanisms, including Conference on Interaction and Confidence-Building Measures in Asia (CICA), China–Arab States Cooperation Forum (CASCF), the Shanghai Cooperation Organization (SCO) Summit, the Dialogue on Strengthening Connectivity Partnership and Asia–Pacific Economic Cooperation (APEC) Meeting, China made full use of "host diplomacy" and launched intensive mobilization efforts, both bilaterally and multilaterally, covering almost all important countries and regional organizations along the Belt and Road. In a number of senior official visits, the "Belt and Road Initiative" was a frequently mentioned term by Chinese high-ranking officials. Consequently, B&R countries have deepened their understanding of the Initiative and expressed their willingness to cooperate.

Jointly Building the Belt and Road with Arab States. The Sixth Ministerial Conference of CASCF held in Beijing on June 5, 2014, was the first major diplomatic move taken by the Chinese government to promote agenda centering on "jointly building the Belt and Road". In the Conference which themed on "joint construction of the new Silk Road towards common development and shared prosperity", China and 22 Arab States reached consensuses on jointly building the Belt and Road. The Conference also laid out plans and deployments on the future directions and priority fields in China–Arab relations for the next 10 years. President Xi Jinping proposed the China–Arab "1 + 2 + 3" cooperation network: to take energy cooperation as the main axis, and infrastructure and trade and investment as two wings, to make breakthroughs in the three high-tech areas of nuclear energy, aerospace satellite, and new energy, so as to build a "community of common interests" and a "community of shared future." Meanwhile, China also proposed to speed up the development of and negotiations on major projects like China–Gulf

Cooperation Council (GCC) FTA, China–United Arab Emirates (UAE) investment cooperation fund, and invited Arab States to join the Asian Infrastructure Investment Bank (AIIB).[2]

Dialogue on Strengthening Connectivity Partnership. On November 8, 2014, the Dialogue on Strengthening Connectivity Partnership initiated by China was held in Beijing. Leaders of countries including Bangladesh, Laos, Mongolia, Myanmar, Tajikistan, Cambodia, Pakistan and leaders of international organizations including the United Nations Economic and Social Commission for Asia and the Pacific (UN ESCAP) and the SCO participated in this dialogue. It is the first time for China to initiate a multilateral international conference on the theme of "Connectivity" and the BRI after the eighth session of the Central Leading Group on Financial and Economic Affairs on November 4, 2014 when construction of the Belt and Road was discussed. In this dialogue, President Xi Jinping made a speech on further deepening B&R cooperation in the new era — to intensify practical cooperation under the BRI, to strengthen connectivity partnership of Asian countries, thus to jointly build a "community of shared future" by making Asian countries as China's priority, making Economic Corridor the support pillar, making breakthroughs in transport infrastructure development, building a financing platform and promoting people-to-people exchanges.[3]

Since 2015, especially after the release of *Vision and Actions on Jointly Building Silk Road Economic Belt and 21st-Century Maritime Silk Road (Vision and Actions)*, policy coordination between China

---

[2] Xi Jinping, "Carrying Forward the Silk Road Spirit, Promoting the Mutual Development — Keynote Speech at the Opening Ceremony of the Sixth Ministerial Conference of the China–Arab States Cooperation Forum", *People's Daily*, June 6, 2014, p. 2. [习近平:《弘扬丝路精神深化中阿合作——在中阿合作论坛第六届部长级会议开幕式上的讲话》(2014 年 6 月 5 日, 北京), 载《人民日报》2014 年 6 月 6 日, 第 2 版。]

[3] Xi Jinping, "Connectivity Spearheads Development and Partnership Enables Cooperation: Address at Dialogue on Strengthening Connectivity Partnership", *People's Daily*, November 9, 2014, p. 2. [习近平:《联通引领发展伙伴聚焦合作——在 "加强互联互通伙伴关系" 东道主伙伴对话会上的讲话》(2014 年 11 月 8日, 北京), 载《人民日报》2014 年 11 月 9 日, 第 2 版。]

and B&R countries has been deepened day by day, shifting from China's sole interpretation to joint discussion between all the parties involved. The agenda has also turned from "what is the Belt and Road Initiative" to "how to realize strategic synergy." With a focus on strategic alignment and a priority on key countries, China's policy coordination has entered a stage of the "BRI Plus".

The China–Pakistan Economic Corridor (CPEC) is a flagship project of the Belt and Road Initiative. On April 20, 2015, President Xi Jinping landed in Islamabad, which not only marked his first visit in this year but also the first official visit to a foreign country by top Chinese leaders since the release of the *Vision and Actions.* The strategic significance of CPEC is self-evident. The two parties agreed to construct a "1 + 4" cooperation pattern focusing on the Gwadar Port, energy, transportation infrastructure and cooperation in industrial parks. The CPEC is made a major project with demonstrative value for connectivity in this region.[4] It is worth noting that, this project highly conforms to the medium- and long-term economic development blueprint — Vision 2025 — released by the Ministry of Planning and Development of Pakistan in 2014. The two countries signed 51 cooperation agreements and memorandums focusing on energy and power and infrastructure construction with an intended investment of 46 billion USD, which amounted to one-fifth of Pakistan's GDP. In January 2016, the government of Pakistan decided to establish a steering committee of construction of the CPEC under the leadership of Prime Minister Sharif. This committee will coordinate provincial works and share information in the construction of the CPEC. Members of the committee include the Federal Planning, Development and Reform Minister, the Water and Power Minister, the Rail Minister, the Transportation Minister as well as Provincial Chief Ministers. Under the principle of "one corridor,

---

[4] Joint Statement on Establishing All-weather Strategic Cooperative Partnership between the People's Republic of China and the Islamic Republic of Pakistan (April 20, 2015, Islamabad) *People's Daily,* April 21, 2015, p. 2. [《中华人民共和国和巴基斯坦伊斯兰共和国关于建立全天候战略合作伙伴关系的联合声明》(2015 年 4 月 20 日, 伊斯兰堡),《人民日报》2015 年 4 月 21 日, 第 2 版。]

multiple passageways", the west passageway of the CPEC is given top priority.[5]

To better coordinate the Silk Road Economic Belt Initiative with Kazakhstan's Bright Road economic policy. Kazakhstan is a big country in Central Asia. It is also the place where the Silk Road Economic Belt Initiative was proposed and a strategic supporting country in the construction of "the Belt". So far, Kazakhstan has formulated the Bright Road strategy aiming at boosting domestic economy. It is estimated that 9 billion USD will be invested to improve infrastructure in domestic transportation, industry, energy, society and culture from 2015 to 2017.[6] In December 2014, Premier Li Keqiang expressed a willingness to actively participate in the Bright Road strategy for the first time and initiated cooperation on equipment and industrial capacity. In March 2015, 28 project documents were signed on major industrial capacity cooperation between China and Kazakhstan in order to deepen integration in industrial fields including steel, cement, plate glass, chemical industry, machinery, nonferrous metal and textile products with a gross investment valued at near 23.6 billion USD, which set a good example of going global for China's advantageous industrial capacity. On May 7, 2015, during President Xi Jinping's visit to Kazakhstan, leaders of the two countries made it clear that they would promote strategic integration of the construction of China's Silk Road Economic Belt with Kazakhstan's economic growth strategy of the Bright Road in an effort to realize common prosperity.

Synergizing China's 21st-Century Maritime Silk Road Initiative with Indonesia's Global Maritime Fulcrum Strategy. Indonesia is

---

[5] Ji Wei, "Pakistan Forms Committee to Oversee China–Pakistan Economic Corridor Project", January 16, 2016, http://news.xinhuanet.com/2016-01/16/c_128633981. htm, log-in time: March 10, 2016. (季伟：《巴基斯坦决定成立中巴经济走廊建设指导委员会》，2016 年 1 月 16 日。)

[6] Huang Dongming and Dong Aibo, "Ambassador of Kazakhstan in China: the Bright Road Plan and the Belt and Road Initiative Neatly are Complementary", April 16, 2015, http://news.xinhuanet.com/world/2015-04/16/c_1114996805.htm, log-in time: April 20, 2015. (黄东明、董爱波：《哈萨克斯坦驻华大使:"光明之路"计划与丝绸之路经济带建设契合互补》，2015 年 4 月 16 日。)

the country where the 21st-Century Maritime Silk Road Initiative was first proposed. As the country with the biggest population and strongest economic power in ASEAN, Indonesia is a strategic pivot in the building of the Belt and Road. Since taking office, Indonesian President Joko Widodo has been dedicated to building Indonesia into a maritime power by promoting infrastructure connectivity, aiming at making the archipelago nation the world's maritime axis. During his visit to China at the end of March 2015, President Joko Widodo and President Xi Jinping issued a joint statement which said that "the two sides hold the view that the 21st-Century Maritime Silk Road, proposed by President Xi Jinping, and the Strategy of the Global Maritime Fulcrum, initiated by President Joko Widodo, are complementary." According to the statement, China and Indonesia agreed to strengthen strategy and policy communication, advance maritime infrastructure connectivity, and deepen cooperation in industrial investment and major project construction. In April 2015, President Xi Jinping attended the Asian–African Summit and activities commemorating the 60th anniversary of the Bandung Conference in Indonesia. The two leaders reaffirmed their commitment to connect China's 21st-Century Maritime Silk Road Initiative with Indonesia's Global Maritime Fulcrum Strategy and to develop a "maritime partnership" together. Meanwhile, China reaffirmed that it would actively participate in Indonesia's infrastructure connectivity construction, including railways, highways, ports, wharfs, dams, airports and bridges. Also, China would be willing to provide financial support in multiple ways to related projects.

Synergizing the Silk Road Economic Belt Initiative with the Eurasian Economic Union (EAEU). The EAEU officially came into being on January 1, 2015. So far, the EAEU includes Armenia, Belarus, Kazakhstan, Kyrgyzstan and Russia. It is essentially a regional organization for economic cooperation led by Russia. Russia has been regarding Central Asia as its own backyard for a long time, hence it had doubts about the increasing influence exerted by China in this region in recent years and had been lukewarm to the Silk Road Economic Belt Initiative. However, in view of the openness and cooperativeness China displayed in advancing the Silk Road Economic

Belt, and the economic sanctions and the diplomatic isolation it faced after the Ukraine Crisis, Russia began to respond positively to the Initiative. On May 8, 2015, President Xi Jinping visited Russia and attended events to commemorate the 70th anniversary of the victory of the Great Patriotic War. The two countries affirmed to continue to seek common ground for regional economic integration under the framework of the Silk Road Economic Belt Initiative and the EAEU. Meanwhile, the two parties signed a joint statement on cooperation in the synergizing of the Silk Road Economic Belt Initiative with the EAEU construction, reaching an agreement to take measures to promote priority fields including investment and trade facilitation, cooperation in industrial capacity, industrial parks, infrastructure construction and settlement in local currency and financial cooperation. On June 20, Russian President Putin said during the St. Petersburg International Economic Forum (SPIEF) that integrating the Silk Road Economic Belt Initiative and the EAEU is of great significance for both Russia and China and it would boost bilateral cooperation in high technology, transportation and infrastructure, and particularly promote the development of the Far East of Russia.[7] On July 9, President Xi Jinping stated in the 15th meeting of the Council of Heads of State of the SCO held in Ufa, Russia, that the two countries needed to use the SCO as a key platform to integrate China's Silk Road Economic Belt Initiative with Russia's EAEU to advance the development, cooperation and prosperity of the whole Eurasia.

Coordinating the Belt and Road Initiative with Russia's Transcontinental Rail Plan and Mongolia's Prairie Road program. During the SCO summit held in September 2014, China, Mongolia and Russia held the first meeting of heads of state, and came up with the proposal to coordinate the Silk Road Economic Belt Initiative with Russia's transcontinental rail plan and Mongolia's Prairie Road program, and to jointly build a China–Mongolia–Russia economic

---

[7]Yue Lianguo and Lu Jinbo, "Integration of Eurasian Economic Union Connects and the Silk Road Economic Belt Brings Huge Opportunities", June 20, 2015, http://news.xinhuanet.com/world/2015-06/20/c_1115678843.htm, log-in time: July 5, 2015. (岳连国、鲁金博：《欧亚经济联盟对接"丝绸之路经济带"可带来巨大机遇》，2015 年 6 月 20 日。)

corridor.[8] Since then, related departments have been maintaining close communication and coordination concerning railway transportation and tourism. During the SCO summit in Ufa in July 2015, the second meeting of heads of state reached a further consensus on deepening trilateral cooperation. During the meeting, the three heads of state approved a roadmap for the development of trilateral cooperation and witnessed the signing of a memorandum on compiling a guideline for building the trilateral economic corridor, a framework agreement on facilitating trilateral trade and a framework agreement on cooperation on ports of entry among the three countries. President Xi Jinping stressed that economic cooperation was the priority area of trilateral cooperation. Noticeably, China called for the docking of the EAEU with trilateral economic corridor on the meeting for the first time.[9]

Synergizing Vietnam's "Two Corridors and One Economic Circle" Plan with China's Belt and Road Initiative. Vietnam is an important neighbor of China. In May 2004, Vietnamese Premier Phan Van Khai proposed to jointly build the "Two Corridors and One Economic Circle" during his visit to China. The two economic corridors form a V-shaped geographic pattern with the east economic corridor linking Kunming in China with Lao Cai, Hanoi, Haiphong and Quang Ninh in Vietnam while with the west economic corridor linking Nanning in China with Lang Son, Hanoi, Haiphong and Quang Ninh in Vietnam. The economic circle, also known as "Gulf of Tonkin Economic Belt", was initiated to cover China's provinces of Hainan, Guangdong and Guangxi as well as Vietnam's Northern coastal area. In November 2015, during President Xi Jinping's visit to Vietnam, the two countries reached an important consensus on integrating the Belt and Road Initiative with the "Two Corridors and

---

[8] Du Shangze and Lin Xuedan, "Chinese President Xi Jinping Meets with Russian President Vladimir Putin and Mongolia's President Tsakhiagiin Elbegdorj", *People's Daily*, September 12, 2014, p. 1.(杜尚泽、林雪丹:《习近平出席中俄蒙三国元首会晤》, 载《人民日报》2014 年 9 月 12 日, 第1版。)

[9] Du Shangze and Lin Xuedan, "Chinese President Xi Jinping Meets with Russian President Vladimir Putin and Mongolia's President Tsakhiagiin Elbegdorj for the Second Time", *People's Daily*, July 10, 2015, p. 2. (杜尚泽、林雪丹:《习近平出席中俄蒙三国元首第二次会晤》, 载《人民日报》2015 年 7 月 10 日, 第 2 版。)

One Economic Circle" plan and strengthening connectivity and cooperation of industrial capacity.

Synergizing the Belt and Road Initiative with EU's Investment Plan for Europe. The European Union is the largest trading partner of China and the most developed region along the Belt and Road. In November 2014, European Commission President Jean-Claude Juncker launched a €315 billion plan to spur investment. It is called Europe's Investment Plan or Juncker Plan. It is aimed to reinvigorate the EU's economy by establishing European Fund for Strategic Investment (EFSI), mainly investing in energy, transportation infrastructure, broadband networks construction and educational projects. In the end of June 2015, during Chinese Premier Li Keqiang's visit to Europe, the heads of state of the two countries decided to integrate the Belt and Road Initiative with the European Investment Plan, and agreed to set up a China–EU joint investment fund and build a China–EU connectivity platform. In fact, there is much potential for the alignment of China and the EU in industries and industrial capacity besides transportation. China now is proactively promoting the strategy of Made in China 2025, which has much in common with Germany Industry 4.0, New Industrial France and UK Industry 2050 in that they all lay emphasis on industrial transformation and upgrading. The trilateral industrial capacity cooperation initiated by China is beneficial to the common development of the upstream, midstream and downstream of industrial chains in China, European developed and developing countries. The Internet Plus plan, the construction of European single digital market and European smart cities are mutually beneficial to each other, too.

Synergizing the Belt and Road Initiative with the development strategies of the 16 Central and Eastern European (CEE) countries — the 16+1 mechanism. The China–CEE 16+1 cooperation mechanism constitutes a new growth driver in China's diplomacy in recent years, which provides a new South–South cooperation platform with the characteristics of North–South cooperation. In June 2015, Foreign Minister Wang Yi and Minister of Foreign Affairs and Trade of Hungary Peter Szijjarto signed the *Memorandum of Understanding (MOU) on jointly promoting the construction of the Silk Road Economic*

Belt and the 21st-Century Maritime Silk Road between China and Hungary. This is the first of such cooperation document signed between China and a European country. Wang Yi said the two countries should work together to promote the strategic integration of China's Belt and Road Initiative with Hungary's policy of "Opening to the East." By signing the intergovernmental MOU, Hungary would become an important pivot for the construction of the Belt and Road in Europe, especially in Central and Eastern Europe. And by taking the construction of the Hungary–Serbia Railway as an opportunity, Hungary could grow into an important logistics hub in the Eurasian continent.[10] Following Hungary, China signed similar intergovernmental MOUs with Poland, Serbia, Czech Republic, Bulgaria and Slovakia during the 4th China–CEE Summit in November 2015.

Integrating China's Belt and Road Initiative with the development strategies of Saudi Arabia, Egypt and Iran. In January 2016, Chinese President Xi Jinping paid a state visit to Saudi Arabia, Egypt and Iran and visited the Arab League headquarters. The three countries are situated in the Western joint zone of the Belt and Road and are with significant influence in the Middle East. During Xi's visit, China and the three countries reached a consensus on synergizing development strategies under the framework of jointly building the Belt and Road and signed *MOU on Jointly Building the Belt and Road* respectively. It is noteworthy that during his stay in Egypt, President Xi Jinping suggested that the two countries should conjoin their development strategies and visions, and focus on cooperation in infrastructure construction and production capacity and turn Egypt into a hub under the Belt and Road Initiative.[11] At the Arab League

---

[10] Ministry of Foreign Affairs of the People's Republic of China, "Wang Yi: China and Hungary Should Connect the Belt and Road Initiative and "Opening to the East" Policy", June 7, 2015, http://www.fmprc.gov.cn/mfa_chn/zyxw_602251/t1271037.shtml, log-in time: June 8, 2015.(中国外交部:《王毅:中匈要对接"一带一路"和"向东开放"》, 2015 年 6 月 7 日。)

[11] Liu Shuiming and Du Shangze, "Chinese President Xi Jinping Holds Talks with Egyptian President Abdel-Fattah al-Sisi", *People's Daily*, January 22, 2016, p. 1.(刘水明、杜尚泽:《习近平同埃及总统塞西会谈》, 载《人民日报》2016 年 1 月 22 日, 第 1 版。)

Headquarters, President Xi Jinping stated that under the framework of the Belt and Road Initiative, China should be builders of peace, promoters of development, boosters of industrialization, supporters of stability and partners of people-to-people exchanges in the Middle East.[12] In Iran, President Xi Jinping elaborated on the four major directions of the strategic integration in the new era. He stressed bilateral cooperation on four fronts: take energy cooperation as ballast; regard connectivity cooperation as a focus; view production capacity cooperation as a compass and take financial cooperation as a promoter.[13]

By the end of 2017, more than 100 countries had expressed interest to support and join the BRI and China had signed 100 agreements to jointly build the Belt and Road with 86 countries and international organizations, covering interconnectivity, energy, investment, trade and economy, finance, technology, society, people's livelihoods and maritime cooperation. China also signed *MOU on jointly building the Belt and Road* with the United Nations Development Programme (UNDP), the UN ESCAP and the WHO. It signed *MOU on Strengthening Cooperation on Jointly Building Online Silk Road* with Turkey, Poland and Saudi Arabia, among other countries. Planning documents on building the China–Mongolia–Russia Economic Corridor and on cooperation between China and Tajikistan and China and Laos have been finished. Documents on cooperation between China and Kazakhstan, China and Belarus and China and Czech Republic have been signed.[14]

---

[12] Xi Jinping, "To Work Together for a Bright Future of China–Arab Relations: Speech at the Arab League headquarters" (January 21, 2016, Cairo), *People's Daily*, January 22, 2016, p. 3.(习近平:《共同开创中阿关系的美好未来——在阿拉伯国家联盟总部的演讲》(2016 年 1 月 21 日,开罗), 载《人民日报》2016 年 1 月 22 日, 第 3 版。)

[13] Du Shangze *et al.*, "Chinese President Meets Iran's Supreme Leader Hassan Rouhani", *People's Daily*, January 24, 2016, p. 2. (杜尚泽等:《习近平同伊朗总统鲁哈尼会谈》, 载《人民日报》2016 年 1 月 24 日, 第 1 版。)

[14] Office of the Leading Group for the Belt and Road Initiative, *Building the Belt and Road: Concept, Practice and China's Contribution*, Beijing: Foreign Languages Press, May 2017, pp. 7–9.

In retrospect of all the efforts made by China to achieve policy coordination since September 2013, three features stand out.

First, relying on the existing bilateral or multilateral cooperation mechanisms between China and B&R countries. As a newly proposed Initiative, the Belt and Road isn't meant to start things all over again. By leveraging and integrating the existing platforms and cooperation mechanisms, China is able to dispel other countries' doubts and effectively reduce political and institutional cost of communication and mobilization. As early as the BRI was proposed, the platforms that China could use were the two most important regional cooperation mechanisms the country has participated in so far: the SCO and ASEAN Plus China (10 + 1). Since then, apart from various bilateral meetings, China has been vigorously dedicated to policy interpretation and mobilization via a series of multilateral mechanisms including China–GCC Strategic Dialogue, Boao Forum for Asia, CICA, CASCF, the SCO Summit, Asia–Europe Meeting (ASEM), APEC Meeting, China–CEE Leaders' Meeting of 16 + 1 mechanism, Asian–African Summit, BRICS Summit, Forum on China–Africa Cooperation etc.

Second, seeking strategic coordination between the BRI and the development strategies of B&R countries. In reality, it is only possible to gain understanding, support and participation from countries and regions along the Belt and Road with relatively low cost when the development strategies of each side are integrated and their interests and aspirations are respected. For example, the construction of the CPEC can provide an optimal solution to Pakistan's most urgent problems regarding energy and transportation; the China–Russia cooperation echoes especially well with Russia's concerns in the EAEU, the construction of transcontinental passage and the development of the Far East and Siberia; the China–Europe cooperation starts first with infrastructure connectivity and industrial capacity; in response to other countries' strategies or policies such as Kazakhstan's Bright Road economic policy, Indonesia's Global Maritime Fulcrum Strategy, Sri Lanka's construction of a maritime transportation center in the Indian Ocean, Vietnam's Two Corridors and One Economic Circle, Egypt's New Suez Canal Economic Corridor, Turkey's Middle Corridor plan,

Poland's Responsible Development Strategy, the EU's Investment Plan for Europe, ASEAN's Master Plan on ASEAN Connectivity 2025, the United Nations' 2030 Agenda etc., China is not only active in seeking cooperation in key fields as infrastructure construction, connectivity and industrial upgrading but also takes care of other countries' ambition to become a regional power or significant hub. As such, policy coordination regarding China's Belt and Road Initiative will focus on strategic integration and prioritize on win–win plans in the future (Table 7.1).

Third, combining key breakthroughs with overall promotion. On the one hand, China continued to launch initiatives in countries and regions along the Belt and Road on various bilateral and multilateral

Table 7.1 Development Strategies or Policies of Countries along the Belt and Road

China's Initiative	Countries/International Organizations	Corresponding Strategies or Policies
The Belt and Road	Pakistan	Vision 2025
	Kazakhstan	The Bright Road Economic Policy
	Indonesia	Global Maritime Fulcrum Strategy
	Russia	The Transcontinental Rail Plan The Eurasian Economic Union
	Mongolia	Prairie Road Program
	Sri Lanka	Maritime Transportation Center in the Indian Ocean
	Vietnam	Two Corridors and One Economic Circle
	Egypt	New Suez Canal Economic Corridor
	Turkey	Middle Corridor Initiative
	Australia	Northern Australia Development Plan
	UK	Northern Powerhouse
	Hungary	Opening to the East
	Poland	Responsible Development Strategy
	EU	Investment Plan for Europe
	ASEAN	Master Plan on ASEAN Connectivity 2025
	UN	2030 Agenda for Sustainable Development

occasions. On the other, China conducted good policy coordination with countries with strategic significance and sound political relations. So far, the list of pivot countries with which China is committed to promote the construction of the Belt and Road has become clear. Among others, countries as Pakistan, Kazakhstan and Russia will serve as the strategic pivots on land while Indonesia on the sea; meanwhile, a few countries in Asia, Europe and Africa will be targeted for some major and flagship projects.

7.2 Infrastructure Connectivity

Facilities connectivity is a priority area in implementing the BRI. It includes the construction of highways, railways, ports, aviation, pipelines, power grids and optical cables. Since the Initiative was proposed, the existing cooperation has received an added boost, yielding fruitful and impressive progress in multiple aspects. By the end of April 2017, China had signed more than 130 bilateral, multilateral and regional transport agreements with countries along the Belt and Road, including railway, road, marine, air and postal transport cooperation contracts, such as *the SCO Intergovernmental Agreement on Creation of Beneficial Conditions for International Road Transportation* and *the China–ASEAN Marine Transportation Agreement*. According to the statistics, there are 356 international cargo and passenger transportation lines between China and relevant countries, connecting 73 ports and road hubs. Marine transportation service is extended to all B&R countries. China has direct air links with 43 countries with around 4,200 flights every week. Formalities for cross-border rail transport have been simplified, which facilities cargo transport between China and Europe and the use of trains to delivery parcel.[15]

---

[15] Liu Zhiqiang, "Promoting Interconnectivity and Building a Bridge for Development: An Interview with Li Xiaopeng, China's Minister of Transport", *People's Daily*, May 13, 2017, p. 4. (刘志强:《推进互联互通 构筑发展纽带——访交通运输部部长李小鹏》, 载《人民日报》2017 年 5 月 13 日, 第 4 版。)

7.2.1 *Highway*

Construction of highways is a significant part of facility connectivity in this Initiative. Although traffic speed on highways is not comparable with that of railways, highway transportation enjoys less restriction from political factors than trans-boundary railways. In recent years, China has been proactively engaged in facilitating transportation in the whole region by making use of various regional cooperative mechanisms and financing platforms while energetically expanding its own highway network at home. On July 10, 2015, during the 15th Meeting of the Council of Heads of State of the SCO Member States, President Xi Jinping stressed that traffic facility connectivity is a priority and the important basis of regional cooperation. In the next few years, China will push for the completion of 4,000 km of railway and over 10,000 km of highway within the region, so that a layout of interconnected transportation will be basically in place.[16] At present, the highway network on the southern corridor (China and the Indo–China Peninsula) is near completion. The construction on the northern and middle corridors is underway.

7.2.1.1 *The Western Europe–Western China International Transit Corridor*

The overall length of Western Europe–Western China International Transit Corridor is 8,445 km. It stretches from Lianyungang in East China, passes through Zhengzhou, Lanzhou, Urumqi in China and enters Kazakhstan via Khorgos. Across the Northern border, it enters Russia and extends to St. Petersburg after passing through Orenburg, Kazan and Moscow and finally joins with European highway network.

---

[16] Xi Jinping, "Strengthening Shanghai Cooperation Organization through Unity, Mutual Support and Joint Response to Challenges: Statement at the 15th Meeting of the Council of the Heads of State of the Shanghai Cooperation Organization Member States" (July 10, 2015, Ufa), *People's Daily*, July 11, 2015, p. 2. (习近平:《团结互助共迎挑战推动上海合作组织实现新跨越——在上海合作组织成员国元首理事会第十五次会议上的讲话》(2015 年 7 月 10 日, 乌法), 载《人民日报》2015 年7 月 11 日, 第 2 版。)

Once the great Northern Eurasian transport corridor is completed, Western China would be connected with the vast area of Western Europe. So far, China's inland part of this project (the Lianyungang–Khorgos Highway) was already completed. The overall length of Kazakhstan's inland part of this project is 2,787 km. When it is completed, the freight volume of highways passing through Kazakhstan would increase to 3.5 million tons from previous 0.9 million tons per year, and the traveling time of Chinese goods exported to Europe would be shortened from the current 45 days (ocean shipping) to 10 or 11 days (land transportation). It is worth mentioning that the total investment of this project amounts to over 6 billion USD (according to the exchange rate in 2009), which is funded by Kazakhstan's national fiscal appropriation, international financing (Asian Development Bank [ADB], European Bank for Reconstruction and Development [EBRD], the World Bank, Islamic Bank and Japan International Cooperation Agency) and franchise investment. The project is considered a good model of cooperative and joint construction.

7.2.1.2 *The Highway Network in Central Asia*

The Tajikistan–China Highway starts from Dushanbe in the west and stretches to the Kulma Pass on the borderline of China and Tajikistan in the east before connecting with the Karakoram Highway (KKH). The overall length reaches near 1,100 km, 70% of which runs through high plateaus and mountain ranges with the maximal altitude of 4,600 m. The renovation of Tajikistan–China highway could contribute to the formation of the highway network in Tajikistan, exert critical influence on its economic development and promote the connectivity of China with countries in Central Asia. According to Luan Guitao, the general manager of the Tajikistan Office of China Road and Bridge Corporation (CRBC), this project will adopt Chinese standard, and be implemented in three stages. The project is estimated to be completed by 2020. Once completed, it could reach the second-level highway standard and the plateaus section could reach the third-level highway standard. The highway is designed to run hundreds of kilometers through the Pamirs where the average altitude could be over 4,000 m.[17]

The Phase I project of Tajikistan–China Highway is 147.64 km long which is designed to be implemented in three stages. On October 1, 2013, the 4,450-m Chormaghzak Tunnel was successfully completed which could shorten the distance by almost 20 km and cut the traveling time from over 4 hours to 1.5 hours. In April 2015, the opening ceremony of Tajikistan–China Highway Phase I Stage 3 Project was held in Danghara City, marking the successful completion of Tajikistan–China Highway Phase I. This is the second project CRBC undertook in Tajikistan under the framework of the SCO and is financed by concessional loans from the Chinese government. It is worth mentioning that President Rakhmon of Tajikistan awarded Order of Friendship to four Chinese including Luan Guitao for their hard and outstanding work, the first of its kind that Tajikistan leaders award Medal of Honor to foreign-owned enterprises. The Phase II of the project has already been initiated, which is believed to make trade and personnel exchanges between the two countries more convenient.

The Alternative North–South Road Project is the largest project, in terms of contract value and engineering quantity, which CRBC contracted in Kyrgyzstan. In September 2013, the Export-Import Bank of China signed the loan agreement on Alternative North–South Road Project with the Ministry of Finance of Kyrgyzstan, marking the beginning of the project. The road is 154 km in length and the duration for this project is 56 months. The construction of this road will not only significantly shorten the distance and traveling time between North and South Kyrgyzstan and alleviate the traffic pressure of highways from the capital Bishkek to the Southern city of Osh, but also greatly improve the transportation capacity of Chinese

---

[17] Zhou Liang and Sha Dati, "China Road and Bridge Corporation Builds Roads and Bridges in Tajikistan", February 20, 2014, http://www.xj.xinhuanet.com/2014-02/20/c_119586753.htm; Jia Xingpeng, "China Road and Bridge Corporation Builds "New Silk Road" in Tajikistan", September 26, 2014, http://finance.people.com.cn/n/2014/0926/c387602-25739299.html, log-in time: July 28, 2015. (周良、沙达提:《在高山之国筑路架桥的中国路桥人》, 2014 年 2 月 20 日; 贾兴鹏:《中国路桥在塔吉克铺设"新丝路"》, 2014 年 9 月 26 日。)

exports to surrounding countries and even to Europe through the land access in Kyrgyzstan. The Around-Lake Issyk-Kul Road Rehabilitation Project is another major project undertaken by CRBC in Kyrgyzstan. The project, with the contract amount of around 39 million USD, is 23.66 km in length, and the construction period is 36 months. On July 22, 2015, the Around-Lake Issyk-Kul Road Rehabilitation Project (Bishkek–Balakchi) was completed. President Atambayev pointed out that the road would not only promote the tourism in Lake Issyk-Kul, but also make Kyrgyzstan a better transit country for regional transportation.[18]

Moreover, with the joint efforts of Chinese enterprises and the host countries, the China–Kyrgyzstan–Kazakhstan Highway (Bishkek–Torugart) Rehabilitation Project (the "60 km Project") and freeway from Ayni to Panjakent in Tajikistan were successfully completed. The quality and progress of tunnel projects, namely, Angren–Pape tunnel in Uzbekistan and Vahdat–Yovon tunnel in Tajikistan have been highly commended by the leaders for many times.

7.2.1.3 *KKH Upgrade Project*

The KKH is also known as "Pakistan–China Friendship Highway". It is a main artery of the CPEC. It starts from Kashgar, a city in the Xinjiang of China, runs through the Karakoram, Hindu Kush and Himalayas, goes through the Khunjerab Pass on the border of China and Pakistan and arrives at the Northern town of Thakot in Pakistan. It is 1,224 km in length with an altitude ranging from 600 to 4700 m. The geological condition is very harsh with frequent occurrences of geological disasters including snow slide, landslide, rockfall, collapse, snow accumulation and earthquake. From 1966 to 1978, hundreds of Chinese engineering technicians had sacrificed their lives

---

[18] China Communications Construction Company Limited, "The President of Kyrgyzstan Kyrgyzstan's President Attends the Opening Ceremony of China Road and Bridge Corporation's Project", July 27, 2015, http://en.ccccltd.cn/pub/cccltd/xwzx/gsyw/201507/t20150727_40164.html, log-in time: July 28, 2015. (中国交通建设股份有限公司:《吉尔吉斯斯坦总统出席中国路桥项目通车仪式》, 2015 年 7 月 27 日。)

for it. There is a Chinese memorial park in the Northern city of Gilgit in Pakistan where 88 Chinese builders were buried. Ali Ahmad Jan, an old Pakistani has been voluntarily guarding the park for almost 40 years since 1978. To commend his devotion, President Xi Jinping conferred the Five Principles of Peaceful Coexistence Friendship Award on him in April 2015.

KKH Upgrade Project Phase I. Considering that the road condition was in bad repair, China and Pakistan decided to reconstruct and extend the KKH at the end of 2006. On August 1, 2008, KKH Improvement Project Phase I (Raikot Bridge to Khunjerab Section) undertaken by CRBC formally started. The overall length is 335 km. In January 2010, landslides in Attabad resulted from an earthquake created a barrier lake over 20 km in length. The lake inundated a large section of the KKH and cut it off. Consequently, people and vehicles could only rely on ferryboats on the lake for transport and accidents occurred frequently, incurring great frustration to the country's import and export trade with China.[19] In July 2012, following CRBC's relocation design of the barrier lake section, construction of relocated section broke ground. On September 14, 2015, having overcome many adversities such as high elevation, frequent occurrences of geological disasters, constant communal conflicts, short construction duration and inconvenient traffic, KKH Upgrade Project Phase I was successfully completed. Five tunnels of 7 km long in total were named China–Pakistan Friendship Tunnels. After the extension, the breadth of the KKH expanded from 10 to 40 m, the speed of vehicles could reach 80 kph and the transportation capability was increased by threefold. From then on, traveling time of automobiles from the Khunjerab Pass in Xinjiang of China to Raikot Bridge in Pakistan was shortened from 14 to 7 hours, the trade logistics time between the two countries was decreased by about eight days and the transportation cost of goods per ton by at least 100 USD.

---

[19] Chen Peng, "Making Efforts for the Re-opening of Karakoram Highway: Visiting KaraKoram Highway Renovation and Extension Project", April 18, 2015, http://news.xinhuanet.com/world/2015-04/18/c_1115011982.htm, log-in time: July 28, 2015.(陈鹏:《通讯:为中巴友谊公路早日复通努力——走访喀喇昆仑公路改扩建项目》, 2015 年 4 月 18 日。)

KKH Upgrade Project Phase II. On December 22, 2015, CRBC contracted with Pakistan's National Highway Authority on KKH Improvement Project Phase II (Havelian to Thakot) in Islamabad. The overall length of the project is 118 km and the duration for this project is 42 months. The contract value is 1.315 billion USD, which is financed by the Export–Import Bank of China. Under the Engineering Procurement Construction (EPC) mode, it would be designed and constructed according to Chinese standard.

7.2.1.4 *The Peshawar–Karachi Motorway in Pakistan*

The Peshawar–Karachi Motorway (PKM) is a 1,152-km-long two-way six-lane motorway with a designed speed of 120 kph. It is now the largest project in transport infrastructure under the framework of the CPEC. This motorway runs through the most developed and populous area of Pakistan. The project is regarded as an Early Harvest Program and strongly supported by the governments of China and Pakistan. On December 22, 2015, China State Construction Engineering Corporation officially signed the EPC project of the Sukkur–Multan Section of the PKM. The overall length of the project section is 392 km, and the duration of this project is 36 months. The contract value is around $2.89 billion. Once it is completed, the traffic condition between the two places would be improved greatly, adding more momentum to the economic and social development of Pakistan.

7.2.2 *Railway*

The railway especially the high-speed rail boasts efficiency, security and convenience as compared with other forms of land transportation. Given the breakthroughs China made in its domestic railway network in recent years and the successful operation of China's high-speed rail, trans-boundary railway becomes a focal point in facilities connectivity. It is reported that along the Belt and Road, Southeast Asia, Central Asia and South Asia are among the top three in terms of their need of railways. The closer they are situated to China, the stronger will they have for interconnectivity. While the Northern corridor and Southern corridor are advancing steadily, the construction in the middle corridor is progressing at a relatively slow pace. In the process, Chinese technologies, standards, equipment, experience on building, operation and management concerning railway construction have gained wide recognition.

7.2.2.1 *The China–Europe Railway*

The China–Europe Railway is an upgrade to the original Eurasian transport corridor rather than a brand new trade route. In March 2011, the Chongqing–Xinjiang–Europe Railway was opened to traffic. It starts from Chongqing, passes through Kazakhstan, Russia, Belarus and Poland before arriving at Duisburg. It takes only 16 days to travel 11,179 km from Chongqing to Duisburg, saving 20 days compared with maritime transport. In quick succession to it, Chengdu, Wuhan, Zhengzhou, Xi'an, Changsha, Kunming, Guiyang, Lianyungang, Suzhou, Yiwu, Qingdao, Guangzhou, Xiamen, etc. opened CRE block trains bound for Central Asia and Europe. Among them, the Zhengzhou–Europe International Block Train takes up over one-fourth of the total trips of the CRE (China–Europe) block train with more than 40% of national volume of freight traffic. Also, it ranks first in China in loading rate, cargo volume, number of trips, frequency of trips and comprehensive influence.[20]

In April 2017, China Railway signed the Agreement for Further Cooperation on China–Europe Container Block Trains with railway companies in Belarus, Germany, Kazakhstan, Mongolia, Poland and Russia. These trains link 28 Chinese cities with 29 cities in 11 European countries, including those from China's Chongqing, Zhengzhou and Yiwu to Duisburg, Hamburg and London respectively. In total, they stretch more than 10,000 km. Within several years, the number of rail lines between China and Europe increased from 0 to 20. They form a new logistics channel across the Eurasian continent. Together with the New Eurasian Land Bridge and the

---

[20] Xia Xianqing and Wang Jinhu, "International Freight Trains Bring Vigor for the Belt and Road Initiative", *Economic Daily*, December 7, 2015, p. 8. (夏先清、王金虎:《国际货运班列为"一带一路"带来活力》, 载《经济日报》2015 年 12 月 7 日, 第 8 版。)

Siberian Land Bridge, there are now three trans-Eurasia railway link-ages, on the West, Middle and East respectively.

According to the National Development and Reform Commission, by the end of 2017, China had opened 61 China-Europe rail routes, entailing the operation of more than 6,000 trains to 36 cities in 13 European countries. As for 2017, there were 3673 China-Europe trains, which rose by 116% over the previous year and exceeded the total number of trains from 2011 to 2016. From Spanish red wine, Holland cheese, Polish fruits to German cars, more and more European goods make their way into the world's biggest consumer market through these block trains. On the other hand, trains loaded with consumer durables, clothes and computers, among other Chinese commodities, hurtle to Europe.

In addition to Chinese commodities, products from South Korea, Japan and Southeast Asia also take these block trains to Europe, proving the public good function of the BRI. According to the China–Europe RAILWAY Express Development Plan (2016–2020), by 2020, all the rail transport lines will be finished, connect-ing China, Europe and countries along the way, in East Asia, Southeast Asia and other regions. Compared with the 1881 trains over the past years, there will be 5,000 every year in the future and trade volume would increase from the 17 billion dollars in six years to several times that figure.

7.2.2.2 *The Moscow–Kazan High-Speed Railway*

In October 2014, Chinese Premier Li Keqiang and his Russian counterpart, Primier Dmitry Medvedev, witnessed the joint signing of a Memorandum on Cooperation on high-speed rail by the Chinese National Development and Reform Commission, the Ministry of Transport of the Russian Federation, China Railway Corporation and Russian Railways. It is designed to advance the building of a Eurasian high-speed transport corridor linking Beijing and Moscow. Also, it is said that the current priority should be given to the high-speed railway between Moscow and Kazan. So far, the 770 km high-speed rail between Moscow and Kazan is the largest Public–Private Partnership (PPP) project in Russia. Except for the different track gauge, it basically adopts the Chinese standard. It is estimated to be completed by the 2018 Russia FIFA World Cup. The traveling time between the two places will be reduced from the current 14 to 3.5 hours. According to Alexander Misharin, the First Vice President of Russian Railways, although Russia provides the materials and labor in the construction, engineers and technologies are all from China.

On May 12, 2015, China Railway Eryuan Engineering Group Co., Ltd. worked in partnership with Russian enterprises and won the bid of the survey and design part of the project, and signed the contract on June 18. This project is not only about design and construction. It is aimed to provide a full life-cycle service for Russia's high-speed railway construction in terms of technical consulting, survey and design, construction management, construction, supervision, integration test and commissioning, equipment matching, operation and maintenance, and technician training. The high-speed railway between Moscow and Kazan lies in a frigid zone with extremely harsh geological and climatic conditions and the max speed can reach 400 kph. The wining of this bid is a good indication of the strength of Chinese railway technologies. It is worth mentioning that, the high-speed railway project in Russia is led by the government and operated by China Railway Corporation with the support of authorities from central and ministerial levels, including the National Development and Reform Commission, Ministry of Foreign Affairs, Ministry of Commerce, China Railway Corporation, National Railway Administration, China Development Bank etc. These authorities are called upon to provide a whole set of solutions ranging from investment and financing, survey and design to construction, operation and maintenance. It can be predicted that this will be an important pattern for China's high-speed railway to go global in the future.

7.2.2.3 *The China–Laos Railway*

Laos is a landlocked state on the Indo–China Peninsula. Transportation has always been a sticking point that restricts this country's economic growth and foreign trade. For a very long time, there is only one 3.5 km railway in Laos, which is situated in Thanaleng Railway Station.

The station is located in the South of the Laos capital city of Vientiane and its size can only be compared with that of a remote town in China. The China–Laos Railway makes up an important part of the Trans–Asian Railway system and China–Indochina Peninsula economic corridor. Since April 2010, the Ministry of Railways of China and Ministry of Public Works and Transport of Laos had begun cooperation on the preliminary work of the China–Laos Railway Project.

On November 13, 2015, after long-time and repeated discussion and debate, Xu Shaoshi, the then director of National Development and Reform Commission, signed the document with Somsavat Lengsavad, deputy prime minister of Laos, representing respectively the two governments on the intergovernmental railway project. Directly connecting with China's railway network, it is the first overseas railway project dominantly invested, constructed and operated by China. With all equipments manufactured in China, the whole line is also constructed according to the Chinese standard. The China–Laos railway has a total length of 418 km, with over 60% of the route connected by bridges and tunnels. The railway connects with the Yuxi–Mohan Railway in the North and the Nong Khai–Bangkok Railway in the South. Construction of the project is scheduled to complete in five years with a total investment of around 40 billion RMB ($\approx$\$5.8 billion). Seventy percent of the fund will come from Chinese investment and the rest 30% from Laos. Utilizing electric traction, the single-track railway with passenger and freight traffic is designed to adopt the National I Class Railway standards and the operating speed on the route is designed at 160 km per hour. In order to better implement this project, the two parties have had full discussion and research on the economic and technological plan. Lao also provided a series of preferential and supporting policies in terms of land, taxation and staff visa.[21]

On December 2, 2015, Zhang Dejiang, chairman of the Standing Committee of China's National People's Congress (NPC) and Lao President Choummaly Sayasone jointly attended the commencement

---

[21] The National Development and Reform Commission, "Construction of China–Laos Railway Project Officially Commences", November 13, 2015, http://www.sdpc.gov.cn/xwzx/xwfb/201511/t20151113_758553.html, log-in time: November 14, 2015. (中国国家发改委:《中老铁路项目正式落地》, 2015 年 11 月 13 日。)

ceremony of the Boten–Vientiane Section of the China–Laos Railway, marking the official beginning of the project's implementation. It is estimated to be completed and open to traffic in 2020. By that time, the traveling time from Vientiane to the border between China and Laos would be reduced from 12 hours to no more than 3 hours, greatly facilitating the personnel exchange and trade contacts between the two countries and offering new opportunities for the economic and social development of Laos and the connectivity of the Indo–China Peninsula.

7.2.2.4 *The China–Thailand Railway*

Thailand, the geographical center of the Indo–China Peninsula, has always been the focus of the construction of the Trans–Asian Railway system, thus the railway cooperation between China and Thailand is of great significance. On December 19, 2014, following the "*rice for high-speed rail*" suspension, Chinese Premier Li Keqiang and Thai Prime Minister Prayut Chan-o-cha witnessed the signing ceremony of the MOU for the railway project and agricultural products trade in Bangkok. The two parties decided to build a railway connecting Northern Thailand Nong Khai and the Southern port of Map Ta Phut.

In the next year, the two countries had been engaged in constant and intensive negotiations. On December 3, 2015, Deputy Head of China's National Development and Reform Commission Wang Xiaotao and Thai Transport Minister Arkhom Termpittayapaisith signed an intergovernmental framework document on railway cooperation at the ninth meeting of the Joint Committee on Railway Cooperation between the Thailand and China. The 845-km railway is Thailand's first standard-gauge dual-track railway that allows trains to operate at top speeds of 180–250 km/h. The railway project will use Chinese technology, standard and equipment. From north to south, the whole project will be divided into four sections, namely, Nong Khai–Nakhon Ratchasima, Nakhon Ratchasima–Kaeng Khoi, Kaeng Khoi–Bangkok and Kaeng Khoi–Map Ta Phut, passing through 10 provinces in Thailand. A joint venture company will be established to take charge of investment, construction and operation and the Chinese side will support the Thai in terms of technology licensing and transfer, human resources training and financing.

On December 19, 2015, Chinese State Councilor Wang Yong and Thai Deputy Prime Minister Prajin Jantong attended the launching ceremony of the China–Thailand railway cooperation project at Chiang Rak Noi Station. According to Zhu Xijun, general manager of the Southeast Asia Branch of China Railway Construction, the construction is estimated to be completed in three years. Once it is completed, the round trip fare for a travel from Kunming to Bangkok would be about THB 3600 (≈RMB 700), which amounts to half or one-third of the airfare. The freight cost could even be one-ninth of the airfare. This project will bring about 2 million more Chinese visitors to Thailand and facilitate the export of Thai agricultural products, making Thailand a traffic hub of ASEAN.[22] In the future, China–Thailand railway will be connected to the China–Laos railway, which would link up the middle corridor of the Trans–Asian Railway system and lay the foundation for the construction of China–Indochina Peninsula economic corridor. Prajin Jantong describes such a prospect of the railway project: highway traffic congestion will be alleviated; visitors from China, Thailand and Laos can enjoy more convenient travel; the cargo trains from Kunming will run through Laos and arrive at Map Ta Phut directly; and the successful application of China's railway technologies will set a good example for neighboring countries.[23]

7.2.2.5 *The Djakarta–Bandung High-Speed Railway Project in Indonesia*

Being the hitherto single largest cooperative project between China and Indonesia, the Djakarta–Bandung High-speed Railway Project is one of the Early Harvest Programs in the docking of China's Initiative with Indonesia's Global Maritime Axis vision. Furthermore, it is the

---

[22] Li Ying, "China and Thailand Railway Cooperation Intends to Sign Framework Agreement in Early September", August 26, 2015, http://news.xinhuanet.com/fortune/2015-08/26/c_1116383729.htm, log-in time: August 27, 2015. (李颖：《中泰铁路合作拟 9 月初签框架协议》, 2015 年 8 月 26 日。)

[23] Yu Yichun and Ding Zi, "To Build a Win-Win Road: An Interview with Prajin Juntong, Minister of Transport of Thailand", *People's Daily*, July 24, 2015. (俞懿春、丁子:《"修建一条互利共赢之路"——访泰国交通部长巴津•占东》, 载《人民日报》2015 年 7 月 24 日, 第 3 版。)

first high-speed railway project initiated by the governments and cobuilt in the form of business-to-business (B2B) model in the world. As for Indonesia, it is the first high-speed railway in this country and in the whole Southeast Asia and thus it delivers immeasurable economic and social benefits. For China, it is the first time to participate in the complete process of planning, building, operating and managing of a high-speed railway overseas with Chinese technologies, standards and equipment. On January 21, 2016, construction of the project began officially, setting up a brand new model for the two countries' cooperation in infrastructure and industrial capacity.

Fairly speaking, this project had gone through twists and turns in the long process from its planning to the implementation. Early in November 2014, Indonesian President Joko had his first taste of the speediness, convenience and safety of China's high-speed railway in his visit to China. On April 22, 2015, the National Development and Reform Commission signed a Framework on Launching the Djakarta–Bandung High-speed Railway Project with Indonesian Ministry of State-Owned Enterprises during President Xi Jinping's visit to Indonesia. According to the Framework, Indonesia agreed to provide related data including the topographic map, earthquake and geological information between Djakarta and Bandung for China's analysis on the feasibility of the project. Early in July, the special envoy of Japan offered an optimized plan during his visit in Indonesia, promising more favorable conditions in loan rate and supporting measures. On August 10, 2015, Xu Shaoshi, President Xi's special envoy and director of the National Development and Reform Commission went to Indonesia with the feasibility report and proposed to form a joint venture, aiming at carrying out all-round cooperation in benefit and risk sharing, building and operating, technology transfer and personnel training. On August 26, Japan sent its special envoy to Indonesia once again to modify and optimize the plan. In late August, the Chinese Ambassador to Indonesia Xie Feng also made his effort on the project. Also, China held a High-speed Railway Achievements Exhibition in Djakarta. On September 4, the Indonesian government suddenly announced the canceling of high-speed railway project and sent back both China's and Japan's plans on high-speed railway. However, the Chinese government didn't quit and finally won the

approval of Indonesia with its technological strength and sincerity.[24]
To develop the high-speed rail project, a consortium of China's enter-
prises led by China Railway Corporation officially signed the agree-
ment of setting up a joint venture with a consortium of Indonesia's
state-owned enterprises (SOEs) led by Wijaya Karya (WIKA) on
October 16. In April 2017, the EPC contract for building the
Jakarta–Bandung High-Speed Rail was signed in Jakarta. During the
Belt and Road Forum for International Cooperation in May 2017,
China Development Bank signed a loan agreement with PT Kereta
Cepat Indonesia China (KCIC), extending 4.5 billion dollars to the
latter. This marked the entry into fast implementation stage of the
first overseas order of Chinese high-speed railway.

The railway, which is expected to be finished in 2019, extends 150
km and boasts a highest speed of 350 km/h. By then, it will shorten
the traveling time from more than 3 hours to 40 minutes, greatly
facilitating people's traveling and alleviating the traffic pressure
between the two cities. In preliminary estimation, the construction of
project is expected to generate 40,000 jobs each year and the railway
will achieve profitability five years after its operation. The comprehensive land development in the eight regions where railway stations are
located will promote tourism along the railway. Thus, an economic
belt of Djakarta–Bandung High-speed Railway will soon come into
shape. In the future, the enterprises from the two countries will
conduct an all-round cooperation in survey and design, engineering
construction, equipment manufacturing and operation and management of high-speedy railway. China's enterprises will help Indonesia
to train professionals in construction, operation and management of
high-speed rail.[25]

---

[24] Gu Di, "XieFeng, Chinese Ambassador in Indonesia: To Win Indonesia High-
speed Rail with Sincerity and Strength", October 16, 2015, http://world.huanqiu.
com/exclusive/2015-10/7771498.html, log-in time: October 17, 2015. (谷棣：《中
国驻印尼大使谢锋:用诚意和实力拿下印尼高铁》, 2015 年 10 月 16 日)

[25] Xi Laiwang and Zhuang Xueya, "Jakarta, Indonesia—Bandung High-speed
Railway Project Officially Commences", *People's Daily*, January 22, 2016, p. 22.(席
来旺、庄雪雅:《印尼雅加达—万隆高铁正式开工》, 载《人民日报》2016 年 1 月
22 日, 第 22 版。)

7.2.2.6 *The Hungary–Serbia Railway*

The Improvement Project of Hungary–Serbia Railway linking Budapest and Belgrade is a flagship project under China–CEE cooperation of 16 + 1 mechanism. The railway was first built in 1882, and thus the infrastructure was already decayed. In November 2013, Chinese Premier Li Keqiang, Serbian Prime Minister Aleksandar Vucic and Hungarian Prime Minister Viktor Orbán reached a consensus of trilateral cooperation on the modernization of the Hungary–Serbia railway at the China–CEE countries leaders' meeting. Then in November 2015, they witnessed the signing of the project cooperation deal in Soochow. The project is undertaken by a consortium of China's enterprises led by China Railway Corporation. On December 23, the launching ceremony of the Serbian section was held, marking the official beginning of the railway project among the three countries.

The railway, linking Budapest and Belgrade, has a total length of 350 km, with 184 km in Serbia and the rest in Hungary. The line is designed for electrified passenger and cargo trains with a maximum speed of 200 km/h. It's estimated that the project will last two years. Upon its completion, the traveling time by train between the two capital cities will be reduced from 8 hours to less than 3 hours. In future, the railway will be connected with the port of Piraeus, Greece, thus forming the China–Europe land–sea fast intermodal transport route. The cargo containers, after arriving at Piraeus Port of Greece by sea, can be transported to Europe conveniently via the Macedonia railway, which gives a boost to the construction of China–CEE economic corridor.

7.2.3 *Oil-and-Gas Pipeline*

The construction of cross-border oil-and-gas pipelines makes up an important part of facilities connectivity. So far, the strategic pattern of China's four import channels of oil and gas respectively distributed in the Northwest, Southwest, Northeast and on the sea (via the Strait of Malacca) has taken shape following the operation and construction of the Sino–Kazakhstan crude oil pipeline, the Central Asia–China natural gas pipeline, the Sino–Myanmar oil-and-gas pipelines and the

Sino–Russia oil-and-gas pipelines. It is significant in the sense that these facilities diversify the energy import sources and channels, and therefore guarantee China's energy security.

7.2.3.1 *The Northwest: The Sino–Kazakhstan Crude Oil Pipeline, the Central Asia–China Natural Gas Pipeline*

The Sino–Kazakhstan crude oil pipeline is China's first direct oil import pipeline. The 2,798-km pipeline runs from Kazakhstan's Caspian shore to Alashankou in China's Xinjiang, and it is designed to carry 20 million tons of oil per year. In September 2013, China National Petroleum Corporation (CNPC) bought an 8.33% share of Kashagan Field from ConocoPhillips for 5 billion USD during President Xi Jinping's visit. The two agreed to cooperate in the exploitation of oil-and-gas fields located offshore in the Caspian Sea. Discovered in July 2000, Kashagan has been described as the largest field found in the past 50 years. It is estimated that the Kashagan Field has recoverable reserves of about 48 billion tons of crude oil and more than one trillion cubic meters of natural gas. The acquisition not only benefited CNPC but also allowed China to get involved in the exploitation of oil and gas in the Caspian Sea. Therefore, the oil from the Caspian Sea can be transported to China directly through the Sino–Kazakhstan crude oil pipeline.

The Central Asia–China natural gas pipeline is the longest natural gas pipeline in the world and also the biggest cooperative project between China and Central Asian countries so far. By delivering resources to a large market, this project can benefit multiple parties. At present, there are four lines respectively connecting China and five Central Asian countries, among which Line A, B and C have been constructed and put into operation. All of the three lines start from the border of Turkmenistan and enter China's Xinjiang via Kazakhstan. On September 13, 2014, the Line D of the Central Asia–China natural gas pipeline started construction in Dushanbe, the capital city of Tajikistan. This line passes two countries of Tajikistan and Kyrgyzstan for the first time, forming the network of the Central Asia–China natural gas pipelines, together with the existing Line A, B and C that connect Turkmenistan, Uzbekistan and Kazakhstan. Upon the completion of Line D and its follow-up facilities, the total gas transportation capacity of the Central Asia–China gas pipelines can reach 85 billion cubic meters per year — the largest gas transportation system in the region, satisfying more than 20% of domestic gas consumption in China. It is worth noting that, Line D has brought about billions of dollars of investment for Uzbekistan, Kazakhstan and Kyrgyzstan. During the 30-year operation period, it will create thousands of jobs along the line, generating billions of dollars for the three countries. Globally-acknowledged technical standards and norms will be introduced into the construction of Line D, which can accumulate precious experiences in natural gas pipeline construction for countries involved and cultivate a host of specialized technical talents. It is believed to promote the development of natural gas pipeline industry in relevant countries in an all-round way.[26]

7.2.3.2 *The Southwest: The Sino–Myanmar Oil-and-Gas Pipelines*

The Sino–Myanmar oil-and-gas pipelines stand as a strategic channel of energy import in the Southwest of China. The crude oil pipeline starts from Maday Island in Kyaukphyu, Rakhine State, and transports crude oil mainly from the Middle East and Africa. It is expected to carry 22 million tons of crude oil to China every year. CNPC South East Asia pipeline Company Limited undertakes the design, construction, operation and management of the pipeline and its supporting facilities. Starting from Kyaukphyu, Rakhine State, the natural gas pipeline is a cooperation project involving investments from six corporations from four countries, including China, Myanmar, India and South Korea. The estimated gas transportation capacity is 12 billion cubic meters per year.[27] The pipelines will run

---

[26] Cui Mo, "Central Asia Gas Pipeline: A Robust Engine of the Energy Silk Road", *China Energy News*, March 16, 2015, p. 14. (崔茉：《中亚天然气管道——"能源丝路"的强劲引擎》, 载《中国能源报》2015 年 3 月 16 日, 第 14 版。)

[27] The six corporations refer to CNPC, Daewoo International Corp, Indian Oil Corporation Ltd., Myanma Oil and Gas Enterprise, Korea Gas Corp and India Gas

parallel to each other and enter China at the border city of Ruili in Yunnan province. The crude oil pipeline extends 771 km, while the natural gas pipeline stretches 793 km within Myanmar's territory. Starting from Anshun in Guizhou province, the two pipelines will go in different directions, with the crude oil pipeline going towards Chongqing, and the natural gas pipeline extending to Guangxi. On October 20, 2013, the trunk line of Sino–Myanmar natural gas pipeline was constructed and put into operation. The Sino–Myanmar natural gas pipeline was connected with China's West–East natural gas transmission project through the Zhongwei–Guiyang natural gas pipeline, linking the channels of Xinjiang gas region, Changqing gas region and Sichuan gas region. Thus, China's oil-and-gas pipeline networks have taken its initial shape.

According to the deal between the two countries, Myanmar could offload some 2 million tons of oil and 20% of gas from the pipelines annually — equaling to 2.4 billion cubic meters of natural gas against its annual delivery capacity of 12 billion cubic meters — for its domestic use after the whole project is completed. In October 2013, the trunk line of Sino–Myanmar natural gas pipeline was constructed and put into operation. Reports said that, the gas power generation brought about by the Sino–Myanmar oil-and-gas pipelines has alleviated the power pressure in Kyaukphyu and as a result, the nearby electric appliances shops have increased their turnover. In Mandalay, the natural gas offloaded from the pipeline benefited the newly built power plant and guaranteed stable and reliable power supply for 6 million people living in the central part of Myanmar — nearly one-tenth of the total population in Myanmar. In Yenangyaung, an important industrial city, the newly acquired natural gas reinvigorated the oldest industrial base in this country.[28] On January 20, 2015, the Sino–Myanmar crude oil pipeline entered trial operation after five years of construction in Maday Island in Kyaukphyu, Myanmar. It is worth noting that this project not only helped train lots of technical

---

Corp. In share allocations, Chinese corporation accounts for 50.9%, Burma accounts for 7.4%, South Korea 29.2% and India 12.5%.

[28] Yu Jinghao, "China-Burma Gas Pipeline Improves People's Livelihood in Burma", *People's Daily (Overseas Edition)*, June 1, 2014, p. 2. (于景浩：《中缅油气管道助力缅甸民生》，载《人民日报海外版》2014 年 7 月 1 日，第 2 版。)

professionals but also made its imprint on environment protection since the places where the pipelines were buried have been revegetated and the marker posts have been totally hidden in green rice fields. According to the deal between China and Myanmar, the two countries will cooperate further on projects of building large refineries and liquefied natural gas (LNG) processing plants in Myanmar. By then, the history of Myanmar's petroleum gas industry will be revolutionized.

7.2.3.3 *The Northeast: The Sino–Russia Oil-and-Gas Pipelines*

The Sino–Russia crude oil pipeline is part of the bilateral loan-for-oil deal reached between the two countries. On February 17, 2009, China and Russia signed a 20-year (2011–2030) contract on oil transportation through crude oil pipeline with an annual supply of 15 million tons. China Development Bank offered Russia a loan of 25 billion USD. On January 1, 2011, the China–Russia crude oil pipeline (aka. the Chinese branch line of the Eastern Siberia–Pacific Ocean oil pipeline) was put into operation, marking the official opening of the strategic channel of crude oil import to Northeast China. The 999-km pipeline starts in the Russian town of Skovorodino in the Far-Eastern Amur region and enters China at Mohe County before continuing to Daqing, with a designed transportation capacity of 15 million tons per year. On June 24, 2013, CNPC released details of the long-term agreement worth 270 billion USD signed with Russia. The contract is the hitherto largest single deal that China has signed with any other country in crude oil trade. Under the contract, the yearly crude oil import from Russia through the Sino–Russia pipeline — the Eastern line — will increase progressively from the current 15 million tons to 30 million tons in 2018. The agreement for additional crude oil supply via the Eastern pipeline will be effective in the next 25 years and could be extended for another five years. Meanwhile, Russia will supply CNPC with 7 million tons of crude oil every year through the Sino–Kazakhstan crude oil pipeline — the Western line — for five years starting from January 1, 2014, and another five years can be extended upon the completion of the current contract. In order to set up an upstream and downstream industry chain, Russia also promised to supply the Sino–Russia joint venture refinery plant in Tianjin with 9.1 million tons of crude oil every year upon its operation. As a result, the maximum of Russia's crude oil export to China in the future can reach 46.1 million tons annually, which amounts to twice the total volume of Sino–Russia crude oil trade in 2013.

In terms of natural gas, CNPC and Russia's top natural gas producer signed *China and Russia Purchase and Sales Contract on East Route Natural Gas Project* on May 21, 2014. According to the contract, Russia will export natural gas to China progressively via the East route pipeline for 30 years starting from 2018 until the annual supply reaches the maximum of 38 billion cubic meters. After being approved respectively by China and Russia's governments in August 2014 and May 2015, the contract has come into effect. This project is the largest pragmatic cooperation project between China and Russia, and an important strategic project in global natural gas cooperation. Given its widespread influence on international energy structure, enormous contract value and a long duration, the deal is called "the gas deal of the century." On September 1, 2014, the Chinese Vice Premier Zhang Gaoli and Russian President Vladimir Putin jointly witnessed the welding of the first roll of pipes on the Russian part of the Sino–Russia East Route natural gas pipeline, which is officially named as "the Power of Siberia" pipeline. The Chinese section of the Sino–Russia East Route natural gas pipeline starts from Heihe of Heilongjiang Province and ends in Shanghai, passing through Heilongjiang, Jilin, Inner Mongolia, Liaoning, Hebei, Tianjin, Shandong, Jiangsu and Shanghai. The 3,968-km pipeline, extending from gas fields in Russia's Far East to Shanghai, is designed to transport 38 billion cubic meters of natural gas from Russia to China every year. On June 29, 2015, the construction of the Chinese section of the Sino–Russia East Route natural gas pipeline began officially. It is scheduled to be completed and put into operation in 2018 and supply natural gas to the Northeast China, Circum–Bohai Sea Region and Yangtze River delta area. At that time, it is expected to relieve the shortage of natural gas in the Northeast China, improve the air quality in Beijing–Tianjin–Hebei region and promote adjustments in energy structure in Yangtze River delta area.

7.2.4 *Ports*

Since the 21st century, China's port and shipping companies have quickened up their steps to go overseas, building and operating ports in foreign countries, and then building industrial parks and special economic zones near ports as well as port cities. Against the backdrop of the Belt and Road Initiative, such activities not only enhance the interconnectivity and trade flow among countries along the routes, but also promote the industrialization of developing countries. As these companies have accumulated more international experiences, their focus overseas shifts from winning construction projects to integrated activities of investing, constructing, operating, developing and managing. In particular, Chinese companies pay increasing attention to the integration and coordination between ports and cities and ports and industrial parks, so that ports assume more diversified functions and thus play a more important role in driving the economic and social development of their host countries.

7.2.4.1 *The Gwadar Port and the CPEC*

The Gwadar Port is situated on the Arabian Sea at Gwadar in Balochistan province of Pakistan. The port is located near Pakistan–Iran border and is only 400 km away from the Strait of Hormuz. The Middle East, South Asia and Central Asia converge in this strategic passage on the Indian Ocean. On February 18, 2013, Pakistani President Asif Ali Zardari announced the transfer of the port's management rights to China Overseas Port Holding Company. Dostain Khan Jamaldini, Chairman of the Gwadar Port Authority said, *"It is the decision of the democratic government to transfer the operation rights of the port to China in 2013, which has little to do with the military. I think the reason for the Pakistani government to choose China is because that China is much more experienced than any other country in port operation. The Chinese experts hold the richest experiences in port construction, operation and sea transportation"*.[29]

---

[29] Zhao Yining, "The Success of China–Pakistan Economic Corridor Depends on the Development of Gwadar Port", *21st Century Business Herald*, April 21, 2015, p. 9.

The 27,000-ton ZI JING SONG container vessel was the first commercial container vessel moored at the port since its completion. It departed from the Gwadar Port, went across Dubai and finally arrived at Qingdao and Tianjin in China. However, the handling capacity of the port so far is only 120 thousand standard containers, an equivalent to about 700 or 800 thousand tons per year, which obviously falls short of the strategic objective set by China and Pakistan. Therefore, as Zeng Qingsong — the general manager of China Overseas Port Holding Company (Pakistan) — said, the most important work at present is to build supporting facilities around the port. On basis of it, Gwadar will be turned into a commercial port and benefit the Northern part of Pakistan and Afghanistan by utilizing the resources in Gwadar Free Trade Zone to develop port-surrounding businesses, raw material processing and finished products export.[30]

So far, a batch of new projects are under construction or expected to launch soon, including a desalination plant, a 300-MW thermal power plant several port roads and a new international airport. On November 11, 2015, the Pakistani authorities formally handed over 300-hectare of Gwadar Port's free trade zone (one-third of the planning area) to the Chinese Overseas Ports Holding Company in the form of a 43-year lease, in order to promote the development of the Gwadar Port and the CPEC. According to official estimate by the Pakistani authorities, the development of the port will create 2 million jobs in the next 8–10 years and there will be 1.7 million economic migrants flowing to the Gwadar Port in the next 30 years.[31] (see Figures 7.1 and 7.2)

(赵忆宁：《"中巴经济走廊成功与否,取决于瓜达尔港的发展"》, 载《21 世纪经济报道》2015 年 4 月 21 日, 第 9 版。)

[30] Zhao Yining, "Gwadar Port Will Move into the Fast Lane of Infrastructure Construction", *21st Century Business Herald*, April 21, 2015, p. 10.(赵忆宁：《瓜达尔港将进入基础设施建设快车道》, 载《21世纪经济报道》2015 年 4 月 21 日, 第10 版。)

[31] Liang Tong, "The Construction of Gwadar Port Brings Significant Development Opportunities: An Interview with Mir Sherbaz Khetran, an Economic and Social Expert from Balochistan, Pakistan", *Economic Daily*, April 20, 2015, p. 4. (梁桐：《瓜达尔港建设带来重大发展机遇——访巴基斯坦俾路支斯坦省经济社会问题专家米尔•舍尔巴兹•赫特兰》, 载《经济日报》2015 年 4 月 20 日, 第 4 版。)

Figure 7.1   Airscape of the Gwadar City
Photographed by Mr. WANG Zhe, October 2015.

Figure 7.2   Gwadar Port's Morning
Photographed by Mr. WANG Zhe, October 2015.

7.2.4.2   *The Ports of Colombo and Hambantola in Sri Lanka*

Sri Lanka was a necessary stop in the ancient Silk Road and an important hub in the 21st-Century Maritime Silk Road. The Ports of Colombo and Hambantola are key access points to the hub.

The Port of Colombo is an age-old port on the Indian Ocean passage, and also Sri Lanka's largest sea port. Cargo shipped through this port to the Strait of Hormuz and Europe takes up about half of the world's ocean-transported cargo. In August 2011, China Merchants Port Holdings Company Limited ("CMPort", formerly China Merchants Holdings International before June 2016) won the bid for the South Container Terminal of the Port of Colombo. The project's investment, totaling 500 million dollars, was contributed by Colombo International Container Terminals Limited (CICT), a joint venture between CMPort and the Sri Lanka Port Authority. CMPort took up 85% of CICT's stake and was responsible for the fund-raising, design, construction, operation and management of the port, with a concession period of 35 years. In April 2014, CICT started operation. It has 4 berths and 12 bridge cranes with annual handling capacity of 2.4 m TEU containers and is the only container terminal in Sri Lanka that is able to accommodate super large vessels (see Figure 7.3).

Since the start of the terminal's operation, the service provided by CICT has improved to match international standard and is the best in the Port of Colombo. In 2014, CICT loaded and unloaded 680,000 tons of cargo, pushing up the throughput of the Colombo Port by 14%, the fastest growth that year in the world. CICT's efficient operation and quality service keep attracting the world's largest container liners. Every week, five liners cruising between Europe and Asia and five South Asia regional liners stop here, which greatly improves Sri Lanka's standing in the international shipping industry. Notably, the terminal's operation brings real benefits to the region. According to its 35-year Build-Operate-Transfer (BOT) contract with the local government, CICT would contribute 1.8 billion dollars in taxes. And its construction and operation would create 3,000 and 7,500 direct jobs respectively and train a large number of professionals.

Figure 7.3   South Container Terminal of the Port of Colombo Operated by CICT Photographed by ZOU Lei (the author), September 23, 2015.

Located 240 km to the Southeast of the Port of Colombo and only 10 nautical miles from the world's busiest European–Far East sea route, The Port of Hambantota is geographically positioned to be an international deepwater transit port.

On October 31, 2007, construction of the Sri Lanka Hambantola port, to be jointly built by two Chinese companies, China Harbour Engineering Company and Sinohydro Group, began. The project, being part of a larger government project, gets 15% its budget from the Sri Lanka government and 85% from the Chinese side. The committed investment during the first phase was 361 million dollars and construction was finished at the end of 2012. It contains two container terminals with the capacity to handle 100,000 tons of cargo, two oil terminals able to handle 100,000 tons of oil, two berths able to moor 10,000-ton tankers and one waterway of 1,000 m. According to some news article, when the main body of the basin was finished, the Chinese Harbour Engineering Company held a water-injecting ceremony, which attracted a lot of attention in Sri Lanka. More than 100,000 spectators witnessed the ceremony, cramming a strip of road extending 10 km. The government had to send police and soldiers to maintain order. According to planning made by Sri Lanka, the port will be finished in three phases which would take 15 years in total. When it is finished, it will become one of the world's largest ports with handling capacity increased from the current 6 to 23 m containers.

On September 16, 2014, the joint venture formed by China Merchants Port Holdings Company and China Harbour Engineering Company closed the deal with the Sri Lanka Port Authority on the second phase of the container terminal project, with leaders from both countries bearing witness to the signing ceremony. Total investment for the project was about $601 million. The Chinese side would contribute $391 m in cash in exchange for 64.98% of the shares. Sri Lanka would contribute $210 m in kind to get 35.02% of the stake. After completion, the Chinese joint venture would get 35 years of concession, extendable for another five years.

In the future, operation of CMPort's overseas ports will move to a "comprehensive development" model. Specifically, it will use ports as a lever, to build industrial parks, logistics parks and free trade zones along them so as to promote the sound interaction among different companies. This will not only facilitate the development of Chinese industrial clusters there, but also create a lot of jobs for local people while promoting economic development of host countries.

7.2.4.3 *Port of Piraeus and the China–Europe Land–Sea Express Line*

To China, Greece acts as a door opening to Europe. The Port of Piraeus is the largest port in Greece and a critical one in Eastern Mediterranean. The Piraeus port enjoys an important geographical location, as it extends inland to the Balkan region and even radiate surrounding areas including the Mediterranean, the Black Sea and North Africa via sea transportation. So far, the European Union has become the largest trading partner of China with more than 80% of China's export arriving at Europe through sea transportation.

On June 12, 2008, China Ocean Shipping (Group) Company won the bid of 35-year franchise rights of Pier II and Pier III at Piraeus and took over the operation rights since October 1, 2009. This is the first time for the COSCO to wholly own an infrastructure facility in Europe. Since then, Piraeus has become one of the fastest growing ports in terms of handling capacity. On June 20, 2014, during his visit to Greece, Premier Li Keqiang and his counterpart witnessed a train, loaded with Huawei and ZTE products, setting off, which marked the official start of sea–railway transportation from the port of Piraeus to Central and Eastern Europe. Previously, cargo had to land at Hamburg or Rotterdam via the Suez Canal, and arrived at Central and Eastern Europe through sea–railway transportation. Today, the new logistics route allows goods to be loaded in the Piraeus Container Terminal of COSCO and arrive at Austria, Slovenia or Czech Republic via Macedonia, Serbia and Hungary. The traveling time is thus shortened to 7–11 days.

On December 17, 2014, Premier Li Keqiang further announced during the Third Cooperation Forum between China and CEE Countries that China, Serbia and Hungary agreed to extend the Hungary–Serbia Railway to the port of Piraeus in order to form the China–Europe Land–Sea Express Line in two years. As the extension and improvement of the Hungary–Serbia Railway, the China-Europe Land–Sea Express Line can exert direct influence on more than 32 million population. Upon its completion, it can open a brand new convenient route for China–Europe goods exchange, which will greatly promote the trade between Asia and Europe. In December 2015, the Hungary–Serbia Railway started construction, and in January 2016, Hellenic Republic Asset Development Fund approved the purchase of 67% stake of the port of Piraeus by COSCO, speeding-up the construction of the China–Europe Land–Sea Express Line.

In brief, from China's Eastern coast to Europe's Baltic Sea, from the Pacific Ocean to the Indian Ocean and the Mediterranean, various cross-border infrastructure or facilities of connectivity, including highway, railway, oil-and-gas pipeline, port, power grid and optical cable and aviation are flourishing and serving as the most symbolic and pragmatic platforms of the Belt and Road.

7.3 Unimpeded Trade

Since the proposal of the Initiative, trade and investment volume between China and countries along the routes have been increasing. According to statistics, from 2014 to 2016, the trading volume between China and relevant countries exceeded 3 trillion dollars and Chinese investment to these countries surpassed 50 billion USD. Even against the backdrop of continuous slump in global trade, in 2016, the trade in goods between China and relevant countries was worth 947.8 billion USD, accounting for 25.7% of China's total commodity trade. Trade in service was worth 122.2 billion USD, accounting for 15.2% of China's total service trade.[32]

7.3.1 *Customs Clearance*

The reform for mutual information exchange, mutual recognized supervision and management and mutual assistance in law enforcement among port management departments has achieved initial progress in China. By far, the coastal provinces have started to promote the "single window" service across the border. Customs in China have realized integrated clearance, and enterprises can autonomously choose the place for declaration, taxation and inspection. It is estimated that the service charge and logistics fee will be reduced by 50% and 25% respectively. The clearance time will also be notably reduced. For example, enterprises in Hefei can finish the clearance process in 20 minutes after their imports arrive in Shanghai.[33]

---

[32] Office of the Leading Group for the Belt and Road Initiative, *Building the Belt and Road: Concept, Practice and China's Contribution*, Beijing: Foreign Languages Press, May 2017, p. 24.

[33] The State Council Information Office of PRC, "The State Council Information Office Held Press Conference about Deepening Customs Reform and Promoting Trade Facilitation", December 24, 2015, http://www.scio.gov.cn/xwfbh/xwbfbh/wqfbh/2015/33938/index.htm, log-in time: December 25, 2015. (中国国务院新闻办公室:《国新办举行深化海关改革与促进贸易便利有关情况发布会》, 2015 年 12 月 24 日。)

The customs cooperation among countries along the routes has also achieved progress. For example, for Chongqing–Sinkiang–Europe International Railway and other railways connecting China and Europe, the General Administration of Customs of the PRC has established direct cooperation mechanism with its counterparts in Russia, Kazakhstan, Belarus, Poland and Germany in an effort to simplify inspection, speed up the process and reduce the cost.

AEO stands for Authorized Economic Operator. Enterprises which have passed the customs verification will be labeled as custom-entrusted enterprises and enjoy clearance facilitation. By far Chinese Customs has implemented mutual recognition of AEO with the Customs in Singapore, Korea, EU and China Hong Kong. The imports and exports from mutually recognized AEO enterprises in China have took up 30% of the total. Enterprises recognized as the Safe Trade Partners and those that have passed assessment by Chinese Customs will enjoy clearance facilitation on either side. Taking Chinese exports to Korea as an example, the average inspection rate is 5.6% and clearance time is 2.3 hours. In contrast, the figures for goods with mutually recognized AEO are 0.1% and 1.5 hours respectively.[34] In the past, it took Chinese enterprises 10 hours to finish clearance, but now it only takes 4 hours. According to General Administration of Customs, Chinese Customs has been in contact with its counterparts in New Zealand, Kazakhstan and other countries in order to achieve the goal that the trade volume of enterprises with mutually recognized AEO will take up to 80% of the total.[35]

---

[34] Wang Shuai, "China and South Korea Achieved AEO Mutual Recognition, Cargo Clearance Efficiency Improved by 50%", *Qilu Evening News*, May 12, 2015, p. W04. (王帅:《中韩海关AEO互认货物通关提速50%》, 载《齐鲁晚报》2015 年 5 月 12 日, 第 W04 版。)

[35] Liu Chu, "AEO Mutual Recognition Between China and Singapore Comes to the 4th Year, Customs Clearance Time Greatly Shortened", December 19, 2015, http://www.thepaper.cn/newsDetail_forward_1410731, log-in time: December 20, 2015.(刘楚:《中国新加坡"海关AEO互认"满三年,通关时效大为缩短》, 2015 年 12 月 19 日。)

Since December 2013, China has sped up the establishment of Green Channels for agricultural products between Xinjiang and neighboring countries such as Kazakhstan, Tajikistan and Kyrgyzstan. Xinjiang is abound in agricultural resources, yet its export enterprises are mostly small and medium-sized and they conduct business in a decentralized way. At Chinese ports, agricultural goods will enjoy priority treatment, nonintrusive inspection and collective declaration. There are special windows for inspection submission and examination of agricultural imports and exports. The declaration documents from those enterprises will be reviewed at the earliest time, and the agricultural products will get through the vehicle inspection channel labeled with Green Channel rapidly. It is reported that the boxed apples from China will take no more than one day to finish clearance. In the last two years, the clearance time for agricultural products in Baketu–Bakhty Port between China and Kazakhstan were reduced by 90%, which ensured the freshness of vegetables and fruits and reduced cost for enterprises. As a result, agricultural products in Xinjiang will enjoy quicker and more convenient access to Russia and European countries via Central Asian countries. Also, more and more fresh agricultural products from Central Asian countries will be brought to Chinese people.

General Administration of Customs is also actively working on a series of relatively mature Customs cooperation projects, such as mutually recognized supervision between border ports in China and Russia, joint Customs supervision between China and Mongolia, Secure and Smart Trade Line Pilot Program between China and Europe, and clearance facilitation on the China-Europe Land-sea Express Line. Successful experiences and institutions can be applied and replicated elsewhere.

7.3.2 *Logistics*

Efficient and convenient logistics service is an important premise for smooth trade. Yet for many inland countries in Europe and Asia, it is the very obstacle that has been blocking their foreign trade for a long time. Therefore, the logistics transit channel provided for related countries is the essence of the Initiative and embodiment of its nature as a public good.

On September 7, 2013, local government of Lianyungang, Jiangsu Province signed Cooperation Agreement on Cross-Border Logistics Channel and Cargo Transit Base with Kazakhstan National Railway. The China–Kazakhstan Logistics Cooperation Base (Lianyungang) became the first platform for international cooperation under the Initiative. With a total investment exceeding 3 billion RMB, the first phase of the project plans to establish a container yard of 220,000 m², with a railway of 3.8 km and an annual maximum handling capacity of 410,000 TEU. The yard will mainly engage in international cargo transport such as intermodal transportation, container handling and transporting, and storage. On May 19, 2014, the first phase of the project started operation. In less than one year, the project finished construction and started operation, and the accumulated container throughput exceeded 100,000 TEU. The cargo throughput reached almost 1 million tons.

On February 25, 2015, the first China–Central Asia train left the China–Kazakhstan Logistics Cooperation Base. There are three trains leaving the base weekly. On December 13, the first China–Europe train started operation. Starting from Lianyungang, the train will go across Kazakhstan and arrive at the destination in Germany. The China–Kazakhstan Logistics Cooperation Base, as a symbol of the bilateral cooperation between China and Kazakhstan, has yielded fruits. There are already more than 20 logistics companies which have signed container storage and transit agreement with the base.

As Mr. Zhu Xiangyang, CEO of the Lianyungang Port Co., Ltd. said "The China–Kazakhstan Logistics Cooperation Base is the model for win–win cooperation between the two countries. With this base, Kazakhstan gains maritime access for its exports, and from the base, the cargo will be transported endlessly to every corner of the world via the New Eurasian Land Bridge."[36]

---

[36] Xie Yahong and Huang Wendi, "Investment of Capital Construction Motivates Asia–Europe Cooperation", *People's Daily*, May 25, 2015, p. 22. (谢亚宏、黄文帝:《基建投资激发亚欧合作新活力》,载《人民日报》2015 年 5 月 25 日, 第 22 版。)

7.3.3 *Free Trade Zone*

Cooperating on the free trade zone with countries along the routes is an important part of the unimpeded trade under the Initiative. At present, international trade protectionism has been on the rise. Against this backdrop, China actively promotes the negotiation on free trade zones and supports the global free trade regime. In December 2015, the State Council issued *Several Opinions on Accelerating the Implementation of the Free Trade Zone Strategy*. The *Opinions* pointed out that China will actively promote the free trade zone development along the Belt and Road. In addition, China will also, along with free trade zone development and international capacity cooperation, actively negotiate and establish free trade zone with B&R countries so as to create a giant market along the routes. By the end of 2015, China has signed free trade zone agreements with 22 economies including ASEAN, Singapore, Pakistan, New Zealand, Chile, Peru, Costa Rica, Iceland, Switzerland, South Korea, Australia and Hong Kong, Macao and Taiwan, accounting for 38% of China's foreign trade in total.

On June 1, 2015, China and South Korea signed a free trade zone agreement. This agreement is by far the widest in scope and biggest in volume among all the free trade zone agreements China have signed with any other foreign government. The agreement serves as an important knot that connects China's BRI and South Korea's Eurasia Initiative. On December 20, the free trade zone agreement between China and South Korea came into effect. As to the cargo trade, China will exempt tariff on 91% of Korean imports, and that accounts for 85% of the value of total imports from South Korea. Korea will exempt tariff on 92% of imports from China, which takes up 91% of the total value of imports from China. The agreement yields obvious and positive effects. For enterprises, they will purchase key parts, electronic components, fine chemical industries, high-end machines, lithium batteries and LCD panels at a lower price from South Korea. For Chinese consumers, they will pay less for Korean-made home appliances such as rice cookers and microwaves, daily chemicals, fashion products such as women's dress and Korean foods. The Korean consumers will enjoy vegetables, fruits, clothing and shoes made in China at a better price.[37]

On June 17, 2015, China and Australia signed a free trade zone agreement. It is one of the free trade zone agreements with the highest level of trade and investment liberalization for both countries. In terms of trade of goods, about 97% of Australian exports to China will be tariff free following the designed timeline step by step. Australia will eventually reduce tariffs to zero on all goods imported from China, as compared to 90% of tax reduction in other free trade zone agreements. As to the service trade, Australia promises to open its service sector to China in "negative list" approach after the agreement takes effect, making Australia the first country offer such promise to China. China in turn promises to open its service sector to Australia in way of "positive list". As to investment, China and Australia will offer most-favored-nation treatment to each other after the agreement takes effect. In the meantime, Australia will lower the inspection level and provide facilitation services for Chinese enterprises who intend to make investment in Australia.[38]

On November 22, 2015, China and ASEAN countries signed the Protocol to Amend the Framework Agreement on Comprehensive Economic Cooperation an upgraded trade cooperation document. It is the first upgrade agreement that China has concluded on the basis of the present FTA, involving trade in goods, trade in service, investment, economic and technological cooperation and other fields. According to Mr. Gao Hucheng, China's former Minister of Commerce, China and ASEAN improved the rules for origin of

---

[37] Gao Hucheng, "Leveraging the China–South Korea Free Trade Agreement to Achieve Regional Prosperity", *People's Daily*, June 2, 2015, p. 12. (高虎城：《借力中韩自贸协定共襄区域发展繁荣》, 载《人民日报》2015 年 6 月 2 日, 第 12 版。)

[38] Gao Hucheng, "Grasp FTA Opportunity, Create a Beautiful Future for China–Australia Economic and Trade Relations", *People's Daily*, July 18, 2015, p. 10. (高虎城：《把握自贸协定历史机遇共创中澳经贸关系美好未来》, 载《人民日报》2015年 6 月 18 日, 第 10 版。)

products, further simplified the custom clearance procedures, and promised to provide efficient and convenient clearance service for enterprises from both sides by making use of automated system and risk management. As to the service trade, China and ASEAN concluded the third round negotiation for service commitments and promised more openness in nearly 70 subdepartments including construction, tourism, finance and communications. As to the investment, China and ASEAN agreed to advance investment promotion and facilitation, simplify investment approval procedure, establish one-stop investment centers, and create a stable, transparent and convenient investment environment. As to the economic and technological cooperation, China and ASEAN agreed to deepen cooperation in more than 10 sectors involving agriculture, information and communications, and include cross-border e-commerce into cooperation agenda. The signing of the protocol will help push up bilateral trade at 1 trillion USD by 2020, and promote the negotiation of Regional Comprehensive Economic Partnership (RCEP) and the development of Free Trade Area of the Asia–Pacific.[39]

At present, China is advancing various free trade zone negotiations, including RCEP, China–GCC FTA, China–Norway FTA, China–Japan–South Korea FTA China–Sri Lanka FTA, China–Maldives FTA, China–Georgia FTA, negotiations on upgrading China–Singapore FTA, the second phase negotiations on China–Pakistan FTA and the follow-up negotiations on Economic Cooperation Framework Agreement (ECFA). China is also engaging in talks on economic and financial cooperation agreement with BRICS countries, EU and EAEU, in an effort to establish systems and schemes for investment and trade facilitation before eventually setting up free trade zones.

---

[39] HuangYin Jjiazi and Shang Jun, "Gao Hucheng's Interview with Xinhua News Agency on the Signing of an Upgraded Protocol of China–ASEAN Free Trade", November 23, 2015, http://news.xinhuanet.com/2015-11/23/c_128455460. htm, log-in time: November 24, 2015. (黄尹甲子、尚军:《高虎城就中国—东盟自贸区升级<议定书>成功签署接受新华社采访》, 2015 年 11 月 23 日。)

7.3.4 *International Capacity and Equipment Manufacturing Cooperation*

In recent years, quality industrial capacity and high-end equipments, in addition to high-speed rail and nuclear power, have been increasingly promoted by Chinese leaders during their visits to foreign countries. The international industrial capacity and equipment manufacturing cooperation is now becoming the highlight and focus of China's economic diplomacy. It serves as an ideal start point for actualizing unimpeded trade and industrial integration under the Initiative.

As China continues to push the BRI, its partners in capacity and equipment manufacturing cooperation keep increasing. As of the end of 2016, China had signed international capacity cooperation documents with 27 countries, including Kazakhstan and Ethiopia, announced *Joint Statement on China–ASEAN Production Capacity Cooperation* together with ASEAN countries, and issued *Joint Statement on Production Capacity Cooperation among LANCANG– MEKONG countries* together with Myanmar, Laos, Thailand, Cambodia and Vietnam, the five countries through which the Mekong River run. Bilateral or multilateral capacity cooperation funds in total exceeded 100 billion dollars. It reached important consensus with France, South Korea, Germany, the United Kingdom and Spain, among other countries on working together to explore third-party markets. It also worked with relevant countries to identify key areas and major projects in production cooperation. With the advancement of the BRI, more and more partners are joining the international industrial capacity and manufacturing cooperation. At present, the international industrial capacity cooperation framework is taking the initial shape. In the framework, China's neighboring countries serve as the axis, key countries in Africa, Middle East and Middle and East Europe as the west wing, and key countries in Latin America as the east wing.

As a form of docking the Silk Road Economic Belt with Bright Road Initiative from Kazakhstan, industrial capacity cooperation between China and Kazakhstan not only promotes the industrialization in Kazakhstan, but also establish a replicable model of bilateral capacity cooperation for other quality industrial capacities in China to expand their international market. Prime Minister Li Keqiang once recalled the moment when two countries agreed to promote capacity cooperation,

> Kazakhstan is in lack of public goods, while in urgent need of more investment to improve its infrastructure. Yet Kazakhstan doesn't have any industrial production line for products such as cement or flat glass. Therefore I suggested we should establish factories in Kazakhstan rather than merely exporting these products. Kazakhstan was excited about my proposal, because the production line from China will help Kazakhstan develop its economy and promote its industrialization.[40]

With support from the central governments, the two countries rapidly set up a coordination committee and a capacity cooperation fund. In December 2014, the first round of dialogue for China–Kazakhstan capacity cooperation was held in Beijing. On March 27, 2015, with the presence of Prime Ministers from both sides, the two countries signed a memorandum for strengthening industrial capacity and investment cooperation, and documents for cooperation in 28 projects including iron and steel, nonferrous metals, flat glass, oil refinery, hydropower and vehicles, with the total value reaching 23.6 billion USD. In the meantime, China and Kazakhstan have decided on 48 early harvest projects with a total investment of 30.3 billion USD. Prime Minister Li pointed out that there was no example for China and Kazakhstan to follow to promote industrial capacity cooperation. He hoped the two countries could follow the guidance of market, choose quality projects, make coordinated efforts, strengthen policy alignment and roll out effective supporting measures in

---

[40] China.org.cn, "Li Keqiang: Just Like Reform, Opening-up Is the Only Way as Well", January 28, 2015, http://www.gov.cn/xinwen/2015-01/28/content_2811397.htm, log-in time: January 29, 2015. (中国政府网:《李克强:开放与改革一样,是我们的必由之路》, 2015 年 1 月 28 日。)

taxation, standards, labor forces, visas, and rights and interests protection for investors.[41]

Indonesia is another key country along the 21st-Century Maritime Silk Road, who shows great interests in quality equipment and industrial capacity from China. In March 2015, China and Indonesia issued a joint statement, agreeing to deepen infrastructure and capacity cooperation, encourage the enterprises from both countries to conduct exchanges and cooperation in areas such as railway, roads, ports, airports, electric power, photovoltaic, iron and steel, ship-building and building materials. China will provide financing support for infrastructure construction and major projects in Indonesia through bilateral and multilateral financing channels. In the meantime, the National Development and Reform Commission and Indonesia Ministry of State-Owned Enterprises signed the MOU on Infrastructure and Industrial Cooperation and MOU on Cooperation on the Jakarta–Bandung High Speed Rail Project. In April, China and Indonesia agreed to take full advantage of their respective strengths and advance in-depth cooperation in industrial capacity such as power, high-speed rail, nonferrous metals, ship-building and building materials. They also agreed to encourage related departments from both sides to finalize the List of Priority Projects at an early date.

Africa is a key area for international industrial capacity and equipment manufacturing cooperation. In May 2014, during Prime Minister Li Keqiang's visit to the headquarters of African Union (AU), China and AU decided to cooperate on the high-speed rail network, express way network and regional aviation network as well as on industrialization. China was willing to provide financing, personnel and technical support. On January 27, 2015, China and AU signed the MOU on major infrastructure networks and industrialization process. When participating in the Johannesburg Summit of Forum on China–Africa Cooperation in December, President Xi Jinping announced 10 major cooperation plans including

---

[41] Li Weihong, "Prime Li Keqiang Meets Karim Masimov, Prime Minister of Kazakhstan", *People's Daily*, March 28, 2015, p. 1. (李伟红：《李克强同哈萨克斯坦总理马西莫夫会谈》, 载《人民日报》2015 年 3 月 28 日, 第 1 版。)

China–Africa industrialization cooperation plan, in a bid to start from the key segments in the upstream and downstream of industrial development and promote coordinated development for industrialization on both sides. In order to ensure the smooth implementation of the 10 plans, China decided to provide 60 billion USD of funding and establish the China–Africa Industrial Capacity Cooperation Fund with the initial capital of 10 billion USD.

Tanzania is one of the first African countries echoing China's call for international industrial capacity cooperation. According to Abdullah Kigoda, minister of Industry and Trade, Tanzania is committed to transforming its development mode from an agriculture-oriented to an industry-oriented one. Despite its rich resources, the industrial production only takes up 9% of the total GDP in Tanzania. He hopes the industrial capacity cooperation between China and Tanzania will help Tanzania improve its industry and create new jobs for the youth.[42] On April 28, 2015, delegations from the NDRC and Ministry of Foreign Affairs visited Tanzania and initiated the agreement on industrial capacity cooperation. Mr. Lv Youqing, the Chinese ambassador to Tanzania, said that China has selected Tanzania as one of the three demonstration countries for China–Africa industrial cooperation. China is willing to help Tanzania develop its potential by providing necessary support of capitals, technologies and industrial capacities so as to further expand industrial capacity cooperation between the two and make Tanzania a model country of China–Africa cooperation.[43]

---

[42] Zhang Ping, "Minister of Industry and Trade of Tanzania: Capacity Cooperation between China and Tanzania Brings Win-Win Results", April 21, 2015, http://news.xinhuanet.com/2015-04/21/c_1115037476.htm, log-in time: April 25, 2015. (张平:《坦桑尼亚工贸部长:坦中产能合作有益双方》, 2015 年 4 月 21 日。)

[43] Ministry of Foreign Affairs of PRC, "The Chinese Ambassador Lv Youqing Accompanies NDRC and Ministry of Foreign Affairs Delegation to Meet Mizengo Kayanza Peter Pinda, Prime Minister of Tanzania", April 30, 2015, http://www.fmprc.gov.cn/mfa_chn/zwbd_602255/nbhd_602268/t1259815.shtml, log-in time: July 7, 2015. (中国外交部:《驻坦桑尼亚大使吕友清陪同发改委、外交部代表团会见坦总理平达》(2015 年 4 月 30 日。)

The Middle East is a new growth point for international industrial capacity cooperation. In January 2016, President Xi Jinping visited the headquarters of League of Arab States (LAS). In his speech, Xi talked about the initiative to advance industrialization in the Middle East and carry out industrial capacity cooperation for the first time. He said, *"production capacity cooperation is consistent with the overall trend of economic diversification in the Middle East. It can help Middle East countries embark on a new path of efficient, people-oriented and green industrialization"*.[44] Under this initiative, China will set up a $15 billion special loan for industrialization in the Middle East to be used on production capacity cooperation and infrastructure projects in regional countries, and provide countries in the Middle East with $10 billion of commercial loans to support production capacity cooperation. China will also provide $10 billion of concessional loans with even more favorable terms for regional countries. Meanwhile, China will launch a $20 billion joint investment fund with the UAE and Qatar to primarily invest in traditional energy, infrastructure development and high-end manufacturing industries in the Middle East. Saudi Arabia, Egypt and Iran are three major countries in the Middle East and founding members of the AIIB. They all expressed interests in the idea of promoting industrialization through capacity cooperation.

Saudi Arabia for long has depended on oil export economically. As oil prices plummet, Saudi Arabia has also been trying to diversify its economy. During President Xi's visit, China and Saudi Arabia signed an MOU on industrial capacity cooperation. The two sides also agreed to promote capacity policy coordination and alignment, and advance technology transfer, industrial upgrade and economic diversification. Having gone through repeated revolutions and coups and with the opening of the new Suez Canal, Egypt has set

---

[44] Xi Jinping, "Work Together for a Bright Future of China-Arab Relations: Speech at the Headquarters of the Arab League" (January 21, 2016, Cairo), *People's Daily*, January 22, 2016, p. 3. (习近平:《共同开创中阿关系的美好未来——在阿拉伯国家联盟总部的演讲》(2016 年 1 月 21 日, 开罗), 载《人民日报》2016 年 1 月 22 日, 第 3 版。)

economic development as its top priority. In the middle of June 2015, China–Egypt industrial capacity cooperation team on the Chinese side held meetings with Egyptian Ministry of Industry, Trade and Small Industries. They nailed down the first List of Priority Projects for industrial capacity cooperation, including 15 projects in key fields such as communications and power, with a total investment of more than 10 billion USD.[45] On September 2, at the presence of President Xi Jinping and President Sisi, China and Egypt signed China–Egypt Production Capacity Cooperation Framework Agreement. In January 2016, two sides confirmed again that two sides should launch practical cooperation on production capacity. China expressed its willingness to help Egypt develop projects to vitalize its economy, and Egypt promised to offer all possible facilitations to Chinese enterprises in order to finalize projects that had been agreed upon or were still under negotiation in accordance with Egyptian laws.

Iran, endowed with rich resources, huge market potential and favorable industrial foundations, is a perfect partner for capacity cooperation. During his visit to Iran, President Xi Jinping suggested that the two countries should take industrial capacity cooperation as the compass, connect their economic and industrial policies, strengthen cooperations between enterprises from both sides with complementary advantages, and establish an all-dimensional, wide-ranging and diversified cooperation pattern. On basis of it, the relevant departments from the two countries signed an MOU for intensifying cooperation in industrial capacity, mineral resources and investment. In the future, China and Egypt will expand mutual investment and cooperation in transportation, railway, port, energy, trade and services.[46]

---

[45] Huang Yuanpeng, "Chinese Embassy in Egypt Held Symposium on Building the Comprehensive Strategic Partnership", July 9, 2015, http://world.people.com.cn/n/2015/0709/c157278-27278018.html, log-in time: July 10, 2015. (黄元鹏:《中国驻埃及使馆举办中埃产能合作专题研讨会》, 2015 年 7 月 9 日。)

[46] Joint Statement between the People's Republic of China and the Islamic Republic of Iran on the Establishment of Comprehensive Strategic Partnership (January 23, 2016, Teheran), *People's Daily*, January 24, 2016, p. 2. [《中华人民共和国和伊朗伊

Besides the above-mentioned bilateral cooperations on industrial capacity with key countries, China also proposed trilateral production capacity cooperation to developed countries, which is a major step forward in China's economic diplomacy. In June 2015, Prime Minister Li Keqiang elaborated on the trilateral cooperation during his visit to Europe. At present, the developing countries are generally in their initial stage of industrialization. With a total population of billions of people, the developing countries, as a whole, have huge potential in market demands. China has a complete range of industrial sectors which are also huge in size. Most developed countries need to expand export for their high-end technologies and equipment. Therefore, the prospect for trilateral industrial capacity cooperation is promising. On the one hand, China's cost-effective products will satisfy the needs of developing countries; on the other hand, China is also in need of key equipments and components from developed countries (e.g., 15% of nuclear power equipments and 30% of high-speed railway equipments are from developed countries). The international industrial capacity cooperation will help developing countries achieve better development at a relatively low cost and a high speed. China, in the middle stage of industrialization, can promote its own industrial upgrading in the process. Developed countries at the upper level of industrialization, or in the stage of postindustrialization will be able to expand international market for their products. The trilateral win–win initiative will enhance South–North and South–South cooperation, accelerate global economic recovery, as well as providing development opportunities for countries in the upstream, middle stream and downstream of the global industrial chain so as to promote inclusive development around the world. China and EU can start with infrastructure, focus on equipment manufacturing and make breakthroughs in the trilateral cooperation involving the Middle and East Europe and the developing countries.[47] So far China has

---

斯兰共和国关于建立全面战略伙伴关系的联合声明》(2016 年 1 月 23 日, 德黑兰), 载《人民日报》2016 年 1 月 24 日, 第 2 版。]

[47] Li Keqiang, "Working Together for New Progress in China–EU Relations: Keynote Speech at China–EU Business Summit" (June 29, 2015, Brussels), *People's Daily*, June

reached agreements with France, Belgium, South Korea and Singapore on trilateral cooperation.

It is fair to say that China is initiating new models of South–South and South–North cooperation models through bilateral and trilateral industrial capacity and equipment cooperation. In the implementation process, China will take into consideration the national strength, willingness and market prospect of different countries, and establish cooperation mechanisms, sign cooperation documents and set up capacity demonstration zones with key countries, in an effort to ensure the success of the Belt and Road Initiative.

7.3.5 *Overseas/Cross-Border Industrial Parks*

Industrial parks are the important carriers of enterprises, equipments, capacities and talents. In recent years, China has been picking up speed in developing overseas economic and financial cooperation zones, which has been high on the agenda when Chinese leaders visit foreign countries.

According to statistics, from 2013 to 2016, Chinese companies' direct investment to B&R countries exceeded 60 billion dollars. As of the end of 2016, Chinese companies had opened more than 56 economic and industrial parks accommodating more than 1,000 companies in 20 relevant countries. Their total output has exceeded 50 billion dollars and they have contributed more than 1.1 billion dollars to their host countries, and created more than 11,000 jobs.[48] For example, the Thailand–China Rayong Industrial Park established by Holley, a Chinese private enterprise, is known as "Industrial China Town". After 10 years' development, Chinese enterprises in the park had made a total investment exceeding 1.5 billion USD and brought

---

30, 2015, p. 2. (李克强:《携手开创中欧关系新局面—在中欧工商峰会上的主旨演讲》(2015 年 6 月 29 日, 布鲁塞尔), 载《人民日报》2015 年 6 月 30 日, 第2 版。)

[48] The State Council Information Office of PRC, "The SCIO's Press Conference on Production Capacity Cooperation among Countries and Regions along the Belt and Road", May 12, 2017, http://www.scio.gov.cn/xwfbh/xwbfbh/wqfbh/35861/36661/index.htm, log-in time: May 12, 2017.(中国国务院新闻办公室:《国新办举行"一带一路"沿线国家和地区产能合作发布会》, 2017 年 5 月 12 日。)

more than 10,000 new jobs. The Sihanohkville Special Economic Zone in Cambodia, with preferential policies in Cambodian apparel industry, has attracted more than 50 Chinese textile and light industrial enterprises. The economic zone has turned into an important production base for textile and light industrial products for export, providing jobs to almost 10,000 natives.[49] It is reported that in Egypt's Suez Canal Special Economic Zone, the workers in a garment workshop named "White Rose" are all local women. On the wall of the workshop are slogans that read in Chinese and Arabian, *"If You Don't Work Hard Today, It Will Be Harder to Find a Job Tomorrow"*. The Haier-invested home appliance industrial park in Pakistan has been upgraded into Pakistan Haier–Ruba Economic Zone. Haier will be responsible for soliciting investment for the first phase of its construction. During this period, the economic zone will mainly engage in home appliances and establish a supporting industrial chain. In the second phase, it will expand into other industrial sectors such as vehicles, building materials and textiles.[50]

More and more countries began to accept the industrial park, which has been successfully practiced by China since its opening up and reform. China is also vigorously advancing such a cooperation mode. During the Ufa Summit of SCO in July 2015, China announced that it would follow market principle, promote SCO member states to cooperate in building industrial parks, and deepen production capacity cooperation in petrochemicals, metallurgy, equipment manufacturing, transportation and logistics, and agricultural development. With the strong effects of agglomeration, radiation and demonstration of industrial parks, a series of flagship projects such as China–Belarus Industrial Park, China–Malaysia Qinzhou Industrial Park and Malaysia–China Kuantan Industrial Park, and

---

[49] Ministry of Commerce of PRC, "A Regular Press Conference Held by Ministry of Commerce", April 28, 2015, http://www.mofcom.gov.cn/article/ae/slfw/201504/20150400954830.shtml, log-in time: April 29, 2015. (中国商务部:《商务部召开例行新闻发布会, 2015 年 4 月 28 日。)

[50] Zhang Yanlong, "Chinese Capacity Export", June 29, 2015, http://www.eeo.com.cn/2015/0629/277402.shtm, log-in time: March 8, 2015. (张延龙等:《中国式产能输出》, 2015 年 6 月 29 日。)

China–Egypt Suez Canal Economic and Trade Cooperation Zone have been gradually launched along the routes.

7.3.5.1 *China–Belarus Industrial Park*

As the biggest joint investment project between the two countries, China–Belarus Industrial Park is also the largest overseas Chinese industrial park. It is another flagship project of the Belt and Road Initiative after the CPEC. In May 2015, President Xi Jinping inspected the park during his visit to Belarus. He called the park a "pearl" on the Silk Road Economic Belt. Such an analogy reveals its strategic and demonstrative significance.

Top leaders of two countries have been pushing for the development of the industrial parks from a strategic vision. In March 2010, when the then Vice President Xi Jinping visited Belarus, President Lukashenko raised the idea of establishing industrial parks in Belarus following the successful example of China–Singapore Suzhou Industrial Park. In September 2011, China and Belarus signed cooperation agreement on China–Belarus Industrial Park when Mr. Wu Bangguo, the then Chairman of the Standing Committee of the NPC, visited Belarus. On August 27, 2012, China–Belarus Industrial Park Development Co., Ltd. was formally established. The Chinese shareholders — China CAMC Engineering Co., Ltd. and Harbin Investment Group Co., Ltd. — take 60% of the shares, and the Belarusian shareholders — Minsk State Government and Belarusian Skyline Holding Group — hold the remaining 40% of the shares.

China–Belarus Industrial Park boasts an advantageous geographic position and convenient transportation. With a planned area of 91.5 km² (about one-third of Minsk, the capital of the Republic of Belarus), the China–Belarus industrial park is located 25 km from Minsk, 500 km to Klaipeda port of Baltic Sea, in close proximity to the Minsk International Airport, Chongqing–Xinjiang–Europe International Railway and the Berlin–Moscow transnational highway. The construction of the park will be proceeded in three phases till 2030 with a total investment of 5.6 billion USD. The first phase (2014–2020) covers an area of 8.5 km². It consists of two stages: the preliminary stage (four years) and development stage (three years). On June 19, 2014, the first phase started with the groundbreaking ceremony. In late September, during Vice Prime Minister Zhang Gaoli's visit to Belarus, China and Belarus decided that Chinese Ministry of Commerce and Belarusian Ministry of Economy would take the lead to establish a coordination team, and make joint efforts with relevant departments, enterprises and financial institutions to advance the development of the park.

According to bilateral agreement, Belarus will provide preferential policies and favorable business environment for enterprises in the park. In June 2012, President Lukashenko enacted a decree, defining benefits offered to residents and investors in the park regarding taxation, land and others, which guaranteed a reduction in cost for doing business. Among the preferential policies, the most notable one is the "10 + 10" taxation policy, which will offer companies an exemption from all corporation taxes in the first 10 years since their registration as residents in the park and a reduction of tax rates by 50% during the subsequent 10 years. Residents in the park will also enjoy exemption of import tariff and import value added tax for their import of equipments and spare parts, and the shareholder can remit their profits outward freely. China–Belarus Industrial Park not only makes Belarus a logistics hub for Middle Europe, China and CIS countries, but also brings opportunities for Chinese enterprises to sell their products tariff-free to Customs Union of Russia, Belarus and Kazakhstan which covers a population of 170 million.

China also encourages Chinese manufacturing and high-tech enterprises to make investment in innovation projects, and establish high and new tech enterprises in the park. According to Mr. Viktor Burya, Ambassador of Belarus to China, Belarus is interested in high-end industries including new materials, electronic information, bio-pharmaceuticals, fine mechanics and precision chemicals. And these industries will be the focus of the industrial park.

In May 2015, China Merchants Group acquired 20% shares of China–Belarus Industrial Park Development Co., Ltd. by increasing its investment. With its ports network across the world and rich experience in industrial park development, China Merchants Group has formulated the strategy for establishing a comprehensive logistics system, which prioritizes the development of ports and aims at opening up a sea gate for Belarus. Furthermore, China Merchants Group also invested to establish a 1-km^2 China–Belarus Commerce and Logistics Park. In December 2015, the first phase of the China–Belarus Commerce and Logistics Park broke ground. With a total investment of 150 million USD, the "park within park" will provide integrated logistics solution — highways, railways, aviation and sea shipping — to support the development of the China–Belarus Industrial Park.[51] According to China Merchant Group, the China–Belarus Commerce and Logistics Park will provide one-stop logistics service to Chinese enterprises settling in the park as well as Belarus enterprises. Ultimately, China–Belarus Commerce and Logistics Park will become "Five Centers", namely commodities exhibition center, distribution center, export processing center, customs clearance integrated service center and cross-border RMB trade settlement center.

By the end of 2015, China Merchants Logistics Holding Co., Ltd., Zhongxing Telecommunication Equipment Corp, Huawei Technologies Co., Ltd., ZOOMLION, China Merchants Group, YTO Group Corporation, Xinzhu Group, Gansu Poly Xin Agricultural Service and Technology Group, and Belarus Nano Pectrin had registered in the park. The total planned investment exceeded 100 million USD, and a total of 117 hectares of the park had been rented. The park has begun to take initial shape. In the future, the China–Belarus Industrial Park will rely on the numerous universities and scientific institutions in Minsk to attract and gather intellectual talents. It will evolve into a modern international eco-city featuring livable environment, robust business, vitality and innovative capacities, creating a new model for integrating industries with the city.

---

[51] China Merchants Group, "Construction of the Preliminary Phase of the China-Belarus Commerce & Logistics Park Officially Commences", December 11, 2015, http://www.cmhk.com/main/a/2015/l15/a30213_30275.shtml, log-in time: March 8, 2016. (招商局集团:《招商局中白商贸物流园首发区工程建设正式动工》, 2015 年 12 月 11 日。)

7.3.5.2 *China–Malaysia Qinzhou Industrial Park and Malaysia–China Kuantan Industrial Park*

China–Malaysia Qinzhou Industrial Park and Malaysia–China Kuantan Industrial Park are two major governmental projects directly initiated and promoted by top leaders of China and Malaysia. They set up a new model for industrial cooperation for the BRI. The China–Malaysia Qinzhou Industrial Park is the third industrial park coestablished by Chinese and foreign governments after China–Singapore Suzhou Industrial Park and China–Singapore Eco-City. In November 2014, President Xi Jinping, when meeting with Malaysian Prime Minister Najib, said that China–Malaysia Qinzhou Industrial Park and Malaysia–China Kuantan Industrial Park should be developed as flagship projects and China–ASEAN cooperation demonstration areas.

China–Malaysia Qinzhou Industrial Park started operation on April 1, 2012. Since 2015, Hebabiz, Sino–Malaysia cooking oil processing project, Malaysia Halal Food Industrial Park have registered and started their construction. A series of industrial cooperation projects between China and ASEAN countries are under negotiation, including Beidou Navigation System Industrial Park, ASEAN Cloud Valley, China–Malaysia Silicon Valley, birds' nest processing, LED chip manufacturing and new substrate materials research and development. Investment involved is expected to exceed 100 billion RMB. By far, the industrial park is able to advance cluster development and accommodate industrial projects immediately. It is expected that by the end of 2017, the park will have 30,000 professionals, accommodate fixed assets worth of 30 billion RMB, and generate 30 billion RMB in industrial output and 1 billion RMB in fiscal revenue.[52]

Malaysia–China Kuantan Industrial Park started operation in February 2013. It is the first state-level industrial park in Malaysia, which is known as the "special area within special area" along the East coast of Malaysia. China and Malaysia established a joint venture to take charge of the operation and management of the park, with the

---

[52] Qi Hui *et al.*, "Qinzhou, Guangxi: Building 'Two Countries, Twin Parks' Cooperation", *Economic Daily*, July 28, p. 3. (齐慧等：《广西钦州:打造"两国双园"合作旗舰》, 载《经济日报》2015 年 7 月 8 日, 第 3 版。)

two sides respectively holding 49% and 51% of the total shares. On December 23, 2014, the first project of the park, Hyundai Steel, broke ground. The total investment of the project was 8 billion RMB, with a designed annual output of 3.5 million tons. The project covers an area of 2.87 km^2, accounting for almost 50% of the first phase of the park. The project mainly produces H beam and other high-tech iron and steel products. After being put into operation, it will be the largest steel factory in Malaysia and the first one producing H beam in ASEAN countries. Also, the project will create 4,000 new jobs for local people. In order to accelerate the development of Malaysia–China Kuantan Industrial Park and Kuantan port, the Malaysian government promised to invest 2 billion MYR in infrastructure development such as roads and other supporting facilities. In the meantime, Guangxi Beibu Gulf International Port Group finished the task of acquiring Kuantan port shares in April 2015, successfully becoming a shareholder of the port. To increase the handling capacity and efficiency of the port, the group is upgrading and reconstructing the port with its Malaysian shareholders and building new deep-water berths.[53]

On February 25, 2014, the Joint Cooperation Council on China–Malaysia Qinzhou Industrial Park and Malaysia–China Kuantan Industrial Park convened the first meeting in Beijing. This marked the establishment of the joint coordination system for the two industrial parks. In order to improve the connectivity and interaction between the two, China and Malaysia opened direct container-shipping route between Qinzhou Port and Kuantan Port. With the comprehensive development of cooperation channels between Chinese and ASEAN port cities, the Qinzhou–Kuantan container-shipping route became a major project of maritime connectivity. In the future, iron ores will be easily exported and transported to Qinzhou port from Kuantan port,

---

[53] Pan Qiang, "China and Malaysia 'Two Countries, Twin Parks' Project Builds 4.0 Version of Free Trade Zone Industrial Park, July 28, 2015, http://news.xinhuanet.com/politics/2015-07/28/c_1116065029.htm, log-in time: March 8, 2016. (潘强:《中马"两国双园"打造 4.0 版自贸区产业园》, 2015 年 7 月 28 日。)

and the latter will become a container transshipment hub and distribution center on the 21st-Century Maritime Silk Road.

Inspired by the "two countries and twin parks" cooperation mode between China and Malaysia, the China–Russia Silk Road Innovation Park has been under busy construction. It consists of two parks in both China and Russia — one in the Fengdong New Town in Xi'an, and the other in Skolkovo Innovation Center in Moscow. The Skolkovo Innovation Center is known as Russia's Silicon Valley, the most successful high and new tech development area in Russia. It is expected that more and more twin-parks or even multiple-parks will emerge along Belt and Road.

7.3.5.3 *China–Egypt Suez Canal Economic and Trade Cooperation Zone*

China–Egypt Suez Canal Economic and Trade Cooperation Zone (SETCZ) is the major carrier of bilateral capacity cooperation, known as the model of the Chinese industrial parks in Middle East and Africa. In January 2016, President Xi Jinping visited the Middle East. In his speech at the Arab League headquarters, he said, "China will take part in the development of industrial parks in the Middle East with priority given to the Suez Economic and Trade Cooperation Zone. By means of personnel training and joint planning and building of factories, we will integrate the whole process from processing and manufacturing to transportation and export."[54]

As a state-level offshore economic and trade cooperation zone approved by the Chinese government, China–Egypt SETCZ was established in 2008. Egypt TEDA Investment Company — a joint venture made up of China–Africa TEDA Investment Co., Ltd., TEDA Suez International Cooperation Co., Ltd. and Egypt–China Joint Venture — is the entity for the development and construction

---

[54] Xi Jinping, "Work Together for a Bright Future of China-Arab Relations: Speech at the Headquarters of the Arab League" (January 21, 2016, Cairo), *People's Daily*, January 22, 2016, p. 3. (习近平:《共同开创中阿关系的美好未来——在阿拉伯国家联盟总部的演讲》(2016 年 1 月 21 日, 开罗), 载《人民日报》2016 年 1 月 22 日, 第 3 版。)

of SETCZ and takes the lead in the investment, development, construction, management and operation of SETCZ. SETCZ has an initially planned area of 7 km² and a total planned area of 20 km².

SETCZ is located next to Suez Canal and Ain Sukhna Port, the third largest port in Egypt. 100 km away from Cairo, the Zone is bestowed with unique and advantageous location. At the end of 2012, with the hard work of Chinese construction team, construction of the 1.34-km² pilot area was completed, with full access to road, water and power, gas, internet and communication services. With its excellent infrastructure, good service, preferential taxation policies and low investment cost, SETCZ has attracted a batch of Chinese manufacturing and service enterprises, including Honghua Drill, XD-EGEMAC High Voltage Electric Equipment Co., Ltd. and Jushi Egypt Fiberglass Stock Company. By the end of 2015, construction of the pilot area was fully completed, realizing a total investment of 105 million USD. It has brought more than 2,000 jobs, and has initially established various industrial subsections for oil equipment, high and low voltage equipment, textile and apparel, new type building materials and mechanic equipment manufacturing, thus forming a complete industrial chain.[55]

In January 2016, President Xi Jinping and President Sisi participated in the unveiling ceremony of SETCZ during President Xi's visit to Egypt. According to the agreement signed by related departments from two sides, China and Egypt will establish work systems for SETCZ in a bid to jointly support and facilitate its construction, investment attraction and operation. China will guide more competent enterprises with scientific and technological dimensions to expand their businesses in the area, encourage financial institutions to provide financing for enterprises settling in the zone, propose development plans, and offer training for Egyptian workers. Egypt will provide policy support concerning public services, tax preferential treatment and the ratio of foreign workers.[56] The expansion area, covering

---

[55] Li Yue *et al.*, "Broad Prospect for China–Egypt Economic and Trade Cooperation", *Economic Daily*, January 21, 2016, p. 4. (黎越等:《中埃经贸合作势头良好前景广阔》, 载《经济日报》2016 年 1 月 21 日, 第 4 版。)

[56] Ministry of Commerce of PRC, "Minister of Commerce Gao Hucheng signs the Agreement on the Suez Trade and Economic Cooperation Zone with Chairman of

6 km², will be developed in three phases with a total investment of 230 million USD in 15 years. The zone is expected to be divided into six areas, including city commercial area, bonded logistics area, processing and manufacturing area, high-end living area and recreational area. By then the Zone is expected to accommodate 200 enterprises, attract a total investment of 3 billion USD, generate a yearly sales volume of around 10 billion USD and create 40,000 jobs.

On August 31, 2015, with the presence of the top leaders of the two countries, China and Laos signed Joint General Scheme of Mohan–Boten Economic Cooperation Zone. According to the Scheme, China and Laos will build a cross-border economic cooperation zone in Yunnan Province in China and Namtha Province in Laos. It is the second cross-border economic cooperation zone after Khorgas Special Economic Zone which was cofounded by China and Kazakhstan. With the advancement of the Belt and Road Initiative, more and more offshore or cross-border industrial cooperation parks will emerge and serve as platforms for industrial capacity cooperation.

7.4 Financial Integration

Up to date, fund-raising for the Belt and Road Initiative has been mainly carried out in two ways: the acceleration of *Renminbi* (RMB) internationalization, and the establishment and operation of new financing platforms.

7.4.1 *Renminbi Globalization*

In recent years, the globalization of RMB has been speeding up, and RMB has continued to expand its share in the global financial system, occupying an increasingly significant position. Till the end of 2015, RMB had become the second largest currency for trade finance, the

---

the General Office of the Special Zone of Egypt Darwiche", January 22, 2016, http://www.mofcom.gov.cn/article/ae/ai/201601/20160101240531.shtml, log-in time: March 8, 2016. (中国商务部:《商务部部长高虎城与埃及特区总局主席达尔维什签署两部门关于苏伊士经贸合作区的协议》, 2016 年 1 月 22 日。)

fourth most-used world payment currency, the sixth largest currency for global foreign exchange transactions, the sixth largest currency for interbank lending globally and the seventh international reserve currency in the world. In the process, the countries and regions along the Belt and Road are the very focus of RMB globalization.

With regard to cross-border trade, the scale of RMB settlement is steadily increasing. According to statistics from the People's Bank of China (PBC), in 2015, the current account using RMB for settlement amounted to 7.23 trillion *yuan*, representing an increase of 10.4% year on year. Specifically, goods trade settled by RMB stood at 6.39 trillion *yuan*, accounting for 26% of the cross-border settlement of foreign currency for goods trade in the same period. In terms of cross-border direct investment, RMB settlement has shown a very significant growth momentum. In 2015, outbound direct investment (ODI) with RMB settlement stood at 736.2 billion *yuan*, a year on year increase of nearly three times. Till the end of 2015, the accumulative ODI using RMB for settlement totaled 1068.25 billion *yuan*. In 2015, foreign direct investment (FDI) settled in RMB reached 1587.1 billion *yuan*, an increase of 84% year on year. Till the end of 2015, the accumulative FDI using RMB for settlement totaled 3275.75 billion *yuan*.[57]

An investigation by Allen & Overy involving senior executives from 150 cross-border corporations engaged in different fields in the United States, Europe and Asia–Pacific region shows that the demand of cross-border companies for RMB has kept expanding and an increasing number of enterprises (especially those having trade and investment relations with Chinese companies) opt to use RMB for trade settlement, risk exposure management and financing management. Ninety percent respondents believed that the use of RMB was important or even particularly important for them; 62% predicted that cross-border transactions conducted in RMB were expected to realize a double increase in the

---

[57] The People's Bank of China, *Annual Report on the Internationalization of Renminbi (2015)*, June 2015; The People's Bank of China, "Report on Financial Statistics in 2015", January 15, 2016, http://www.pbc.gov.cn/goutongjiaoliu/113456/113469/3004953/index.html, log-in time: March 8, 2016.(中国人民银行:《人民币国际化报告(2015年)》, 2015 年6 月；中国人民银行:《2015 年金融统计数据报告》, 2016 年 1 月 15 日。)

following five years. Currently, more than half of the non-Chinese transnational enterprises make RMB payment in the offshore market outside China. For Volkswagen, Daimler, Ford and General Motors and other carmakers in Europe and the United States, RMB has become the second mostly used currency after their local market currencies. In the future, an increasing number of transnational companies will expand their use of RMB in such sectors as commodities, mechanical manufacturing and services.[58]

In recent years, China has speed up the development of RMB cross-border settlement network to facilitate the use of RMB in overseas market and reduce the trading costs for individuals and enterprises. As of the end of 2016, there were 36 overseas RMB business clearing banks, including six in countries along the Belt and Road. Nine Chinese banks had opened 18 subsidiary, 35 branches and 9 representative offices in relevant countries. China had signed local currency settlement agreements for border trade with Vietnam, Mongolia, Laos and Kyrgyzstan. It had signed general agreements on local currency settlement for trade and investment with Russia, Kazakhstan, Belarus and Nepal.[59] In addition, the PBC had signed a series of bilateral currency exchange agreements with overseas central banks or monetary authorities in order to facilitate the use of RMB for investment and trade settlement. These agreements stipulated that under certain conditions, any party could use some local currencies in exchange for equivalent counterpart currencies for bilateral trade investment settlement or short-term liquidity in the financial market, and when the transaction matured, both sides got back their local currencies and the fund user paid the interests accordingly. As of the end of 2016, the PBC had signed bilateral currency swap agreements with central banks or monetary authorities in 22 countries or regions along the routes, with the agreed amount reaching 982.2 billion RMB.

---

[58] Li Yingqi and Guan Kejiang, "Multinational Enterprises Love to Use RMB to Settle International Trade", *People's Daily*, May 5, 2015, p. 22. (李应齐、管克江:《跨国企业爱上人民币结算》, 载《人民日报》2015 年 5 月 5 日, 第 22 版。)

[59] Office of the Leading Group for the Belt and Road Initiative, *Building the Belt and Road: Concept, Practice and China's Contribution*, Beijing: Foreign Languages Press, May 2017, pp. 32–33.

In 2015, the PBC and the European Central Bank successfully carried out a test on the use of euro and RMB funds, and in the future China and European countries can swap currencies instantly when necessary. The PBC swapped for a total of RUB 10 billion with local currencies in two times, mainly for Sino–Russian bilateral trade settlement, the Bank of China issued the first Tenge loans to Kazakhstan companies under the bilateral currency swap agreement, facilitating the globalization of RMB as well as Sino–Kazakhstan trade and investment.[60]

More importantly, in order to satisfy the demands for RMB-related business development in major time zones of the world and further integrate the existing RMB cross-border payment and settlement channels and resources, the Phase I Cross-Border Interbank Payment System (CIPS) initiated by the PBC was successfully launched in October 2015, marking a historic milestone in RMB globalization. According to the PBC, the main features of CIPS include: (1) using real-time gross settlement to deal with remittance businesses for both individual customers and financial institutions; (2) direct participants having access to the system through one platform, thus centralizing liquidation business, shortening the clearing path and improving the efficiency of clearing; (3) cross-border businesses being handled directly under the international ISO 20022 messaging standard; (4) operating time covering Europe, Asia, Africa, Oceania and other major RMB business time zones; (5) providing direct access to domestic direct participants.[61] As the BRI involves a large span of time zones, the launching of CIPS will bring about great convenience for the cross-border RMB clearing business.

---

[60] Ministry of Commerce of PRC, "2015 Business Review X: Active Advancement of Silk Road Economic Belt Construction in Eurasian Region", January 15, 2016, http://www.mofcom.gov.cn/article/ae/ai/201601/20160101235094.shtml, log-in time: April 20, 2016. (中国商务部:《2015年商务工作年终综述之十:丝绸之路经济带建设在欧亚地区积极推进》, 2016 年 1 月 15 日。)

[61] People's Bank of China, "The Important Milestone of RMB's Internationalization–Cross-border Payment System (First Phase) Running Successfully", October 8, 2015, http://www.pbc.gov.cn/goutongjiaoliu/113456/113469/2960452/index.html, log-in time: October 9, 2015. (中国人民银行:《人民币国际化重要里程碑人民币跨境支付系统(一期)成功上线运行》, 2015 年 10 月 8 日。)

RMB is also on the way to be an important financing currency. For instance, on June 5, 2015, the Russian pharmaceutical giant "Synthetic" acquired the RMB-denominated L/C from the largest Russian state-owned commercial bank Sberbank to pay for the imported drugs with a total valve of RMB 290 million *yuan*. This is the first time for Sberbank to obtain financing from the Export–Import Bank of China in the form of RMB-denominated L/C, significantly saving the cost of trade settlement between China and Russia, and exerting a direct impact on trade import and export enterprises. Since 2015, China Development Bank and Export–Import Bank of China have signed loan agreements with Sberbank, Vnesheconombank, VTB Bank and other financial institutions, jointly supporting the construction of large-scale projects. It was the first time for Russian construction projects to use RMB loans.

In addition to settlement and financing, the function of RMB serving as a reserve currency has also been intensified. For example, in October 2014, the British government successfully issued a sovereign bond of RMB 3 billion *yuan* with a term of three years. This is the first RMB-denominated sovereign bond issued by Western countries, as well as the largest sum of non-China-issued RMB bond. The UK Treasury made it clear that the bond issuance income would be included into the British foreign exchange reserves. In October 2015, 38 countries reported that RMB was a part of their international reserves. On November 30, 2015, the IMF's Executive Board decided to include RMB into the SDR basket of currencies as the fifth special draw currency after the dollar, euro, sterling and yen, another milestone on the road of RMB internationalization. In the SDR basket, RMB accounts for 10.92%, ranking third after the dollar and euro.

7.4.2 *Establishment and Operation of New Financing Platforms*

7.4.2.1 *Asian Infrastructure Investment Bank*

Initiated by China, AIIB is a multilateral development bank, boasting broad representativeness, the focus of which is to provide financial support for infrastructure development in Asia. To some extent, the AIIB also represents an important cooperative platform and public product provided by China for the global development. Just as what President Xi Jinping said at the Inauguration Ceremony of the AIIB,

> The demand for infrastructure development in Asia is enormous. The initiative to establish the AIIB is a constructive move. It will enable China to undertake more international obligations, promote improvement of the current international economic system and provide more international public goods. This is a move that will help bring mutual benefits and win-win outcomes to all sides.[62]

In early October 2013, when visiting Southeast Asia, President Xi Jinping and Premier Li Keqiang successively put forward the establishment of the AIIB. In early 2014, China started to take the lead in conducting extensive communications within Asia and in countries outside Asia. On October 24, the first group of 21 Prospective Founding Members including China, Bangladesh, Brunei, Cambodia, India, Kazakhstan, Kuwait, Laos, Malaysia, Mongolia, Myanmar, Nepal, Oman, Pakistan, Philippines, Qatar, Singapore, Sri Lanka, Thailand, Uzbekistan and Vietnam signed the MOU on establishing the AIIB. The amazing expansion of the AIIB's "friend circle" began in March 2015. On March 12, the United Kingdom submitted a confirmation letter to China to join the AIIB, becoming the first major European and world power to apply as a founding member. On March 18, France, Germany and Italy jointly announced that the three countries would participate; since then, South Korea, Australia, Brazil, Russia, South Africa and other major countries have submitted applications. Up to March 31, the number of Prospective Founding Members of the AIIB had risen to 57, covering Asia, Europe, Oceania, Latin America and Africa. Within just a month, the AIIB

---

[62] Xi Jinping, "Address at the Inauguration Ceremony of the Asian Infrastructure Investment Bank" (Diaoyutai State Guesthouse, 16 January, 2016), *People's Daily*, January 17, p. 2. (习近平:《在亚洲基础设施投资银行开业仪式上的致辞》(2016 年 1 月 16 日, 钓鱼台国宾馆), 载《人民日报》2016 年 1 月 17 日, 第 2 版。)

advanced irresistibly, becoming the most flamboyant superstar in the international political arena.

On May 22, 2015, China's Ministry of Finance announced that all sides had reached a consensus on the Articles of Agreement of the AIIB. The Cabinet of Germany said at the time of its approval, "*The AIIB contains a balanced power, and its agendas and standards are in line with the European Bank for Reconstruction and Development (EBRD) and the Asian Development Bank (ADB). China and the AIIB have met the requirements of Western countries.*"[63] On June 29, the signing ceremony was held at the Great Hall of the People in Beijing. Financial ministers or their authorized representatives from 57 Prospective Founding Members attended the signing ceremony and 50 of them officially signed the Articles of Agreement of the AIIB.

With respect to the list of member states, 37 countries are from Asia, including Azerbaijan, Bangladesh, Brunei, Cambodia, China, India, Indonesia, Iran, Israel, Jordan, Kazakhstan, South Korea, Kuwait, Kyrgyzstan, Laos, Malaysia, Maldives, Mongolia, Myanmar, Nepal, Oman, Pakistan, the Philippines, Qatar, Saudi Arabia, Singapore, Sri Lanka, Tajikistan, Georgia, Thailand, Turkey, UAE, Uzbekistan, Vietnam, Australia, New Zealand and Russia. In the meantime, 20 countries are from areas outside Asia such as Europe, Latin America and Africa, including Austria, Denmark, France, Finland, Germany, Iceland, Italy, Luxembourg, the Netherlands, Norway, Poland, Portugal, Spain, Sweden, Switzerland, the United Kingdom, Malta, Brazil, Egypt and South Africa. AIIB member states include all BRIC countries, four of the five permanent members of the UN Security Council, four of the G7 and 13 of the G20. It can be said that the world's most influential powers have all joined the AIIB, except the United States and Japan.

---

[63] Zhou Ailin, "Germany Will Become the Fourth Largest Shareholder of AIIB and Back Up the Constitution in Accordance with International Standards", June 11, 2015, http://www.yicai.com/news/2015/06/4630993.html, log-in time: June 12, 2015. (周艾琳: 《德国将成亚投行第四大股东力挺章程符合国际标准》, 2015 年 6月 11 日。)

The participating countires have different expectations for the Bank. Countries from Southeast Asia, South Asia and Central Asia will gain access to new infrastructure financing channels in addition to the World Bank and the ADB; BRICS countries have enhanced their voice in international financial discourses; the Middle East oil-producing countries obtain a new oil investment platform; Britain, France, Germany and other Western powers maintain their traditional influences while sharing the opportunities brought about by the development of Asian infrastructure through taking part in the constitution of the new financial institution.

On December 25, 2015, after more than 800 days of preparation, with the Articles of Agreement of the AIIB meeting the legal threshold for entry into force (i.e., at least 10 signing parties' approval and the proportion of initial capital subscription by signing parties accounting for no less than 50% of the total capital subscription), the world saw the establishment of the first multilateral financial institution initiated by China and the AIIB was thence officially founded in the legal sense.

According to the articles, the authorized capital of the AIIB is USD 100 billion. The paid-in ratio will be 20 percent, that is, USD 20 billion. Within the scope of 75:25, the capital subscription of members in and outside Asia is assigned based on their GDP proportion (weighted average calculation by the 60% market exchange rate method and 40% purchasing power parity method). The total voting power of the AIIB consists of the share voting right, the basic voting right and the founding members' special voting right. The proportion of the voting right of each member equals to its AIIB shares, and the basic voting right accounts for 12% of the total voting power, distributing evenly among all the members (including the founding members and the subsequent ordinary members). Each founding member holds 600 votes as their special voting right. Calculated in such a way, since China subscribes USD 29,780.4 million, accounting for 30.34% of the total capital subscription, currently constituting the biggest shareholder of the AIIB, the voting right of China accounts for 26.06% of the total voting right, also the highest voting power at the stage. And the following countries on the list are India (7.51%), Russia (5.93%, joined as an Asian country), Germany (4.15%) and South Korea (3.5%).

When it comes to the governance structure, the AIIB has set up a three-tier management structure consisting of the board of governors, the board of directors and the management. The board of governors is the highest decision-making body of the AIIB. The board of directors is responsible for the daily operation of the AIIB, with 12 nonresident directors (nine within the Asia-Pacific region and three representing members outside the region). Such an arrangement, as compared to the World Bank and the ADB, is more streamlined and efficient. The AIIB has one president elected from the member states within Asia, whose term of office is five years. The president can be reelected consecutively only once. As the main promoter in the preparation, Jin Liqun, the former Vice Minister of Finance of China and Vice President of the ADB, commanding public respect and support, was elected as the first President of the AIIB.

According to Jin Liqun, the AIIB would seek AAA credit rating and strive to maintain it, so the investment strategy would be "very conservative", with the leverage ratio lowered to 1:1 and maximally 1:2.5 in the next 10–20 years. In terms of project selection, the AIIB would first focus on electricity, transportation and water supply.[64] As for the relationship between the AIIB and the BRI, Jin Liqun also pointed out that although the AIIB was not specifically established for the purpose of serving the BRI, many projects of the Initiative would definitely be supported by the AIIB.[65] As of the end of 2017, AIIB had 84 members. Since its official operation, AIIB had financed 24 infrastructure projects in 12 member states such as Philippines, India, Pakistan, Myanmar and Indonesia. The total lending amounted to 4.2 billion USD, with more than 20 billion USD in investment induced from co-investors, both in private and public sectors. These projects have been in energy, transport and urban infrastructure sectors.

---

[64] Shi Yan, "AIIB Needs to Pursue Higher Goals and Firstly Aims at Electricity, Transportation and Water Supply", *21st Century Business Herald*, November 11, 2015, p. 16. (师琰:《亚投行要追求更高层次目标开张瞄准电力交通供水三领域》,载《21世纪经济报道》2015 年 11 月 11 日, 第 16 版。)
[65] Guancha.cn, "Jin Liqun: Internet Construction Also Being the Focus of AIIB", December 16, 2015, http://www.guancha.cn/JinLiQun/2015_12_16_344896.shtml, log-in time: January 8, 2016. (观察者网:《金立群: 互联网建设也是亚投行的题中之意》, 2015 年 12 月 16 日。)

7.4.2.2   *The BRICS New Development Bank*

In March 2013, at the fifth BRICS Summit, the leaders reached a consensus on the establishment of the BRICS New Development Bank (hereinafter the "New Development Bank") to support infrastructure development and sustainable development projects in the BRICS countries and other emerging economies as well as developing countries. In July 2014, after seven rounds of negotiation by the finance authorities of the five countries, the articles of agreement for the new development bank were signed during the sixth meeting of the BRICS leaders.

According to the articles of agreement, the authorized capital of the New Development Bank is USD 100 billion, with an initial capital subscription of USD 50 billion, distributed evenly among the five founding members. The headquarters is in Shanghai, and the regional center of Africa in located in South Africa. As for the organizational structure, the New Development Bank sets up a board of governors, a board of directors and the President and vice-Presidents. The first chairman of the board of governors is nominated by Russia; the first chairman of the board of directors is from Brazil and the first president from India. Such arrangements embody equal rights of the member states of the New Development Bank. The board of governors is at the top of governing structure, members of which are constituted by ministers of finance and a meeting will be held every month. Membership in the New Development Bank is open to members of the United Nations and new members are required to be approved of by the board of governors.

In July 2015, board of governors of the New Development Bank held its first meeting in Russia, and the Russian finance minister, Anton Siluanov, served as the first chairman of the board of governers. The meeting appointed the members of the board of directors and the first management, and decided that the board of directors and the President and vice-Presidents are permanently stationed at the Shanghai headquarters. The President and vice-Presidents are in charge of the daily management and its subordinate departments are responsible for the execution of daily routines. The NDB President will be elected on a rotational basis from one of the founding members, specifically, in the order of India, Brazil, Russia, South Africa and China. Except the founding member that selects the President, there will be at least one Vice President from each of the other four founding members and both the President and vice-Presidents serve the office for five years each term (the first vice president shall serve for six years). The New Development Bank adopts a model of "one president, four vice presidents", including President Kamath (Indian), Vice President Zhu Xian (Chinese, also the Chief Operating Officer), Batista Jr. (Brazilian, also the Chief Risk Officer), Maasdorp (South African, also the Chief Financial Officer), and Kazbekov (Russian, also the Chief Executive Officer).

On July 21, 2015, the BRICS New Development Bank launched business in Shanghai. Both China's Minister of Finance Lou Jiwei and the first President Kamath stressed that, instead of posing a challenge to the existing international financial system, the new development bank is committed to complementing and improving the current system. Kamath also suggested that BRICS countries should make full use of their local capital market in financing, including issuing RMB-denominated bonds in China at first stage.

7.4.2.3 *The Silk Road Fund*

On November 4, 2014, at the eighth meeting of the Central Leading Group for Financial and Economic Affairs, the proposal to establish the Silk Road Fund was first brought up. On November 8, at the Dialogue on Strengthening Connectivity Partnership, President Xi Jinping officially announced that China would invest USD 40 billion to set up the Silk Road Fund to provide investment and financing support for connectivity projects such as infrastructure, resource development, industrial collaboration and financial cooperation in B&R countries, and welcome investors in and outside Asia to actively participate in the establishment of subfunds specifically designated for certain region, industry or project.

On December 29, 2014, Silk Road Fund Company Limited was founded in Beijing and formally put into operation with a registered capital of RMB 61,525 million *yuan*. It is reported that the initial capital of the Silk Road Fund is USD 10 billion, including the USD 6.5 billion, USD 1.5 billion, USD 1.5 billion and USD 0.5 billion respectively contributed by the State Administration of Foreign Exchange (SAFE), China Investment Corporation (CIC), Export–Import Bank of China and China Development Bank through their affiliated investment platforms. In terms of the management team, the former assistant governor of the PBC Jin Qi was appointed as the legal representative and the Chairman; the former Division Chief of the Entrusted Loan Office of the SAFE Wang Yanzhi was appointed as the General Manager and the Director. Representatives from the four contributors, including Liu Wei (Director General of the Comprehensive Department of the SAFE), Yuan Xingyong (Vice President of Export–Import Bank of China), Zhang Qing (Director of Special Investment Department of CIC) and Fan Haibin (Chief Financial Officer, China Development Bank) as well as Liu Jinsong (Associate Director General of the Department of International Economics, Ministry of Foreign Affairs), Guo Tingting (Deputy Director General of the Finance Department, Ministry of Commerce), Tian Jinchen (Director General of the Western Development Department of National Development and Reform Commission) and Hu Xuehao (Deputy Director General of Finance Department, Ministry of Finance) were appointed as directors. The high profile of the Silk Road Fund is thus evident.

With respect to its positioning, China's central bank governor Zhou Xiaochuan said in an interview that the Silk Road Fund was neither a multilateral development bank, nor China's sovereign wealth fund, but an equity investment fund aiming at cooperation projects and the host countries' industrial projects.[66] It works as kind of PE Fund with a longer investment period. With regard to the principles of the investment, Jin Qi puts it in this way: the first principle is integration, that is, investment shall accommodate the national development strategies and planning of the countries involved;

---

[66]Yang Yanqing, "Interview with Zhou Xiaochuan: The Silk Road Fund Starts Operation", *China Business News*, February 16, 2015, p. 1. (杨燕青等:《专访周小川:丝路基金起步运作》, 载《第一财经日报》2015 年 2 月 16 日, 第 1 版。)

second, profit which means that investment shall be directed to profitable projects under the standard of marketization, internationalization and specialization to achieve middle and long-term investment returns; third, cooperation, that is, to cooperate with domestic and foreign enterprises and financial institutions to carry out diversified investment and financing; fourth, openness, which refers to welcoming all countries that are interested in joining, or having cooperation at the sub-fund level.[67]

On April 20, 2015, CPEC, the flagship project of the BRI, received the first investment from the Silk Road Fund. During Xi Jinping's visit to Pakistan the Silk Road Fund, China Three Gorges Corporation (CTGC) and Pakistan's Private Electricity and Infrastructure Committee signed *the MOU on Developing Pakistani Hydropower Projects*. According to the Memorandum, the Silk Road Fund would invest in the CTGC South Asia Company, which is controlled by the CTGC, to provide financial support for the Karot Hydropower Project, and the Pakistani Private Electricity and Infrastructure Committee would help to facilitate the work of the Silk Road Fund and the CTGC. Karot Hydropower Project, located at the Jhelum River of Pakistan, was planned to have a 720,000-kilowatt installed capacity, 3,213 million-kwh annual generating capacity, and the total investment was about USD 1.65 billion. As one of the priority energy projects of the CPEC, this project adopted the "Build-Operate-Transfer" (BOT) model. Started at the end of 2015, the project was planned to be put into operation in 2020, and after 30 years' operation, it would be transferred to the Pakistani government for free.

For this project, the Silk Road Fund adopted the "equity + claims" way of investment. On the one hand, the Silk Road Fund, together with the International Finance Corporation which is affiliated to the World Bank, poured money in the CTGC South Asia Company to provide financial support for projects. On the other

---

[67] Jin Qi, "Financial Support and Cooperation of the Belt and Road Initiative", *Tsinghua Financial Review*, no. 9, 2015. (金琦:《"一带一路"战略中的金融支持与合作》, 载《清华金融评论》2015 年第 9 期)。

hand, the Silk Road Fund, Export–Import of Bank, CDB and the International Finance Corporation formed a syndicate to provide loans to the chosen projects.

Then why did the first investment of the Silk Road Fund go to the China–Pakistani hydropower project? Main reasons probably include: (1) As the flagship project of the BRI China–Pakistan Economic Corridor is the key area for the Silk Road Fund to seek investment and financing opportunities. (2) The Pakistan power industry has a huge market potential, and it is a priority sector in the next 10-year development plan of Pakistan. In addition, the Pakistani government also promised that the investors would get good returns besides reasonable construction and operating cost recovery. (3) The cooperative partners have a wealth of international business expertise. CTGC is a world-class hydropower development group and a leading enterprise in the Chinese clean energy industry, and the International Financial Corporation is the largest global development institution whose objective is to encourage the development of the private sectors in developing countries. With the three sides working together, risks can be better shared, managed and controlled.[68]

In June 2015, through the same approach of "equity + claims", the Silk Road Fund lent its support to China National Chemical Corporation in a takeover bid for an Italian tire maker. This was the first investment in the high-end manufacturing sector in developed countries made by the Silk Road Fund, as well as its first takeover project in support for Chinese enterprises' "going-global" and acquisition of advanced technologies and management.[69]

---

[68] People's Bank of China, "Head of Silk Road Fund Meets the Press about the Initial Investment", April 20, 2015, http://www.pbc.gov.cn/goutongjiaoliu/113456/113469/2811749/index.html, log-in time: April 21, 2015. (中国人民银行:《丝路基金负责人就启动项目投资有关情况答记者问》, 2015 年 4 月 20 日。)

[69] Zhang Guilin and Zhang Chi, "Deputy General Manager of Silk Road Fund: the Silk Road Fund Will Go to Four Major Areas", August 30, 2015, http://news.xinhuanet.com/fortune/2015-08/30/c_1116416993.htm, log-in time: September 8, 2015. (张桂林、张翅:《丝路基金副总经理:丝路基金将重点投向四大领域》, 2015年 8 月 30 日。)

On September 3, 2015, witnessed by President Xi Jinping and President Putin, the Silk Road Fund signed a framework agreement with the largest shareholder of Russia's Yamal LNG Integration Project — Novatek — on the purchase of a 9.9% stake of the project. This was the first investment in Russia made by the Silk Road Fund, as well as its first investment in the field of oil and gas, and the "equity + claims" investment model was also adopted.[70]

On December 14, 2015, the Silk Road Fund and KAZNEX INVEST JSC signed a framework agreement in Beijing. Under the agreement, the Silk Road Fund would invest USD 2 billion in establishing the China–Kazakhstan Production Capacity Cooperation Fund in support of the production capacity cooperation between China and Kazakhstan and relevant projects. This was the first special fund set up by the Silk Road Fund since its founding.[71] On the same day, the Silk Road Fund and BAITEREK JSC also signed an MOU in search of cooperative opportunities in priority areas such as capacity, innovation and information technology.

By the end of 2017, the Silk Road Fund had signed 17 projects, with promised investment amounting to around 7 billion dollars. These investments would support projects in Russia, Mongolia, Central Asia, South Asia, Southeast Asia, West Asia, North Africa, Europe and other regions.

It is reported that through its contact with relevant departments and enterprises, the Silk Road Fund has identified a number of key follow-up projects and some potentially feasible investment projects. At the next stage, the Fund will continue to explore mutually

---

[70] The Silk Road Fund, "Silk Road Fund Signed Stock Purchase Framework Agreement with Novatek", September 3, 2015, http://www.silkroadfund.com.cn/cnweb/19930/19938/20112/index.html, log-in time: September 7, 2015.(丝路基金:《丝路基金与诺瓦泰克公司签署购股框架协议》, 2015 年 9 月 3 日。)

[71] The Silk Road Fund, "Silk Road Fund Signed Framework Agreement about Setting Up China-Kazakhstan Capacity Cooperation Fund with Department of Export of Kazakhstan", December 14, 2015, http://www.silkroadfund.com.cn/cnweb/19930/19938/31691/index.html, log-in time: January 8, 2016. (丝路基金:《丝路基金与哈萨克斯坦出口署签署关于设立中哈产能合作专项基金的框架协议》, 2015 年 12 月 14 日。)

beneficial cooperation models which are replicable and sustainable under the principle of marketization, internationalization and specialization.

In addition to the AIIB, the New Development Bank and the Silk Road Fund, China has also actively strived to broaden other financing channels. For example, China has been dedicated to the establishment of a variety of capacity cooperation funds and investment cooperation funds, and provided a large amount of special loans. At the Chinese–CEE leaders' meeting held in November 2015, Prime Minister Li Keqiang proposed to establish a 16 + 1 financial firm. China has appointed the Industrial and Commercial Bank of China, the largest commercial bank in China, to take the lead, and together with the participation of China Development Bank and Export–Import Bank, in discussing how the multilateral financial firm would take part in the China–CEE capacity cooperation. In January 2016, China officially became a member of the EBRD, which paved the way for China to integrate the Belt and Road Initiative with European Investment Plan, to invest in cooperative projects, and to deepen industrial and technical cooperation in Central and Eastern Europe, Eastern and Southern Mediterranean, Central Asia, North Africa and other regions.

In the meantime, developmental, policy and commercial financial institutions actively provide financial support. As of the end of 2016, China Development Bank extended more than 160 billion dollars of loans to countries along the Belt and Road, with balance exceeding 110 billion dollars. Most of the finance went to support infrastructure connectivity, production capacity cooperation, energy and resources projects and projects that will benefit the livelihood of the people. The Export–Import Bank of China provided support to more than 1,200 relevant projects, promising more than 700 billion RMB to support projects in transportation, electricity, hydrology and telecommunications infrastructure connectivity, high-tech products, large equipment set and mechanical and electrical projects export and energy and resource development. China Export and Credit Insurance Corporation underwrote export and investment projects exceeding 320 billion dollars made by countries along the belt and road. It underwrote all major capacity cooperation projects. The Bank of China extended 100 billion dollars to relevant countries and followed up on 420 major oversea projects. The Industrial and Commercial Bank of China had signed 412 projects, with total investment exceeding 337.2 billion dollars. The China Construction Bank had signed 180 major projects, with credit extended worth 90 billion dollars.[72]

During the Belt and Road Forum for International Cooperation held on May 14, 2017, Chinese President Xi Jinping announced that China would increase financial support to projects related to the BRI and increase contributions to the Silk Road Fund by 100 billion RMB. He encouraged financial institutions to engage in overseas RMB funds business with money raised expected to reach 300 billion RMB. The China Development Bank and the Export–Import Bank of China would provide loans worth 250 billion and 130 billion RMB equivalent respectively to support projects in infrastructure, energy and financial cooperation. China would work with the AIIB, the BRICS New Development Bank, World Bank and other multilateral development institutions to support relevant projects. To facilitate more efficient financing cooperation, financial departments from 27 countries, including China, jointly approved *the Guiding Principles on Financing the Development of the Belt and Road*. These new measures will provide more financing support to the BRI.

7.5 Closer People-to-People Bonds

People-to-people cultural exchanges are the "soft infrastructure" for deepening international relations. It is a "popular project" that promotes friendship between countries and peoples, thus bringing vitality, popularity and passion to the construction of the Belt and Road. But at the same time, compared with infrastructure, industrial parks

---

[72] The State Council Information Office of PRC, "SCIO's Press Conference on Results from the Banking Industry's Support of the Belt and Road", May 11, 2017, http://www.scio.gov.cn/xwfbh/xwbfbh/wqfbh/35861/36645/index.htm.(中国国务院新闻办公室:《国新办举行银行业支持"一带一路"举措成效发布会》, 2017 年 5 月 11 日)

or financing platforms, the area of cultural exchanges is also the most difficult one with the lowest efficiency. Since the B&R Initiative was put forward, China has been making further efforts to promote cultural exchanges on the basis of past experiences. As of the end of 2016, China had provided 10,000 government scholarships to B&R countries every year. It had signed education cooperation agreements with more than 60 countries, set up 30 China Culture Centers, signed 46 intergovernmental technology cooperation agreements and opened 16 Traditional Chinese Medicine Overseas Centers in B&R countries.[73]

7.5.1 *Exchanges with Southeast Asian and South Asian Countries*

China shares a similar culture with Southeast Asian countries, and people-to-people cultural exchanges could date back to long long ago. In 2015, bilateral tourism exceeded 20 million person-times with over 1,000 flights coming back and forth every week.

In September 2013, Chinese leaders announced that in the next three to five years, China would provide ASEAN students with 15,000 government scholarships, and set up more education centers in China for ASEAN countries; China would invest an special fund of RMB 200 million *yuan* to enhance regional cooperation in Asia, which would be used mainly on deepening people-to-people cultural exchanges and capacity build-up on both sides; China would continue to support the building of China–ASEAN Center, China–ASEAN Think-Tank Web, China–ASEAN Public Health Cooperation Fund and other platforms. In 2014, the two sides successfully held the first China–ASEAN cultural exchange year, which included more than 150 programs, covering various fields such as press, film, publication and sports. In April, *China–ASEAN Cultural Cooperation Initiative (2014–2018)* was passed, clarifying the plans and goals for both sides in the next five years. In November, China proposed the following measures: to

---

[73] Fan Hengshan, "Striding towards a Prosperous Future by Supporting the Grand Vision", *People's Daily*, May 10, 2017, p. 22.(范恒山:《助推宏伟构想迈向辉煌未来》,载《人民日报》2017 年 5 月 10 日, 第 22 版。)

launch a second round of building of China–ASEAN education and training centers and invest more in "China–ASEAN education exchange week"; to build agricultural technology demo centers in ASEAN countries, carry out poverty reduction cooperation in rural areas, and implement the "100 public health talents training program"; to continue to carry out "China–ASEAN Technological Partnership Plan" and build the China–ASEAN Technological Innovation Center, supporting 100 ASEAN young scientists to come to China for short-term research program in the next three years.

By 2014, there were approximately 120,000 Chinese students studying in ASEAN countries and up to 70,000 ASEAN students pursuing education in China. Up to now, higher education institutions in China have courses covering all national languages spoken in ASEAN countries, and in 10 ASEAN countries, there are 30 Confucius Institutes and 30 Confucius Classrooms in primary and middle schools. An increasing number of youngsters are learning each other's language and culture. At the China–ASEAN Summit (10 + 1) in November 2015, both sides agreed that the year of 2016 would be China–ASEAN Year of Education Exchange. In the next three years, China would provide another 1000 government scholarships to ASEAN countries besides the existing scholarships.[74] For Great Mekong Subregion countries (i.e., the five countries in the Indo–China Peninsula), China proposed to provide them with 3,000 training opportunities from 2015 to 2017 to help train specialists in areas of agriculture, health and livelihood.

Currently, the China Cultural Center, covering an area of 1352.6 m² in downtown Singapore, is under construction which will be China's biggest overseas cultural center with the most advanced infrastructure. The Indonesian government decided to grant Chinese citizens the right of Visa-free travel and invite Chinese tourists to appreciate its new tourism package to trace the voyage of Admiral Zheng He in Indonesia. Both sides are actively promoting the cooperative research program on Chinese pandas and ensure the success of relevant

---

[74] Ding Zi *et al.*, "Opening a New Chapter for China–ASEAN Relations", *People's Daily*, November 5, 2015, p. 2. (丁子等:《开启中国—东盟关系新篇章》, 载《人民日报》2015 年 11 月 5 日, 第 22 版。)

exchange activities, such as "Experience China" and "Seminar on China–Indonesia Relations" etc. China will continue to invite Indonesian religious figures to visit China.

In South Asia, when Chinese President Xi Jinping made a state visit to India in 2014, the two countries decided to host "Visit India Year" in China in 2015, and "Visit China Year" in India in 2016. In May 2015, Chinese Premier Li Keqiang and Indian Prime Minister Narendra Modi attended the "Yoga Meets Tai Chi" Event in Beijing. Fudan University set up the Centre for Gandhian and Indian Studies. Sichuan Province and Karnataka State became friend province/state. The City of Chongqing and Chennai, Qingdao and Hyderabad, Dunhuang and Aurangābād became sister cities respectively. Both countries decided to take turns to host "China–India Think Tank Forum" on a yearly basis. In the second half of the year, each country sent 200 young people to visit each other. During his visit to Pakistan in April 2015, President Xi Jinping announced that in the next five years, China would provide 2,000 training opportunities. The two countries would hold China–Pakistan Year of Friendly Exchanges in 2015. China would set up a China Culture Center in Islamabad. It would build a National Joint Research Center for Small Power Plants Technology and a Joint Marine Science Research Center in Pakistan together with the latter. Chinese cities Chengdu, Zhuhai and Karamay would become sister cities with Pakistani cities Lahore, Gwadar and Gwadar respectively. China's China Global Television Network (CGT) and CCTV-9 would set up branches in Pakistan and broadcast to the Pakistani people. And China Radio International (CRI) would set up a "FM98 China–Pakistan Friendship" studio there.

In Sri Lanka, the number of Chinese tourists is soaring thanks to the adoption of e-VISA. The China Cultural Center in Sri Lanka is officially open to the public and the Confucius Institute in University of Colombo is in preparation. The number of overseas students studying in each other's country is increasing steadily and the two sides are considering carrying out joint underwater archeological studies to explore the sunken ships of Admiral Zheng He's Fleet. In Maldives,

Chinese visitors constitute the bulk of foreign customers and the number of Chinese restaurants is on the rise in its capital Malé.[75]

7.5.2 *Exchanges with Russia, Mongolia and Central Asian Countries*

In recent years, thanks to the regular meeting mechanism between Chinese and Russian Prime Ministers and under the promotion of Sino–Russian Cultural Cooperation Committee, people-to-people cultural exchange between China and Russia has been expanding to nine sectors covering education, culture, health, sports, tourism, press, film, archives and youth. The two countries have successfully held Year of Nation, Year of Language, Year of Tourism, Year of China–Russia Youth Friendly Exchange. Thousands of events attracted the participation of millions of people, which has greatly promoted understanding and friendship between the two peoples. It is worth noticing that according to the consensus reached by leaders from both sides, the two countries jointly held the "Year of Youth Friendly Exchange" in 2014 and 2015. During that time, young artists, writers, translators and scientists from the two nations worked together to stage shows, translate books, conduct joint research and development. Besides, young politicians, athletes, doctors, journalists and entrepreneurs made mutual visits, and online exchange programs attracted millions of followers. The microfilm *"Chinese Makers"*, one episode of the series *"Hello China"* produced by Chinese filmmakers, has won wide praise and received over 100 million audiences in Russia. By the year 2020, there will be up to 100,000 mutually dispatched students in both countries, with 50,000 sent by China to study science, technology, culture, language and art in Russia, and the other half sent by Russia to China. Furthermore, Russia has become China's third largest tourist source with China being the largest

---

[75] Du Haitao, *et al.*, "South Asia: New Opportunities for Win-Win Cooperation", *People's Daily*, October 23, 2014, p. 13.(杜海涛等:《南亚:合作共赢新契机(丝路观察)》, 载《人民日报》2014 年 10 月 23 日, 第 13 版。)

source of travelers in Russia's capital, Moscow, where there is 1 Chinese tourist out of every 15 foreign tourists.

China and Mongolia have been maintaining close cultural exchanges. In 2013, mutual visits between the two countries amounted to 1.3 million person-time, with 1 million Mogolian people visiting China. In August 2014, during President Xi Jinping's state visit to Mongolia, he stated that China would warmly welcome more Mongolian citizens to come to China for education, sightseeing, business and medical care; in the next five years, China would provide Mongolia with 1,000 training opportunities and add an additional 1,000 government scholarships, help the Mongolian Army train 500 cadets, invite 500 Mongolian youngsters and 250 journalists to visit China, and offer 25 translated version of excellent Chinese films for free.[76]

The *Medium-Term Roadmap for Development of Trilateral Cooperation between China, Russia and Mongolia* stated that the cultural exchanges and cooperation will be further strengthened. The three countries will jointly hold cultural festivals, encourage exchanges and cooperation among experts and scholars in culture and arts; launch trilateral academic cooperation in Mongolian Studies and Buddhism; expand tourism cooperation, including setting up a special committee to jointly develop an international tourist line called "10-Thousand-Mile Tea Route" and promoting cross-border tourist routes such as "Lake Baikal (Russia) — Khovsgol Lake (Mongolia)". In the trilateral cultural exchanges, China's Inner Mongolia Autonomous Region (IMAR) plays a vital part. In 2014 alone, 30 schools in IMAR recruited approximately 4,000 students from Russia and Mongolia, and strengthened cooperation with the Confucius Institute at National University of Mongolia (NUM) and Russian Confucius Institute; over 30,000 Mongolian patients were received and treated in IMAR and the volunteer medical services provided by

---

[76] Xi Jinping, "Open Up New Horizons for China-Mongolia Relations through Mutual Assistance: Speech at the State Great Khural of Mongolia", *People's Daily*, August 23, 2014, p. 2. [习近平:《守望相助,共创中蒙关系发展新时代——在蒙古国国家大呼拉尔的演讲》(2014 年 8 月 22 日, 乌兰巴托), 载《人民日报》2014 年 8 月 23 日, 第 2 版。]

the Inner Mongolia International Hospital of Mongolian Medicine were warmly welcomed in Mongolia; IMAR opened border tourism services at Arxan, Zhuengadabuqi and Ari-Harsha-Te ports; "Grassland Star", "Manchuria–Siberia", "Revisiting the Tea Road" and other cross-nation tourist trains have been put into service.[77]

In Central Asia, on June 22, 2014, the project of "Silk Roads: the Routes Network of Chang'an-Tianshan Corridor", jointly applied by China, Kazakhstan and Kyrgyzstan, was officially included in the UNESCO World Heritage List. This is a grand milestone of cultural cooperation among the three countries. In December 2015, the Chinese and Kazakhstan Prime Ministers reached a consensus to build an Eurasian Center for Chinese Studies; to support the cooperation between Beijing Dancing Academy and Kazakhstan National Dancing Academy; to expand media cooperation and strengthen cooperation on literature translation and film coproduction; to encourage universities and cultural institutions in both countries to establish direct contacts with each other; to establish a consultation mechanism between the two country's tourism authorities and make the "China Tourism Year 2017" in Kazakhstan a great success.[78] What's more, Xi'an City (Shaanxi Province) became a sister city with Mare City of Turkmenistan and Samarkand City of Uzbekistan respectively and the opera "Zhang Qian" was widely acclaimed in its city tour.

In addition, the Chinese leaders has declared within the framework of the SCO that China is willing to provide 2,000 training opportunities for officials, management and technical personnel of the SCO members between 2015 and 2017; invite 50 young leaders from SCO members every year to study in China for the next five consecutive years; provide a total of 20,000 government scholarships in the next five years starting from the 2016 to 2017 academic year.

---

[77] Hong Yan, "China, Mongolia and Russia Economic Cooperation Corridor Extends Quickly in the Belt and Road Initiative", *Neimenggu Daily*, October 17, 2015, p. 1. (红艳:《在"一带一路"战略中加速延伸》, 载《内蒙古日报》2015 年 10 月 17 日, 第 1 版。)

[78] China-Kazakhstan Joint Communique, *People's Daily*, December 15, p. 3.(《中华人民共和国政府和哈萨克斯坦共和国政府联合公报》, 载《人民日报》2015 年 12 月 15 日, 第 3 版。)

These will bring new opportunities for deepening the people-to-people exchanges between China and Russia, Mongolia and Central Asian countries.

7.5.3 *Exchanges with Middle-Eastern Countries*

In June 2014, Chinese President Xi Jinping proposed to jointly build the Belt and Road and establish a "1 + 2 + 3" cooperation mode in the CASCF. At the beginning of 2016, China and Arab states had jointly held the "Year of Friendship", signed the first agreement on building joint universities, and launched cooperation between over 100 cultural institutions of the two parties. The number of Arabic students in China exceeded 14,000 and the number of Confucius Institutes in Arab increased to 11. The number of flights between China and Arab states increased to 183 per week.

At the beginning of 2016 when President Xi Jinping visited the headquarters of the LAS, he further proposed to carry out the "Hundred, Thousand and Ten-Thousand" Project, which included translating 100 Chinese and Arabic classic works, inviting 100 scholars to visit each other's country; providing 1,000 training opportunities for Arabic young leaders and inviting 1,500 Arabic Party leaders to visit China; offering 10,000 scholarships and 10,000 training opportunities and inviting 10,000 Chinese and Arabic artists to exchange visits.

During his state visit to Egypt, Chinese President Xi Jinping and Egyptian President Abdel Fattah el-Sisi attended the event commemorating the 60th Anniversary of the establishment of diplomatic ties between the two countries. They announced that the "Year of Chinese Culture" would be held in Egypt and the "Year of Egyptian Culture" would be held in China. In 2015, the first Confucius Class teaching mandarin via television was officially open in Egypt, reaching hundreds of millions of audiences in 22 Arabic countries.

In Iran, Chinese is becoming one of the most popular foreign languages. Many Iranian universities, including University of Tehran, Shahid Beheshti University, Allameh Tabataba'i University, all have a Chinese Department or Chinese Major. According to the agreement signed by both governments, a certain number of Iranian students will be granted Chinese government scholarships to study in China every year. In 2014, the leaders of the National Library of China visited Iran and they reached consensuses with the National Library and Archives of Iran on cooperation in press publication. Tehran held the "Day of Chinese Film". Puppet show troupes of Zhejiang, Fujian and Jiangxi Province formed a delegation and attended the 15th International Puppet Show Festival in Iran. The delegation of Chinese National Women's Federation and the Iranian Women's Federation sponsored the second China–Iran Women's Seminar. In 2015, a signing ceremony was held in Tehran of a bilateral contract for the two countries to coproduce the film "Shaolin Dream". The China Philharmonic Orchestra "Silk Road Tour" visited Iran and performed together with Tehran Symphony Orchestra. Now a year has passed since CRI coproduced the Persian program "Oriental Pearl" with the Iran Culture Broadcasting Company, which is broadcasted every week at a fixed time to introduce Chinese culture and today's China to the Iranian audience.[79]

7.5.4 *Exchanges with African Countries*

In recent years, the people-to-people cultural exchange between China and Africa is increasing rapidly and mutual visits per year amount to nearly 3 million person-times. In December 2015, at the Johannesburg Summit of the Forum on China–Africa Cooperation, President Xi Jinping proposed that in the next three years China would cooperate with Africa to carry out "10 Cooperation Plans", which include setting up a group of regional vocational education centers and several capacity-building colleges to help Africa train 200,000 professionals while providing Africans with 40,000 training opportunities in China; carrying out "Agriculture Leads to Prosperity" projects in 100 African villages and sending 30 teams of Chinese

---

[79] Liu Shuiming, "The Belt and Road Initiative Helps to Build a New Blueprint", *People's Daily*, January 19, 2016, p. 22. (刘水明等:《"一带一路"共铸发展新梦想》, 载《人民日报》2016 年 1 月 19 日, 第 22 版。)

agricultural experts to Africa; supporting African countries to build five transportation universities; implementing 200 "Happy Life Projects" and poverty reduction projects in Africa that mostly benefit local women and children; supporting cooperation between 20 hospitals of china and Africa and upgrading hospital departments; continuing to dispatch medical teams to Africa, such as the "Brightness Action" and assistance in maternal and child health; providing Africa with doses of anti-malaria compound artemisinin; building five cultural centers and giving 10,000 African villages access to digital television; offering 2,000 degree education opportunities in China and 30,000 government scholarships to African countries; inviting 200 African scholars to visit China and 500 young Africans to study in China every year; training 1,000 African media professionals every year; operating more nonstop flights between China and Africa to promote tourism cooperation.

China's Africa policy paper, released in the same period, stated that China would continue to set up more Confucius Institutes in African countries, and encourage and support the opening of Chinese cultural centers in Africa and African cultural centers in China; support the holding of the "Year of China" events in Africa and the "Year of an African Country" events in China, raise the profile of the "Chinese/African Cultures in Focus" events, and enrich the program of China-Africa mutual visits between cultural personnel and the China-Africa Cultural Cooperation Partnership Program; provide support for the sound development of the China-Africa Press Center, strengthen technological exchanges and industrial cooperation with Africa on radio, film and television; encourage the implementation of the Proposals on China-Africa People-to-People Exchanges and Cooperation, China-Africa People-to-People Friendship Action and China-Africa People-to-People Friendship and Partnership Program, etc.

7.5.5 *Exchanges with European Countries*

People-to-people cultural exchange is the "Third Pillar" of Sino–Europe cooperation, besides political mutual trust and economic and trade cooperation. Each year, mutual visits between China and Europe amount to 5 million person-times. In April 2014, when President Xi Jinping visited the European Union, he suggested that the two parties should make full use of the high-level cultural exchange mechanism, continue to carry out "Year of Sino–Europe Cultural Dialogue" and other events, and further strengthen exchanges and cooperation in education, science and technology, culture, media, think tank, tourism, women and youth etc. In July 2015, when Premier Li Keqiang attended the China–EU Summit, the leaders reached new consensus on simplifying VISA procedures, and China approved the setting up of VISA application centers in 15 Chinese cities without consular presence. In addition, *China's Policy Paper on the EU*, published in 2014 stated specifically that China would expand exchanges between students and scholars, and strive to expand the interflow of students between the two sides to 300,000 person times per year by 2020; enhance cooperation in the teaching of Chinese and European languages and training of teachers; support the establishment of centers for Chinese studies and centers for European national and regional studies by European and Chinese higher learning institutions; encourage European and Chinese universities to carry out high-quality cooperation in running schools; produce documentaries and publish books and news articles that reflect each other's economic development, history, culture and customs; push for the establishment of China-EU tourism cooperation mechanism, and work for the early signing of the Memorandum of Understanding on Bilateral Tourism Cooperation.

China and East European countries are strengthening cultural exchanges under the "16 + 1" framework. In 2015, in accordance with the *Belgrade Guidelines for Cooperation between China and CEE Countries* (hereinafter referred to as "CEEC" or "CEECs"), the second China–CEEC Seminar on Innovation, Technology Cooperation and International Technology Transfer was held in Slovakia; the second China–CEEC Cultural Cooperation Forum was held in Bulgaria; "China Art Festival" was held in Lithuania, Estonia and Latvia; the Ministry of Culture of PRC organized a delegate to visit Hungary, Salvia and Romania to purchase programs; the cartoon series "Panda and Little Mole", co-produced by China and the Czech Republic, made its debut in Czech; the first China–CEEC Summer Dance Camp was organized in Shaanxi Province; CEEC artistic directors of international jazz festivals visited China; the China–CEEC radio and television seminars were held in Shanghai and Hu'nan Province; the launching ceremony of the Year of Promotion of China-CEEC Tourism Cooperation was held in Hungary; the First Working Meeting for the China-CEEC Association of Governors of Provinces and Regions was held in Hebei Province; the Beijing–Budapest and Beijing–Prague nonstop flights were opened; the second China–CEEC Young Political Leaders' Forum was held in China; the third China–CEEC High-Level Symposium of Think Tanks was held in Beijing; delegations of CEEC journalists visited Zhejiang Province, Henan Province and Beijing; the first traditional Chinese medicine center was established in Czech.

7.5.6 *Exchanges with South Pacific Countries*

The South Pacific Region is a natural extension of the 21st-Century Maritime Silk Road. In November 2014, during President Xi Jinping's visit, he declared that in the next five years China would provide 2,000 scholarships and 5,000 training opportunities for the island countries; China was willing to strengthen exchanges and cooperation with all sectors and would keep sending medical teams to work there. China would encourage more tourists to visit these island countries.[80]

During the Belt and Road Forum for International Cooperation held on May 14, 2017, Chinese president Xi Jinping announced that in the next three years, China would provide 60 billion RMB of assistance to developing countries and international organizations that participate in the Belt and Road Initiative, provide 2 billion RMB of

---

[80] Du Shangze and Yan Huan, "Chinese President Xi Jinping Delivers a Keynote Speech During a Group Meeting with Eight Pacific Island Countries", *People's Daily*, November 23, 2014, p. 1. (杜尚泽、颜欢:《习近平同太平洋岛国领导人举行集体会晤并发表主旨讲话》, 载《人民日报》2014 年 11 月 23 日, 第 1 版。)

emergency food assistance to developing countries along the Belt and Road, increase its contribution to the South–South Cooperation Assistance Fund by 1 billion USD, build 100 "happy homes", carry out 100 "poverty assistance" projects and 100 "medical assistance" projects in B&R countries, contribute 1 billion dollars to relevant international organizations to carry out cooperation projects designed to benefit these countries. These measures will enhance the people-to-people bonds between China and other relevant countries.

In conclusion, with joint promotion from China and B&R countries, the BRI has been gaining global acceptance and influence. From coordination of development strategies to the implementation of cooperation projects, from deepening existing cooperation mechanisms to establishing new financing platforms, from free trade zones to overseas industrial parks, from using RMB as settlement for crude oil trade to the operation of CIPS, from CPEC to China–Europe Land–Sea Express Line, from infrastructure, rules and regulations to people-to-people exchange, new progresses have been made in the B&R cooperation. It is worth noticing that the capital, technology, equipment, engineering, standard and currency of China are gaining more and acceptance among B&R countries, and the experience that China has accumulated from the global economic cooperation since the Reform and Opening up provides a valuable reference. Fruits of joint efforts perfectly demonstrate the win–win cooperative nature of the Belt and Road Initiative.

Chapter

8

Risk Management in the Building of the Belt and Road

As an ultralarge international cooperation proposal covering a vast geographical area, the Belt and Road Initiative involves a good number of countries as well as numerous complex matters. The implementation of it will hardly be achieved at one stroke or in a smooth way. Although the BRI has been comprehensively moving forward, various risks — inherent or concomitant, structural or unexpected — will surface accordingly, which calls for rational understanding and deliberate management.

8.1 Internal Risks in B&R Countries

Except for Western Europe, most of the B&R countries are developing or transforming nations. Due to historical disputes and current conflicts, there are severe standoffs among ethnics, religions, regions and factions inside these countries. As a result, a cycle of political crises is emerging, with one crisis coming after another. For key countries with strategic standings, the internal political standoffs are always entangled and mutually reinforced with external superpower struggles, which makes the internal tension structural, regular and repetitious.

For example, Thailand, the geological hub on the China–Indochina Peninsula Economic Corridor, has been vexed by severe domestic political conflicts among different classes and regions. The Yellow Shirts, consisting of urban middle classes, and Red Shirts, consisting of rural residents, frequently resort to radical measures such as large-scale street protests to seek political change. Conflicting interests of different classes, contradicting political appeals and uncompromising zero-sum game make the army the final arbitrator for democracy.

Take the China–Pakistan Economic Corridor, the flagship project of the BRI, as another example. Since its independence in 1947, Pakistan has been torn by conflicts between different tribes, sects, local governments and army. The Talibanization in tribe areas and Pakistanization of Al Qaida started in 2004. The rise of Tehrik-i-Taliban Pakistan (TTP) fueled the radical religious forces and Islamization of politics in Pakistan, seriously weakening the central government's control over domestic affairs. With their influence and power gradually expanding from the tribal areas to inner land and coastal cities, the TTP began to stand up to the central government as an equal. The political turbulence helps create fertile ground for the spread of radical groups such as Al-Qaida, and in turn, it impacts politics in Pakistan, making it the frontline for anti-terror war. Against such a background, the already fragile political system is increasingly falling apart. Due to the gloomy political outlook, Pakistan is increasingly dubbed as a "failed state" and undergoing "Balkanization."[1]

As to the Bangladesh–China–India–Myanmar Economic Corridor, the Myanmar central government and local armed forces are still far away from striking package deals about the latter's status and settlement. Military conflicts occur now and then. In recent years, the United States, European Union (EU), Britain, Japan and other

---

[1] Wang Lian, "Comments on the Penetration of Taliban into Pakistan", *Contemporary International Relations*, no. 8, 2009, p. 28. (王联:《评塔利班对巴基斯坦的渗透》, 载《现代国际关系》2009 年第 8 期, 第 28 页。)

countries scaled up their political engagement and resource inputs in Myanmar. Regions controlled by ethnical minorities, which are also bestowed with rich water and mineral resources, are major destinations for China's investment in recent years. It will be a major issue for China to appropriately deal with the domestic situation in Myanmar.

Along the China–Central Asia–West Asia Economic Corridor, West Asia tops the world in terms of political and security risks. In Central Asia, although Kazakhstan and Uzbekistan are enjoying overall political stability, both countries are going to go through a power transition in the next few years. As a major party of China–Kyrgyzstan–Uzbekistan railway, Kyrgyzstan has been in frequent regime changes since its independence in early 1990s. Except the Tulip Revolution in 2005 and political disturbances in April and June of 2010, Kyrgyzstan has had 14 prime ministers and eight major alterations to its constitution in 20 years.[2] In essence, the root for structural political dilemma lies at the North–South political divide that is hard to be bridged. Different tribes are the main actors in these conflicts, and their struggle for a national regime has been a norm in the country's political life. In Afghanistan, the withdrawal of United States and North Atlantic Treaty Organization (NATO) forces heralded a new phase of reconstruction. During the process, the central government in Kabul, North Union, Taliban, local warlords and Al-Qaida are in intense competition for power distribution and dominance, and their relations with each other are increasingly complex. Strategic competition in Afghanistan among the United States, Russia, India, Pakistan and Iran is also getting acute than ever. The outlook for Afghanistan's politics, security and economic transition is still filled with uncertainty.

The six international economic corridors are facing risks posed by internal political, security and societal situation of the countries along the Belt and Road, though to varying degrees. West European countries, usually deemed the safest and stablest places in the world, are

---

[2] Xu Haiyan, "State Governance and Political Stability: From the Perspective of Kyrgyzstan's Transition", *Issues of Contemporary World Socialism*, no. 2, 2011, p. 78. (徐海燕：《国家治理与政治稳定——以吉尔吉斯斯坦转轨为视角》，载《当代世界社会主义问题》2011 年第 2 期，第 78 页。)

now in great panic. The terrorist attack in Paris in November 2015 revealed the dilemma in Europe, which is also an alarm for the building of the New Eurasian Land Bridge Economic Corridor. With the influx of refugees from West and North Africa, chances that the security situation in West Europe will further deteriorate. To make things worse, domestic extremists are hard to guard against.

At present, the implementation of the BRI is mainly through major strategic and demonstrative projects. However, the past and present experiences from China–Thailand railway, Letpadaung copper mine project and Myitsone hydropower station project in Myanmar, Piraeus Port in Greece, China–Kyrgyzstan–Uzbekistan railway and Colombo Port City project in Sri Lanka have shown that the building of such projects is always influenced by or bound with domestic affairs of the host countries. China's interests are even compromised or sacrificed in their political struggles, resulting in huge political and economic loss. In the case that the political crisis turns into violence, regime change or even wars, investment from Chinese enterprises will be in great need for protection. The war in Libya stood as an evidence for that.

What is worth mentioning is that in some countries along the Belt and Road, resource nationalism, economic nationalism and trade protectionism are on the rise. The resource and energy development and infrastructure projects invested by China are readily labeled as resource plundering, new colonialism and environmental pollution. Misbehaviors of some Chinese enterprises fuel criticism as well. Chinese enterprises are condemned by local groups or people when conflicts of interest arise or Chinese enterprises fail to take care of the interests of all parties in choosing the location and route for the projects. Aided by foreign media and nongovernmental organizations (NGOs), local governments finally wade in to suspend or even cancel the project. Due to resource nationalism, the fiscal and tax laws in some countries change frequently, which raises the risk cost for Chinese energy enterprises. Similarly, resource nationalization policies are expected to cause continuous negative impact on the business conduct of Chinese enterprises abroad.

In the past, many developing countries were faced with capital shortage; therefore, it was common practice for Chinese enterprises to cooperate with them in models such as "resources for projects", "loans for oil", "gold mine for road", and "infrastructure construction-resources and energy development-financial cooperation". The essence of such cooperation models is that China's development finance institutions provide loans while the recipient countries put up resources and energies as a guarantee to pay Chinese infrastructure enterprises for engineering, equipment and labors. Although cooperation of this type has created new ways of financing for developing countries, it nevertheless invited constant criticism, and even caused diplomatic passiveness for China. In fact, with the rise of economic nationalism, the international industrial capacity cooperation sponsored by China faces the issue of how to be accepted and implemented in the B&R countries.

In some countries, not only are China's projects subject to non-market risks, but also the safety of Chinese citizens are under threat. In recent years, there are almost 30,000 overseas Chinese enterprises, with a total asset exceeding 3 trillion dollars. However, according to incomplete statistics from the Ministry of Commerce (MOFCOM), the number of security incidents related to overseas Chinese enterprises and institutions amounted to 345 during the period from 2010 to 2015.[3] In the terrorist attack in Mali in November 2015, three senior executives from China Railway Construction Corporation (CRCC), who were on a business trip for a communication cooperation project, were shot to death. It sounded an alarm for overseas protection of both Chinese enterprises and citizens. In accelerating the building of the Belt and Road, more and more Chinese industrial capacities and labor services will go global, especially to developing countries. It will be a critical issue to ensure personal security for overseas Chinese.

8.2 Cross-border Security Risks

Historically, the decline of the ancient land Silk Road was largely attributed to enduring wars and unrest in areas along the route. Since

---

[3] Ministry of Commerce of the People's Republic of China, "Regular Press Conference of the Ministry of Commerce", December 2, 2015, http://www.mofcom.gov.cn/article/ae/slfw/201512/20151201199367.shtml, log-in time: Feburary 14, 2016. (商务部:《商务部召开例行新闻发布会》, 2015 年 12 月 2 日。)

the 21st century, although the possibility of massive military conflicts has been greatly reduced, the cross-border political mobilization and operation networks, represented by "the Three Forces", are a great impact on the political system in multiethnic countries in Central and West Asia and North Africa. They constitute a constant threat to the security and stability of the Northwest frontier of China. Since the land trade involves frequent people and cargo exchange and cross-border infrastructure construction, the radical acts of "the Three Forces" — explosion, assassination and kidnapping, and so on — could seriously deteriorate security environment along the Silk Road Economic Belt, and shatter confidence of the visitors and foreign investors.

In China, South Xinjiang has been targeted by East Turkistan terrorists, which also gradually expands their activities into East and North Xinjiang and other parts of China.[4] A number of major terrorist attacks have signaled that China has entered a new phase in which terrorism will become a constant phenomenon. In the meantime, the East Turkestan Islamic Movement stationed in South, Central and West Asia are adopting various ways to spread terrorist ideas, instigating, plotting and carrying out terrorist acts, which has become the most direct and realistic security threat.

In West Asia and North Africa, the impact of the Arab Spring is far from being over. The ethnic reconciliation and national reconstruction in Iraq are facing various difficulties after the withdrawal of the US army. The enduring Syrian war witnesses the rise of the IS (Islamic State), which is permeating into North Africa, Central Asia, South Asia, Southeast Asia and Europe at a fast pace. Through Syrian war and Yemen civil war, the deep-rooted sect conflicts between Shi'a, led by Iran, and Sunni, led by Saudi Arabia, have intensified. Both sides support their own "proxy" and provide arms to them. In

---

[4] Guriazti Tulsson, "Analysis on the Characteristics and Development Trend of the Terrorist Forces in East Turkistan", *Contemporary International Relations*, no. 1, 2014, pp. 56–62. (古丽阿扎提•吐尔逊:《"东突"恐怖势力个体特征及其发展趋势评析》, 载《现代国际关系》2014 年第 1 期, 第 56–62 页。)

January 2016, Saudi Arabia's execution of Sheikh Nimr, a Shia cleric, aroused strong repercussion in Iran, leading to the termination of diplomatic relations between the two countries. As a result, Bahrain, Sudan and United Arab Emirates decided to terminate or lower the level of diplomatic relations with Iran, making the regional situation even more complex.

In Central Asia, due to rapid expansion of IS and the spillover effect of the Afghanistan war, the extremist ideas and religious forces are obviously on the ascent. More violent terror attacks appear in Kazakhstan, Kyrgyzstan and border areas between Tajikistan and Afghanistan. While looming large in the East and South of Afghanistan, Afghanistan Taliban joined hands with "the Three Forces", such as the Islamic Movement of Uzbekistan (IMU) and Islamic Jihad Union (IJU) in Central Asia, to move into the Northern Province of Kondoz. The IMU, while having lain low in Afghanistan, regrouped itself and integrated with extremists from Taliban, Chechnya and Middle East and East Turkistan Islam Organization, and headed south to the border area between Kyrgyzstan, Tajikistan and Afghanistan. It stayed in the north while Afghanistan Taliban in the south. The Fergana Valley, the tri-border area of Uzbekistan, Kyrgyzstan and Tajikistan, became a primary target of terror.

In contrast with the security challenges arising from internal unrest in countries along the Belt and Road, "the Three Forces", with its cross-border or internationalized activities, is harder to be cracked down. It is a necessity for countries involved to jointly launch cross-border governance.

First, as to the guiding ideology, "the Three Forces", with various political backgrounds and interest appeals, refused to recognize the existing multiethnic national systems or territorial borders in the region, and tried to redraw the political map based on specific religions or ethnics. The pan-Islamism advocates uniting all Islamic countries and ethnics to overthrow the existing secular state and establish Caliphate with Caesaropapism. The IS, with its increasingly globalized ideology and presence, embodies a direct implementation of the concept. Correspondingly, pan-Turkism believes in the notion that all Turks in the world belong to one ethnic group, and encourages all Turkish-speaking people to unite in West and Central Asia, to establish the Great Turk Empire with Turkey as its center. As cross-border ideologies, pan-Islamism and pan-Turkism have divided their belief or ethnic map into a central region and border areas. Countries in the central region, such as Saudi Arabia, Turkey and other Middle East countries, are exerting constant influence on Central Asia, South Asia and Xinjiang. Apart from being ideological guiders, those countries also serve as "patrons" for the latter. The oil dollar in the Middle East is secretly linked with the Three Forces in Central Asia, South Asia and Xinjiang.

Second, as to sphere of influence, rather than limiting itself in one nation, "the Three Forces" spread in border areas between countries. For example, since 1990s, Fergana Valley at the border areas between Uzbekistan, Tajikistan and Kyrgyzstan became a camp for religious radical extremists in Central Asia. Persisting turbulence in Afghanistan facilitated cross-border activities for IMU, the East Turkistan Islamic Movement (ETIM), IJU, Hizb ut-Tahrir al-Islami and other radical groups.[5] As to China, since Xinjiang shares long borders with Pakistan and Afghanistan, East Turkistan organizations in these three countries are closely linked.

Third, as to the functioning mode, "the Three Forces", although with different requests and demands, are able to establish a set of mobilization and cooperation networks based on shared political and religious ideas. These networks are either loose or tight in structure, both independent and complementary in relations with each other, making "the Three Forces" more complicated and internationalized. In China, the East Turkistan terrorism has developed a cross-border act pattern and an "assembly line" of terrorism. Namely, the radical forces overseas upload video clips in Uyghur onto the Internet as a

---

[5] Chen Jing and Wang Mingye, "Causes and Possible Impacts of Islamic Extremism in Fergana", *Social Sciences in Xinjiang*, no. 6, 2012, pp. 80–87.(陈靖、王鸣野:《费尔干纳的伊斯兰极端主义:产生的原因与可能的影响》, 载《新疆社会科学》2012 年第 6 期, 第 80–87 页); Yang Lei, "Analysis on the Current Security Situation of Five Central Asian Countries", *Contemporary International Relations*, no. 11, 2012, pp. 24–27. (杨雷:《当前中亚五国安全形势评析》, 载《现代国际关系》2012 年第 11 期, 第 24–27 页。)

guide for terror attacks, provide bomb-making manuals or sell illegal products, recruit Chinese terrorists and train them overseas, and send them back to China with funds and weapons to conduct violent terrorist attacks. The escalation of the Syrian civil war and the cruelty of IS have provided opportunities to practice war fighting for terrorists globally. At present, many Uyghur terrorists have stolen into Vietnam and Myanmar from Yunnan and Guangxi. Helped by smugglers, they travel to Thailand and Cambodia through land route and waterway, fly to Turkey from Malaysia and Indonesia and then head for Syria and Iraq to join the IS. Once these "jihadists" go back to China to wage terrorist attacks, they will cause severe damage and casualty.

What is worth mentioning is that the "Golden Crescent" at the border of Afghanistan, Pakistan and Iran has replaced the "Golden Triangle" as the main source of drugs in the world. The cross-border drug trafficking network centering on Afghanistan is increasingly permeating to Xinjiang. Evidences show that the collusion between cross-border drug trafficking groups and East Turkistan terrorist group is intensifying. The vicious cycle of terrorism–drug linkage has taken shape.

Simply speaking, while the possibility of large-scale international military clashes is diminishing, the threat of "the Three Forces" is increasing. Due to the resurrection of global political Islamism, the enduring turbulence in Afghanistan and Pakistan, the fund support and ideology output from Saudi Arabia and Turkey, the double standards and appeasement policies of the United States and European countries, and fighting experience gained from wars in Iraq and Syria, "the Three Forces" are getting strengthened, becoming a long-standing threat to China and the countries along the Belt and Road. In the meantime, it is likely that the rapid flow of commodities, funds and people, and the connectivity of infrastructure will facilitate the activities by "the Three Forces", and cross-border crimes as well. It is the very scenario that China should try to avoid.

8.3 Risks Deriving from Great Power Competition

Great power competition is a major issue for building the Belt and Road Initiative. The competition usually happens in key regions and countries. If China fails to work with major powers to manage differences and frictions or achieve strategic understanding and cooperation, the building of the Belt and Road will be negatively impacted. Contrarily, enhanced cooperation between major powers will ease concerns of middle and small countries, and prevent certain countries from harvesting benefits from major power competition. Specifically, there are two types of competitions facing China in building the Belt and Road Initiative: competition with global power (the United States), and with regional powers (Russia, India and Japan)

The power shift between China, the second largest economy and largest developing country, and the United States, the largest economy and the largest developed country, has accelerated the internationalization of their bilateral relations. Currently, competition between them concerning Belt and Road Initiative centers on the Asia-Pacific region and the financial area.

The Asia-Pacific is believed to be the region where China and the United States have the most overlapped interests, the most frequent interactions and the greatest risk for conflict. With the rebalancing strategy in Asia-Pacific, the United States rolled out a series of political, military and economic measures against China. The strategic competition between China and the United States is growing. Politically, the United States remains partial to Japan at Diaoyu Island, added resources support for Myanmar, and gets increasingly involved in the territorial disputes between China and Vietnam, or between China and the Philippines. Militarily, the United States adjusted its military deployment in Japan proper, Okinawa, Korea, Guam, Australia, the Philippines and Singapore, held frequent military exercises with Asian allies to improve the amphibious warfare and cooperative combat capacities, and tries to develop its Airsea Battle strategy against the so-called Anti-Access/Area Denial strategy from China.[6] Economically, the United States advocated Trans-Pacific Partnership Agreement (TPP), in an effort to gain dominance in

---

[6] Ruan Zongze, "Analysis on the Prospects of Asia Pacific Rebalancing Strategy", *World Economics and Politics*, no. 4, 2014, pp. 8–9.(阮宗泽:《美国"亚太再平衡"战略前景论析》, 载《世界经济与政治》2014 年第 4 期, 第 8–9 页。)

Asia-Pacific economic cooperation by establishing new rules, and to weaken China's influence and competitiveness in regional economic integration. Later, TPP was trashed by the Trump Administration.

The United States is the major player in the existing international financial system. But China has recently been intensifying financial cooperation with the rest of the world, and promoting reforms in the international financial governance structure. First, China has been steadily promoting bilateral currency swap, settlement and direct transaction, achieving great progress in renminbi (RMB) internationalization. The rising influence of RMB in Association of Southeast Asian Nations (ASEAN) has weakened the traditionally advantageous US dollar and Japanese Yen. Since 2013, China has signed deals with the Bank of England and the European Central Bank on currency swap and direct transaction between RMB and Pound or Euro. An RMB cross-border network has been established, covering European financial centers such as London, Frankfurt, Paris and Luxembourg. More significant landmark events include the successful launch of RMB Cross-border Interbank Payment System (CIPS) Phase One and the inclusion of RMB in the Special Drawing Right (SDR) Currency Basket of International Monetary Fund (IMF). Second, China draws on its huge foreign reserve to provide new financing channels, especially for Asian and developing countries. The Asian Infrastructure Investment Bank (AIIB), the New Development Bank, the Silk Road Fund, the projected Shanghai Cooperation Organization (SCO) Development Bank and various special funds established jointly by China and relevant countries will offer new options of financing for developing countries, besides the World Bank and the Asian Development Bank. Third, China, having participated in the multilateral currency swap and contingent reserve arrangement, is providing short-term liquidity to developing countries in times of disequilibrium of international payment balance. Such a move helps to achieve joint management of financial risks. It is fair to say that internationalization of RMB and financial cooperation between China and relevant countries are restructuring global financial governance scenario, which is not warmly welcomed by the United States.

Russia is a key country on the Silk Road Economic Belt and holds great significance for the New Eurasian Bridge Economic Corridor and the China–Mongolia–Russia Economic Corridor. Central Asia is the place where China and Russia might have strategic competition. For a long time, Russia has been viewing Central Asia as its backyard and maintaining high alert for any attempts by other major powers to strengthen their influence in this area. Centering on the Eurasian Economic Union, Russia has developed a set of clear, definite and progressive ideas and measures to promote trade, investment and financial cooperation with Central Asian countries. Just as other integrated groups, the Eurasian Economic Union, while promoting the free flow of various elements among its members, erects system barriers for nonmembers. The industry, investment and trade protectionism will make access harder for Chinese commodities, capitals and labor. Therefore, although China and Russia have achieved consensus on the alignment of the Silk Road Economic Corridor and Eurasian Economic Union, competition for Eurasian economic integration still exists between the two countries.

What is worth mentioning is that the cooperation and competition between China and Russia are also delicate in the financial sector. As to the currency exchange, China and Russia have shared interests in breaking down the US dollar monopoly. Nevertheless, as China deepens currency cooperation with other SCO members, it should face the issue of RMB–Ruble competition. As to the financing support, the obstacles for setting up SCO development bank mainly come from disagreement over proportion of votes among members, especially by China and Russia. As early as in 2006, Russia joined hands with Kazakhstan, Tajikistan, Kyrgyzstan, Armenia and Belarus to establish the Eurasian Development Bank, a development bank to finance infrastructure projects in member countries. In the future, it would be necessary for the SCO Development Bank to find a way to work with the Eurasian Development Bank.

As a regional power in South Asia, India is a key component of the Bangladesh–China–India–Myanmar Economic Corridor, and a major party concerned in the China–Indochina Peninsula Economic Corridor, China–Pakistan Economic Corridor and China–Central

Asia–West Asia Economic Corridor. Due to territorial disputes, China–Pakistan relations, and competition for regional dominance, India has long viewed China as its major strategic competitor after Pakistan. With its advantageous geographical location, India is confident in its dominance in South Asia, and shows great interest in the regional affairs of neighboring areas, such as Central Asia (especially Afghanistan), South East Asia (such as Myanmar), the Middle East and Africa, which is manifested by its intensified resource input and business effort in these areas. Against such a backdrop, China's port construction in Pakistan, Myanmar, Bangladesh and Sri Lanka in recent years has alerted India to the so-called String of Pearl Strategy and the rising Chinese influence in the Indian Ocean. Following China's Belt and Road Initiative, India put forward the Monsoon Plan as a response.

Due to the structural conflict in China–Japan relations, Japan is a possible challenger to the Belt and Road Initiative. Since Shinzo Abe took office, Japan has been continuing its provocation in Diaoyu Island and the East China Sea, as well as trying to establish anti-China alliance by involving Vietnam and the Philippines in issues related to the South China Sea. All these are done in a clear attempt to disrupt the building of the 21st-century Maritime Silk Road. As to the infrastructure connectivity, China Railway High-Speed (CRH) and Japan's Shinkansen have been in fierce competition for the railway development plans in a number of Asian countries such as Thailand, Cambodia, Vietnam and India. Moreover, Japan refused to join the AIIB under the pretext that AIIB, aiming at offering financial support for Asian developing countries, is overlapping in function with Asian Development Bank — a development financing institute led by Japan. All signs point to the fact that China and Japan not only fail to ease the tension around the East China Sea, but also upgrade their competition in the South China Sea, Southeast Asia, Central Asia and South Asia.

In one word, although China has repeatedly stressed that no exclusive geopolitical purposes are attached in the Belt and Road Initiative, relevant major powers are still concerned with China's rising political influence. Whether China can reach strategic understanding or deepen practical cooperation with other major powers will largely determine how the Belt and Road Initiative will be implemented.

8.4   Policy Recommendations

As the Belt and Road has been advancing comprehensively, it is necessary to understand and manage risks in a rational way.

On the one hand, China should be fully prepared for the fact that building the Belt and Road is a long, complicated and difficult journey. Therefore, a multilevel and comprehensive security support system should be established. Although China is vigorously promoting the BRI in key aspects, countries, regions and projects, it should pay close attention to and guard against possible designated attacks.

On the other hand, China should not overstate the risks along the Belt and Road, or blame the BRI for all the challenges arising from Chinese enterprises and citizens' going global. Neither should China reject the BRI in times of temporary failure, nor should it lose itself in skepticism and defeatism.

In order to properly manage the realistic and potential risks along the Belt and Road, following suggestions are put forward:

The first is to pay close attention to political, economic, religious and ethnic changes in key B&R countries. For countries with high security risks and unstable political environments, China should pay close attention to their domestic political situation, make appropriate assessments and take precautions against possible political risks. In cases where China's political and military strength cannot ensure effective protection, it should take caution and prudence in getting involved, and get ready to pull out when necessary. Apart from the guidance for "going global" from the MFA and the MOFCOM, China should encourage relevant chambers, enterprises, universities and research institutes to conduct dynamic assessments on various security risks facing the B&R. Their research should include all the influence variables on the political stability in countries along the Belt and Road, such as ethnics, religions, regional differences, classes, political fractions, military and politics, and central–local government relation; policies and attitudes to China or Chinese investors of specific countries and governments; possible cross-border security risks; and exterior major powers.

The second is to develop friendly relations with different political forces in key B&R countries so as to minimize the impact arising from regime changes. In implementing the Belt and Road Initiative, China should identify convergence of interests with these countries, and prioritize infrastructure projects of as power and communications so as to ease concerns of the host government and its people. Lessons from the demonstration against Letpadaung copper mine project and Kyrgyzstan's refusal to accept financing proposal for China–Uzbekistan–Kyrgyzstan railway show that, concerning major strategic cooperation projects, China should work closely with the local people, take local social and economic development into consideration and avoid the public being manipulated by some political fractions or foreign forces. The B&R countries commonly have a political structure of weak central government versus strong religion/tribe/local government, which makes it necessary for China to defend its overseas interests through both formal channels — bilateral relations between governments and nations — and informal channels — interactions with sectional, religious and local forces in host countries. China should fully understand the importance of tribal and religious leaders in their political life, especially at the local level, and therefore take advantage of the rich cultural resources to strengthen people-to-people bonds and public diplomacy, and achieve acceptance and popularity at the grassroots level.

The third is to strengthen international cooperation and crack down "the Three Forces" and collusion between drug and terror. Given the internal unrest in Afghanistan, increasing international activities of "the Three Forces", and intensified collusion between drug and terrorism, China may draw on the experience from joint law enforcement on Mekong River launched by China, Thailand, Myanmar and Laos, and propose to SCO members and observer states — especially India, Pakistan and Iran — to establish joint operation mechanism for combating terror and drug trafficking. China may help Pakistan to establish its national counter terrorism ability, intensify policy coordination with Saudi Arabia, Turkey and other Middle

East countries, and eradicate the overseas training camp and funds, ideology and recruitment network of "the Three Forces". China may intensify intelligence and border control cooperation with Southeastern Asian countries to prevent religious extremists from going to the Middle East through Guangxi and Yunnan, or from returning to China to carry out violent acts of terror. While seeking investments from the Middle East, local Chinese governments should firmly guard to prevent Wahhabism, pan-Islamism and pan-Turkism from infiltrating China.

The fourth is to enhance policy coordination with other major countries, and to conduct pragmatic cooperation in specific regions or fields. While the conflicts between Russia and the West over Ukraine are getting acute, China should intensify its cooperation with Russia in Central Asia and the Far East, and accelerate the establishment of the SCO Development Bank and Development Fund. In the meantime, China may accept the Russian proposal to invest in Eurasian Development Bank led by Russia. Since its shareholders can settle with their own currencies, the Eurasian Development Bank could serve as a new platform for RMB internationalization. China's investment will boost the bank in its credit rating, improve the discourse power of China and Russia in the international financial system and offer members better infrastructure financing. When it comes to major investment projects in Central Asia, South Asia, Southeast Asia, Middle East, Central and Middle Europe, China may learn from the cooperation mode of China-Myanmar Oil and Gas Pipelines project, which features "six party of four countries". By involving enterprises from Russia, India, United States, EU and Korea, China can share the risks with and lessen the concerns of all parties. Although the strategic competition between China and United States in Asia-Pacific is getting intense, with the US troops gradually withdrawing from Iraq and Afghanistan, the two countries have shared interests in maintaining regional stablity and protecting overseas investments and citizens. There is still room for expanding Sino–US cooperation in the Middle East and Central Asia. At present, China and the United States may center their cooperation on the stability and reconstruction in Afghanistan, and seek convergence of interests between China's Belt and Road Initiative and America's New Silk Road. Since 2012, China and the United States have started to hold annual meeting on the Middle East affairs, which has achieved initial progress. Such a cooperation mechanism should be enhanced in the future.

In conclusion, complexities in the situation along the Belt and Road make it highly difficult for China to implement the Initiative. The risks involved are diverse in their nature, type and level. In terms of nature, emergent risks coexist with structural and long-term ones; in terms of type, political, economic, social and cultural risks are mixed together; in terms of level, domestic risks in B&R countries, cross-region threats and major power struggles are mutually reinforced. Therefore, instead of underestimating or overstating them, China should manage the risks with reason and prudence.

Conclusion

As a major national development strategy and international cooperation initiative proposed by China in the new era, the "Silk Road Economic Belt" and "21st-Century Maritime Silk Road" represent the Chinese government's new vision on equal and win-win cooperation between China and relevant countries with the ancient maritime and land Silk Roads as a reference. As we dig deeper into this initiative's relationship with the ancient Silk Road and the Modern Silk Road, its strategic importance gradually manifests itself. It is not a simple reincarnation of the ancient Silk Road, but China's guiding principle in opening up and conducting international cooperation. It is the "Chinese Proposal" and an international public good that will promote a win-win cooperation in the world.

1.1 Vision and Actions on Jointly Building the Belt and Road

As an overall plan for international cooperation and opening-up, the Belt and Road Initiative puts China's economic transformation and upgradation in the context of global economic cooperation and envisions a new type of opening-up that brings together China's coastal and inland areas, reaches out toward countries to China's West as well as East. Meanwhile, it will bring together China's capital, production capacity, equipment, technology, merchandise, labor force, standards, management experience, and currency and the natural resources, energy, and markets of B&R countries. It outlines a new model of win-win cooperation that features equality, shared and mutual benefits.

Nicknamed the "Chinese Proposal", it is by no means dominated by China alone. Rather, it is thus named because the plan consists of key strategic decisions made by China as its comprehensive national strength increases and its development model shifts, taking into consideration prevailing domestic and global circumstances. It is a reflection of China's definition of a new type of international relations. The concept of the Belt and Road Initiative features an emphasis on win-win cooperation rather than confrontation and dominance. The implementation of the BRI will prioritize much-needed infrastructure connectivity and industrialization in B&R countries, with whom China will share the development experience it has gained since the start of its reform and opening-up.

The fact that the BRI is termed an international public good for countries along the Belt and Road does not suggest that China will provide all funds needed for relevant projects. Rather, the Initiative is a public good in a more fundamental sense of the term. As President Xi Jinping pointed out, "the Belt and Road Initiative is an inclusive, large-scale development platform that China is providing to the region and the world", "capable of bringing together the common interests of a rapidly developing China and B&R countries".[1] Operating on this platform, China and B&R countries can utilize their own strengths in capital, industrialization, infrastructure construction, natural resources and energy to meet each other's demands; China and developed countries will be able to jointly explore and open up new markets;

---

[1] Xinhua News Agency, "Accelerating the Construction of the Silk Road Economic Belt and 21st-Century Maritime Silk Road", *People's Daily*, November 7, 2014, p. 1.(新华社:《加快推进丝绸之路经济带和二十一世纪海上丝绸之路建设》,载《人民日报》2014 年 11 月 7 日,第 1 版。)

South–South and North–South cooperation will gain new momentum and have at its disposal a new vehicle; European and Asian countries, especially developing ones, will be able to greatly improve their business environments and transportation and logistics networks, and promote industrialization; countries all over the world will discover opportunities to cooperate with partners on the Eurasian continent, participating in the region's development.

The founding of the Leading Group for the Belt and Rod Initiative and the release of the *Vision and Actions on Jointly Building Silk Road Economic Belt and 21st-Century Maritime Silk Road* indicate that top-level design of the BRI has been completed by the central government of China. Components of the BRI will be implemented gradually, through the expansion of successful small-scale attempts. Efforts will be made mainly in the areas of policy coordination, facilities connectivity, trade and investment, financial integration and cultural exchange, with a priority on key routes, countries, sectors and projects. Implementation is progressing according to plan on all levels and in all areas, from central to local government, in the public and private sectors, and within and beyond the borders of China. Relevant support structures and institutions are gradually being put in place.

There is now increasing acceptance and positive response toward the Belt and Road Initiative in the international community, thanks to the support of relevant participants. Many countries have gone from merely passively observing from the sidelines to being active participants and proponents of the BRI. Through the "BRI Plus" strategy, China has concluded memorandums of understanding and cooperation agreements with a number of countries, "identifying pivotal nations and core participants in key areas for itself."[2] Furthermore, under the Initiative, a new type of financing platform has been successfully established and is now in operation, a number of landmark projects that will serve as a blueprint for future endeavors have been launched, and work on the six economic corridors

---

[2] National Development and Reform Commission of PRC, "Belt and Road Construction Achieves Concrete Results", August 3, 2015, http://www.sdpc.gov.cn/xwzx/xwfb/201508/t20150803_744051.html, log-in time: August 5, 2015. (中国国家发改委:《"一带一路"建设取得实实在在成果》, 2015 年 8 月 3 日。)

promoting Eurasian connectivity has already begun. In addition, much progress has been made in terms of promoting infrastructure connectivity, regulation compatibility and personnel exchanges.

In fact, great progress in the Initiative's implementation can be observed across multiple regions and sectors, from China's eastern coastline all the way to its northwestern frontiers. Examples include industrial parks such as the China–Malaysia Qinzhou Industrial Park, Malaysia–China Kuantan Industrial Park, China–Belarus Industrial Park; free trade zones (FTZ) such as the Shanghai FTZ and Gwadar Port FTZ; rail lines such as the proposed China–Thailand railway and Moscow–Kazan high-speed rail; Chinese investment in Colombo Harbor and the Port of Piraeus; the China-Europe RAILWAY Express and China–Europe Land–Sea Express Line; China's conclusion and implementation of mutual recognition of authorized economic operator (AEO) programs with various countries around the world and setting up of "green channels" at Customs to facilitate agricultural product imports; joint projects such as the Karot Hydropower Project and YASREF refinery; China's establishment of Asian Infrastructure Investment Bank (AIIB) and joining of European Bank for Reconstruction and Development (EBRD); the acceptance of the Renminbi for commodities trading by more and more countries and companies; the launch of China's Cross-Border Interbank Payment System (CIPS); and cultural initiatives and events such as the China–Russia Youth Year of Friendship, European Union (EU)–China Year of Intercultural Dialogue, "Revisiting Zheng He's Voyages", and "Revisiting the Tea Road".

Through observation and analysis of the activities carried out under the Belt and Road Initiative, the integration of five sets of factors can be observed and inferred.

First, the combination of progress in selected areas and overall progress. The Belt and Road Initiative strives to be a cooperative initiative that is comprehensive and overarching, yet considering that China's capabilities are not unlimited, and that its efforts may sometimes be restrained by the internal and external factors it faces, China will likely focus on a select group of countries, sectors, projects and pathways in the implementation of the Initiative. Cooperation with countries that have favorable conditions, display greater willingness, are located strategically and have greater influence will be prioritized. Such cooperation will be directed toward bottleneck-breaking landmark projects located in key regions and crucial to promoting connectivity.[3]

Second, the combination of long-term vision and near-term results. As President Xi Jinping pointed out, the BRI is not merely rhetoric, but can lead to substantive results, of which the AIIB, the New Development Bank, Silk Road Fund, China–Thailand Railway, China–Laos Railway, Jakarta–Bandung High-speed Rail, Hungary–Serbia Railway, Gwadar Port, China–Belarus Industrial Park and the industrial capacity cooperation between China and Kazakhstan are all good examples. In fact, the sooner concrete results can be produced through the BRI, the more support and participation there will be.

Third, the combination of new platforms and existing mechanisms. Even though many new proposals were made under the auspices of the BRI, China does not seek to establish a new, separate global or regional order. This is why, in addition to initiating new financing platforms such as the AIIB, the New Development Bank and Silk Road Fund, China is very much inclined to making full use of and upgrading existing bilateral or multilateral cooperation mechanisms, platforms and processes to better join up its own development strategy with those of B&R countries, thereby complement each other's strengths.

Fourth, the combination of government and market forces. In the early stages of building the Belt and Road, most of the top-level planning, policy coordination and platform building will be done by national governments. However, it will be private enterprises that shoulder the bulk of the responsibility for the actual launch and operations of the projects that make up the BRI. Since the Initiative's inception, the Chinese private sector has shown great enthusiasm for exploring new markets and optimizing existing business abroad, achieving great results in both regards. Notably, Chinese companies

---

[3] Fan Hengshan, "Five Dos and Don'ts in the Construction of the Belt and Road", *China Economic & Trade Herald*, no. 31, 2015, p. 42. (范恒山：《"一带一路"建设的"五忌五要"》, 载《中国经贸导刊》2015 年第 31 期, 第 42 页。)

are doing much more than simply selling products or contracting projects in B&R countries; they are now exporting sophisticated solutions that include equipment, designs, standards, project construction, project operation and management experience. Furthermore, it has to be noted that all projects, including government-led ones, will play by market rules, taking costs and earnings into full account. The BRI is not a handout, nor will it employ loss leader strategies.

Fifth, the combination of central and local government efforts. China's central government has devised a top-level design for the BRI, while at the same time cabinet-level ministries and local governments have all placed the promotion of the Initiative at the top of their agendas, coming up with their own plans for work. Provincial and municipal-level governments have put forward a number of road-maps centering on infrastructure construction, trade promotion, investment, energy, natural resources, financial cooperation, environmental protection, maritime cooperation and cultural exchanges. Local governments have displayed great eagerness in participating in the Initiative, regarding it as the start of another round of favorable policies. Many large-scale project plans have been drawn up. To prevent the rise of a potential homogenous market, the central government is stepping up efforts in guiding and coordinating local endeavors, encouraging each region to position itself appropriately, with a clear focus on key areas, and put their respective comparative advantages to full use.[4]

1.2 Understanding the Belt and Road from Historical and Comparative Perspectives

1.2.1 *Land–Sea Relations*

To better understand the Belt and Road, it is important to first look at the relationship between the East and West throughout history and the rise and fall of the sea and land routes that connect China to

---

[4] Xinhua News Agency, "To Ensure a Sound Start for the Belt and Road", *People's Daily*, July 22, 2015, p. 1. (新华社:《确保实现"一带一路"建设良好开局》,载《人民日报》2015 年 7 月 22 日, 第 1 版。)

the rest of the world. The rise of the overland Silk Road came to a halt with the An Lushan Rebellion in the mid-Tang dynasty, and began a gradual process of historical decline. In the meanwhile, sea routes began to be more frequently used by travelers and became increasing well developed. Previously, most travelers between Tang China and Persia, the Arab Empire, the Byzantine Empire and other regions took the land route, over which people, regional goods and regional religions travelled throughout the continent. However, as the Tang dynasty entered a phase of decline, the Arab Empire continued to expand, and instability spread throughout Western and Central Asia, the overland route fell out of favor with merchants conducting trade between the East and West. The sea route gradually became the preferred route of trade between China and West Asia. During the same period, the center of China's economy experienced a southward shift, with the provinces along the southeastern coast becoming the government's main source of fiscal revenue and the country's largest production hub. These factors, along with the rise of maritime trade, contributed to the emergence of major port cities such as Quanzhou, Guangzhou, Yangzhou and Mingzhou (present-day Ningbo). As customs duties and its proportion of government income continued to grow, the Southern Song government became much more supportive of maritime trade than previous dynasties. In the succeeding Yuan dynasty, the significance of the maritime Silk Road reached a new level as it became an important route for trade and cultural exchanges between China and Southeast Asia and West Asia. Even though the northwestern land route remained in use, it had by then lost much of its former renown and glory. The expeditionary voyages of Zheng He during the Ming dynasty marked the peak of the ancient maritime Silk Road's influence, as well as China's then status as a maritime power to be reckoned with.

With the rise of the Western world in the 19th and early 20th century, seaborne trade became the main form of international trade and the overland trade route that spanned the Eurasia continent fell completely out of use. This new world order also contributed to the existing development gap between coastal and inland China. Many efforts, such as adjustments to relevant institutions and the geographical distribution of industrial activities, have been made since the founding of the People's Republic of China to correct this imbalance. However, the eastern, coastal regions maintained its leading position in China's export-oriented economy, in part due to the country's reentry after the launch of the reform and opening-up policies into a global market that was mostly dominated by Western powers. The concentration of economic activity in coastal areas then became a main feature of China's economic geography landscape. During this period, there was much overlap between the country's industrial development policy (which put great emphasis on export-oriented, labor-intensive manufacturing), regional development policy (which gave priority to eastern coastal regions) and opening-up strategy (which saw coastal regions being opened up to the outside world first). As this book's investigation of the "Modern Silk Road" that connects China and the Middle East suggests, although such a development may seem like a revival of the sea routes that served as the vehicle for trade between ancient China's eastern coastal regions and lands such as the Arab Empire and Persia, it is in essence the result of China's post–reform opening-up of national development strategy in response to the modern international political and economic landscape. This resulted in an overreliance on the economies of coastal areas, maritime trade and maritime transportation, which in turn brought about a certain amount of risk and restrictive factors. Such circumstances reflect the grander structural issues that China faces today.

It is in this context that the Belt and Road Initiative proposes a change to China's current regional development and opening-up strategies, one that seeks to align the development speeds of eastern and western China and correct the imbalance between coastal and inland regions. The BRI maps out a new trade route between China and the Belt and Road countries and proposes to link the eastern and western regions to such countries via the overland "Belt" and maritime "Road", respectively. The BRI is a development scheme that is much more inclusive than the subregional cooperation of the past that saw coastal and border provinces work in tandem with China's neighboring countries, takes into consideration both the eastern and western parts of China, and therefore has greater potential waiting to be unleashed. The Silk Road Economic Belt and the 21st-Century Maritime Silk Road shall not seek to outcompete or replace one another. That they were proposed together speaks to the fact that during this current, new phase of development, China intends to pursue a strategy that puts matching emphasis on both its eastern and western regions, and on both land and maritime fronts.

Originally, the Belt and Road Initiative was to involve Central Asia and Southeast Asia only, but as circumstances changed and developed, the geographic scope of the Initiative expanded accordingly to encompass a larger geographic area. The three major routes of the Silk Road Economic Belt (northern, central and southern), with western China as their starting point, will span the Eurasian region, connecting Asia, Europe and Africa. The two major routes of the 21st-Century Maritime Silk Road will link the ports of eastern China with the Pacific and Indian Ocean Rim. One corridor will stretch across the South China Sea and Indian Ocean to reach Europe and the other toward South Pacific. Compared to the "Anxi Passage to the West" and "Guangzhou Sea Route to Foreign Lands" of the Tang dynasty or the routes that Zheng He took during his expeditions, the modern day Belt and Road connect China to many more countries and spans across a much larger region.

It cannot be denied that for a long time to come, the eastern coastal regions of China will remain the throbbing heart of the country's economy, and that the opening-up of coastal regions, maritime trade and maritime transport will maintain its prominent position in existing national strategies and the current international order. The maritime Silk Road's great economic significance and potential will no doubt continue to be highlighted as maritime connectivity is enhanced, port cooperation conducted and port industries developed. However, the Silk Road Economic Belt, a brand new overland channel facilitating the flow of capital, energy, professionals, technology, goods and currency between China and Belt and Road countries, will compensate for the inherent risks and inadequacies of the maritime trade route, correct the imbalance between China's coastal east and inland west that has proven to be a restriction on the country's development, in addition to serving as a revival of the ancient trade passage. This is why the Silk Road Economic Belt is much more of a historical breakthrough than the 21st-Century Maritime Silk Road, and much more telling of China's proactive long-term vision in this new era of development.

1.2.2 *Economic and Trade Ties*

Cross-border trade and economic cooperation have always been at the heart of the Silk Road, both the ancient and modern-day ones. A comparison of the economic ties embodied by the ancient Silk Road, the "Modern Silk Road" between China and the Middle East and the Belt and Road Initiative reveals the profound changes that overtook the international political and economic landscape through the ages.

In ancient times, trade between China and countries along the Silk Road was more or less balanced, with the former exporting finished goods and latter raw materials. Most of the consumers for the products traded on the Road, such Chinese silk, porcelain, Middle Eastern spices, jewels, rhino horns and ivories came from the upper echelons of society. Even though international trade had been a significant source of fiscal income in the Southern Song, such trade had limited impact on the national economic structure and people's quality of life in China at the time. The currencies used to settle transactions along the ancient Silk Road included the Chinese copper coin, Chinese silk, as well as gold/silver coins minted in Persia, the Arab Empire or the Byzantine Empire. Despite copper being a nonprecious metal, the Chinese coin saw extensive circulation abroad and demand for the currency stayed high, mainly due to people's trust in and acceptance of China's then status as a reliable major power. However, for the most part, the currencies used along the ancient Silk Road were chosen only for their availability in trade. No country had attempted to link the value of their currency to the price of main commodities during this time.

International trade underwent a series of profound changes with the rise of Western countries in the last few centuries. A clear line between "central" and "peripheral" regions was drawn; previously there had been no rigid structures in place and most countries conducted trade on an equal basis. In such a climate, it was the developed countries that dominated the scene, setting the rules for international trade and determining monetary policies and pricing standards, whereas developing countries served as their source of raw materials and market for industrial products. In the 1980s, the economies of East Asian countries, including that of China, witnessed rapid growth and soon the "center vs. periphery" structure gave way to a new, triangular structure, with the developed countries in North America and Europe in the role of consumer nations, China and other East Asian countries as manufacturing nations and Middle Eastern oil-producing countries as resource-providing nations. Within this new structure, the manufacturing countries import raw material from resource-provider nations, then export finished goods back to these countries and consumer countries. The consumer countries provide capital, technology and services to manufacturing countries that, along with resource-provider countries, pay consumer countries with great quantities of their trade surplus and forex reserves. This meant that the trade between consumer and resource-provider countries became indirect, and that the exploitation of resource-provider and manufacturing countries by consumer countries became less apparent yet more profound. As this study shows, the "Modern Silk Road" that China set up with Middle Eastern countries upon entering the 21st century was actually a response to the US-dictated rules of international trade and US-dominated payment mechanisms, pricing mechanisms, global political order and security landscape. This new triangular trading system that saw crude oil, US dollars and products manufactured in China flow between resource-providers (the Middle East), consumers (the United States) and producers (China) speaks of the inequality that existed between the three.

Most countries along the Belt and Road are developing countries. As the implementation of this Initiative continues, the economic cooperation between China and these countries may well enter a new phase. More specifically, China has capital to spare and ample experience in industrial production, construction and infrastructure-building, whereas Belt and Road countries possess rich natural resources, much untapped market potential and a strong demand for industrialization and urbanization coupled with an urgent need for funding in building infrastructure for transportation, energy, telecommunication, power generation and agriculture to improve quality of life for their peoples. If a truly diverse, inclusive and mutually beneficial financial cooperation platform could be set up to promote infrastructure connectivity and cross-border production capacity cooperation, it might herald the beginning of a brand new chapter in South–South cooperation. On the one hand, such a platform would be able to address China's shortage of natural resources, excess capacity and excess capital. Through large-scale construction projects, it may be possible for China to export its capital, capacity, equipment, technology, standards and management practices, and promote the globalization of the RMB. The BRI would be China's significant step forward from simply exporting goods and a more balanced approach to going global and allow the country to have a more institutionalized voice in the global economic governance structure. On the other hand, the BRI could help the countries along the Belt and Road improve the quality of infrastructure, tap into natural resource and energy reserves, accumulate capital, industrialize and enhance their overall capacity to develop. Such a cooperation model is much more sustainable and addresses the issues faced by developing countries at a deeper level than the South–South Cooperation of the past, which mainly sought to boost development through trade and foreign aid. Undoubtedly, the US-dominated triangle of international trade will continue to exist for a long time to come, but using the Belt and Road Initiative as an opportunity, China might be able to break free of its role as the producer of cheap "Made-in-China" manufactured goods and the traditional model of trade that sees China exchange finished goods for energy with other developing countries. A new type of South–South Cooperation will be fostered, with B&R countries working with each other on the basis of equality and mutual benefit.

Moreover, it should be noted that in addition to bringing about a new type of South–South Cooperation, the BRI will redefine the economic ties between China and developed countries, injecting new vitality into North–South Cooperation. On the one hand, China can work hand-in-hand with developed countries to open up markets elsewhere in the world, especially in places that have historic ties with the latter, which will allow for a certain level of complementarity. On the other hand, as Chinese capital buys up more leading enterprises and technologies in Western Europe, Chinese presence in Western European infrastructure projects will only grow stronger, allowing Chinese equipment to make a debut on the world stage. At the same time, more efforts to promote the globalization of the RMB will be made in the financial hubs of Europe, in countries such as the United Kingdom, Germany, France and Luxemburg.

1.2.3 *Religious Factors*

Understanding the interplay between religion and trade, the spread of faith and changes in the global political landscape are crucial to analyzing the changes that came over the Silk Road through the ages. The strong presence of Islam over the ancient land and maritime Silk Roads brought profound changes to the diverse religion landscapes in regions the Roads passed through. A "corridor of Islam" that stretched from the East to the West was formed, and many of the regions along the corridor remain predominantly Islam to this day. The main driving forces behind the spread of Islam during the heyday of the ancient Silk Road were trade and the expansion of Islamic states. Later on, it was the political unrest in Central Asia caused by the rise of Islam that contributed to the decline of the overland Silk Road. In the 21st century, the ties between religion, trade and politics remain closed, as can be seen from the China–Middle East "Modern Silk Road" and the Belt and Road Initiative. These ties bear distinct hallmarks of the times we live in and their features display a sort of continuity over time.

If one looks at the city of Yiwu in Zhejiang province and the Ningxia autonomous region of China, it is possible to see how religion and trade affect each other. On one hand, opportunities for trade can turn into opportunities for a certain religion to spread. As

Muslim merchants from the Middle East and China's northwestern regions made their way to Yiwu throughout the centuries, the city's religious makeup and society in general went through significant changes. The growth of the Muslim population, the establishment of multiple mosques around the city and *Fan-fang* (lit. "foreigners' neighborhoods", which persist to this day), speak of a thriving Muslim community during the heyday of the ancient Silk Road. On the other hand, religion can pave the way toward more opportunities for economic cooperation. Ningxia, a largely Muslim region of China, has always maintained a special link to the Arab/Islamic world on the basis of religion and culture. In recent years, with the hosting of the China–Arab States Expo in Ningxia, many new ideas for China's westward opening-up have been proposed, targeting Arab states and predominantly Muslim countries. Therefore, it is possible for a region to make up for its unfavorable geographic location with ties based on a shared religion.

However, as this book's analysis of the China–Middle East "Modern Silk Road" reveals, the triangular flow of crude oil, US dollars and "Made-in-China" products still lies at the heart of many phenomena, be it the growth of the Muslim population, cropping up of mosques in Yiwu or the popularity of Made-in-China Islamic products in Middle Eastern countries. Religion does play an important role here, but it is by no means a central factor in this triangular trade. The fact that China is stepping up Ningxia's cooperation with the Arab world suggests that religion as an influential factor is being integrated into China's overall national strategy. There had been voices from the media and academia proposing that China use its ties with the Muslim world to attract more petrodollars from the Middle East to develop the economy of its northwestern regions as early as the 1990s. However, this only became an actual policy option after "opening-up to the west" and the BRI were proposed by the national government. Such a policy saw the economic potential of religious ties being put to full use. It can be inferred that the interplay between trade and religion in the 21st century is by no means a duplicate of what took place in the past. With religion being so closely coupled with economics and politics, the rise and fall of religion will most likely continue to be profoundly influenced by developments in the latter two.

Furthermore, this study shows that the expansion and revival of religion has always had a negative bearing on the trade routes and regimes. This is true for the Silk Road in both ancient and modern times. Many factors had contributed to the interruption of trade on the ancient Silk Road, but the rise of Islam and Muslim military conquests in relevant regions was definitely one of the most prominent. Today, the risk of major international armed conflict is significantly lower, yet the spread of faith continues to be a major challenge that China will have to face in the implementation of the Silk Road Economic Belt.

On one hand, political Islam is on the rise, while sectarian conflicts persist — two factors that greatly impact the internal stability and development potential of a number of B&R countries. Continued political unrest poses significant security concerns for China as it implements its strategy abroad. Due to its geopolitical location and richness in oil and gas, the "corridor of Islam", which stretches from the Middle East to Central Asia, has always been facing an incredibly complex situation, in which sectarian strife, ethnic conflict and intervention from major powers all play a part. Since the mid- and late 1970s, political Islam has been on the rise and actively attempting to reshape the political landscape of sovereign states by enforcing their brand of logic. Many B&R countries face long-term, structural hurdles in development as well as political and security risks, what with cross-border religious groups actively spreading their beliefs and recruiting members, sectarian confrontation (both domestic and cross-border) and an increasingly fierce competition for control between major power that have great influence over the region. The "weak state vs. strong religion" situation persists and is getting more apparent.

On the other hand, many B&R countries and China's western frontiers are plagued by the troika of religious extremism, ethnic separatism and terrorism, which also threaten to negatively impact overland trade routes. Although large-scale riots such as those that took place throughout China's history in its northwest and southwest are unlikely to repeat in the future, the terrorist attacks that targeted part of Xinjiang autonomous region in recent years suggest that the threat of extremism/separatism/terrorism to state power still persists in this multiethnic country. With instability reigning in Afghanistan, the Golden-Crescent-based opium trade is funneling money into terrorism for the purchase of arms, forming a vicious cycle. As overland trade routes are expanded and infrastructure connectivity promoted under efforts of the Silk Road Economic Belt, it may indeed become easier for forces of extremism, separatism and terrorism to infiltrate Xinjiang and for terrorist organizations to be even more closely involved in the drug trade. It would be wise for China to remain vigilant, considering how certain Middle Eastern countries maintain close relationship with extremist/separatists/terrorist groups, supporting their ideology and providing funds. China must remain guarded against infiltration, especially infiltration by religious extremism through the flow of petrodollars.

1.3 Future Prospects for the Belt and Road Initiative

The Belt and Road Initiative embodies a set of sophisticated opportunities for development. Because it meets the demands for global development and China's own development, it is also an excellent platform for businesses and individuals. There is ample reason to be optimistic about the future of the BRI.

However, it is worth noting that as an intercontinental economic cooperation proposal unprecedented in geographic scale, the challenges posed by complex geopolitical relations, ethnic strife and religious conflicts between B&R countries are not to be underestimated. Each country has its own and widely varying development goals and interests. Risk factors are present in every country, including transnational ones. Furthermore, major world powers are constantly vying for control in relevant regions. Challenges during the implementation of the BRI will also be unprecedented, especially in the case of the Silk Road Economic Belt. The Belt spans a huge number of countries and factors such as territory, ethnicity, religion, population and natural environment will play a much more influential role than in the Road;

the risks will be greater, as will the costs of cooperation. Throughout history, trade on the Silk Road had been interrupted multiple times due to armed conflicts. Such risk is significantly lower today on the Eurasian continent. However, it has to be noted that extremist/separatist/terrorist organizations (which are often transnational these days) still pose a major threat to the stability of China's northwestern border, the safety of Chinese companies and citizens abroad and the stability of Central Asia, West Asia and North Africa. It is likely that such organizations may even expand their influence and begin operating in Europe and Southeast Asia.

Taking all these into consideration, it is necessary for us to view the risks that the BRI faces or will face with a clear head. China must be mentally prepared for the challenges up ahead, challenges that may persist for a very long time, that are highly complex and extremely difficult to tackle. On the one hand, we should avoid becoming over-optimistic, take efforts one step at a time, not take on commitments that we cannot fulfill, not waste too much strategic resources in locations with high security risks and establish a multidimensional mechanism to ensure the overall security of the Initiative's implementation. On the other hand, we must not harbor a sense of defeatism and associate all risks that Chinese businesses and citizens face in going global with the BRI, or reject the Initiative in its entirety citing temporary setbacks.

The Belt and Road Initiative is a cause that China shares with other participant countries. But most importantly, China should still focus on getting its own affairs right, because only when China's growth is ensured can it actually provide continuing support for the BRI. And only when Chinese businesses and citizens gain substantive benefits from the Belt and Road can the Initiative have enough substantive support. Now that China's economic development is entering a "New Normal", it is particularly important to keep these two points in mind.

At the same time, China should step up strategic cooperation with B&R countries, identify common interests and devise mutually beneficial plans for cooperation that actually targets the needs of the countries involved. Only when participating countries feel they can gain benefits and opportunities from the BRI will they really develop an enthusiasm for it.

It should be made known to major powers such as Russia, India and the EU that the BRI does not seek to weaken their existing influence in certain regions; rather, it may well pave the way toward a larger platform for cooperation. In the future, China should actively pursue opportunities for substantive cooperation with Russia in the Far East, with India in Southeast Asia and the Middle East and with the EU in Central and Eastern Europe as well as Africa. In particular, when participating in major projects along the Belt and Road, Chinese companies should be encouraged to work with those from the United States, Russia, India, the EU, South Korea and Singapore to explore new markets, shouldering risks together and sharing the gains.

When working with smaller B&R countries, China should take into consideration the varying interests of different ethnic groups, social classes, regions and parties, seek to establish stable, long-term ties and avoid becoming ensnared by such countries' internal political strife. In the past, there had been cases where major projects (often infrastructure projects) undertaken by Chinese companies in the B&R countries suffered a backlash from the local community and significant financial losses. It is possible that China will still be criticized for perpetrating "neo-colonialism", seen as a "resource plunderer" or deemed guilty of "polluting the environment" as future infrastructure, capacity cooperation and energy utilization projects are launched under the Belt and Road Initiative. In addition, Chinese businesses might also face pressure from nationalist, economic nationalist and trade protectionist forces abroad. There is one thing that we must be clear on, and that is China will not promote a model of industrialization that brings along high levels of pollution and energy consumption. Even though China seeks to achieve economic complementarity with B&R countries, it should be noted that these countries would also like to maintain their autonomy over their own economies and do not want their economies to be fragmented (which is an entirely reasonable demand). China should avoid creating new equalities as it disrupts the existing global division of labor. China should also be aware that infrastructure connectivity does not naturally lead to goodwill. It will take a lot of wisdom and hard work to convert the public goods that China is providing to goodwill, appeal and influence.

Compared with the ancient Silk Road, this new Silk Road that we are building is veritably a push for cooperation within the Eurasian continent and beyond. The United States, though not part of the region, will most definitely be involved in one way or another, given its status as the global superpower. The expanding scope of Sino-US ties means that some strategic coordination will have to take place between the two countries over the Belt and Road Initiative at some point in the future. Politically, the BRI is not China's "Marching Westwards" intended to counter America's "Pivot to Asia", nor is it China's version of the Monroe Doctrine, one that seeks to expel US influence from the Eurasian continent. Economically, the BRI is not China's attempt to create a new Marshall Plan or Comecon with the intention of confronting US influence. Nor is it China's intention to create a new global economic order that sees China replacing the United States and the RMB replacing the US dollar. As the balance of power between the United States and China begins to shift, the BRI is more than capable of providing a platform for the two to establish a new type of major power relations, cooperate and achieve win-win results. Although China and the United States remain in competition over each other in the Asia-Pacific, there is a strong likelihood the two will work together in maintaining stability in Central Asia and the Middle East.

Following the successful conclusion of the Belt and Road Forum, a long-term cooperation mechanism is gradually being set up. In the future, China will adhere to the principle of extensive consultation, joint contribution and shared benefits, and continue to focus on key corridors, countries, sectors and projects. Under the framework of "six corridors, six means of communication, multiple countries and multiple ports", and with promoting infrastructure connectivity as the first part of the efforts, China will first initiate cooperation with countries that have friendly relations with China, possess favorable industrial conditions, display greater willingness, are located strategically and have greater influence — together building the New

Eurasian Land Bridge Economic Corridor, the China–Mongolia–Russia Economic Corridor, the China–Central Asia–West Asia Economic Corridor, the China–Indochina Peninsula Economic Corridor, the China–Pakistan Economic Corridor and the Bangladesh–China–India–Myanmar Economic Corridor — promote connectivity in rail, high-ways, seagoing transport, aviation, pipelines and aerospace integrated information network and build a number of important ports along the Belt and Road. Promoting connectivity and capacity cooperation will be the two dominant themes during the Initiative's implementation. A number of demonstrative projects and industrial zones will be built to further enhance industrial cooperation. At the same time, China will improve its tax, financial, customs and quality inspection policies, strengthen strategic cooperation with other countries, enter into investment protection agreements with other countries, establish better platforms for facilitating cultural exchanges and exchanges of other types and build a comprehensive support mechanism for the implementation of the Initiative.

Building the Belt and Road is one of the most important steps in China's economic transformation and upgrading, all-round opening-up and progress in becoming a major world power. It is a long-term, difficult, yet honorable cause. As President Xi Jinping pointed out:

> Building the Belt and Road is an important way to take China's opening-up to the next level, as well as part of China's top-level design for economic diplomacy. The right breakthroughs must be identified, with small-scale attempts paving the way for bigger endeavors. We will forge ahead one step at a time, and we shall persevere. [5]

Cooperation, mutual benefit and perseverance — this is perhaps the most accurate description of the vision and actions of the Belt and Road.

---

[5] Xi Jinping, "Speech at the Second Plenary Meeting of the 5th Plenary Session of the 18th CPC Central Committee(Excerpt)", *Qiushi*, no. 1, 2016. (习近平:《在党的十八届五中全会第二次全体会议上的讲话（节选)》, 载《求是》2016 年第 1 期。)

Bibliography

1. Official Documents in Chinese

习近平:《携手推进"一带一路"建设——在"一带一路"国际合作高峰论坛开幕式上的演讲》(2017 年 5 月 14 日, 北京), 载《人民日报》2017 年 5 月 15 日, 第 3 版。Xi Jinping, "Work Together to Build the Silk Road Economic Belt and the 21st Century Maritime Silk Road: Speech at the Opening Ceremony of the Belt and Road Forum for International Cooperation" (May 14, 2017, Beijing), *People's Daily*, May 15, 2017, p. 3.

习近平:《共担时代责任共促全球发展——在世界经济论坛 2017 年年会开幕式上的主旨演讲》(2017 年 1 月 17 日, 达沃斯), 载《人民日报》2017 年 1 月 18 日, 第 3 版。Xi Jinping, "Jointly Shoulder Responsibility of Our Times, Promote Global Growth: Speech at the Opening Session of the World Economic Forum Annual Meeting 2017" (January 17, 2017, Davos), *People's Daily*, January 18, 2017, p. 3.

习近平:《共同开创中阿关系的美好未来——在阿拉伯国家联盟总部的演讲》(2016 年 1 月 21 日, 开罗), 载《人民日报》2016 年 1 月 22 日, 第 3 版。Xi Jinping, "Work Together for a Bright Future of China-Arab Relations: Speech at the Arab League Headquarters" (January 21, 2016, Cairo), *People's Daily*, January 22, 2016, p. 3.

习近平:《在亚洲基础设施投资银行开业仪式上的致辞》(2016 年 1 月 16 日, 北京), 载《人民日报》2016 年 1 月 17 日, 第 2 版。Xi Jinping, "Address at AIIB Inauguration Ceremony" (January 16, 2016, Beijing), *People's Daily*, January 17, 2016, p. 2.

习近平:《在党的十八届五中全会第二次全体会议上的讲话(节选)》, 载《求是》2016 年第 1 期。Xi Jinping, "Speech at the Second Full Assembly of the Fifth Plenary Session of the 18th CPC Central Committee (Excerpt)," *QiuShi*, no.1, 2016.

习近平:《迈向命运共同体开创亚洲新未来——在博鳌亚洲论坛 2015 年年会上的主旨演讲》(2015 年 3 月 28 日, 海南博鳌), 载《人民日报》2015 年 3 月 29 日, 第 2 版。Xi Jinping, "Towards a Community of Common Destiny and a New Future for Asia: Keynote Speech at the Boao Forum for Asia Annual Conference 2015", (March 28, 2015, Hainan), *People's Daily*, March 29, 2015, p. 2.

习近平:《联通引领发展伙伴聚焦合作——在"加强互联互通伙伴关系"东道主伙伴对话会上的讲话》(2014 年 11 月 8 日, 北京), 载《人民日报》2014 年 11 月 9 日, 第 2 版。Xi Jinping, "Connectivity Spearheads Development and Partnership Enables Cooperation: Address at Dialogue on Strengthening Connectivity Partnership" (November 8, 2014, Beijing), *People's Daily*, November 9, 2014, p. 2.

习近平:《弘扬丝路精神深化中阿合作——在中阿合作论坛第六届部长级会议开幕式上的讲话》(2014 年 6 月 5 日, 北京), 载《人民日报》2014 年 6 月 6 日, 第 2 版。Xi Jinping, "Carrying Forward the Silk Road Spirit, Promoting the Mutual Development: Keynote Speech at the Opening Ceremony of the Sixth Ministerial Conference of the China-Arab States Cooperation Forum" (June 5, 2014, Beijing), *People's Daily*, June 6, 2014, p. 2.

习近平:《携手建设中国—东盟命运共同体——在印度尼西亚国会的演讲》(2013 年 10 月 3 日, 雅加达), 载《人民日报》2013 年 10 月 4 日, 第 2 版。Xi Jinping, "Hand in Hand Building a China-ASEAN Community of Shared Destiny: Speech at the Indonesian Parliament" (October 3, 2013, Djakarta), *People's Daily*, October 4, 2013, p. 2.

习近平:《弘扬人民友谊共创美好未来——在纳扎尔巴耶夫大学的演讲》(2013 年 9 月 7 日, 阿斯塔纳), 载《人民日报》2013 年 9 月 8 日, 第 3 版。Xi Jinping, "Promote Friendship between Our People and Work Together to Build a Bright Future" (September 7, 2013, Astana), *People's Daily*, September 8, 2013, p. 3.

李克强:《在澜沧江—湄公河合作首次领导人会议上的讲话》(2016 年 3 月 23 日, 三亚), 载《人民日报》2016 年 3 月 24 日, 第 2 版。Li

Keqiang, "Address at the First Lancang-Mekong Cooperation Leaders' Meeting" (March 23, 2016, Sanya), *People's Daily*, March 24, 2016, p. 2.

李克强:《在上海合作组织成员国总理第十四次会议大范围会谈时的讲话》(2015 年 12 月 15 日,郑州),载《人民日报》2015 年 12 月16 日,第 2 版。Li Keqiang, "Remarks at the Extended Session of the 14th Meeting of the Council of Heads of Government of Member States of the Shanghai Cooperation Organization" (December 15, 2015, Zhengzhou), *People's Daily*, December 16, 2015, p. 2.

李克强:《在第四次中国—中东欧国家领导人会晤上的讲话》(2015 年 11 月 24 日,苏州),载《人民日报》2015 年 11 月 25 日,第 3 版。Li Keqiang, "Remarks at the Fourth Summit of China and Central and Eastern European Countries" (November 24, 2015, Suzhou), *People's Daily*, November 25, 2015, p. 3.

李克强:《携手开创中欧关系新局面——在中欧工商峰会上的主旨演讲》(2015 年 6 月 29 日,布鲁塞尔),载《人民日报》2015 年 6 月 30 日,第 2 版。Li Keqiang, "Working Together for New Progress in China-EU Relations: Keynote Speech at China-EU Business Summit" (June 29, 2015, Brussels), *People's Daily*, June 30, 2015, p. 2.

《"一带一路"国际合作高峰论坛成果清单》,2017 年 5 月 15 日,北京。*List of Deliverables of Belt and Road Forum*, Beijing, May 15, 2017.

《"一带一路"国际合作高峰论坛圆桌峰会联合公报》,2017 年 5 月 15 日,北京。*Joint Communique of Leaders Roundtable of Belt and Road Forum*, Beijing, May 15, 2017.

《"一带一路"融资指导原则》,2017 年 5 月 14 日,北京。*Guiding Principles on Financing the Development of the Belt and Road*, Beijing, May 14, 2017.

推进"一带一路"建设工作领导小组办公室:《共建"一带一路":理念、实践与中国的贡献》,北京:外文出版社,2017 年 5月。Office of the Leading Group for the Belt and Road Initiative, *Building the Belt and Road: Concept, Practice and China's Contribution*, Beijing: Foreign Languages Press, May 2017.

推进"一带一路"建设工作领导小组办公室:《中欧班列建设发展规划(2016–2020 年)》,2016 年 10 月。Office of the Leading Group for the Belt and Road Initiative, *Construction and Development Planning of CHINA RAILWAY Express (2016–2020)*, October 2016.

中华人民共和国政府:《深化互利共赢的中欧全面战略伙伴关系——中国对欧盟政策文件》,2014 年 4 月。Government of the People's Republic of China, *China's Policy Paper on the European Union: Deepen the*

China-EU Comprehensive Strategic Partnership for Mutual Benefit and Win-win Cooperation, April 2014.

中华人民共和国政府:《中国对阿拉伯国家政策文件》, 2016 年 1月。Government of the People's Republic of China, *China's Arab Policy Paper*, January 2016.

中华人民共和国政府:《中国对非洲政策文件》, 2015 年 12 月。Government of the People's Republic of China, *China's Africa Policy Paper*, December 2016.

中华人民共和国国家发展改革委、外交部、商务部:《推动共建丝绸之路经济带和 21 世纪海上丝绸之路的愿景与行动》, 2015 年 3 月。The National Development and Reform Commission, Ministry of Foreign Affairs, and Ministry of Commerce of the People's Republic of China. *Vision and Actions on Jointly Building Silk Road Economic Belt and 21st-Century Maritime Silk Road*, March 2015.

中华人民共和国商务部、国家统计局、国家外汇管理局:《中国对外直接投资统计公报》(2013–2016), 北京:中国统计出版社, 2014–2017 年。Ministry of Commerce, National Bureau of Statistics, and State Administration of Foreign Exchange of the People's Republic of China, *Statistical Bulletin of China's Outward Foreign Direct Investment (2013–2016)*, Beijing: China Statistics Press, 2014–2017.

中华人民共和国国务院:《国务院关于推进国际产能和装备制造合作的指导意见》(国发(2015)30 号), 2015 年 5 月 16 日。The State Council of the People's Republic of China, *Guiding Opinion of the State Council on Promoting International Cooperation on Production Capacity and Equipment Manufacturing* (No. 30 Document of State Council (2015)), May 16, 2015.

《中华人民共和国政府和哈萨克斯坦共和国政府关于"丝绸之路经济带"建设与"光明之路"新经济政策对接合作规划》, 2016 年 9 月 2 日, 中国杭州。*Cooperative Plan between the Government of the People's Republic of China and the Government of the Republic of Kazakhstan for Synergizing the Silk Road Economic Belt Initiative and the Bright Road Policy*, Hangzhou, China, September 2, 2016

《中华人民共和国与俄罗斯联邦关于丝绸之路经济带建设和欧亚经济联盟建设对接合作的联合声明》, 2015 年 5 月 8 日, 俄罗斯莫斯科。*Joint Communique between the People's Republic of China and Russian Federation on Synerizing the Silk Road Economic Belt Initiative and the Eurasian Economic Union*, Moscow, Russia, May 8, 2015.

《建设中蒙俄经济走廊规划纲要》, 2016 年 6 月 23 日, 乌兹别克斯坦塔什干。*Outline for Building China-Mongolia-Russia Economic Corridor*, Tashkent, Uzbekistan, June 23, 2016.

《中国—东盟产能合作联合声明》, 2016 年 9 月 7 日, 老挝万象。*Joint Statement between ASEAN and China on Production Capacity Cooperation*, Vientiane, Laos, September 7, 2016.

《加强互联互通伙伴关系对话会联合新闻公报》, 2014 年 11 月 8 日, 北京。*Joint Press Statement on Dialogue on Strengthening Connectivity Partnership*, Beijing, China, November 8, 2014.

《中国—中东欧国家合作中期规划》, 2015 年 11 月 24 日, 中国苏州。*Medium-term Plan for Cooperation between China and Central and Eastern European Countries*, Suzhou, China, November 24, 2015.

2. Research Literature in Chinese

白寿彝:《中国伊斯兰史存稿》, 银川:宁夏人民出版社, 1983 年。Bai Shouyi, *The History of Islam in China*. Yinchuan: Ningxia People's Publishing House, 1983.

陈炎:《海上丝绸之路与中外文化交流》, 北京:北京大学出版社, 2002 年。Chen Yan, *Maritime Silk Road and Cultural Exchanges between China and Foreign Countries*. Beijing: Peking University Press, 2002.

陈高华:《海上丝绸之路》, 北京: 海洋出版社, 1991 年。Chen Gaohua, *The Maritime Silk Road*. Beijing: China Ocean Press, 1991.

陈慧生:《中国新疆地区伊斯兰教史》, 乌鲁木齐: 新疆人民出版社, 2000 年。Chen Huisheng, *History of Islam in Xinjiang*. Urumqi: Xinjiang People's Publishing House, 2000.

戴志康:《"反剪刀差"时代的全球战略考量》, 载《文化纵横》2013 年 第 2 期, 第 23–26 页。Dai Zhikang, "Consideration on Global Strategies in the Age of Reversed Price Scissors", *Beijing Cultural Review*, no. 2, 2013, pp. 23–26.

邓浩:《中国与中亚国家关系:回眸与前瞻》, 载《国际问题研究》2002 年第 3 期, 第 7–12 页。Deng Hao, "China-Central Asian Relations: Retrospect and Prospect", *China International Studies*, no. 3, 2002, pp. 7–12.

邓廷良:《丝路文化》(西南卷), 杭州:浙江人民出版社, 1995 年。Deng Tingliang, *The Silk Road Culture (The Southwest Volume)*. Hangzhou: Zhejiang People's Publishing House, 1995.

董小君:《中国下阶段产业转移的道路选择——基于产能国际转移日美两种模式的创新探索》,载《人民论坛·学术前沿》2013 年 12 月下,第 69–77 页。Dong Xiaojun, "Selecting the Path for China's Next Phase of Industrial Transfer—Based on the Japanese and US Models for International Transfer of Production Capacity". *People's Forum: Frontiers*, no. 2, December 2013, pp. 69–77.

方豪:《中西交通史》,长沙:岳麓书社,1987年。Fang Hao, *The History of Sino-foreign Relations*. Changsha: Yuelu Press, 1987.

冯承钧:《西域南海史地考证译丛》,北京: 中华书局 1958 年。Feng Chengjun, *Collections of Translated Works for the Study on Historical Geography of the Western Region and Regions Surrounding the South China Sea*. Beijing: Zhonghua Book Company, 1958.

范恒山:《从八方面落实"一带一路"战略》,载《中国发展观察》2015 年第 8 期,第 18–19 页。Fan Hengshan, "Implementing the Belt and Road Initiative from Eight Aspects", *China Development Observation*, no. 8, 2015, pp. 18–19.

范恒山:《助推宏伟构想迈向辉煌未来》,载《人民日报》2017 年 5 月 10 日,第 22 版。Fan Hengshan, "Propelling the Great Idea for a Bright Future", *People's Daily*, May 10, 2017, p. 22.

范若兰:《伊斯兰教与东南亚现代化进程》,北京:中国社会科学出版社,2009 。Fan Ruolan, *Islam and Modernization in Southeast Asia*. Beijing: China Social Sciences Press, 2009.

冯并:《一带一路:全球发展的中国逻辑》,北京:中国民主法制出版社,2015 年。Feng Bing, *One Belt and One Road: The Chinese Logic for Global Development*. Beijing: China Democracy and Legal System Publishing House, 2015.

高柏:《高铁与中国 21 世纪大战略》,北京: 社会科学文献出版社,2012 年。Gao Bai, *The High-speed Rail and China's Grand Strategy in the 21st Century*. Beijing: Social Sciences Academic Press, 2012.

高虎城:《完善对外开放战略布局》,载《人民日报》2015 年 12 月 10 日,第 7 版。Gao Hucheng, "Refining China's Strategic Plan for Opening Up", *People's Daily*, December 10, 2015, p. 7.

高虎城:《促进全球发展合作的中国方案》,载《人民日报》2015 年 9 月 18 日,第 7 版。Gao Hucheng, "The Chinese Proposal to Promote Global Development Cooperation", *People's Daily*, September 18, 2015, p. 7.

高虎城:《从贸易大国迈向贸易强国》,载《人民日报》2014 年 3 月 2 日,第 7 版。Gao Hucheng, "From a Trader of Quantity to a Trader of Quality", *People's Daily*, March 2, 2014, p. 7.

高荣盛:《元代海外贸易研究》, 成都: 四川人民出版社, 1998 年。Gao Rongsheng, *Research on Overseas Trade in Yuan Dynasty*. Chengdu: Sichuan People's Publishing House, 1998.

高永久:《西域古代伊斯兰教综论》, 北京: 民族出版社, 2001 年。Gao Yongjiu, *A Comprehensive Discussion of Ancient Islam in the Western Regions*. Beijing: The Ethnic Publishing House, 2001.

古丽阿扎提·吐尔逊:《中亚跨国犯罪问题研究》, 北京: 中央民族大学出版社, 2013年。Tulsson Guriazti, *Research on Transnational Crime in Central Asia*. Beijing: Minzu University of China Press, 2013.

胡怀邦:《开发性金融与"一带一路"建设》, 载《中国金融》2017 年第 9 期, 第 25–27 页。Hu Huaibang, "Development Financing and Construction of the Belt and Road Initiative", *China Finance*, no. 9, 2017, pp. 25–27.

胡晓炼:《政策性金融服务"一带一路"的优势》, 载《中国金融》2017 年第 9 期。Hu Xiaolian, "The Advantages of Policy-based Finance Serving the Belt and Road", *China Finance*, no. 9, 2017, pp. 28–30.

黄志刚:《丝绸之路货币研究》, 乌鲁木齐:新疆人民出版社, 2010年。Huang Zhigang, *Research on Currency on the Silk Road*. Urumchi: Xinjiang People's Publishing House, 2010.

黄纯艳:《宋代海外贸易》, 北京: 社会科学文献出版社, 2003 年。Huang Chunyan, *Overseas Trade in Song Dynasty*. Beijing: Social Sciences Academic Press, 2003.

黄群慧:《工业化蓝皮书:"一带一路"沿线国家工业化进程报告》, 北京: 社会科学文献出版社, 2015 年。Huang Qunhui, *Blue Book of Industrialization: Report on National Industrialization Process of Countries along the Belt and Road*. Beijing: Social Sciences Academic Press, 2015.

何芳川:《中外文化交流史》, 北京: 国际文化出版公司, 2008 年。He Fangchuan, *A History of Culture Exchanges between China and Foreign Countries*. Beijing: China International Culture Press, 2008.

黄新亚:《丝路文化》(沙漠卷), 杭州:浙江人民出版社, 1995 年。Huang Xinya, *The Silk Road Culture (Desert Volume)*. Hangzhou: Zhejiang People's Publishing House, 1995.

胡伊:《中国新疆与中亚区域经济贸易》, 乌鲁木齐:新疆人民出版社, 2006 年。Hu Yi, *The Regional Economic and Trade Relations between China's Xinjiang and Central Asia*, Urumqi: Xinjiang People's Publishing House, 2006.

韩香:《隋唐长安与中亚文明》, 北京:中国社会科学出版社, 2006 年。Han Xiang, *Chang'an in the Sui and Tang Dynasties and the Central Asian Civilization*. Beijing: China Social Sciences Press, 2006.

蒋新卫:《冷战后中亚地缘政治格局变迁与新疆安全和发展》，北京: 社会科学文献出版社, 2009 年。Jiang Xinwei, *The Changes of the Geopolitical Pattern in Central Asia and Xinjiang's Security and Development after the Cold War*. Beijing: China Social Sciences Press, 2009.

金立群、林毅夫:《"一带一路"引领中国》，北京: 中国文史出版社, 2015 年。Jin Liqun and Li Yifu, *The Belt and Road Leading China*. Beijing: Wenshi Press, 2015.

李建红:《落地生根开花结果——招商局集团践行"一带一路"倡议的探索实践》，载《求是》2017 年第 9 期, 第 59–61 页。Li Jianhong, "From Striking Roots to Blossom and Fruits: China Merchants Group Makes Explorations Proposed by the Belt and Road Initiative", *Qiushi*, no. 9, 2017, pp. 59–61.

李进新:《丝绸之路宗教研究》，乌鲁木齐: 新疆人民出版社, 2010 年。Li Jinxin, *Research on Religions on the Silk Road*. Urumqi: Xinjiang People's Publishing House, 2010.

李明伟:《丝绸之路贸易研究》，乌鲁木齐: 新疆人民出版社, 2010 年。Li Mingwei, *Research on Trade on the Silk Road*. Urumqi: Xinjiang People's Publishing House, 2010.

李金明、廖大珂:《中国古代海外贸易史》，南宁: 广西人民出版社, 1995 年。Li Jinming and Liao Dake, *History of Overseas Trade in Ancient China*. Nanning: Guangxi People's Publishing House, 1995.

李向阳:《"一带一路":定位、内涵及需要优先处理的关系》，北京:社会科学文献出版社, 2015 年。Li Xiangyang, *"One Belt One Road": Orientation, Contents and Challenges*. Beijing: Social Sciences Academic Press, 2015.

李兴华:《中国伊斯兰教史》,北京:中国社会科学出版社,1998 年。Li Xinghua, *History of Islam in China*. Beijing: China Social Sciences Press, 1998.

李忠民:《欧亚大陆桥发展报告》，北京: 社会科学文献出版社, 2012 年。Li Zhongmin, *The Eurasian Continent Bridge Development Report*. Beijing: China Social Sciences Press, 2012.

林梅村:《丝绸之路十五讲》,北京:北京大学出版社, 2006 年。Lin Meicun, *Fifteen Lectures on the Silk Road*. Beijing: Peking University Press, 2006.

林天蔚:《宋代香药贸易史》，中国台湾台北: 中国文化大学出版部, 1986 年。Lin Tianwei, *A History of Spice Trade in the Song Dynasty*. Taipei City: Taiwan Chinese Culture University Press, 1986.

刘赐贵:《发展海洋合作伙伴关系推进 21 世纪海上丝绸之路建设的若干思考》，载《国际问题研究》2014 年第 4 期, 第 1–8 页。Liu Cigui, "Reflections on Maritime Partnership: Building the 21st Century Maritime Silk Road", *China International Studies*, no. 4, 2014, pp. 1–8.

刘冬:《中国与海合会货物贸易的发展现状、问题及其应对》, 载《阿拉伯世界研究》2012 年第 1 期, 第 91–107 页。Liu Dong, "The Development and Problems of China-GCC Commercial Goods Trade", *Arab World Studies*, no. 1, 2012, pp. 91–107.

刘欣如:《丝绸之路上佛教和伊斯兰教的传播》, 收入余太山、李锦绣:《丝瓷之路 I: 古代中外关系史研究》, 北京: 商务印书馆, 2011 年, 第 67–91 页。Liu Xinru, The Spread of Buddhism and Islam along the Silk Road, in Yu Taishan and Li Jinxiu eds., *Silk and Porcelain Road I: Study on Sino-foreign Relations in Ancient Times*. Beijing: The Commercial Press, 2011, pp. 67–91.

刘迎胜:《丝路文化》(海上卷), 杭州:浙江人民出版社, 1995 年。Liu Yingsheng, *The Silk Road Culture (The Sea Volume)*. Hangzhou: Zhejiang People's Publishing House, 1995.

刘迎胜:《海路与陆路: 中古时代东西交流研究》, 北京: 北京大学出版社, 2011 年。Liu Yingsheng, *Maritime and Continental Routes between East and West*. Beijing: Peking University Press, 2011.

刘卫东等:《"一带一路"战略研究》, 北京:商务印书馆, 2017 年。Liu Weidong *et al.*, *Research on the Belt and Road Strategy*. Beijing: The Commercial Press, 2017.

楼继伟:《打造二十一世纪新型多边开发银行》, 载《人民日报》2015 年 6 月 25 日, 第 10 版。Lou Jiwei, "Building the New-type Multilateral Development Bank in the 21st Century", *People's Daily*, June 25, 2015, p. 10.

陆如泉等:《"一带一路"话石油》, 北京: 石油工业出版社, 2015 年。Lu Ruquan *et al.*, *Petroleum and the Belt and Road Initiative*. Beijing: Petroleum Industry Press, 2015.

卢苇:《中外关系史研究》, 兰州: 兰州大学出版社, 2000 年。Lu Wei, *Research on the History of Sino-foreign Relations*. Lanzhou: Lanzhou University Press, 2000.

马文宽:《从考古资料看中国唐宋时期与伊斯兰世界的文化交流》, 收入中国社会科学院考古研究所《汉唐与边疆考古研究》编委会:《汉唐与边疆考古研究》(第一辑), 北京:科学出版社, 1994 年, 第 231–249 页。Ma Wenkuan, "An Examination of the Cultural Exchanges between China's Tang and Song Dynasties and the Islamic World Unveiled by Archaeological Findings", *Archaeological Research on Han and Tang Dynasties and Border Areas*, Beijing: China Science Publishing & Media, 1994, pp.231–249.

(明) 马欢:《瀛涯胜览校注》, 冯承钧校注, 北京: 中华书局, 1955 年。(Ming Dynasty) Ma Huan, *Collation and Annotation of Vision in Triumph in a*

Boundless Sea (collated and annotated by Feng Chengjun). Beijing: Zhonghua Book Company, 1955.

梅新育：《中国制造业向何处去》，昆明：云南教育出版社，2013 年。Mei Xinyu, *Where Do China's Manufacturing Industries Head?* Kunming: Yunnan Education Publishing House, 2013.

敏贤麟：《蒙古游牧文明与伊斯兰文明的交汇》，北京：宗教文化出版社，2010 年。Min Xianlin, *The Intersection of Mongolian Nomadic Civilization and Islamic Civilization*. Beijing: China Religious Culture Publisher, 2010.

穆虹：《推进"一带一路"建设》，载《人民日报》2015 年 12 月 11 日，第 7 版。Mu Hong, "Advancing the Belt and Road Initiative", *People's Daily*, December 11, 2015, p. 7.

欧晓理：《政策沟通：为"一带一路"唱出共鸣》，载《求是》2017 年第 11 期，第 11–12 页。Ou Xiaoli, "Policy Coordination: Creating Resonance for the Belt and Road Initiative", *QiuShi*, no. 11, 2017, pp. 11–12.

全汉昇：《中国经济史研究. 2》，北京：中华书局，2011 年。Quan Hansheng, *Research on Chinese Economic History*, Volume. 2. Beijing: Zhonghua Book Company, 2011.

任宗哲等：《丝绸之路经济带发展报告 (2014)》，北京：社会科学文献出版社，2014 年。Ren Zongze *et al.*, *Development Report on the Silk Road Economic Belt (2014)*. Beijing: Social Science Academic Press, 2014.

沈福伟：《丝绸之路：中国与西亚文化交流研究》，乌鲁木齐：新疆人民出版社，2010 年。Shen Fuwei, *Research on Cultural Exchanges between China and West Asia*. Urumqi: Xinjiang People's Publishing House, 2010.

苏波：《向高端装备制造业强国登攀》，载《求是》2014 年第 13 期，第 51–53 页。Su Bo, "Develop into a High-end Equipment Manufacturer", *QiuShi*, no. 13, 2014, pp. 51–53.

苏北海：《汉、唐时期我国北方的草原丝路》，乌鲁木齐：新疆美术摄影出版社，1994 年。Su Beihai, *Prairie Silk Road in Northern China in Han and Tang Dynasties*. Urumqi: Xinjiang Photographic Art press, 1994.

孙光圻：《中国古代航海史》，北京：海洋出版社，2005 年。Sun Guangqi, *History of Navigation in Ancient China*. Beijing: China Ocean Press, 2005.

上海博物馆：《丝绸之路古国钱币暨丝路文化国际学术研讨会论文集》，上海：上海博物馆，2011 年。Shanghai Museum, *Proceedings of the Symposium on Ancient Coins and the Culture of the Silk Road*. Shanghai: Shanghai Museum, 2011.

史丹:《中国能源安全的国际环境》, 北京: 社会科学文献出版社, 2013 年。Shi Dan, *International Environment of China's Energy Security*. Beijing: Social Sciences Academic Press, 2013.

田卫疆:《丝绸之路与东察合台汗国史研究》, 乌鲁木齐: 新疆人民出版社, 1997 年。Tian Weijiang, *Research on the Silk Road and the History of the Eastern Chagatai Khanate*. Urumqi: Xinjiang People's Publishing House, 1997.

王小甫等:《古代中外文化交流史》, 北京: 高等教育出版社, 2006 年。Wang Xiaofu *et al.*, *History of Sino-foreign Cultural Exchange in Ancient Times*. Beijing: Higher Education Press, 2006.

王炳华:《丝绸之路考古研究》, 乌鲁木齐: 新疆人民出版社, 2009 年。Wang Binghua, *Archaeological Studies on the Silk Road*. Urumqi: Xinjiang People's Publishing House, 2009.

王介南:《中外文化交流史》, 北京: 书海出版社, 2004 年。 Wang Jienan, *A History of Culture Exchanges between China and Foreign Countries*. Beijing: Shuhai Press, 2004.

王湘穗:《倚陆向海: 中国战略重心的再平衡》, 载《现代国际关系》2010 年庆典特刊, 第 54–64 页。Wang Xiangsui, "Lean on the Land and Face to the Sea: Rebalance of China's Strategy Emphasis", *Contemporary International Relations*, 2010 Celebration Special Issue, pp. 54–64.

王永兴:《唐代经营西北研究》, 兰州: 兰州大学出版社, 2010 年。Wang Yongxing, *Research on the Governance of Northwest China in Tang Dynasty*. Lanzhou: Lanzhou University Press, 2010.

王琳:《共同的声音: "一带一路"高端访谈录》, 北京: 商务印书馆, 2017 年。Wang Lin, *Wang Lin's Top Interviews with Global Leaders on the Belt and Road*. Beijing: The Commercial Press, 2017.

汶江:《古代中国与亚非地区的海上交通》, 成都:四川省社会科学院出版社, 1989 年。Wen Jiang, *Maritime Communication between Ancient China and Asian-African Countries*. Chengdu: Publishing House of Sichuan Academy of Social Sciences, 1989.

魏良弢:《喀喇汗王朝史稿》, 乌鲁木齐: 新疆人民出版社, 1986 年。Wei Liangtao, *History of QaraKhanid Dynasty*, Urumqi: Xinjiang People's Publishing House, 1986.

魏革军、张驰:《开创"一带一路"投融资合作新格局——访丝路基金董事长金琦》, 载《中国金融》2017 年第 9 期, 第 20–23 页。Wei Gejun and Zhang Chi, "Creating A New Pattern for Belt and Road Investment and Financing Cooperation—Interviewing Jin Qi, Chairman of the Silk Road Fund", *China Finance*, no. 9, 2017, pp. 20–23.

徐绍史、何立峰主编:《"一带一路"与国际产能合作》，北京: 机械工业出版社, 2017 年。Xu Shaoshi and He Lifeng. *The Belt and Road Initiative and International Capacity Cooperation*. Beijing: China Machine Press, 2017.

徐以骅等:《宗教与当代国际关系》，上海:上海人民出版社, 2012 年。 Xu Yihua *et al.*, *Religion and Contemporary International Relations*. Shanghai: Shanghai People's Publishing House, 2012.

邹磊:《"一带一路":合作共赢的中国方案》，上海: 上海人民出版社，2016 年。Zou Lei, *The Belt and Road: China's Global Initiative for Win-Win Cooperation*. Shanghai: Shanghai People's Publishing House, 2016.

邹磊:《"一带一路"上宗教与贸易的互动》，收入蒋坚永、徐以骅主编:《中国宗教走出去战略论集》，北京: 宗教文化出版社, 2015年, 第 94–108 页。Zou Lei, "Interaction between Religion and Trade on the Belt and Road", in Jiang Jianyong and Xu Yihua eds., *The "Going Out" Strategy of Chinese Religions*. Beijing: China Religious Culture Publisher, 2015, pp. 94–108.

邹磊:《中国与伊斯兰世界"新丝绸之路"的兴起》，收入徐以骅、邹磊主编:《宗教与中国对外战略》，上海: 上海人民出版社，2014 年, 第 86–124 页。Zou Lei, The Rise of the New Silk Road Connecting China and the Islamic World, in Xu Yihua and Zou Lei eds., *Religion and China's Foreign Policy*. Shanghai: Shanghai People's Publishing House, 2014, pp. 86–124.

余振贵:《中国历代政权与伊斯兰教》， 银川: 宁夏人民出版社， 1996 年。Yu Zhengui, *Ancient Chinese Regimes and Islam*. Yinchuan: Ningxia People's Publishing House, 1996.

殷晴:《丝绸之路经济史研究》，兰州: 兰州大学出版社, 2012 年。Yin Qing, *Research on the Silk Road Economic History*. Lanzhou: Lanzhou University Press, 2012.

于向东、施展:《全球贸易双循环结构与世界秩序—外交哲学对谈之四》，载《文化纵横》2013 年第 5 期, 第 46–55 页。Yu Xiangdong and Shi Zhan, "The Dual Circle Structure of Global Trade and the World Order: Dialogue on Diplomatic Philosophy No. 4", *Beijing Cultural Review*, no. 5, 2013, pp. 46–55.

杨建新、卢苇:《丝绸之路》，兰州:甘肃人民出版社 1988 年。Yang Jianxin and Lu Wei, *The Silk Road*. Lanzhou: Gansu People's Publishing House, 1988.

杨光:《中国与中东国家政治经济关系发展》，北京 :社会科学文献出版社 2013 年。Yang Guang, *Development of the Political and Economic*

Relations between China and Middle Eastern Countries. Beijing: Social Sciences Academic Press, 2013.

杨光:《解析中东非洲国家的"向东看"现象》, 北京 :社会科学文献出版社 2011 年。Yang Guang, *Analysis on the Phenomena of Middle East and African Countries Looking Eastward.* Beijing: Social Sciences Academic Press, 2011.

张广达:《西域史地丛稿初编》, 上海: 上海古籍出版社 1995 年。Zhang Guangda, *Collection of Papers on History and Historical Geography of the Western Regions,* Shanghai: Shanghai Classical Publishing House, 1995.

张丽娟:《中亚地区民族问题与中国新疆民族关系》, 北京: 社会科学文献出版社 2014 年。 Zhang Lijuan, *Ethnic Problems in Central Asia and Ethnic Relations in Xinjiang.* Beijing: Social Sciences Academic Press, 2014.

张维华:《中国古代对外关系史》, 北京: 高等教育出版社, 1993 年。Zhang Weihua, *History of Foreign Relations of Ancient China.* Beijing: Higher Education Press, 1993.

张俊彦:《古代中国与西亚、非洲的海上往来》, 北京: 海洋出版社 1986 年。Zhang Junyan, *Maritime Communication among Ancient China, West Asia and Africa.* Beijing: China Ocean Press, 1986.

张一平:《丝绸之路》, 北京: 五洲传播出版社, 2005 年。Zhang Yiping, *The Silk Road.* Beijing: China Intercontinental Press, 2005.

张忠山:《中国丝绸之路货币》, 兰州: 兰州大学出版社, 1999 年。Zhang Zhongshan, *The Chinese Currency on the Silk Road.* Lanzhou: Lanzhou University Press, 1999.

张锡模:《圣战与文明: 伊斯兰与西方的永恒冲突》, 北京: 三联书店 2014 年。Zhang Ximo, *Jihad and Civilization: The Eternal Conflict between Islam and the West.* Beijing: SDX Joint Publishing Company, 2014.

赵丰:《唐代丝绸与丝绸之路》, 西安:三秦出版社, 1992 年。Zhao Feng, *Silk in Tang Dynasty and the Silk Road.* Xi'an: San Qin Press, 1992.

赵常庆等:《中亚五国与中国西部大开发》, 北京: 昆仑出版社, 2004 年。Zhao Changqing *et al., Five Countries of Central Asia and China's Western Development Strategy.* Beijing: Kunlun Press, 2004.

(宋)赵汝适:《诸番志校释》, 杨博文校释, 北京: 中华书局, 2000 年。(Song Dynasty) Zhao Rushi, *The Book of Collation and Annotation of Chu Fan Chi-Records of Foreign Countries* (collated and annotated by Yang Bowen). Beijing: Zhonghua Book Company, 2000.

(宋)周去非:《岭外代答校注》, 杨武泉校注, 北京: 中华书局, 1999 年。(Song Dynasty) Zhou Qufei, *The Book of Collation and Annotation of Lingwai Daida* (collated and annotated by Yang Wuquan). Beijing: Zhonghua Book Company, 1999.

中国人民大学重阳金融研究院:《欧亚时代——丝绸之路经济带蓝皮2014–2015》,北京:中国经济出版社,2014 年。Chongyang Institute for Financial Studies, Renmin University of China. *The Era of Europe and Asia: Blue Book of Silk Road Economic Study (2014–2015)*. Beijing: China Economic Publishing House, 2014.

查道炯:《中国石油安全的国际政治经济学分析》,北京:当代世界出版社,2005 年。Zha Daojiong, *The International Political Economic Analysis of China's Petroleum Security*. Beijing: Contemporary World Press, 2005.

章巽:《我国古代的海上交通》,北京:商务印书馆,1986 年。Zhang Xun, *The Maritime Communication in Ancient China*, Beijing: The Commercial Press, 1986.

张文木:《丝绸之路与中国西域安全——兼论中亚地区力量崛起的历史条件、规律及其因应战略》,载《世界政治与经济》2014 年第 3 期,第 4–27 页。Zhang Wenmu, "The Silk Road and Security of China's Western Regions: Historical Conditions, Law and Coping Strategies of the Rise of Central Asia", *World Economics and Politics*, no. 3, 2014, pp. 4–27.

赵忆宁:《大战略:"一带一路"五国探访》,杭州:浙江人民出版社,2015 年。Zhao Yining, *Grand Strategy: Inside the Belt and Road*. Hangzhou: Zhejiang People's Publishing House, 2015.

中国现代国际关系研究院:《"一带一路"读本》,北京:时事出版社,2015 年。China Institutes of Contemporary International Relations, *Interpreting the Belt and Road Initiative*. Beijing: Current Affairs Press, 2015.

(宋）朱彧:《萍洲可谈》,北京:中华书局,1985 年。(Song Dynasty) Zhu Yu, *Pingzhou Ketan*. Beijing: Zhonghua Book Company, 1985.

[法]阿里•玛扎海里:《丝绸之路:中国—波斯文化交流史》,耿昇译,乌鲁木齐:新疆人民出版社,2006 年。[France] Mazalleri A, *La Route De La Soie* (translated by Geng Sheng). Urumqi: Xinjiang People's Publishing House, 2006.

穆根来等译:《中国印度见闻录》,北京:中华书局,1983 年。*Ancient Accounts of India and China* (translated by Mu Genlai et al.). Beijing: Zhonghua Book Company, 1983.

[日]三上次男:《陶瓷之路》,李锡经、高善美译,北京:文物出版社,1984 年。Mikami Tsugio, *The China Road* (translated by Li Xijing and Gao Shanmei). Beijing: Culture Relics Press, 1984.

［日］桑原骘藏:《唐宋贸易港研究》, 杨鍊译, 上海: 商务印书馆, 1935 年。Kuwabara Jitsuzo, *Study of Trading Ports during Tang and Song Dynasties* (translated by Yang Lian). Shanghai: The Commercial Press, 1935.

［日］桑原骘藏:《中国阿剌伯海上交通史》, 冯攸译, 上海: 商务印书馆, 1934 年。Kuwabara Jitsuzo, *History of Maritime Transportation between China and Arab* (translated by Feng You). Shanghai: The Commercial Press, 1934.

［摩洛哥］伊本·白图泰:《伊本·白图泰游记》, 马金鹏译, 银川: 宁夏人民出版社, 1985 年。Ibn Battuta, *The Travels of Ibn Battuta* (translated by Ma Jinpeng). Yinchuan: Ningxia People's Publishing House, 1985.

［阿拉伯］伊本•胡尔达兹比赫:《道里邦国志》, 宋岘译注, 北京: 中华书局, 1991 年。Ibn Khordadbeh, *The Book of Roads and Kingdoms* (translated by Song Xian). Beijing: Zhonghua Book Company, 2001.

3. Research Literature in English

Abdel-Khalek, Gouda, and Korayem Karima, "The Impact of China on the Middle East." *Journal of Developing Societies*, vol. 23, no. 4, 2007, pp. 397–434.

Abu Dhabi Investment Authority, *ADIA Review*, 2010–2012.

Al-Tamimi, Naser, *China-Saudi Arabia Relations, 1990–2012: Marriage of Convenience or Strategic Alliance?* New York, NY: Routledge, 2013.

Alterman, Jon B., and John W. Garver, *The Vital Triangle: China, the United States, and the Middle East.* Washington, DC: Center for Strategic and International Studies, 2008.

Andrews-Speed, Philip, and Roland Dannreuther, *China, Oil and Global Politics.* New York, NY: Routledge, 2011.

Asian Development Bank Institute, *Infrastructure for a Seamless Asia.* Tokyo, Japan: Asian Development Bank Institute, 2009.

Asian Development Bank, *Asian Infrastructure Financing Initiative.* Manila, Philippines: Asian Development Bank, 2008.

Bank for International Settlements, *Triennial Central Bank Survey 2013*, September 2013.

Bentley, Jerry H., *Old World Encounters: Cross-cultural Contacts and Exchanges in Pre-modern Times.* New York, NY: Oxford University Press, 1993.

Bhattacharyay, Biswa N., Masahiro Kawai, and Rajat Nag, eds., *Infrastructure for Asian Connectivity.* Cheltenham, UK: Edward Elgar Publishing, 2012.

Boulnois, Luce, and Bradley Mayhew, *Silk Road: Monks, Warriors and Merchants*. Hong Kong, China: Odyssey Books & Guides, 2012.

BP, *BP Statistical Review of World Energy*, 2010–2014.

BP, *BP Energy Outlook 2030*, 2012.

BP, *60 Years BP Statistical Review of World Energy (1951–2011)*, 2013.

Carter, Hannah, and Anoushiravan Ehteshami, eds., *The Middle East's Relations with Asia and Russia*, New York, NY: RoutledgeCurzon, 2004.

Calabrese, John, *China's Changing Relations with the Middle East*. London, UK: Pinter, 1991.

Chen, Gang, and Ryan Clarke, *China's Intensified Energy Engagement in the Middle East*. Singapore: National University of Singapore, 2010.

Cooley, Alexander, *The Emerging Political Economy of OBOB: The Challenges of Promoting Connectivity in Central Asia and Beyond*. Washington, DC: Center for Strategic and International Studies, 2016.

Crews, Robert D., and Amin Tarzi, eds., *The Taliban and the Crisis of Afghanistan*. Cambridge, MA: Harvard University Press, 2008.

Curtin, Philip D., *Cross-Cultural Trade in World History*. New York, NY: Cambridge University Press, 1984.

Davidson, Christopher, *The Persian Gulf and Pacific Asia: From Indifference to Interdependence*. London, UK: Hurst & Co., 2010.

Das, Sanchita Basu, and Catherine Rose James. "Addressing Infrastructure Financing in Asia." *ISEAS Perspective* (Singpore), no. 27, May 2013, pp. 1–15.

Djankov, Simeon, and Sean Miner, *China's Belt and Road Initiative: Motives, Scope, and Challenges*. Washington, DC: Peterson Institute for International Economics, 2016.

Dorraj, Manochehr, and James English, "China's Strategy for Energy Acquisition in the Middle East: Potential for Conflict and Cooperation with the United States." *Asian Politics and Policy*, vol. 14, no. 2, April 2012, pp. 173–191.

Downs, Erica S., *Inside China, Inc: China Development Bank's Cross-Border Energy Deals*. Washington, DC: John L.Thornton China Center at Brookings Institute, 2011.

Economist Intelligence Unit, *Near East Meets Far East: The Rise of Gulf Investment in Asia*. New York, NY: The Economist Group, 2007.

Eisenman, Joshua *et al.*, eds., *China and the Developing World: Beijing's Strategy for The Twenty-first Century*. Armonk, NY: M.E. Sharpe, 2007.

Elisseeff, Vadime, eds., *The Silk Roads: Highways of Culture and Commerce.* New York, NY: Berghahn Books, 2000.

Elverskog, Johan, *Buddhism and Islam on the Silk Road.* Philadelphia, PA: University of Pennsylvania Press, 2010.

Ernst, Young, *World Islamic Banking Competitiveness Report 2011–2012,* 2011.

———, *World Islamic Banking Competitiveness Report 2012–2013,* 2012.

Esposito, John L., et al., *Asian Islam in the 21st Century.* New York, NY: Oxford University Press, 2008.

Foltz, Richard C., *Religions of the Silk Road: Overland Trade and Cultural Exchange from Antiquity to the Fifteenth Century.* New York, NY: St. Martin's Press, 1999.

———, *Religions of the Silk Road: Premodern Patterns of Globalization.* New York, NY: Palgrave Macmillan, 2010.

Friedberg, Aaron L., "'Going Out': China's Pursuit of Natural Resources and Implications for the PRC's Grand Strategy." *NBR Analysis,* vol. 17, no. 3, 2006, pp. 5–34.

Glain, Stephen., "The Modern Silk Road." *Newsweek,* May 26/June 2, 2008, pp. 32–33.

Hamilton, Carl., *The New Silk Road to Europe: New Directions for Old Trade,* Adelaide, Australia: Centre for International Economic Studies, 1989.

Hansen, Valerie., *The Silk Road: A New History.* New York, NY: Oxford University Press, 2012.

Hedin, Sven., *The Silk Road: Ten Thousand Miles through Central Asia.* London, UK: Tauris Parke Paperbacks, 2009.

Henry, Clement M., and Rodney Wilson, *The Politics of Islamic Finance.* Edinburgh, Scotland: Edinburgh University Press, 2004.

Herberg, Mikkal E, et al., *The New Energy Silk Road: The Growing Asia-Middle East Energy Nexus.* Washington, DC: The National Bureau of Asian Research, 2009.

Hickey, Dennis, and BaogangGuo, eds., *Dancing with the Dragon: China's Emergence in the Developing World.* Lanham, MD: Rowman & Littlefield-Lexington Books, 2010.

Johnson, Christopher K., *President Xi Jinping's "Belt and Road" Initiative: A Practical Assessment of the Chinese Communist Party's Roadmap for China's Global Resurgence.* Washington, DC: Center for Strategic and International Studies, 2016.

Karrar, Hasan H., *The New Silk Road Diplomacy: China's Central Asian Foreign Policy Since the Cold War.* Vancouver, Canada: University of British Columbia Press, 2009.

Kemp, Geoffrey, and Abdulaziz Sager, eds., *China's Growing Role in the Middle East: Implications for the Region and Beyond.* Washington, DC: The NixonCenter, 2010.

Kemp, Geoffrey, *The East Moves West: India, China, and Asia's Growing Presence in the Middle East.* Washington, DC: Brookings Institution Press, 2010.

Khan, Riaz Mohammad, *Afghanistan and Pakistan: Conflict, Extremism, and Resistance to Modernity.* Baltimore, MD: Johns Hopkins University Press, 2011.

Kim, Hodong, *Holy War in China: The Muslim Rebellion and State in Chinese Central Asia, 1864–1877.* Stanford, CA: Stanford University Press, 2004.

Levathes, Louis, *When China Ruled the Seas: The Treasure Fleet of the Dragon Throne, 1405–1433.* New York, NY: Oxford University Press, 1996.

Lin, Christina, *The New Silk Road: China's Energy Strategy in the Greater Middle East.* Washington, DC: Washington Institute for Near East Policy, 2011.

Liu, Xinru, *Connections across Eurasia: Transportation, Communication, and Cultural Exchange on the Silk Roads.* Boston, MA: McGraw-Hill, 2007.

——, *The Silk Road in World History.* New York, NY: Oxford University Press, 2010.

——, "A Silk Road Legacy: The Spread of Buddhism and Islam." *Journal of World History*, vol. 22, no. 1, March 2011, pp. 55–81.

Luft, Gal, *It Takes A Road—China's One Belt One Road Initiative: An American Response to the New Silk Road.* Washington, DC: Institute for theAnalysis of Global Security, 2016.

Marantidou, Virginia, "Revisiting China's 'String of Pearls' Strategy: Places 'with Chinese Characteristics' and Their Security Implications." *Issues & Insights*, vol. 14, no. 7, June 2014, pp. 1–39.

Mckinsey Global Institute, *Bridging Global Infrastructure Gaps.* June 2016.

——, *The New Power Brokers: How Oil, Asia, Hedge Funds, and Private Equity Are Shaping Global Capital Markets.* 2007.

Mehden, Fred R., *Two Worlds of Islam: Interaction between Southeast Asia and the Middle East.* Gainesville, FL: University Press of Florida, 1993.

Millward, James A., *The Silk Road: A Very Short Introduction.* New York, NY: Oxford University Press, 2013.

Mufti, Mariam, *Religion and Militancy in Pakistan and Afghanistan.* Washington, DC: Center for Strategic and International Studies, 2012.

Olcott, Brill M., *Roots of Radical Islam in Central Asia.* Washington, DC: Carnegie Endowment for International Peace, 2007.

Olimat, Muhamad S., *China and the Middle East: From Silk Road to Arab Spring.* New York, NY: Routledge, 2012.

OPEC. *OPEC Annual Statistical Bulletin 2012–2013.*

Pantucci, Raffaello, and Alexandros Petersen, "China's Inadvertent Empire." *The National Interest,* 2012, pp. 30–39.

Pew Research Center's Forum on Religion & Public Life, *The Future of the Global Muslim Population: Projections for 2010–2030,* 2011.

Pham, Peter J., "China's 'Surge' in the Middle East and Its Implications for U.S. Interests." *American Foreign Policy Interests,* vol. 31, no .3, 2009, pp. 177–193.

Plummer, Michael G *et al.*, eds., *Connecting Asia: Infrastructure for Integrating South and Southeast Asia.* Cheltenham, UK: Edward Elgar Publishing Limited, 2016.

Rolland, Nadège,"China's 'Belt and Road Initiative': Underwhelming or Game-Changer?" *The Washington Quarterly,* Spring 2017, pp. 127–142.

Rumer, Eugene, Dmitri Trenin, and Huasheng Zhao, *Central Asia: Views from Washington, Moscow, and Beijing.* Armonk, NY: M.E. Sharpe. 2007.

Ruthven, Malise, *Historical Atlas of the Islamic World.* Cambridge, MA: Harvard University Press, 2004.

Sanderson, Henry, and Michael Forsythe, *China's Superbank: Debt, Oil and Influence-How China Development Bank is Rewriting the Rules of Finance.* Singapore: John Wiley & Sons, 2013.

Shambaugh, David, eds., *Tangled Titans: The United States and China.* New York, NY: Rowman & Littlefield Publishers, 2012.

Sheives, Kevin, "China Turns West: Beijing's Contemporary Strategy Towards Central Asia." *Pacific Affairs,* vol. 79, no. 2, Summer 2006, pp. 205–224.

Simpfendorfer, Ben, *The New Silk Road: How A Rising Arab World is Turning Away from the West and Rediscovering China.* New York, NY: Palgrave Macmillan, 2009.

Smith, Martin, *State of Strife: The Dynamics of Ethnic Conflict in Burma.* Singapore: Institute of Southeast Asian Studies, 2007.

Starr, Frederick S., *Xinjiang: China's Muslim Borderlands,* Armonk, NY: M.E. Sharpe, 2004.

——, *The New Silk Roads: Transport and Trade in Greater Central Asia.* Washington, DC: Johns Hopkins University, 2007.

van der Putten, Frans-Paul *et al.*, eds. *Europe and China's New Silk Roads,* December 2016.

Wakefield, Bryce, and Susan L. Levenstein, eds., *China and the Persian Gulf: Implications for the United States.* Washington, DC: Woodrow Wilson International Center for Scholars, 2011.

Whitfield, Susan, and Ursula Sims-Williams, *The Silk Road: Trade, Travel, War and Faith.* Chicago, IL: Serindia Publications, 2004.

Zhao, Huasheng, *China and Afghanistan: China's Interests, Stances, and Perspectives.* Washington, DC: Center for Strategic and International Studies, 2012.

Ziegler, Charles E, "The Energy Factor in China's Foreign Policy." *Journal of Chinese Political Science*, vol. 11, no. 1, Spring 2006, pp. 1–23.

Zweig, David, and Bi Jianhai, "China's Global Hunt for Energy." *Foreign Affairs*, vol. 84, no. 5, September–October 2005, pp. 25–38.

Index